The
Ongoing
Present

The Ongoing Present

A Critical Look at the Society
and World in which I Grew Up

Micheál Mac Gréil SJ

Messenger Publications 2014

ISBN 9781910248065

Designed by Messenger Publications Design Department
Printed by Nicholson & Bass Ltd

MESSENGER
PUBLICATIONS
JESUITS in IRELAND

Messenger Publications,
37 Lower Leeson Street, Dublin 2
www.messenger.ie

This book is dedicated, in the first place,
to the memory of the late
Pádraic Naughton, former Director of the
Pioneer Total Abstinence Association,
on whose encouragement this attempt to record
a personal view of Irish and world society
over three-quarters of a century was undertaken.

The work is also dedicated to all my third-level students
who taught me more than I taught them.

TABLE OF CONTENTS

ACKNOWLEDGEMENTS

I would like to acknowledge the support I received in the writing and preparation of this book which covers seventy-eight years of my life from 1936 until 2014. It is but right that I begin with my family who encouraged me to write this personal account of the world in which I grew up. This does not mean that the members of my family necessarily agree with (all of) my views. The support of my brothers Austin, Owen and Pádraig was essential to me in my decision to proceed with this project.

The encouragement and support of my 'second family', i.e. my Jesuit brothers are also very gratefully acknowledged. Father Derek Cassidy SJ, and other Jesuit colleagues, kindly agreed to read the text and gave me the confidence to complete the manuscript. The support of the Irish Jesuit Provincials, Fr Tom Layden SJ, and his predecessor Fr John Dardis SJ, enabled me to devote time to writing the text. I am particularly grateful to Fr Fergus O'Donoghue SJ, who has supported this project.

I am also very thankful to Ms Máiréad Mahon, Ms Paulyn Marrinan-Quinn, Ms Sheila O'Donnell, Mrs Maureen Griffin and Mr Éanna Ó Caollaí who read the text and helped me with their comments on both style and content. Despite all these valuable suggestions, I alone am wholly responsible for what is written below and I apologise for any errors or misreading of events or happenings recorded in the course of the text.

The person who influenced me most to write *The Ongoing Present* was the late Mr Pádraic Naughton, former chief executive of the Pioneer Total Abstinence Association (PTAA). I could not resist his gentle and argued persuasion. For that reason I have dedicated the book to his memory. I also acknowledge the support of his wife, Mary and her late father, Proinsias Uas Ó Laoire, who agreed with Pádraic and constantly encouraged me to complete the text.

Among the persons who contributed most to the preparation of the book for publication were Mrs Teresa Hunt (originator) and Ms Angela Burt (proof-reader). I also wish to thank Liam Killion of Crotare Printing Limited for his advice and help. The advice and guidance of Ms Pat

Coyle, director of Jesuit Communications; and Ms Cecilia West, Ms Sarah Brady, and Ms Paula Nolan of Messenger Publications were most valuable. Thanks are also due to Mr Ardal O'Hanlon and Archbishop Michael Neary of Tuam, for agreeing to launch the book in Dublin and Westport respectively.

Finally, I wish to thank my friends and neighbours, especially the Heraty, O'Connor, Walsh and Gavin families, who helped to keep my 'home fire burning' as I delved into three-quarters of a century of the world around me in the seclusion of the old family cottage, in the quiet beauty of Loughloon (Laghloon). I am especially grateful to my late brother Seán, his late wife, Eileen, and his son Austin, his daughter Kathleen and her husband Mártín Ó hIarnáin for letting me have the use of the cottage over a number of years.

Go raibh maith agaibh go léir.

Micheál Mac Gréil SJ,
Leac Chluain,
Cathair na Mart,
Co Mhaigh Eo.

THE ONGOING PRESENT
A Critical Look at the Society and World in which I Grew Up

AUTHOR'S PREFACE

The following pages contain or recall reflections on the world around me as I grew up, lived and worked in Ireland (with short stays abroad) over more than three quarters of a century. The book is not intended to be an autobiography as such. It is rather an account, largely from memory of conscious awareness of what has been happening in Ireland and in the world since the mid-1930s. The author's perception has been influenced by what he read, heard and studied, in addition to the actual experience of his own limited life, relationships and work experience.

Of course, such a personal account has many shortfalls due to the limitations of the perceptual ability of the author, his life experience and the inevitable normative points of view on value-laden issues. It is impossible for anyone who is interested in cultural, political, social and religious affairs to be value-free in his or her outlook. We are not robots. In my opinion our values are our most important human (and uniquely human) characteristics and give a meaningful context to life and to our views.

My motivation in attempting this substantial work has been mixed. Let me say, in the first instance, the initiative came from my friend, the late Pádraic Naughton, who wanted me to look back at the society in which I lived and worked and record my comments as well as attempting an accurate description from my perspective at the time. Secondly, commentators have presented images of Irish society through the decades, which aroused my interest. My reaction to some of these commentators has been quite varied. Some appear to be very good and intelligent. Others were over-the-top and romanticised too much, while some were downright biased in a negative sense and lacked socio-cultural understanding.

The third reason why I have decided to write this reflection has been influenced by my respect for Ireland and its people, living and dead. It appears to me that a number of writers have tended to suffer from *'the apostate complex'*, namely, they have expressed a 'compulsive alienation' from what they were originally and an over-identity with what they have become later in life[1]. In a sense, they have written with an 'ex' mentality, i.e. ex-Republican, ex-Loyalist, ex-Catholic, ex-British, ex-socialist, ex-capitalist, etc. This is very understandable in times of acute social change and leads to successive bouts of various forms of revisionism.

How can I avoid this trap? I must leave that to the reader. Maybe, by being aware of this psychological danger and trying to address personal, social and cultural change in a positive and integrated manner, I will still respect the views of those I may not now appreciate as strongly as I once did. Ireland's reputation has been greatly damaged (unwittingly I hope) by the negative influence of those (from among modern writers) suffering from the 'apostate complex'. There does not seem to be a correlation between this condition and intelligence. At times, in my life, I may have drifted into the trap of becoming alienated 'from the old in favour of the new', but experience has shown me the wisdom of seeking the true value of both!

A fourth motive for reflecting in print on experience is the innate wealth of the encounter of living through different challenges and opportunities. In truth there are no such realities as the 'past' or the 'future'. There is only the 'ongoing present'. What we see as the past is in our memory and in our records, while the future is in our minds. This more existential view of time makes the recalling of the notion of 'ever-becoming life' always alive in the mind and on the pages. What happens is never over, which, incidentally was seen by St Paul in *Romans 8*, and of course, by the great evolutionist, Fr Teilhard de Chardin SJ. To repeat the view of Aristotle, as commented on by my esteemed professor, Fr Maurits de Tollenaere SJ, in Leuven, time as such does not exist; it is but a measure of activity with reference to before and after! The photograph distorts dynamic history because it freezes life at a particular moment. Since, therefore, we are our past, to distort our history would be to distort ourselves!

The content of this book is a mix of personal experience and commentary on Irish society and on the world since the 1930s. It is largely descriptive and evaluative. It follows a chronological order (more

---

1 See sociologists Talcott Parsons (*The Social System*) and Robert K Merton (*Social Theory and Social Structure*) on 'Reference-Group Theory'.

or less) with a chapter devoted to each decade. As already noted, the descriptive narrative is a recording of one person's experience of living, i.e. including (in alphabetical order):

achieving;	laughing;	searching;
arguing;	learning;	serving;
campaigning;	listening;	suffering;
consoling;	losing;	talking;
debating;	loving;	teaching;
enjoying;	mourning;	visiting;
exploring;	playing;	winning;
failing;	praying;	working;
finding;	preaching;	worshipping;
interacting;	reading;	writing

and other particular activities that went to make up a fairly active life blessed by reasonably good health, thank God. It is a unique combination of events and interactions, as is the case of any individual's experience of encountering the challenges of ongoing human living.

While attempts are made to substantiate conclusions with reasoned arguments, the opinions expressed below do not purport to be the last word on particular issues and situations. The reader is free to arrive at different interpretations of similar experiences, happenings or combinations of facts. The author will feel to have achieved his purpose in writing *The Ongoing Present* once he has raised the awareness of the events described and issues discussed in the mind of the reader.

I hope the readers will find this frank critique of the world I grew up in of interest, especially in the case of my thousands of graduates. I look forward to the comments of the readers and encourage them to get involved in their 'ongoing present'.

Dáta: Lá Bealtaine 2014   *Micheál Mac Gréil SJ*

Prologue

MY LIFE IN BRIEF

I was born in a log cabin in a forest in Clonaslee, *Contae na Laoise* on 23rd March 1931. My father was Austin McGreal from Loughloon, (Laghloon on the map), Westport, County Mayo, and my mother was Máire Ní Chadhain from *An Cabhar, An Mám, Contae na Gaillimhe*. At the time, my father was in charge of cutting the mature trees on the Dunne estate (Brittas) on the side of the Slieve Bloom Mountains at Clonaslee. He worked for a Scottish timber company, McAinish Limited. Prior to her marriage to my father in 1928, my mother was a nurse in St Ultan's Children's Hospital, Charlemont Street, Dublin under Dr Kathleen Lynn from 1919 until 1928. My godparents were Mary King (*Ráighe*) and Jimmy Dunne (Clonaslee).

I was second of a family of six, i.e. Seán (born April 1930), Austin (born February 1934), Owen (born June 1935), Mary (born August 1936) and Pádraig (born December 1942). Seán and I were born and baptised in Clonaslee. Austin, Owen and Mary were born and baptised in Portumna, County Galway, and Pádraig was born in Loughloon and baptised in Westport, County Mayo. My father was transferred to Portumna in the early 1930s on promotion within McAinish's, when he had overall responsibility for woods throughout Munster, part of Leinster and Connaught. The principal sawmill was along the Shannon River in Portland near Portumna.

My grandparents on my father's side had died before I was born. My grandfather, John ('Big John') McGreal died in 1930 aged seventy years, and his wife, Katie (née Mortimer of Borris, Lecanvey, Westport) died in 1912 aged fifty years. I barely remember my mother's father, *Meaidhc Michil Ó Cadhain* (who died on 6th February 1936). My mother's mother, *Méiní Eoghain Nic an Rí* died at the age of eighty-six years in 1956. Our grandparents on my mother's side were always addressed as *Daideó* and *Máimeó*. During my childhood I spent most of my summer holidays with my *Máimeó* and my uncle *Tomás* (Tommie) in the Maam Valley.

My family lived in Portumna (first in Dominic Street and later in

Abbey Street) from 1932 until 1936 when we moved to my father's family home in Loughloon, Westport, County Mayo. We lived in the original cottage, built after the marriage of my great-grandfather Padney McGreal to his next-door neighbour's daughter, Kitty Conway, on 3rd April 1847. It was re-roofed and extended in 1936 with two small rooms added to the rear. The walls were raised and some other minor modifications were also made. Seán, Austin, Owen, Mary and I attended Brackloon National School. While in Portumna, Seán and I received our first Confession and Holy Communion (at the ages of six and five respectively). Honorah (Onnie) Conway lived with us in Loughloon after her husband Willie died.

In 1940, it was decided to renovate Brackloon National School, which was originally built at the end of the Famine (1849). Rather than lose the few months' schooling caused by the interruption, our parents decided to send my brother, Seán and myself to the Christian Brothers' Primary School in Castlebar Street, Westport, County Mayo. The distance to school was about four miles each way.

In 1946 our family bought two small holdings (thirty-one acres and nine acres respectively) in Drummindoo, approximately one mile on the east side of Westport. There was a small, slated house on the larger holding (owned by the Geraghty family). This holding was where General Joe Ring (who was killed in the Civil War in 1923) was reared. Joe Ring was a leader of the local IRA during the War of Independence. His family home was burned by the Black-and-Tans and the house we bought had been built by the 'White Cross Fund' in the 1920s. The mother of the family from whom we bought the house, Mrs Elsie Geraghty, was a sister of the late General Joe Ring. The land in Drummindoo was relatively poor and not very productive, with the exception of a few fields.

After four years I was to leave Drummindoo for Dublin in 1950, where I trained to become a stores' manager in Joseph Lucas Limited, North Portland Street, Dublin 1, and in McCairns Motors, Tara Street, Dublin 2. On return to Westport in the summer of 1950, I went to work at Hastings Garage, the Fairgreen, Westport, and helped to develop the stores on a systematic basis.

In October 1950, I left Westport to join the Defence Forces as a Cadet in the *Coláiste Míleata* (Military College). My brother, Seán, had become a cadet two years previously. After two years, in November

1952, I was commissioned as a Second Lieutenant and two years later in 1954, promoted to the rank of First Lieutenant. I served as an officer in the Third Battalion ('The Bloods') on the Curragh from 1952 to 1959. During the 1950s, the three siblings next to me left home, i.e. Austin went to America (where he ended up a lawyer), Owen went for the priesthood (in the Oblates of Mary Immaculate), and my sister, Mary, joined the St Louis Convent in Monaghan.

In 1959, after my brother Owen was ordained a priest, I was forced to address the question of the meaning of life itself. The net result of the self-searching was my decision to resign my commission in the Defence Forces in order to become a priest.

I joined the Jesuit Noviceship in Emo Park, *Contae na Laoise*, on 7th September 1959, having resigned my military commission on 30th August 1959. In 1961, I was sent to Tullabeg (Rahan) outside Tullamore, County Offaly to study philosophy.

In 1962, I was sent to the Jesuit Philosophate at Heverlee, Leuven, in Belgium, to continue the study (through Flemish) of philosophy to the Licentiate level. In 1964/65 I did a Bacheloriate in Social and Political Sciences in the Catholic University of Leuven, i.e. a two-year course in one year. In 1961 my brother Pádraig joined the Defence Forces as a Cadet and was duly commissioned as a Second Lieutenant.

During 1965 to 1966 (five terms) I was awarded a 'graduate assistantship' in Kent State University, Ohio, thanks to Professor Larry Kaplan from that University, who was a visiting Professor in Leuven. While at KSU, I completed an MA in Sociology and began my serious study of intergroup relations, i.e. social prejudice and tolerance.

In September 1966, I registered for a four-year course in Theology at Milltown Park in Dublin (later known as the Milltown Institute of Theology and Philosophy). It was immediately after Vatican Two and it was an exciting time to be a student of theology. In 1966 I was invited to lecture (part-time) in Sociology in the College of Industrial Relations, in the Milltown Institute (philosophy) and in Kimmage Manor the Holy Ghost Scholasticate in addition to my studies.

On 31th July 1969, I was ordained a priest in St Mary's Church, Westport, by the Most Reverend Dr Joseph Walsh, Archbishop of Tuam, who had just retired.

On completion of Theology in 1970 I was posted to the College of

3

Industrial Relations, Sandford Road, Dublin. In October 1970, I registered in the Department of Social Science, University College Dublin, for a PhD (Doctorate) in Sociology. My research would be into Intergroup Relations in Ireland. I was given a junior post as lecturer in Sociology in UCD at the same time.

In 1971, Professor Liam Ryan invited me to become a junior lecturer in Sociology in the NUI section of St Patrick's College, Maynooth. I continued as part-time lecturer in Sociology in UCD, the College of Industrial Relations, and in the Milltown Institute for a further ten or more years. In December 1975, I completed my PhD and submitted my thesis to UCD. I was awarded the PhD in 1976 and the text of my thesis was published, i.e. *Prejudice and Tolerance in Ireland*, in 1977.

In July of 1979, I offered Mass in Irish at St Patrick's Well and Bed at *Mámean*, on the Maamturk Mountains and, with the support of local people, began the restoration of this traditional pilgrimage, which had been neglected for years.

In 1979, another new campaign began for me. It was the inter-regional (Regional Development Organisations of Sligo-Leitrim, Galway-Mayo and Clare-Limerick-Tipperary NR) Railway Committee whose aim was to restore the cross-radial rail services from Sligo to Limerick and on to Rosslare. CIE had ended the rail services from Collooney to Claremorris in 1975.

In 1982, I was elected Chairperson of the Academic Staff Association (i.e. shop steward to the local university teachers' union) – a position I held for nine years.

In 1988-89, I organised a second major survey of prejudice in Ireland and commissioned the ESRI to carry out a national survey (sample of 1,350 with a response of 1,005) of attitudes and prejudices in the Republic of Ireland. The average length of interviews was almost one and a half hours. The attitudes measured in the 1972-73 survey were replicated and the findings were published in 1996, i.e. *Prejudice in Ireland Revisited*.

In January 1992, I was appointed Chairperson of the Interim Board of Management of the Pioneer Total Abstinence Association (PTAA). The Board was asked to carry out a 'root and branch review' of the Association. The PTAA was founded on 28th December 1898 and would soon be celebrating its first centenary. An interim report was published in December 1992 and a final report was published at the end of the following year in 1993. I edited *Monsignor Horan, Memoirs*, which was published in 1992.

I retired as a Senior Lecturer in NUI, St Patrick's College, Maynooth in 1996. That same year *Prejudice in Ireland Revisited* was published, which was based on the findings of the 1988-89 national survey. I continued lecturing part-time in the NCIR until 1999.

In 1996, I was invited by the Archbishop of Tuam, Dr Michael Neary, to help carry out a pastoral audit of the needs and resources of the Archdiocese which was later published as *Quo Vadimus* in 1998.

In August of 1998, I was transferred from the NCIR Community to Gardiner Street Jesuit Community. The whole NCIR, now renamed as NCI (National College of Ireland), was being transferred to the North Wall Docklands.

In 2002, I was invited by the Bishop of Meath, Dr Michael Smith, to help carry out a survey of the pastoral needs and resources of the Diocese of Meath (with its quarter of a million members). The first report was circulated to the priests of the Meath diocese in April 2004. The final Report was presented in 2005, i.e. *Our Living Church*.

A third national survey of Irish attitudes and prejudices was carried out in 2007-08. The recent in-migration of different ethnic, racial and religious people makes Ireland far more diverse, especially in the larger cities. It was published in 2011 under the title, *Pluralism and Diversity in Ireland*. A fourth survey of Westport as a visitor/tourist destination was carried out in 2011 and 2012 and published in 2013 under the title *Westport Eleven-Twelve*.

Conclusion

Thus ends the synoptic biographical note of my life. In addition to the events and features noted above, I would like to add the very privileged experience of pastoral work in various parishes since ordination in 1969. I was always available for parish relief work at weekends. The reader will be able to gather from the above chronology the perspective from which I was in a position to view first-hand the world around me. Of course, hindsight can always enable the observer to add to the diagnosis and the explanation of what was actually happening around one. Nevertheless, it should be possible to distinguish between the memory of my perception of events around me and a later layer of meaning and analysis and the contribution of comparative experiences by other observers in different or similar socio-cultural environments.

Because of the inevitable subjective nature of the narrative below and also because of my own personal values and convictions, this is not a strictly 'sociological' text. At the same time, my experience of the psychological, sociological and anthropological disciplines must help me in my perceptions and evaluation of perceptions. My religious background and training in philosophy, theology and spiritual formation have also enriched my perception of life around me and informed my criticism and appraisal where applied. Most of the material that I have published to date has been governed by the rules of empirical research and theory. This text, therefore, is a new experience for me and may be problematic. I trust the reader will be tolerant of my new venture. Hopefully, it will provide an original nuance on a multi-varied reality, i.e. society as it was lived in and observed by one who passed on the way with his eyes opened and his ears listening. It has been a wonderful journey. I would not have wished to live at any other time or with other relationships, neighbours, friends, colleagues, comrades or even 'enemies'! Hopefully, the reader will excuse any errors or misinterpretations he or she encounters in the course of this text. Some of the details noted in this *Prologue* will be repeated and developed at greater length throughout the following chapters as part of the 'ongoing present'.

Chapter One

THE 1920S AND 1930S
AFTER INDEPENDENCE AND BEFORE THE WAR

1. REARED ON A HILL FARM IN COUNTY MAYO

The 1930s was the decade in Ireland in which the people were still experiencing the aftermath of the War of Independence. My mother, for instance, had fought in the War of Independence from 1919-1921 (in a covert manner) from St Ultan's Hospital, Charlemont Street, Dublin, with Dr Kathleen Lynn, Ann Duggan, the Countess Markievicz, the Ryans of Wexford and others. Later she supported the Republican side in the Civil War and agreed with the ending of hostilities and the return of Republican (*Fianna Fáil*) TDs to *Dáil Éireann*. My father's experience of the War of Independence was less involved. He did take part in the 1918 General Strike against conscription into the British Army. He was very much opposed to the Civil War and tended to blame de Valera and his followers for not going the 'democratic way'. The destruction of local industry and communications during the Civil War appalled him.

As we grew up at home, we always got both sides of the argument. My mother regretted the Civil War but was much closer to the Republican fighters. During our childhood the leaders of the War of Independence were household names (although I do not remember meeting the early leaders, when a child in the 1930s). We certainly got both sides of the political point of view at home. Two of my father's brothers were in the IRA, Pat (who died in 1919) and John. My mother had 'autograph books' from the Frongoch Prison where Republicans were interned.

It was not until we came to live in Loughloon, in the summer of 1936 that I began to observe society around me. Our farm comprised two half holdings (Conway's and McGreal's) which together consisted of 214 acres of hill land, i.e. fifty-two acres around the house and 162-acre share of a commonage. It was mixed farming with cattle, sheep, a horse and a donkey, hens, turkeys, geese and ducks. Most children were inducted into the chores of farming. Each season had its own duties.

Spring was ploughing, sowing, manuring the meadows and picking the stones. Also, we had the task of 'getting the newly born lambs' and putting 'gas tar' on their breasts in order to repel the fox from taking them. There was a bounty of one egg for each male lamb 'found' and two eggs for each female lamb discovered. Should we come across a neighbour's lamb, we would demand our egg bounty. We would go to the hills at dawn, around six o'clock in the morning in search of the lambs.

Cleaning out the barns was a task for the hardier children. The stable manure would be taken in *pardógs* carried by donkeys, i.e. baskets with releasable buttons, and deposited in the meadows and on the ridges and drills prepared for potatoes. Children were also given the tedious task of picking the stones off the meadows. Otherwise, the smallest stones would damage the edge of the scythes at mowing time. There would be many small stones in fields, which had been stubble the previous year.

The sowing of potatoes involved every generation. The old women would 'cut the slits', i.e. cut the potatoes into a number of parts with 'an eye' in each. The 'slits' would then be dipped in lime (to deter insects). The older men would make the holes for each slit and the child would 'pitch the slits' into the hole dug by the older man who would use the earth from the next set of three holes (in each ridge), to cover the 'slits' pitched by the child. If you missed the holes, the old man would scold you. Pitching slits was a task that demanded one's constant attention. Early potatoes had to be sown by the first Friday in March if one was to have them ready for digging by the 29th June, the Feast of Saints Peter and Paul.

Weeding and thinning turnips and mangels were also chores given to older children. It happened in the late spring and could be quite unpleasant if the flies and midges were biting. Driving and bringing home the cows was a task for children. I remember I was driving the cows on 3rd September 1939 when the 'wool-gatherer' passed by and told me that it 'came upon the wireless' that the War was on, i.e. Britain had declared war on Germany. (The 'wool-gatherer' was a woman, who bartered carrageen moss, 'dillisk' and 'crannach' for wool. She would have a long 'bran-bag' on her back. Most wool-gatherers in North Connemara came from the *'cladach'* or the 'shore'. They visited the hill farmers once a year and received a great reception.) Very often, we had to drive the cows to their grazing fields in the mornings before going to school in the weekdays or after going to early Mass on the Sundays. Each family received their full supply of milk and butter from their own cows. Calves were weaned off the cows at infancy. Feeding the calves with milk was also a job for the nine- and ten-year-olds. You would steep your fingers in the milk and then the calf would suck them. Gradually, you would lower your fingers into the bucket until the calf would suck up the milk directly.

Growing up on the land we were totally familiar with cows going to the bull when in heat ('bulling') and calves being born from the womb of a cow. In fact, I delivered my first calf at the age of ten. I cut the 'bed' from around the calf's front feet and pulled gently as the cow was in labour. I was lying on the ground behind the cow with my feet against her hips. After I delivered the calf on top of me, as I was lying behind the cow, she got up and licked both the calf and me. I knew her as 'the Kimeen Cow'. At the time, cows were very domesticated and friendly and gentle. They accepted our acts of kindness. (Today, because of slatted sheds and letting the calves suck on the cows, they have become 'wild' again.) We also helped to deliver lambs from ewes in labour. We knew when things were going wrong, i.e. if the hind legs or the head came first. Then the calf would be pushed back in and turned around so that the front legs and head came first. This would be a job for an adult and, in rare situations a veterinary surgeon would be called, or, as in our case, an amateur veterinary surgeon, Mr Frank Murphy of Bohea, would be sent for. He was a genius with cattle. Despite our familiarity with the 'facts of life of animals', we never applied them to humans. Domestic animals were quasi-pets and on the occasion of the death of an animal, it would be buried in a corner of a field with deep soil. This was a sort of graveyard. Our dogs and cats were both pets and 'beasts of burden'. Sheep dogs were treasured very much and cats' functions were the control of vermin, especially rats and mice. Dogs were also there to scare off foxes.

2. Other Seasonal Chores

From May Day until September we went without shoes or boots, except when visiting the local town. It was liberating to be without shoes! Of course, we suffered from thorns, stone bruises and nettle stings. In late spring and early summer, we had to work on the bog, i.e. spreading, footing and 'putting out' the turf. The bog was a wonderful place except when there were 'midges' or horseflies. Gathering for lunch and tea with neighbours along the roadside was always memorable. Bog-water seemed to make tasty tea! Days in the bog were long, and hard work. Yet, we enjoyed them. It was the aim of each family to have new turf for the bonfire on the eve of St John's Day (24th June) as we hoped for new potatoes for the feast of Saints Peter and Paul (29th June and my father's birthday).

With regard to the sowing of grain, every farmer had fields (gardens) of oats, which supplied food for horses, fowl, cattle (crushed oats) and people (in the form of oatmeal porridge). Some farmers sowed wheat in order to have ground wheat for mixture with white flour in baking brown bread. There would be a rotation of crops, i.e. potatoes, grain, grass for meadows. The seeds would be scattered by experienced and skilled farmers. In the thirties in my village (Loughloon), there was little or no farm machinery. The horse plough had been introduced a generation before my time. We also had wooden harrows with iron spikes and rollers usually made from a smooth length of a trunk of a tree with steel pins bored in at each end. It was a real skill to plough in rocky land. A first cousin of my father's, Michael Flynn of Kimeen, Lanmore, was a 'contract' farmer who would plough, etc. for different farmers (on hire) after he did his own work. He was a genius in negotiating a plough over and around rocks in our land.

Farmers did not have much time for flower gardens or indeed for ornamentation in general. There was very little 'congealed wealth', i.e., ornaments, even in the houses of the people. Everything was functional, while at the same time being artistic and pleasing to the eye. Attitudes towards trees and shrubs were almost indifferent. Each household had a 'sally garden', i.e. rods for making baskets, etc. There was a minimum of waste or rubbish. All was biologically degradable. Farming was practically totally organic. In an earlier generation my grandfather would harvest seaweed ('wrack') on the shore off Killadangan and use it as manure and 'top-dressing' for the fields. The level of land husbandry was really impressive and there was space for young and old to do 'whatever they could' on the land. The idea of holidays was foreign to most people. Summer holidays were viewed as a middle-class or *bourgeois* convention. I have tried to avoid taking holidays, as such, all my life. In fact, there was very little commercialisation of leisure in my early youth. The bifurcation of 'work' and 'leisure' was minimal. This was most healthy and gave a fuller life and more integration to those who were fully part of the family, neighbourhood and community. Unfortunately, the level of poverty was such that the majority of young people were forced to emigrate to England, Scotland, Wales, the United States, Canada, Australia, New Zealand and elsewhere in Ireland and leave the closely-knit community behind. For the duration of the Second World War and immediately afterwards, many young people stayed at home in Ireland, which was great for us all!

Summer and early autumn were busy on the land. The normal farmyard chores were greatly reduced because the cows and calves as well as the horses and donkeys were grazing outside. In fact, we milked the cows outside (sitting on a bucket turned upside down). Our sheep were sent out to *Gleann a Chailligh* in the Erriff Mountains (Willie Reilly's) and to *Tawneyard* in the Sheeffry Mountains (Martin Joyce's) for the summer. We also had cattle grazing in the *Deerpark* near Murrisk (Martin Thornton's) during summer and autumn.

The saving of the hay and the bringing home of the turf featured much during the late summer and early autumn. All the hay was cut with the scythe. It had to be shaken, turned, 'lapped', hand-cocked and 'fork-cocked' or 'tramp-cocked' during the mixed weather. In a very fine season some of the intermediate stages could be skipped. The children's roles were determined by their ages. We sometimes shook the hay with our hands. Often, we would come across a wild bees' hive in a dry spot in the meadow. Sometimes we would rob the hive of its honey – running the risk of being well and truly stung (which we deserved). There would be a wonderful odour of new-mown hay from the grassy meadows, which would drift across the valley in the gentle breeze. While this romantic dimension was most aesthetically enjoyable, there was a degree of serious hard labour there also. The bringing in of the hay ('ricking') to the 'haggard' when it was saved in the cocks was a day of great excitement. It took place in late August usually. A *meitheal* of neighbours attended and certain acknowledged elders supervised the building of the 'rick'. When finished it was a real work of art, and, when settled it was thatched with 'rushes' and held down by rows of hemp ropes. The 'ricking of the hay' was also a major social event.

The reaping of the corn was also an annual event, which usually took place in the second half of August. It involved mainly the cutting of the oats. The man of the house usually cut into the standing crop with the scythe. The mother and the other adults would come behind and lift the sheaves around and tie them with a few blades of oats ensuring that the head of the binder was up with the oats. The sheaves were then gathered together into 'stooks' (to ripen fully). Later the 'stooks' would be capped with four sheaves and made into 'barts'. After some time the 'barts' of oats would be collected into the 'haggard', where stacks of oats or wheat or corn would be built according to a well-established design. As in the case of the ricks of hay, brambles would be put under the stacks to prevent the dampness from 'heating' the crop. Not infrequently rats would nest at the bottom of the stacks. When bringing in the ripened and dried oats or wheat or corn into the barn there would be the cruel sport of setting terriers and other dogs on the poor unfortunate mother rat and her brood. I have always felt sorry for the poor rats or mice for the inhumane way we killed them. Occasionally a donkey (ass) would 'poke into' the stack of oats in order to get to the grain at the centre. All we would see sticking out would be his/her hindquarters. The tail would be wagging contentedly as he/she relished the rich oats!

In the 1930s and early in the 1940s all oats and wheat were threshed in the traditional way, usually in the kitchen/living room of the house. A sheet would be put over the dresser and one over the fireplace. A special round boulder would be placed on a chair without a back rest. The sheaves would be 'scutched' and most of the grain would be beaten out of the heads. After being duly 'scutched', the sheaves were put lying on the ground and the farmer would drive the remaining grain out of them with the 'flail', i.e. *'a manual threshing device, consisting of a long wooden handle or staff and a shorter free swinging stick attached to its end'* (*Universal Dictionary*, 1987). The grain then would be put through a 'riddle' to get rid of the short pieces of straw. The next event was the 'winnowing' of the oats, which was done on a day with a gentle breeze. A big sheet would be laid out on the 'winnowing patch' and the grain would be dropped in a controlled manner. The breeze did the rest. The 'chaff' would blow away furthest. The heavier grain would fall closest to the person winnowing. The lightest grain would

be fed to the horses and the cattle. The good grain would be preserved
in suitable bags or containers and kept away from access by rats. Oats
would be fed untouched to horses. Crushed oats would also be given to
horses and to cows. Oatmeal would be used for feeding chickens or for
making porridge. Oats were a very important staple food for man and
beast in rural Ireland in the 1930s. The threshing was also a *meitheal*
event in my early youth.

The late autumn months were busy for the farmers in that they were
engaged in saving the root crops and fruit, especially apples. The digging
of the potatoes was quite a laborious task. Very often the smaller children
had the job of picking the *póiríní* (small potatoes). The larger potatoes
would be stored in a 'pit', i.e. a long pile of potatoes with straw under
them and around them and a thick layer of soil neatly packed around
them. This would save the potatoes through the winter's frost and also
deter the rats from boring into them. Sometimes, a cunning rat would
bore through the soil wall of the pit.

Thatching was a very important annual task for the people who
had barns and cottages with thatched roofs. Wheaten straw was the
most popular thatch for the cottages. Good strong rushes were used
for barns. 'Scallops' were cut from hazel shoots (sally rods would be
unsuitable because they would take root in the thatch). Most men could
thatch a house to a reasonable standard. Birds, especially the wrens,
would nest in the 'bunthop' of the thatched roof. During the 1930s a
most successful public scheme of house-building took place across the
West of Ireland. Old thatched cottages were replaced by sturdy, well-
appointed, slate-roofed houses. The walls were made of dry stone. (My
grandfather, Mike Coyne, and my mother's brothers, John and Tommie
Coyne, were stonemasons.) Minister Seán T Ó Ceallaigh TD, was a
most progressive minister who succeeded in transforming the housing
conditions of a depressed people at a time of economic scarcity and
poverty. The 'Economic War' between Ireland and Britain was quite
severe at this time. In the long term it was a *felix culpa* ('happy fault'),
in that it forced the Irish people to become more self-reliant. The de
Valera Governments of the 1930s were quite radical and socialist,
despite the depressingly right-wing regimes in the European mainland
at the time.

3. Living as Part of a Neighbourhood

The long nights (of late autumn, winter and early spring) were characterised by visiting neighbours' houses, and being visited in return. The family rosary was recited every evening around seven o'clock. We knelt on the concrete floor and each member had to 'call out' a decade. We had the usual trimmings. The visitors would arrive after the rosary was said and anyone going on a visit to another house would not leave until the rosary was over. In my youth, the Catholic Church was, unlike today, very much a 'domestic Church'. The people would go to Westport Church once a week for Mass.

We also had house entertainment on occasion. When Johnsie Thornton and his mother, Maggie (from the Deerpark, a distance of over two miles) would come, Johnsie would sing from his repertoire of traditional ballads with the competence of a professional singer. We had a good gramophone and a collection of John McCormack's records, comedy sketches by Jimmy O'Dea, records of Irish music by the Ballinakill Céilí Band and others. Some nights we would be entertained to a 'gramophone concert'. The wireless was turned on only for news bulletins, as batteries were hard to come by during 'the Emergency'.

In winter, cattle, horses and donkeys were kept in their respective stables or barns during the hours of darkness. The chores associated with their 'indoor state' included giving the animals hay and other feeds in buckets, i.e. mangels, turnips, potatoes, crushed oats, etc.

Pulling hay off the rick on a cold frosty morning was not easy! Cleaning out the barns was another toilsome task – usually given to the younger teenagers. After cleaning out, a bedding of straw, ferns (bracken) or rushes was spread so that the animal could lie down in comfort. The bedding also absorbed the urine, which would be valuable manure. In the farmyard nothing was wasted!

Winter and early spring was a time for repairing fences, which in our case were mainly drystone walls with a strip or two of barbed wire on top of them. The fences between farms were known as 'mairns' and each farmer was responsible for the maintaining of half of the fence. In the old 'Rundale System' of half-holdings almost every second garden or field belonged to a different owner. This led to serious conflict between neighbours because of trespassing sheep or poorly maintained fences. In addition to paying attention to walls and fences, farmers also used the short days to open and repair drains. Because of the 'hard times' many young fathers had to emigrate for work, mostly to England during the winter and summer months. They would return home for the spring and harvest time. They would also return home for Christmas. This seasonal migration was very painful and put heavy burdens on the migrating fathers and on the mothers forced to rear their usually large families and keep a close eye on the land.

Most of the food consumed at home was grown and produced on the farm, i.e. milk, butter, potatoes, vegetables, oatmeal, fowl, bacon (every family killed and preserved a fattened pig = three hundredweight in weight), mutton (occasionally sheep would be killed), hen and duck eggs, some fruit, etc. All of this food would be classified as organic today. The townlands (called villages) were informal or communal welfare systems. For instance, should one neighbour's cow die, another neighbour would give the unlucky family milk and butter freely (as far as they could). Also, should a young father or mother become ill, neighbours and relations would come to their assistance. For example, they would help with the spring or the harvest as the case may be. Whenever a family went to visit a relation they would always bring food gifts with them, i.e. bread, butter, tea and sugar, etc. This would avoid embarrassment for the hosts as the people were for the most part just surviving. At wakes, neighbours 'chipped in' as they did at stations, i.e. a seasonal neighbourhood Mass system. In addition to food, people would lend chairs, stools, cups, etc. whenever the occasion would demand. Also, neighbours would take turns to stay up at night and keep vigil with a neighbour who was sick or dying. People also bartered many items and lent instruments such as ploughs, harnesses, etc. When a neighbour died, farm work would stop immediately and would not resume until the person's remains were buried. The clock was stopped and mirrors covered while the corpse was over-board in the house!

Because of the system of neighbourhood cooperation, money was not as central as it became later when the neighbourhood system broke down. Looking back at it all now, some seventy years later, I feel we got much more out of less. The current Welfare State, despite its generous monetary and other provisions, has failed to replace the qualitative aspect of the informal welfare system of what appeared to be a much poorer (in money terms) system. This is not romantic nostalgia. The '*cailleach*' (the bed in the alcove in the kitchen) was a more satisfying and natural place to spend one's declining years than even in most up-to-date old people's home, in my opinion. Society in the 1930s was much more family-orientated than it became later!

The level of material poverty among the small farming community was very severe during the 1930s. My own family was among the more privileged because of my father's good job. For instance, he had a private motor car and was in a position to enable his children to go to school (as far as the Leaving Certificate). Some people, however, just barely existed.

Where the '*meitheal* system' did not work or where a childless couple (without the support of an extended family) was forced to eke out a living on their own, they would sometimes endure great hardship. The widow's and old age pension did help somewhat. Prior to the building of the slated houses, some of the thatched cottages were very congested because of the larger number of children.

4. DOMESTIC LIFE

The house in which we lived in Loughloon, Westport, was a thatched cottage originally built at the end of the farm. It was the traditional Mayo cottage (in the vernacular architectural sense) with heavy walls. There was a single chimney (with two flues) between the kitchen/living room and the 'room above'. The room below was smaller and had a loft over it. There was a '*cailleach*' (alcove, the width of a double bed, near the fire in the kitchen. There was a spring well near the rear of the house. As stated earlier, my father had the house re-roofed with iron in 1936. The outside walls were raised and two small rooms built at the rear of the house. The walls between the kitchen and the new rooms and that between the kitchen and the 'room below' were replaced by wooden partitions (to give more space). The net result of the renovation was the increase of space and a decrease of snugness. My father intended that we stay in Loughloon only until he could purchase a farm nearer to Westport, but the Emergency intervened.

With regard to amenities, there were no indoor toilets or running water, yet the people maintained a good standard of personal hygiene.

Fleas and lice were problematic – partly because of the people's proximity to domestic animals but also due to lack of facilities. When DDT came later it would help to control these problems. The absence of electricity meant that we were totally dependent on paraffin oil lamps and lanterns and wax candles for light at night. The dim light provided shadows and ghostly images. The scarcity of space in the relatively small houses was coped with by the use of 'settle-beds' in the kitchen and canopy beds ('tent-beds') in the rooms. The old couple would sleep in the '*cailleach*'.

All food was cooked on the open fire. Iron pots of various sizes were used. The pot-oven was used for baking the bread, with coals under and over. Some pots were big enough to boil a stone of potatoes or roast a turkey or a leg of mutton. People would rarely kill lambs or chickens – it was always adult sheep and hens. The killing of a goose was normal for a feast or celebration. The fat of the goose, i.e. 'goose grease', was a valuable lubricant for the axles of cartwheels. Flour was bought in ten-stone bags. When the flour bag was empty it would be used for bedclothes, either as a pillowslip or part of the sheets. Feathers were used for the making of a large sack for under the sheet in the settle-beds and in other beds, i.e. the 'feather tick'. It was very comfortable and warm, even on a cold night.

The fire was never quenched. Turf was the main fuel. At night, the fire would be 'raked', i.e. the coals would be covered with ash and in the morning the coals would be still burning. The raked fire was also a form of central heating, which kept the fireplace and kitchen warm. The fireplace was open with a stone seat on each side, i.e. the 'hobs'. These seats were usually reserved for the 'man of the house' and the 'woman of the house'. We children would love to get a chance to occupy the 'royal thrones'. Over the fireplace you had the 'chimney board' or the 'mantelpiece' on which would be two brass candlesticks (to be used for Mass in the house, or for beside the corpse at the wake). There would also be a crucifix in the place of honour. A sally rod would sometimes be lying on two pegs under the mantelpiece, which was the deterrent to misbehaving children. (Corporal punishment was acceptable in moderation.) The parents' and grandparents' rosary beads would also hang from the supports of the 'chimney board'. Each kitchen had a picture of the Sacred Heart, usually with a small red globed lamp in front of it on a small stand. There would be a holy water font inside the front door. A picture of the 'holy family' was also hanging in each home. Holidays were holydays.

The kitchen table was a most important piece of furniture. The family always assembled around the kitchen table for meals. The idea of members eating casually would be very rare. The dinner was in the middle of the day and would be presided over by the 'man of the house'. Potatoes would be the staple diet. Meat and fish would not be available every day. The main vegetables would be cabbage, turnips and onions. Peas, carrots and parsnips would be available less frequently. The occasional rabbit would be very popular. When meat or fish were absent, we would have potatoes with butter and milk. Fried potatoes were also popular. Jam was also sometimes available. I rarely saw fruit, i.e. apples, bananas, oranges, pears, etc. on the table for supper. The breakfast menu consisted mainly of oatmeal porridge, bread and butter and (sometimes) an egg or two. From time to time, families would add extras including currant cake, or a dessert of some kind. Having a 'fry' for breakfast would be a feature of a feast day, i.e. Christmas, Easter, etc. Tea was the only beverage on offer. Coffee was very rare, even during times of rationing. The annual killing of the pig was an occasion for sharing (with neighbours) of the parts of the carcass not suitable for salting. There were no refrigeration facilities available. The absence of waste was a feature of country life. Food leftovers, which were not re-cooked for a later meal, would be fed to dogs or to the fowl. The food fed to the pig included 'swill' from leftovers after meals. Onnie Conway would 'try the hens' to detect those 'laying out'.

5. THE VILLAGE SCHOOL

Going to school in rural Ireland in the 1930s was obligatory until the age of fourteen years. My eldest brother, Seán, eleven months my senior, and I began our schooling in the convent school in Portumna, County Galway in 1935. One year and a half later we came to Loughloon and were sent to Brackloon National School. The teachers were Mr Joseph Maher and Mrs Ellen Gibbons. The school, which was built in 1849, was quite rudimentary. On our first day we sat on the long forms or stools behind the door in the junior half of the school. There was only one fireplace in the school building and it was on the master's side. An oven of red coals, taken from the master's fire would be placed on an iron sheet in our side and we would heat our hands over the oven. Each pupil had a slate with a special type of marker (not chalk). There were quite a number of children in attendance. Everyone had to walk to school. There was an obligation on every family with children in attendance to give a cartload of dry turf to the school every year. Otherwise, one would be required to bring two sods of turf each day. The playground was a bushy hill at the back of the school with the boys on one side and the girls on the other. The girls and the infants had access to a small yard. Toilets were on the outside of the building. As in all schools at the time, the teachers had the right to use corporal punishment.

The standards of teaching and learning were good and pupils were well grounded in the basics of religion, reading, writing, numeracy and general knowledge. I would judge that those pupils who finished their schooling in Brackloon National School and took their lessons seriously reached the standard of the Junior Certificate today in the subjects taught. The rapport between pupil and teacher varied. Most of us loved Mrs Gibbons as she was very sympathetic. Our relationship with Mr Maher was a mixture of fear and respect. Not every family was in a position to keep their older children in school every day because of domestic pressures. Absence from school was treated very seriously by the State and we had the threat of being sent to an 'industrial school' if we 'mitched' from school or our parents kept us at home too much.

From an academic point of view, I owe much to the convent school in Portumna, County Galway, and to my four years in Brackloon National School. We were taught well how to calculate and how to read and write. We were challenged and introduced to new topics. At school our world expanded. We were also taught to appreciate nature. I remember the master criticising those farmers who would cut a holly tree to put it in a gap. We were taught how to vote, i.e. the proportional representation system. Current affairs were also discussed once a week. In 1939, when the Second World War broke out, we were trained how to respond to an air-raid, etc. In fact, our games were often war games. At the time few children wished to play the part of the British soldier. The people had not realised the malign disposition of the Hitler regime at the time and the memory of the treatment of the 'peasant' Irish (Catholics) by the 'colonial occupying forces' and local ascendancy left an anti-British legacy, which was intuitively internalised by the vast majority of the children. While this latent anti-British disposition was present, I would, in retrospect, interpret the message of our teachers and parents in a more positive sense. They were trying to instil into us a greater pride in our own country and culture.

After so long a colonisation and persecution we had become a 'captured people' with very low self-esteem. Looking-up to the British was looking-down on ourselves. *Sinn Féin,* under Arthur Griffith and *Fianna Fáil* under Éamon de Valera, had preached a gospel of Irish self-worth. So also had movements like the GAA, *Conradh na Gaeilge,* the Co-operative Movement, Trade Union Movement, *Muintir na Tíre,* The PTAA and others. Other political leaders subscribed to this necessary corrective philosophy. The partial success of the independence movement also contributed to this sense of emancipation. The success of Irish neutrality in the Second World War also added to our sense of self-worth. We had to become independent in mind before we could become voluntarily interdependent. All suppressed minorities, it appears to me now, must go through the process of achieving a sense of self-esteem. Unfortunately, many of our learned historians and commentators have failed to appreciate what was happening in this regard during the 1920s, 1930s, 1940s, 1950s and even later in Ireland. In my own studies, I was later to find evidence of this 'post-colonial attitudinal schizophrenia' in the Irish population (see *Prejudice and Tolerance in Ireland* 1977 [pp 374-5] and *Prejudice in Ireland Revisited,* 1996, pp 262ff). The explicit nationalist phase in Irish history has been an essential one.

At the level of social class, most of us pupils in Brackloon School could be classed as belonging to the rural (small farmer) working class. Some would end up with skills or crafts and the odd one would enter the white-collar professional classes – largely due to our continuing in education (schooling). Therefore, there was a tendency for many to suffer from 'induced submissiveness' while those in the middle class and among the professionals, i.e. priests, teachers, pension officers, and others, would manifest their 'induced dominance'. This class condition has been one of the great impediments (universally) to true equality and full personal development. Of course, some of our most critical commentators from privileged-class backgrounds, and their new associates who have experienced a level of upward class mobility tend to fail to understand the need for 'collective class emancipation'!

The teaching of religion was central in the national school curriculum. This is something for which I am personally very grateful. The pedagogy of the Christian doctrine classes was most effective. The annual visit of the Diocesan Inspector, a priest of the diocese, who would examine each of us, was prepared for with diligence and care. We were asked to learn 'off-by-heart' answers from the Catechism and quotations from the Gospels. What used to amaze us was how well our parents and other adults in the village remembered the Catechism answers, when we would be rehearsing them while working in the fields. On later reflection, it struck me that the contemporaries of Christ in his time knew their Old Testament in a similar manner.

Something has gone seriously wrong with the manner in which religion is being taught today in the home and in the schools, in my opinion. We (of my generation) were very fortunate in having received such a solid grounding in our faith. Of course, our understanding of certain tenets of Church teaching have improved since the 1930s, because of the sad experience of the failure of Christian Churches to prevent the atrocities of the Second World War and the positive clarifications and changes of Vatican Two. Also, the advances in the study of Sacred Scripture have enriched our understanding of the text. All that having been admitted, I would still contend that the teaching of religion in my pre-Second World War days in Brackloon National School gave me and others a sound foundation in our faith, which I do not detect in the younger generation today.

When Seán and I arrived in Brackloon School, we were told when we would be doing our 'First Holy Communion', i.e. when we reached the age of seven years. We told the teachers that we had already received our First Communion and Confession in Portumna (where the age of seven was not the rule and we were invited to receive when we came 'to the age of reason'). Most Rev Dr Deignan, bishop of Clonfert, had laid down the 'use-of-reason rule'. I was only five years and three months old when I went to my First Holy Communion, in June 1936. The master in Brackloon would not believe us. So I came home and told my mother what the teacher had said. She wrote a fairly curt letter to the master advising him not to accuse her sons of telling lies without knowing the facts. She attached a copy of our First Communion Certificates. Mr Maher's reaction lives in my memory (seventy-five years later). He said: '*I see the Connemara woman can write!*' and he accepted that we had already been admitted 'to the rails'. He probably disagreed with Bishop Deignan's innovation. The master was supposed to have a policy of delaying Confirmation as long as possible. This would ensure that all parents would keep their children at school until they were confirmed. In the case of Seán and myself, we were delayed until we were in sixth class (at the ages of twelve and thirteen) before we were confirmed. (By that time we were in the Christian Brothers' School in Castlebar Street, Westport.) So, in the end, Mr Maher got the final say!

6. POLITICAL AWARENESS IN LOUGHLOON

The political issues of the 1930s that entered my consciousness were rather limited. We were going through the so-called 'Economic War' with Britain because we halved the annuities paid to compensate for the return of the land to the Irish farmers. I have a recollection of the 1937 referendum establishing *Bunreacht na hÉireann* and the inauguration of Dr Dubhghlas de h-Íde as the first President of Ireland in 1938. There was a photograph in the daily newspaper of the Cavalry Guard of Honour on horses. The Spanish Civil War was not discussed with us children. The two TDs who were household names were Micheál Ó Cléirigh (of Oldhead, Westport and living in Ballyhaunis) and Dick Walsh. They were known to my mother, probably because of her involvement in the War of Independence and in the Civil War in the early 1920s. They were both *Fianna Fáil* TDs. There would be fairly robust arguments between supporters of *Fianna Fáil* and *Fine Gael*. The latter incorporated *Cumann na nGael*, i.e. the party that was in power between 1922 and 1932. *Fianna Fáil* took over power in 1932.

My uncles, Pat and John McGreal, as already noted, were both 'old' IRA men. Uncle Pat died in 1919 and was buried 'in the tricolour'. He and a blacksmith, Mr Tony Hoban, James Street, (whose brother, Harry Hoban, was clerk of the Church in Westport) had a secret forge on the Loughloon commonage, near Doirín in '*Taobh a'Riabhach*' where they made pikes for the volunteers. Uncle John (affectionately known as 'the Major') was 'a runner' at the time of the Carrowkennedy Ambush. John told me that every able-bodied young man in the valley was in support of the volunteers (old IRA) during the War of Independence. The Civil War had a very negative impact on the solidarity, which prevailed between

1919 and 1922. The pain of the divisions and the deaths and injuries that took place during the Civil War were still raw in the people's memory. (Westport once had a strong Republican presence during the Civil War under General Michael Kilroy, from Newport, while General Joe Ring, from Drummindoo, Westport, was on the Free-State side and tragically lost his young life on the Ox Mountains during the conflict.) Although republican, we were never strongly anti-British or anti-Protestant in my family. My father's company was Scottish and its manager was Presbyterian.

As the decade drew to a close the clouds of war in Europe were gathering. The Third Reich in Germany, under Adolf Hitler, had taken over from the Weimar Republic in 1933 and became an aggressive dictatorship. The *Treaty of Versailles* humiliated the defeated German people and built up resentment, which the charismatic (demagogic) Adolf Hitler and his ruthless colleagues exploited. He built a war machine and preached an ideology of Aryan racial superiority in his book *Mein Kampf*. This generated a false pride among the German lower-middle classes. His original plan was to extend the Reich to all German peoples. The League of Nations was incapable of checking Hitler's expansionist ambitions. The scapegoating of the Jews for most of Germany's evils was based on a lie, but there was a strong residue of anti-Semitism, which was also used in a most evil manner. The legacy of the 1929 Wall Street Crash also had negative effects throughout the Western World.

On 3rd September 1939 Britain declared war on Hitler's Germany. This marked the beginning of six years of the bloodiest war fought to date. Éamon de Valera, when Chairperson of the League of Nations, tried to check the advance of Germany. When the war broke out in 1939, he opted for neutrality, with the support of *Dáil Éireann*. Irish support for Britain's war efforts was indirect, i.e. Irish migrant workers worked in British industry and services during the war. Also, there were food exports to Britain on a 'credit basis'. Northern Ireland, as part of the United Kingdom, took an active part in the war. Many Irish men and women from the Twenty-Six Counties joined the British Army. Others became casualties in the British Merchant Navy. Two of the reasons why the Irish Government could not see itself entering the war on the side of Britain, were the fact that the 1922 Treaty resulted in the Six Counties being divided from the rest of Ireland, and the presence of the British Army as an occupying force on Irish soil. The maintenance of Irish neutrality was an adroit exercise by Éamon de Valera and his government. Once the war broke out in Europe, a State of Emergency was declared in Ireland and the Defence Forces were increased accordingly. We followed the events of the war at home on the wireless, i.e. *Raidió Éireann*, 'Germany Calling' (Lord Haw Haw) and occasionally the BBC (which was difficult to receive). I feel, looking back now, that many Irish people were 'taken in' by the propaganda of the German government at the time.

7. FAMILY, FAITH AND LAND

Growing up on a mountain hill farm in the West of Ireland under the shadow of Croagh Patrick was a relatively happy time for me, my brothers and sister and peers. Our recreation was informal. *Bhíodh muid níos mó ag sugradh ná ag imirt cluichí*. Our games were spontaneous. We explored the hills and loved to come across foxes' and badgers' dens. We were very much in touch with older generations. There was very little exclusive peer socialisation or association. We also did not have to endure an extended adolescence. We were always curious about nature – animals, plants, birds, fish, etc. There was a rich supply of ghost stories and we had the usual 'haunted' places. Behind our cottage in Loughloon there were ruins of a stable (the roof had been taken off it). Two elderly grey-haired women were seen in it. The cows were supposed to be frightened in it. It was unoccupied save from being used as a pen for sheep and lambs.

There was a garden over one hundred yards above the cottage (which was the original site of the cottage but had to be abandoned because they failed to find water), which we called 'The Gold Garden'. Originally, it was known as *'Garra Mhicheáil'* (my great-great grandfather was Micheál). My grand-aunt (later Mrs Mary Flynn of Kimeen, Lanmore) had a dream that there was a crock of gold under a certain spot in the field. She was told in her dream where to dig and that she would come across a snake-like worm before reaching the crock of gold. She was warned not to take anybody with her. The next day she took a spade with her and proceeded to the spot and started to dig. The dog followed her. After some time she came across the monster worm. The dog ran away with fright and my grand-aunt Mary followed the dog with even greater fright. When she returned there was no gold to be found. As children, we all tried our hand at digging for gold but to no avail! Numerous other such stories were told to us around the fire on a winter's night. Of course, all this opened up our imagination and created a sense of wonder. We had no comics or movies and we went to Westport only for Mass on Sundays and occasionally for shopping. We always called to my late grand-uncle's shop, Austin McGreal's Pub and Grocery on the Quay Road. One member of the family was a very popular local doctor, Michael McGreal. Later (when I was in secondary school) I would spend time with the old widow (my grand-aunt through marriage) of the corner pub and grocery, Mrs Bridget (née Moran) McGreal.

There was a subcultural difference between the 'townies' and us 'country mugs'. This urban/rural divide was something that I have never really succeeded in crossing! I still see myself as a 'country peasant' and I have always been proud of it. The quality of life of the much-derided peasants with their primacy of the personal relationships is, in my opinion, superior to the more sophisticated bourgeois lifestyle of the urbanised middle and upper-middle classes. Wealth and sophistication cannot compensate for the loss of the richly personal relationships of family, neighbourhood and community. Rural peasant culture is not without its very serious faults and jealousies, but, at least, it is human! Of course, there are also humanly rich pockets of 'urban peasantry', which bear qualities of the life of their rural counterparts. Had I been reared in such environments, I would remain attached to the urban version. The current capitalist, free-market model of society appears to me not to be supportive of family, neighbourhood and community living. Geographic and social mobility, which are characteristic of our current social model, make the creation and maintenance of stable domestic and community life well nigh impossible. The human casualties of our current 'progress' are enormous. Power today is in the hands of wealth and arrogance, while there is an illusion of democracy. The rule of law is a good thing but its function can be very destructive, i.e. the rule of liberal-capitalist law obstructed the relief of the starving people during the Irish Famine. Current law facilitates the market priorities often at the expense of family, neighbourhood and community.

Returning to the 1930s, I would like to comment on the life cycle of the people around us at the time. The first marriage I remember was that of a neighbour, Broddie O'Connor, to Mary Elizabeth Heraty from Owenwee, the next village over the hill. It took place on a Sunday afternoon in 1940 after a nuptial ceremony in St Mary's Church, Westport. The married couple came in a 'hackney' motor car. That night, there was a party in the groom's house. My uncle John was Broddie's best man. My parents were at the wedding and at the party. The following Monday morning there were 'two straw masks' on the pillars of the gate into the house. This indicated that the 'straw boys' had been present the night before. Honeymoons were quite rare for the ordinary people in those days. The new woman, Mary O'Connor, was a great addition to Loughloon and became one of my mother's closest friends and neighbours. She became just like a member of an extended family. (Of course, Broddie O'Connor and my father were second cousins anyhow.)

There were a few births in the village/valley every year. Families ranged from six to ten on average. Fourteen children would be considered large. All births that I knew of at the time took place at home. I was not yet aware of the 'facts of life'. My mother, who was a retired children's nurse, was present at practically all the births in a purely voluntary capacity. My father's first cousin, Dr Michael McGreal, who had a great reputation for confinement (delivering babies), would also be present. (We thought he found the baby under a head of cabbage and brought him or her to the mammy!) Baptism would take place within two or three days, with the mother not being able to attend. In fact, there was a 'churching' ceremony, which a mother had to attend in the church, before she could visit a neighbour's house.

During the last few years of the 1930s and early 1940s, there were babies born in four other houses in the valley, i.e. to Eddie and Nora O'Malley (Bofara), to Michael and Annie Heraty (Brackloon), to Pat and Katie Walsh (Loughloon) and to Broddie and Mary O'Connor (Loughloon). Sadly, young Peter Walsh died and went to heaven a short time after his birth. We children were not made familiar with the details of the baby's death. All I remember is the great sadness. I learned very early in life that *every child is an only child to his or her parents* (no matter how many children were in the family). The rearing of children and babies was integrated into the daily routine of the family. Grannies would play a big part in the rearing and would watch the infant while the mother did her work in the home or in the farmyard. The custom of residence was 'patrilocality' and, at times, 'matrilocality', i.e. the young couple living in the home of the groom's or bride's parents. Today, neolocality seems to be almost universal, i.e. newlyweds have their own residence. This leads to a big increase in houses and is, in my opinion, quite wasteful. The division of the parents' residence so as to provide a granny flat or apartment could be a good compromise. In the 1930s, children, male and female, wore skirts until they were three or four years old, i.e. until they were toilet trained. The big advantage of being reared on a small farm in the 1930s was the great play space in the fields and gardens. Also, with so many siblings and children in neighbouring homes, we were introduced to peers early in life and in a safe and controlled manner. There was little pampering (generally) of children.

Death was a normal but desperately sad event in the valley. Once a person died, the clock in the house of the deceased was stopped and would remain so until the remains were buried. Special elders would assist the dying person with prayers. The priest would be sent for when things were nearing an end. Extreme Unction was seen as the sacrament of the dying. (Today it is seen as the *Sacrament of the Sick.*) On the death of a neighbour, all work stopped, except routine jobs such as milking, feeding, etc. Some farmers would not complete a cock of hay on hearing of the sad news or finish a 'bay' of hay they were mowing. People returned from the bog or from the hill where they would be working as soon as they heard the news. Such tasks as dipping sheep or shearing them would be discontinued on the death of a neighbour. In fact, this was evidence that we were all one family. In a real sense, death made brothers and sisters of all of us! Even before the death of the deceased, neighbours would stay up at night keeping vigil with the person about to depart. Communal prayers were recited. It was on such occasions we young people witnessed faith in life after death with God. This was better than a thousand sermons or Catechism lessons. The way people approached death also taught us their value for the life of the loved one while alive on earth.

In the 1930s the majority of those who died were waked in their homes and were not brought to the Church before burial (that rule came in under the reign of Archbishop Joseph Walsh only in the 1940s). The two nights' wake was an important social event. It provided the family of the deceased time to grieve with the support of neighbours. Wakes were all-night affairs. When a very old person died, the wake was also a celebration of their life and games would be played to mark the occasion. When a young person died such actions would be more restrained. Two deaths took place in the valley in the 1930s that I remember. The late Mrs Bridget McGreal (née McNally) was the first person I saw 'over-board'. She was laid-out beautifully in a canopy (tent) bed lined with linen sheets. I noticed the mirror in the room was covered with a white cloth. The second person was the late Mr Ned Heraty (Brackloon), who died suddenly. I did not see his remains over-board. I remember the motor hearse came to the valley to bring the corpse to the church (for one night) the evening before the funeral; and 'high Mass'. The route the hearse took to the church was 'the long way around', so as to avoid passing the graveyard.

Most coffins were carried on the 'well' of the sidecar (drawn by a horse) with the mourners sitting on both sides of the remains. In March 1940, I accompanied my mother to the funeral of the late Mr Affie Gannon of Belclare (quite close to the graveyard). His remains were laid out in the coffin. When they took the coffin outside the door of the cottage they placed it on two chairs and an elder called out three 'Hail Marys'. The local men then shouldered the coffin and the two chairs were knocked in opposite directions. I remember asking an old man why the chairs were knocked in opposite directions. *'To confuse the "good people" so that they will not know which way he was taken,'* he said. The remains were carried shoulder high to Aughaval graveyard, about four hundred yards away, and I witnessed a burial for the first time. The use of snuff and clay pipes at wakes was probably to suppress any unpleasant odours, although the people had ways of preventing the remains becoming warm, which would cause problems over forty-eight hours. The mode of transport at local funerals was by means of sidecar. Motor cars were very scarce before the Second World War.

In the 1930s, many young men and women had to emigrate for work to England, the United States and elsewhere. There were a number of factories in Westport, i.e. Shoe Factory, Thread Factory, 'Cosiwear Garments' Factory and Pollexfen Flour Mills at the Quay. A number of other businesses employed workers also such as Charles Hughes Limited, PJ Kelly Limited, JJ O'Malley, John Gibbons, M Molloy & Sons and others. Cargo ships would bring goods into Westport Quay and local men would unload the ships and haul the cargo (by horse and cart) to the warehouses. A number of men would work for the County Council on the roads. Some would hire out their labour on the land and on the bog. Wages in most of the jobs were very poor and the work was very hard. The 1930s were tough times in Ireland.

In the late 1930s, a number of local families were transferred up to County Meath from Bolybreen, where they were settled on better land. Their places were duly subdivided among the families left behind. Of course, it was an attempt by the Government of the day to make up for the injustice done to the ancestors of these poor people when they were expelled from their lands in Ulster and elsewhere by Oliver Cromwell and others to make way for the 'planters'. My own ancestors were expelled from County Armagh (in the Blackwater area) by Cromwell's *Act of Settlement 1654* and forced to eke out a living on the almost barren land on the side of Croagh Patrick and its foothills. In modern day language this would be known as 'ethnic cleansing' of the 'native Irish Catholics' to make way for the Scottish Presbyterian and English Protestants. This move was popularly referred to as *'to Hell or to Connaught!'*

An Taoiseach Éamon de Valera tried to reverse this migration of people. Unfortunately, he did not have access to the landed estates of Ulster, with the result that our family could not return home! This mass settlement of dispossessed Irish Catholics in the seventeenth century was akin to the refugee settling in Palestine and elsewhere. The native Irish Catholics were dealt a very cruel deal by their colonial masters. The seventeenth century was a horrific time for the native Irish! The folk memory of this ethnic cleansing became somewhat blurred, probably because of the further waves of persecution which followed the refugees' arrival here. What was done to the Catholic clergy and to the people who protected them by the eighteenth-century Irish Parliament in Dublin was so unjust and cruel, that it is difficult to record. May God forgive the perpetrators of such collective cruelty. Because of this I have avoided entering the old Irish Parliament building in College Green, which is now occupied by the Bank of Ireland. Liberal-capitalist dogma prevented the authorities from giving the starving poor the necessary support during the Great Famine.

The persecution of Roman Catholics in Ireland continued from the reign of Elizabeth I until the end of the eighteenth century. The backlash on the defeat of the 1798 Rising in Connaught was followed by the Act of Union in 1801 and was crowned by the experience of the Great Famine. An example of the impact of the latter was the change in the number of dwellings in the valley (of Loughloon, Brackloon and Bofara) between 1841 and 1851, from thirty-eight to eight dwellings. The Famine was aptly defined by someone as an act of passive genocide by our colonial masters and others who greedily exploited the poor peasant Catholics.

The Westport Rural Area was very much involved in the Land War (1879-1906) led by Mayo man, Michael Davitt, who was one of the greatest Irish leaders, in my opinion. There was also an involvement of the local people in the Fenian Movement. I was always given to understand that my grandfather, 'Big John' (McGreal), was at the time, implicated with the Fenians. I could not confirm this information. It was clear to me growing up that we were 'outsiders' in relation to the British rule in Ireland. The people had suffered so much over so many generations to feel very hurt deep down inside. At the same time, they did not resent those who possessed the good land or who were now in positions of privilege – from the old regime. Revisionist historians have glossed over the human misery caused by successive generations of colonial and other rulers. We should never forget that some strong Catholic farmers also benefited from the exodus of their weaker colleagues after the Famine.

Life expectancy was greatly reduced by widespread pulmonary tuberculosis, which decimated many families over the years. In fact, the family of my grandmother from Borris (behind Croagh Patrick), Katie Mortimer, was forced to abandon their home because of tuberculosis in the early 1900s. It was mostly young people who died from TB. Creagh House near Ballinrobe was the nearest sanatorium to our village. The untimely death of so many young people cast a shadow of gloom over us all. The discovery of a cure for this killing disease at the end of the 1940s was a great relief to us all. Credit is due to the then Minister for Health Dr Noel Browne TD, (himself a victim of TB), and his Department for their energetic approach to the treatment of those likely to succumb to tuberculosis. In the 1930s we had no such cure. Popular ballads highlighted the tragic scourge of TB, e.g. 'Noreen Bawn', 'Little Boy Blue' and others.

8. THE DOMESTIC CHURCH

Religion occupied a central role in the lives of most people. My mother's sister, Aunt Annie, Sr Gregory, was a nun in the St Louis Order. My father's nephew, James McDonnell of Philadelphia, was an ordained priest. Sr Gregory and Fr James were much admired in the family. A priest or a nun in the family gave an advantage to a young family, because it removed the false mystique associated with a vocation. It also gave witness to faith in God. The religious practice of the people was centred on family prayer. There were religious objects and pictures in the houses. Weekly Mass attendance rate was almost one hundred per cent. The men's and women's sodalities were very popular and young people could join when they reached fourteen years. Membership of the sodalities involved monthly Confessions and Holy Communion. Sermons were thematic, rather than commentary on the Sunday Gospel, i.e. themes would include family, honesty, purity, etc. A list of themes for the year would be published each Advent. A parish mission was held every three years with a women's week followed by a men's week. The missioners preached with fiery eloquence at times. The ten o'clock Mass each Sunday was for schoolchildren.

The image of the priest was one of authority and of being somewhat distant from the ordinary people. Priests' material standards of living appeared 'middle class'. Their houses were big and imposing. Although the priests came from the people, i.e. from the strong farmer and business and professional classes, the training seemed to have the effects of making them a 'tribe of Levi', i.e. a tribe apart. Ordinary families could not afford to send their sons to the diocesan minor seminary (St Jarlath's) to ensure that they would be eligible for St Patrick's College, Maynooth, which was the major seminary. The sanctity and humility of some priests enabled them to relate to the people in a non-patronising way. At times, priests displayed a disposition of 'righteous anger', which made us afraid of them. Some of this may have reflected the medieval village, which was dominated by the church, the manor and the guild; although in Ireland the troubled years of the persecution of Catholics resulted in the manor and the guild becoming Protestant and Anglo-Irish. The sons of the poorer families with vocations to the priesthood had to go to the missionary societies and religious orders. (This class distinction within the clergy and religious has been reduced somewhat over the past twenty-five years because of the rise in secularism and the reduction in vocations. Once the diocesan vocations began to dry up, Maynooth broadened its intake and the missionary seminaries were the first to feel the pinch.)

Prayer, fasting and pilgrimages were key elements of the devotional life of the people around us. Some older people became mystics and lived in constant conscious presence of God. Despite this intensity of their prayer life, they were quite discreet and were not over-pious. The older women in particular spent the last years of their lives praying and (those who could read) reading devotional magazines, such as the *Messenger of the Sacred Heart*, the *Far East* and others that they could get or borrow. Oral prayer was more common than silent meditation. Grandparents played a large part in handing on the faith to the children. (This was the advantage of patrilocality, living in the same house.) Pilgrimages were an integral part of our liturgical life. Being reared on the foothills of Croagh Patrick ensured that the annual pilgrimage on the last Friday in July, Garland Friday or on Reek Sunday, the last Sunday in July, would be a must for us as we grew up.

I think I climbed the Reek for the first time in 1940 (on 'Reek Sunday') at the age of nine years. An annual pilgrimage to St Patrick's Shrine in Mámean in Mámean was also an early experience for me. (Mámean was on the Maamturk Mountains near the home of my Connemara grandparents.) A third traditional shrine, which was very popular in my youth, was the holy well in Kilgeever, near Louisburgh, which was one of the last pre-Norman Patrician establishments. Knock Shrine was becoming very popular after the war in the 1950s. It did not loom large in our liturgical year before the War. Maybe, it was not in the traditional ascetic mode.

A feature about Croagh Patrick, Mámean and Kilgeever was their predominantly lay nature. *They were the people's shrines*. In fact, there was a degree of clerical opposition to some of the native shrines during the reign of Cardinal Cullen in the late nineteenth century. This opposition was part of the movement to bring the people back to worship in the churches, especially, the adoration of the Blessed Sacrament. The building of the chapel on Croagh Patrick in 1905 (and in Mámean in 1985) may have gone someway to integrate the traditional and the modern emphasis. (Pope John Paul II's encouragement to return to worship at our traditional shrines in 1979, while in Knock, had also given a welcome boost to the revival of our truly traditional pilgrimages.)

When Archbishop Gilmartin died in 1939, Archbishop Joseph Walsh from Newport, County Mayo (and affectionately known as 'Tiny' since he was quite tall) succeeded as Archbishop of Tuam. Some had thought that Bishop Michael Browne, a native of Westport, could have got the Tuam appointment. The public reception for the new Archbishop in Westport in 1939 was enormous. There was a procession from the station to St Mary's Church, which included all schoolchildren, sodalities, Children of Mary, Urban Councillors, religious brothers and nuns and a large section of laity. There were bands and bunting. I took part in the reception. There were a number of priests in surplices and soutanes. It was as if a Pope or an Emperor had arrived in town. This demonstrated the prestige of the Archbishop and the power of the clergy at the time. People listened closely to the Archbishop's words and his message was discussed later among the adults. At the time we children were mainly interested in spectacle. (Thirty years later, in 1969, Archbishop Joseph Walsh ordained me in St Mary's Church, Westport. Some said it was his last 'hurrah'.)

While a degree of 'induced dominance' was evident in the way the clergy expected a high degree of docility from the faithful, they were also good friends of people in need. They sought to protect the vulnerable from abuse. In recent times there have been a number of very serious scandals committed by a minority of priests, who were found guilty of the sexual abuse of children. In fact, the priests, in my experience, were the great defenders of children from sex abuse and would confront anyone who would ever touch a child – be he or she a relative of the child or a stranger. Such defence of children and of the vulnerable was and still is an important pastoral role of the parish clergy. The tragedy of recent scandals has been the inclination in the media to stereotype clergy as deviant because of the sins of a minority. This has revealed a level of what appears to be an anti-clerical prejudice in some of our media, both print and electronic.

The priests would visit the villages twice a year to celebrate Mass in the people's houses. (This has now ceased in our parish.) This practice was known as the 'stations'. In our area we had three villages (townlands) clustered together, i.e. Loughloon, Brackloon and Bofara. The stations were held in spring and in autumn. In good times and bad, this excellent practice brought the Church to the grassroots society. For months before the stations, the house and its environs were prepared, whitewashed, painted and wallpapered, floors washed, curtains hung, etc. As the day approached there was the borrowing of tablecloths, cups, saucers, cutlery, teapots and kettles, chairs and stools. On the morning of the stations, two priests would arrive accompanied by the clerk of the church, Mr Harry Hoban, and two altar boys. The priests heard the confessions of everyone present. After that one of the priests (usually the curate) would visit the housebound in the district, while the parish priest would offer the Mass on the kitchen table. After Mass, the station subscriptions, or dues, would be collected by the parish priest. The dues would be two shillings or a half-a-crown.

It was important that each house would be represented at the 'stations'. When the other priest returned and all the dues were collected, the priests, clerk and selected elders and senior members of the family would be invited to the 'room above' for formal breakfast. Very appetising meals were prepared for the dignitaries. The remaining members of the congregation were given food in the kitchen. Depending on the policy of the clergy, a drink would be offered to enhance the *agape*. Of course, preparations for the 'stations' were a *meitheal* operation. Neighbours would have generously chipped in and given a helping hand to the host family. This was very necessary in the case of very poor families living in very small houses. One of the latent effects of the Stations was the incentive it gave to people to do up their houses every seven years. A social (dance or party) would be held on the night of the Stations in some houses. Musicians would attend. All dancing on the concrete or flagged floors was in the form of half-sets or Irish dancing. Ballads would be rendered with gusto. Children would rarely perform except the odd Irish step-dancer.

Relationships between neighbours were generally quite close. The trespassing of animals was the main cause of disputes. The Rundale System of land division was conducive to trespassing. At times, it was sad to see neighbours taking each other to court over very small issues. When the dispute was resolved there would be a residue of resentment between families. Occasionally, some families would refuse 'to talk to' members of a neighbouring family. One of the latent functions of the stations would be to restore neighbourhood solidarity. Some parish priests would refuse to accept dues from anyone but a member of the family. This was very important because animosity over even a trivial dispute could even be carried forward to a second generation. The mechanism of the stations was a very positive structure in the spiritual as well as the social sense. Animosity between some families also followed the divisive hostility of the Civil War.

Protestant-Catholic relationships would be described as cordial but a little distant. After the departure of the British security forces in 1922, there was an exodus of Protestants from the Republic. Westport, being a garrison town, suffered a share in the departure of some of its Protestant citizens. During the 1930s, many of the managerial jobs were in the hands of Protestants. In the scenic parts along Clew Bay, i.e. Rossbeg, Rossmalley, etc., many of the luxury homes were owned by families of the Protestant ascendancy or Catholic merchant classes. Knappagh was a settlement of Protestants within two miles of Loughloon. The Protestant families had good two-storey slated houses and possessed the best lands. They had a 'pump in the yard'. Some of these families had the reputation of being pro-Unionist, which was their right. We were told that there used to be mini Orange Parades in Knappagh on the 12th of July, in years past. The political difference was further added to by the mutual suspicion caused by negative ecumenical attitudes and rules. Folklore was rife with stories of Protestant proselytism after the Famine. Hungry Catholic children were supposed to have been offered food and shelter and encouraged to become Protestants. There was a hostel of some kind near Leenane (in *Gleann na nÉan*) known as the 'Bird's Nest'. Hardly a trace of it was left after it was knocked down in the 1920s, and the stones of its walls were put into the building of the Leenane-to-Westport Road. There were also stories of Protestant proselytism in Achill during the late nineteenth century. The Catholic clergy reacted very negatively to the situation. We were forbidden, under the pain of serious (reserved) sin, to attend a Protestant Church service or even put a foot inside the Protestant graveyard for the funeral of a friend or neighbour. I remember going to Westport (on a horse cart) one day and hearing the following rhyme:

> *On Paddy's Day we'll all be gay,*
> *And kick the 'left-footers' out of the way.*

Such popular expressions of anti-Protestantism prejudice, while understandable in the light of our history of political and religious bigotry and violence, were regrettable. In our family, however, we did not give assent to anti-Protestantism. Both my father and my mother had worked with Protestants and made it clear to us that they were as good as Catholics, if not better. One other story that I heard in my youth was about a certain person who was possessed by four devils or evil spirits, i.e. Cain, Judas, Luther and Cromwell. This again manifested the bitter resentment in the Catholic folk culture of Protestantism, probably inflamed by the persecution of Catholics by the Protestant Irish Parliament in the late seventeenth and eighteenth centuries. While these residues of a bitter colonial past history stood out in my memory, they did not dominate our childhood experiences of the 1930s. The election (unopposed) of a Protestant, Dubhghlas de hÍde, as the first *Uachtarán na hÉireann* (President of Ireland) in 1938 was evidence of an ecumenical tolerance, which was most welcome. Also, the allocation of half of the University *Seanad* seats to the University of Dublin (Trinity College) in the 1937 Constitution was an ecumenical gesture.

9. THE IRISH NATION STATE

The enactment by the people of *Bunreacht na hÉireann* (the Irish Constitution) in 1937 did not feature that much in my childhood memory. I do remember, as I have already said, the photographs in the newspaper of Dubhglas de h-Íde's inauguration ceremonial horse-parade to Áras an Uachtarán. I also remember the commemorative postage stamp to mark the occasion. Personally, as I grew older, I came to admire the wisdom expressed in our 'Bill of Rights'. At a time when despotism and dictatorships were winning approval in Europe, our Constitution protected the democratic prerogative in giving the President the right and obligation to disband the *Dáil* when its full legal period was up, even if the Government of the day should wish to stay in office. Also, it gave the President the right to test the constitutionality of a Bill passed by the two houses of the *Oireachtas* or deemed to have been passed by them. These two powers protected the country from slipping into a dictatorship. The authors of *Bunreacht na hÉireann* resisted the temptation or the pressures to make Ireland a 'confessional State', as was the case of the United Kingdom and some Scandinavian countries with their State religions.

The often-criticised Article 44, which acknowledged the Catholic faith as that of the vast majority (90% plus) and identification of the other Churches and religious collectivities in the State at the time, was very enlightened and was praised by Jewish believers as a constitutional right to their protection as a religious group – at a time when much of continental Europe was anti-Semitic. There were groups in the 1930s (clergy and laity) who aspired to a confessional State. The preamble and Article 44 were akin to Articles 2 and 3 in giving recognition of the concrete situation without interfering with exclusively democratic and legal foundation of our relatively new State. Articles 2 and 3, which recognised the unity of the island of Ireland, had the intention and the latent effect of 'taking the gun out of Irish politics'. The late Seán MacBride told me that *Bunreacht na hÉireann* enabled him to embrace fully the Irish state as reconstituted.

Of course, there were other features in the Constitution that I would like to have been modified. For example, the protection of private property was too strong and has constrained the State from such necessary actions as the municipalisation of the ground space of towns and cities, which would put community interests before those of speculators. (The obscenely high cost of housing during the recent boom was largely due to the unqualified right to private property in *Bunreacht na hÉireann*.) I also admire *Bunreacht na hÉireann* for enshrining the rights of the family, but I regret such rights have not been adequately enshrined in law. (The recent 'individualisation of income tax' allowance is, in my opinion, anti-family and against the spirit of *Bunreacht na hÉireann*.) Allowing for its inevitable shortcomings here and there, our Constitution has served the country well to date.

Hopefully, *Bunreacht na hÉireann* will not lose its relevance in the years ahead because of the moves towards the 'United States of Europe', which I would totally oppose. As the anthropologist, Sahlins, so wisely observed, superpowers have a shorter life-span, than more modest sized nations or cultures. Superpowers have imploded or failed after over-reaching themselves. Cultural diversity is something to be appreciated. At the same time, socio-economic interdependence between sovereign States can enrich all countries and prevent inter-State conflict. Sociologist, Emile Durkheim, saw this interdependence ('division of labour') as a new basis of social solidarity.

At the time, I was not that much aware of the full implications of the dominant political ideology of the 1930s. There was a strong, almost radical, socialist dimension to the de Valera Government. The ambitious house-building schemes coupled with the transfer of people from the congested poor land in the West of Ireland up to the former estates of the 'landed gentry' in Meath and elsewhere were evidence of this dimension. We also were forced to depend on our own resources. Unfortunately, the British left our country in a very underdeveloped state. Migration from the countryside did not result in the building up of local urban areas, such as Westport, Castlebar or Ballina. The cities to which Irish rural migrant workers went were Boston, Philadelphia, New York, London, Coventry, Liverpool, Manchester, Cardiff, Swansea, Glasgow, Melbourne, Sydney, Wellington, etc. The Irish migrant workers built cities in other countries rather than their own. The British saw Ireland as an almost exclusively agricultural colony and failed to industrialise it in the nineteenth century. Some might say, that 'Ireland was useful for the production of navvies, soldiers and cattle needed for the expansion of "mainland Britain"'. This guaranteed our continuous out-migration and depopulation at home once agriculture developed into agri-business and ceased to be labour-intensive. These forces of national underdevelopment were beyond the capacity of even the best political leadership. Without dispersed urban and industrial development (with the necessary infrastructure) and the building up of strong cities in each province, even the modicum of development, which happened, would be distorted. This distortion has resulted in top-heavy Dublin and Belfast.

On the 3rd of September 1939, Great Britain declared war on Germany following its invasion of Poland and Czechoslovakia. This began one of the most horrific wars ever fought to date. All the killing power of advanced science and technology was to be released in a cold-blooded and callous manner both on military personnel (mostly conscripted) and civilians for the next six years. The following chapter deals with this dark event.

Chapter Two

THE 1940S
A DECADE OF DISASTER AND CHANGE

1. THE WAR IS ON

Looking back on the 1940s with one's memories and hindsight, it is very difficult to find words to describe the decade. In one sense, it was a nightmarish time during the first five years, i.e. living through a World War of savage proportions. In the beginning the main perpetrators of destruction were Germany, Japan and, to a lesser extent, Italy, while in the final years the Allies, mainly Britain, Russia and the United States, were the unleashers of death and destruction with their overkill of Dresden, Berlin, Warsaw, Hiroshima, Nagasaki and other less extensive cases of wilful destruction of civilian populations. Historians and analysts have not yet, to my knowledge, carried out an objective and critical examination of the causes, the effects and the *modus operandi* of the Second World War. There are many serious questions that have not been answered going back to the infamous *Treaty of Versailles*, (after World War I) and beyond. There seemed to have been gross inadequacies in the political, social, military and religious leaderships in the so-called 'developed world', especially of Europe and the United States throughout the early part of the twentieth century. This was manifested in the First World War, the decadence of the 1920s, the comic tragedy of the Wall Street charade in 1929, the ineptitude of the League of Nations to check the incremental rise of the Third Reich and the excesses of Joseph Stalin's totalitarianism in the USSR.

When one reads the literature of the time, it is amazing to find so many commentators living blindly in semi-complacency. There were notable exceptions. Among the latter I would include the article published in *Studies* in the early 1930s by the Irish Ambassador to the Weimar Republic of Germany, Mr Daniel A Binchy, prior to the rise to popular power of Adolf Hilter and his associates. He read the situation very accurately. In fairness to Mr de Valera, his interventions at the League of Nations were prophetic, but to little avail. The Churches also seem, in hindsight, to have missed the plot, although Pope Pius XI and others publicly expressed concern about the way the world was going.

Among the many lessons that should be learned from the costly failure of the world's leadership, I would underline two root causes of situations and the happenings leading up to the Second World War. The first would be the blatant social injustices within and between the nations, which were promoted and defended by the power elites. This lesson has not been learned. The whole idea of 'superpowers' and the defence of serious disparity of wealth between peoples and within countries, are still with us today as a basic cause of inter- and intra-national conflict. Until the world accepts, at least in principle, that *'the superfluities of the rich are the rights of the poor'* (attributed to St Ambrose) and seeks to operate this level of social justice – war and destructive conflict are inevitable, in my opinion. Religious leadership can help this 'cause of peace' by exhorting the faithful to see justice as the first expression of faith in a just God. Religious Communities should never accommodate blatant injustice.

The second root cause of war and destructive conflict is structural, or should I say, infrastructural. World peace and justice require a United Nations with power, capacity and objectivity to monitor social justice and take measures to intervene in time when such justice is not being maintained. The United Nations should be financed by means of direct taxation of the citizens of the world. The current structure of the United Nations is dominated by the victors of the Second World War and is under-resourced, which prevents it exercising a dominant role in defence of justice and peace. While regional 'blocs' of nations, such as the European Union, can help to prevent internal wars between the member States, they could just become 'superpowers' over time. The Constitution of the United Nations would need to be sufficiently comprehensive to meet the needs of its mission as the collective protector of international peace and justice. I realise that this is a utopian ideal. The lesson of the Second World War and subsequent destructive conflicts would seem to indicate that such a world body is required to keep the peace and correct injustice. The United Nations should also have a monitoring role in relation to wealth distribution and prevention of exploitation through the manipulation of credit, *et cetera*.

2. Surviving Under Rations

Let me return to my little world at the beginning of the decade under review. The War was soon to take its toll on our lives. The motor car was necessary for my father's job but he did not qualify for a petrol allowance. For a while he tried to keep going by doing long journeys on the train and on the bicycle. He had to stay away from home during the week and the burden of rearing five children and keeping an eye on the farm was left to my mother. A young man was employed to help out on the land and to take care of the sheep and the cattle. At this stage, I think my father would have been pleased to get a transfer from Loughloon up to Meath under the Land Commission Scheme. At the same time, he wished that we be educated by the Irish Christian Brothers and the Sisters of Mercy in Westport. He did not approve of 'boarding schools'.

From 1940 to 1948 my brother, Seán, and I attended the CBS Primary and Secondary Schools in Westport, a distance of four miles from Loughloon and one and a quarter miles from Drummindoo, where we lived from 1946 onwards. As time went on I got more attached to the simple life on the hill farm and looked forward to the day when I could leave school and spend all my time tilling the land and looking after the livestock. Of course, the teachers and my parents were (indirectly) encouraging me to do well at school and end up with a good 'pensionable' professional job. Such an aspiration did not appear so attractive to a youngster embedded in life on the land in a closely-knit neighbourhood. It nearly broke my heart to bid goodbye to Loughloon in 1946. I was fifteen years old when I left the village I had come to know and love as my own. Was I so romantic? I was, and I do not apologise for such attachment to the land and to the neighbourhood. This is not to say that I did not relish learning in itself. I suppose I was drawn between different aspirations and beginning to realise that choice in life is limited.

Despite the clouds of War raging all over Europe and in the Atlantic Ocean, which we could gaze upon from the top of our hill, we struggled on in Loughloon. During the summer holidays I would spend most of my time in my grandmother's (*Máimeó's*) house in Curr, Maam, in North-West Connemara in County Galway. Irish was the spoken language of the people there at the time, although English was fast becoming the daily language of the youth. It was also a most wonderful neighbourhood.

During the Emergency (War years) not so many young people emigrated and this meant that life at home was much better. The local football teams were stronger and social life was much richer. A source of income for the older teenagers was the sale of rabbits, which we snared on the Curr hill and on the Maam Hills. Rabbits were very plentiful at the time and there was a great demand for them in England. While in Curr we young lads would spend much time with my *Daideo's* sister, Babs Coyne (Babs Michil) who lived in one room of the old house. She was self-sufficient. She spun her own thread, knitted her clothes and even her blankets. Her hens were perched on a frame inside the back door. She saved her own turf and sowed her own potatoes. She told us many stories.

The spade (or *lái*), the slane (or *sleán*) and the scythe (or *speal*), were main agricultural instruments in Curr. Nobody used ploughs in Curr at that time. Asses (donkeys) and baskets (cleeves) were used for bringing home the turf, and putting out the stable manure. Hay and corn were carried into the haggard on the men's and women's backs. *Súgáin*, i.e. ropes woven from hay or straw, were used to tie down the cocks of hay and also tie down the thatch on the barns. The land in Curr was, if anything, even less arable than that of our farm in Loughloon. And yet, it produced potatoes, vegetables, hay and oats (in small fields) of the highest quality. The diet was much the same as at home. The potatoes, mainly 'Kerr's Pink', were delicious and 'bursting out all over'. Much of our time would be spent looking after sheep. The commonage was in *Gleann Fhada* between the Maamturk Mountains and Curr Hill. My brother, Seán, and I would 'go to the hill' with my uncle Tommie in search of sheep for dipping, shearing, or changing pasture. We would also go to the bog with him (further down the glen near Willie Lydon's homestead). We often fished in the river and would swim and bathe in the deeper holes.

My cousin, Mary Coyne, stayed with *Máimeó* before my uncle Tommie married Babbie (Barbara) King from 'far *Ráighe*'. Mary's brother, Mickey Coyne, whose family lived in *Corr na Móna (Éadon)* during the war because of the bombing in England, would also join us for the summer break. The Coynes (my cousins) were among a number of Irish families who were living in England before the War and returned to Ireland for the duration of 'the Emergency'. The fathers sometimes remained in England working and sending home the money to keep their families going. The great thing for us about 'the Emergency' was, as I said, the fact that the local schools were full, football teams had many players, and we all had a great time – despite the rationing and the inevitable hardship and poverty. The adage was true, i.e. 'nobody is poor when everybody is poor!' It is when some have more than others that poverty becomes hard to bear, i.e. 'relative deprivation'.

Despite the fact that we in the West of Ireland were spared the horrors of war and bombing and so forth, we were subjected to a severe rationing regime. This extended to all household consumables, i.e. food, clothing, paraffin oil, candles, shoe polish, soap, footwear, bicycle tyres, *et cetera*. The fact that we had a limited supply of paraffin oil for our lamps meant serious difficulties with our homework and study late at night. I remember at times trying to read my school books by the light of the fire. We used to use little strips of 'bog deal' as emergency tapers to assist us with our work.

We on the land had an advantage over the poor people living in towns and cities in that we had our own milk, butter, potatoes and vegetables, oatmeal, fowl and meat (i.e. killing the pig each year). The flour we bought in the shop was brown and contained bran. My mother would separate the bran from the flour by filtering it through the pores of a 'silk-stocking' so as to get sufficient white flour to make pastries and sweet cakes. The Emergency proved another adage: '*Necessity is the mother of invention.*' When I discovered after the war that Ireland continued to export food to Britain during it (on a credit basis), I felt happy about this gesture of solidarity with our neighbours across the water, who were suffering the hardships of war. At the same time, I agreed with Ireland's neutrality stand, although our workers were free to go to England to work and we continued to send England beef and other foods.

The ass and the horse came into their own during the Emergency as the motor car withdrew into garages, except for the doctor, the veterinary surgeon and the priest, who were given a modest ration of petrol. Private trucks used 'gas' derived from charcoal instead of petrol. The gas apparatus was usually constructed between the lorry's cab and the body. Sidecars pulled by horses were the common mode of passenger travel from the villages to towns on a Sunday morning. Not every house had the luxury of a sidecar. We did not have one, since we had a motor car before the War. We had to go on 'shank's mare' for the four miles to Mass. My mother would sometimes get a seat on a neighbour's side car. At times, I would sit on the well of Michael Heraty's (of Brackloon) sidecar, with the adults sitting up on each side. I still feel the thrill of going down by Phil Grady's of Cloona as the grey mare trotted briskly. The springs of the sidecar responded so perfectly to the bumps in the road that one felt that one was travelling on a stabiliser. The sight of a funeral coming down the Owenwee Road (from Kerrigans to Dan Heraty's) was something to see with 'the remains' on the well of the leading sidecar and the chief mourners sitting each side of the coffin, followed by the able-bodied on foot and thereafter, maybe twenty sidecars bearing the older neighbours and friends. Even the noise of the horse's hooves on the gravel road sounded like the drumbeat of a funeral march. The whole scene conveyed an air of dignity and sadness, which suited the occasion. This was something that the motor limousine or the four-wheel drive could not replace!

For those who were 'more important', there would be a horse-hearse, with the jarvey wearing a high hat while there would be a black plume standing on the head of the horse. The horse-hearse had its own attraction and dignity but, in my opinion, it was not as 'natural' as the well of the side-car with the chief-mourners accompanying the remains of their loved-one 'on board'. (Incidentally, I remember later when the motor hearse took over, the redundant horse-hearse was parked outside Paddy Joe O'Malley's house in Carnalurgan and young chickens were reared in it, enjoying the heat of the sun, sheltered from the winds of spring.)

3. A TEENAGE FARMER IN LOUGHLOON!

At the age of fourteen years, I began ploughing with a one-horse plough in the hilly and stony fields or gardens of Loughloon. Our horse, Paddy, was an extraordinarily friendly horse. He was very sensitive when ploughing, especially when the 'culter' or the 'sock' of the plough would come up against a concealed rock or strong root. When that would happen, Paddy (the horse) would halt, reverse a little, while I would swing on the handles of the plough to raise the 'sock' over the obstructing rock or root and then lift up the handles to enable the plough to sink again to the depth permitted by the wheel. Paddy, on a signal from me, would resume his steady pace ahead until the 'mould board' reached the 'headland', when we would turn right and start again in the opposite direction until we reached the end of the ploughed portion. When the field was ploughed, the patches missed around exposed rocks would be dug by the spade (or *lái* as it was called). When ploughing we would love to see a sheen on the sod turned. Crows and sea gulls would always be hovering overhead when we were ploughing in order to pick up the fat worms exposed, before they had time to burrow their way down to safety. The main ploughing at home was done by Michael Flynn (a first cousin of my father) from Kimeen, Lanmore. I would do only a portion of it.

When the ploughing was complete, the next operation was the 'shaking of the oats'. This was a real skill, which could be done only by an experienced farmer. It meant that the grain would be scattered at the proper density to ensure an adequate spacing between each sprig of oats in order to yield the best crop. After the oats were shaken, it was time to 'harrow'. This was an instrument with timber posts about three-feet long, criss-crossed with iron pins driven through the timber at regular intervals (six to eight inches apart, I would say) and sticking out about eight inches. These iron pins would break up the soil when pulled over it by the horse and enable the grain to sink into the earth where it would, in time, take root and produce a rich crop. When the young oat sprigs were well over the ground, the field would be 'rolled' in order to keep in the dampness, make the roots more firm and push down any small stones or pebbles which could damage the edge of the scythe at harvest time.

'Scarecrows' would be erected to prevent birds from picking up the exposed seeds after harrowing and when the crop would ripen. I was always doubtful about the extent to which these contraptions would deter the wise 'old crow' or 'jackdaw' or 'grey-back'. I always felt that we had to live and let live. Farmers used very little fertiliser (other than stable manure and seaweed known as 'wrack'). The 'bag manure' bought on occasion was known as 'duano' which was supposed to be dried bird-droppings from Guáno or somewhere in North Africa. It used to be imported into Westport Quay in two-hundredweight bags (which only the strongest men could carry on their backs). I used to hear stories of certain 'strong men' who could carry 'duano bags' up the ladder from the hold of a cargo ship! That separated the men from the boys! I carried a bag of 'duano' once and its weight made me breathless.

When I reached fifteen years of age I had as much interest in the land as I had in school. My brother Seán preferred looking after the sheep. It was said of him that he could run faster than a sheep on the mountain! My younger brothers, Austin (three years younger) and Owen (four years younger) were also very athletic in being able to cover a wide stretch of hill in a short time. In some parts of the hill you would have to jump from '*tortóg*' to '*tortóg*' as you ran after the sheep. In fact, we could run miles over the hills although we were never able to train for games or sport because of the distance from school and our chores on the land. You might say of us and of all our companions in the hill country that we were naturally athletic without being athletes! We had very little time for formal training.

Once we reached fourteen we shared responsibility also for the sowing of potatoes and other root crops, such as turnips or mangel-wurzels (known as mangels). Cabbage, onions, carrots and parsnips were sown in the vegetable garden near the house, as were early potatoes (Duke of York). Cabbage (producing heavy white heads) was also sown on the sides of potato ridges at regular intervals. The sowing of the main crop of potatoes was considered 'real farming' while vegetable gardening would be left to the care of old men or younger women, partly because of its proximity to the house.

Potatoes were sown in three types of ground, i.e. green fields (ley land), stubble (after a crop of oats) and ridges (after a crop of potatoes). In the case of 'ley land' we would score the field with a scoring line and turn the 'ferrabeen', i.e. just one sod or 'scraw' in towards the ridge. The width of a '*sioch*' away, another 'ferrabeen' would be turned (parallel) in the opposite direction. The whole operation would be replicated within the width of a ridge (wide enough for three 'slits') until the whole field was scored into straight ridges. (One can see the tracks of these ridges on the lower slopes of the mountains today. They are called 'lazy-beds'.) The next operation was the scattering of farmyard manure and/or seaweed on the ridges. The manure would be brought out in *párdógs*, i.e. baskets on the ass whose load could be released by pulling a ring from the end of a fork of timber. When the manure was spread, the 'slits' i.e. pieces of potatoes with 'eyes' in them, would be placed in rows of three wide with one foot between the rows. The heavy work then began with the opening of the new '*siochs*' and the covering of the 'slits' with soil. After a few weeks, the potato-stalks would break through the ground.

Then it would be time 'to mould' the potatoes. First one would dig the mould in the '*sioch*' and beat it fine with the spade. After this, one would spread the fine soil around the stalks with a shovel and provide cover and space for the new potatoes to grow out of the direct rays of the sun. Potatoes would turn green if exposed to the direct light of the sun. The sowing of potatoes in 'stubble soil' or in fields where potatoes grew the previous year was not so laborious as on ley land. The practice of crop rotation would mean that sowing potatoes two years in succession in the same field would be rare enough.

Turnips and mangels would normally be sown in drills rather than ridges. The reason why ridges were preferred to drills for potatoes was due to their advantage for spade cultivation and the provision of a dryer bed for the crop. Also, one would get more potatoes out of a field of ridges than from one of drills. Potato crops would be sprayed (to prevent blight) with bluestone and lime or washing soda in late June or during the month of July. Before the arrival of the shoulder pump-spraying vessel (carried on the farmer's shoulders), spraying was done by means of sprinkling the stalks with a 'besom', i.e. a bunch of heather tied together like a sprinkler. The bluestone would prevent the blight from rotting the stalks, as happened during the Famine in the 1840s. The prevention of blight was something that every farmer would take very seriously. The barrel for the spray would be on the headland and we, young teenagers, had the task of drawing water to fill the barrel. A measure of bluestone would be tied in the cloth (bag) and left dipped in the barrel until all the bluestone was 'melted' into the water. Then, before the actual spraying began, the washing soda or lime would be mixed into the solution turning it into a bright blue-green colour.

Drawing water to the 'dipping box', where the sheep would be dipped in a large concrete tub filled with some twenty to thirty gallons of water mixed with 'McDoughills' or 'Coopers' dip was another laborious chore for young teenagers. I could never understand at the time why the communal 'dipping box' was not built closer to the stream flowing through the village. Of course, looking at it now from the context of prevention of polluting the stream, the 'dipping box' was the right distance from the running water. The 'dipping box' was built in the ruins of an early nineteenth-century cottage (owned by Padney Gibbons and family). The small 'room above' was turned into a 'dripping chamber', which channelled the dip back down to the concrete tub located in the centre of what was once the kitchen, living room and 'room below' of Gibbon's peasant cottage. The dipping-box was shared by the sheep farmers of the village/ townland. The purpose of dipping was two-fold, i.e. to improve the skin and wool of the sheep and to remove and prevent 'maggots' from injuring the sheep and causing them great discomfort. 'Maggots' were the scourge of sheep in the hot, sultry and damp climate of summer and autumn in Ireland. This was especially true before the shearing of sheep was carried out in the summer.

During the 1940s my father had a relatively large flock of sheep grazing in Loughloon, *Gleann an Chailligh* and Tawneyard. Shearing was by a *meitheal* of expert shearers. I remember the late Martin Joyce from Tawneyard, who was able to shear sheep more rapidly than other experts. Martin would not have to turn the sheep as he could shear with both hands. I would 'pull' sheep for him and admire his great skill. The wool would be packed in large canvass wool-packs and sold to JM Joyce of Leenane, who was an agent for some wool merchants. During the War the price of wool was considered good at one shilling and three pence a pound.

Every family kept some wool for the domestic needs of knitting socks, scarves, jerseys and even blankets. The soft wool growing on the belly of the sheep was very good for spinning and knitting socks, etc. The wool would be 'carded' and 'spun' at home. The old widow staying at our house, Honorah (Onnie) Conway, spun woollen thread on our spinning wheel (each house had a spinning wheel in the 1940s). The wool thread was made grey by mixing black and white wool when carding. There was also a special dye (brownish in colour), which was made from lichens found on the rocks. This colour was a popular colour for socks. In earlier times the women would knit caps and other items of clothing. As I grew up, practically all of our socks were knitted from our own wool carded and spun by Onnie Conway. This was especially true during 'the Emergency'.

It should be noted that for a time during these years of rationing, clogs, i.e. shoes with wooden soles, were popular. The clogs were made by fitting boot leather 'uppers', which were tacked on to the wooden soles. An iron strip was nailed on the sole of the clog to prevent the wood from wearing. The clogs were noisy when those wearing them walked on the road. They were also noisy on the concrete or flagged kitchen floors. Some people would tack on strips of old bicycle tyres to the soles of the clogs to reduce the noise. After a while, I got to like wearing clogs. The old people held the view that they were particularly healthy for the feet.

My father took early retirement from McAinish and Company Limited, in 1941, at the age of forty-eight years, partly because of the loss of the use of his motor car for the long journeys. He also felt the need to be at home to look after his growing family and take over the running of the farm etc. He rented conacre for tillage and continued to have stock scattered in many places. He was hit with two very serious setbacks in relation to stock. In early 1940s he lost some fine heifers, bullocks and cows from 'bracken poison', which causes a perforation of the smaller intestine. The second 'disaster' happened during the 1947 snowfall (following the bad harvest of 1946), which led to the loss of up to fifty ewes trapped under the drifts in the valleys between the hills in the commonage. Some surviving ewes were too weak to feed their lambs when the snow abated at the end of March. At that time, there was no compensation scheme for such losses, and we had to bear those losses. This certainly made things very difficult for my father rearing a family of six plus three adults. He returned for a few years to his job of cutting woods in the late 1940s. Thank God, he did not neglect his family and willingly took on extra work.

In 1946 he bought two holdings of land and a house and a glasshouse in Drummindoo on the Castlebar side of Westport and the family moved there to live. He did not sell the Loughloon farm but continued to stock it until he died in 1976. As I grew older I came to appreciate the enormous sacrifices that my father and mother made for their family. This was true love, which was lived to the full. We had to endure many privations living in a small cottage during the war with little or no disposable income.

In 1940, the National School in Brackloon was closed for some months for renovation. My parents thought that such a disruption would be bad for Seán and me so they decided to send us to the CBS Primary School in May or June of that year. We were finishing fourth class at the time. I was very sorry to be leaving Brackloon School and all my pals, but soon got used to Westport, where we 'country lads' were never fully integrated. Although Seán and I had no difficulty in keeping up with our classmates in the Christian Brothers' School (thanks to the high standards of Brackloon School) I did not really like going to school all that much. Corporal punishment was a factor in the unpleasantness of school in those days, but it would be wrong in hindsight to overemphasise it, i.e. we took our slaps from the teachers in a brave and stoical manner. In fact, I preferred the slap to some of the psychological embarrassment used in its place. Once one had got one's slap, one felt it was over and the balance was restored. At times, however, I felt that some teachers over-relied on negative sanctions, and did not use positive rewards enough to increase our motivation. (They had not interpreted Skinner correctly!)

Looking back on our schooldays from the standpoint of adult life is not always that objective an exercise. Some pupils were more intimidated than others. Also, corporal punishment was an accepted aid to the rearing of children in most families at the time. Most parents and teachers genuinely believed that is was an essential method of helping the young to become responsible later in life. It was for them a way of loving the youth to ensure that they developed a capacity to defer satisfaction, control their emotions and perform better as students. On reflection, I would have been happier if teachers had used positive sanctions more. There was not that much corporal punishment in our home.

During the 1940s the length of adolescence, i.e. the period between childhood and adulthood, was very much shorter than it is today. I would define adulthood as being expected to take responsibility in terms of work and relationships. Young people who emigrated as young as sixteen and seventeen years of age in search of employment were literally on their own. They were expected to act responsibly – and they did so behave (with the rare occasion of energetic waywardness). At home we were thrown in at the deep end, beginning at the age of fourteen years. There were the usual 'adult-incorporating rituals', i.e. finishing formal education, working (job), starting a steady line leading to marriage, etc. As matchmaking had all but died out even before the War, the practice of dating and of individual mate-selection was well established. In the majority of cases, the *'principle of propinquity'* seemed to operate, i.e. one was free to court widely so long as you ended up marrying your neighbour's son or daughter. (Neighbour covered a wide area!) This principle applied to many emigrants as well!

4. ADVANCING IN FAITH AND RELIGION

When I was growing up, being accepted into the *Men's Sodality of the Sacred Heart* was one such adult-incorporating ritual. I still remember my 'application' for membership to the local sodality leader, Mr Martin Walsh of Faughburren (Prospect). It went something like this. I approached Martin one Sunday morning as we walked down the hill from Loughloon to early Mass:

Mise:	*I am fourteen years (allowed to wear long trousers) and I would like to join the Sodality.*
Martin:	*What are your priorities, son?*
Mise:	*I don't know the meaning of the word.*
Martin:	*What comes first for you?*
Mise:	*I want to be a steamroller driver like PJ McMenamin.* (my uncle-in-law).
Martin:	(Not impressed with my reply) *If you want to be a true Irish Catholic it is, first, your God, second, your country (and community), and third, your mother (and family). These are the priorities of a true Irish Catholic.*

I hope I am relaying the conversation accurately. He explained the meaning of these priorities. What struck me later was that I myself (as a priority for me) did not find a place in the 'top three' of Martin Walsh. I have meditated on Martin Walsh's priorities many times since, and after much reflection, I would more or less agree with them. Martin Walsh was a tall bony hard-working hill farmer. I looked up to him. His late mother, Mary, was a very old woman and was always praying. Like many of her generation she lived in the continuous conscious presence of the Living God. Martin accepted me into the Men's Sodality and I would walk up to Holy Communion once a month as part of the Loughloon-Prospect section. Each of us wore our Sodality Medal for the purpose. Confession on the previous Saturday evening was a required duty.

Once a person was accepted for membership of the Men's Sodality, it meant that we could attend the *Men's Week of the Parish Mission*, which came to Westport every three years. These missions were given by priests of Religious Orders/Congregations. The Redemptorists were well known for their colourful rhetoric when preaching about sin and sanctity. The third evening would focus on sins of the flesh and the missionary would frighten the life out of us. We would be talking, on the road home, about the images of hell and the temptations that we would have to resist. On the positive side, we were encouraged to become more devout and loyal to our prayers, to Mass and the Sacraments, and the importance of justice and charity. Devotion to Our Lady was the high point of the mission on the last night of the men's week. A massive altar would be erected in honour of Our Lady. The Redemptorists always promoted devotion to *Our Lady of Perpetual Succour*. Many of the 'trimmings' attached to the family rosary had their origin at one or other of the Missions.

The parish mission was a very valuable institution for the evangelisation of the faithful. Missions were taken very seriously by the vast majority of the people, as far as I could see in the 1940s. These were thrilling events and while the preachers tried to put the 'fear of God into us', they may not have succeeded in making sinless saints out of us but they helped us to internalise a wise moral code. I often say jokingly, *'I would have been in jail, were it not for the Ten Commandments'*! The Missioners reinforced the teaching of our parents and what we learned in school and at Sunday Masses. When we did something wrong against our neighbour, we knew it was a sin and felt compelled to confess it. In my judgment this was the real test of faith. The faith dies as a moral force when expediency replaces morality. This in turn, leads to normlessness or 'anomie', which threatens the basic fabric of society. It would be very difficult for people in society to trust each other without a basic morality internalised by the members. Such a common morality existed in our parish in the 1940s, thanks to the parents, the teachers, the priests and the missions. We were rooted in the faith. God's existence and relevance for our lives were as real as the air that we breathed or the food that we ate. Christ was implicitly 'The Way, the Truth and the Life' of most of the people. It was a privileged social and domestic environment in which to be reared. It was the people's religion. This belief prepared us for life at home in Ireland or abroad in England, the United States or elsewhere.

Pilgrimages were a very important part of the liturgical yearly calendar. As noted earlier, there were three popular local pilgrimages for us, i.e. Croagh Patrick, *Mámean* and Kilgeever. Croagh Patrick (known locally as 'The Reek'), and Mámean were penitential pilgrimages. Since our farm was at the foothills of the Reek, we were introduced to it when quite young. I am not sure whether my first pilgrimage was in 1940 or 1941. (In all, I calculated that I made the pilgrimage some forty-six times.) We loved climbing at night, or should I say, early in the morning. Our route was to walk through Faughburren (Prospect) up the road towards Skelp and cut to the right up to the Deerpark Wall (a folly built during the Famine as a relief work) and left towards the first Station. We would join the pilgrims coming up from Murrisk at the beginning of the flat piece of the path at *Paddy McGreal's tent* where he sold tea and minerals. After completing the first Station we would climb the peak of the Reek. At that time, the path was fairly firm and the pilgrim did not deviate from it (unlike in recent years where climbers have ceased to respect the mountain, in my view). On reaching the top we would do the second Station, i.e. walk fifteen times around the summit ending by going on our naked knees into St Patrick's Bed. We would then go to confession to a priest sitting on a clump of stones and attend Mass. After Mass we would go down the western side of the peak to a third Station, i.e. *Garra Mór*, where we would go around seven 'cairns' of stones seven times and the whole of *Garra Mór* seven times also. During these 'walks around' each of the three Stations we would continuously pray the *Pater, Ave* and *Gloria*. On completion of the third Station we would re-climb the peak and descend the way we came and walk fairly tired but enjoying a great inner feeling

In those years almost everyone seemed to be a genuine pilgrim and very few climbed for non-spiritual reasons. Most pilgrims would have very serious requests to make to God through the intercession of St Patrick. Others were making pilgrimages of thanksgiving for favours received, i.e. getting married, the birth of a child, a recovery from illness, etc. Many people of all ages climbed in their bare feet. It was quite normal for young people to be making pilgrimages to the Reek that 'were put on them' by their parents at some time earlier. I once heard a worried mother say about a very ill child: '*If he recovers the young lad is "bound" to make a pilgrimage of thanksgiving.*' It was also wonderful to see a newly married couple climbing the Reek together in their bare feet. Probably, they were thanking God for their marriage and praying that He would send them a child. During the War years we would always pray for peace in Europe and in the Far East. Going to Confession at the top of Croagh

Patrick made great sense. It completed the penitential dimension of this wonderful act of reparation and reconciliation. I feel that the decline of the sensed need for reparation and reconciliation in society in recent decades may have weakened the moral fibre of our Catholic faith.

The annual pilgrimage to *Mámean* (Pass of the Birds) a Patrician shrine on a pass on the Maamturk Mountains between the Maam Valley and Recess in North Connemara took place on the same days as the Croagh Patrick Pilgrimage. The shrine was on the eastern slopes of *Ben Mhairg* (the north side of which was part of the commonage shared by my uncle Tommie Coyne of Curr, Maam). *Máimeó* (my grandmother *Méiní Eoghain*) would tell of the great preparation she would make for all the visitors who would call on their way to *Mámean* every year. She would be baking bread for days! In some houses there would be much celebrating around the pilgrimage day. During the nineteenth century, *poitín* (home-made spirits) would be available in long tents at the shrine. In 1932, my grandfather built a temporary altar at the Shrine for a celebration of thanksgiving for the new Irish State. The Mass was served by the late William T Cosgrave, head of the first Free State Government, and his two sons: one of whom, Liam, was to become *An Taoiseach* in 1973. There are a number of accounts of *Mámean* written by visitors to North Connemara in the nineteenth century.

During the 1930s and the 1940s, there were still a good few regular pilgrims making the '*turas*' each year on *Mámean* Sunday – the last Sunday in July or on the last Friday of the same month. I often joined these pilgrims. The shrine is over a thousand feet above sea level. Access to it is by means of a path (*casán*) of almost two miles from the Maam side and one mile from the Recess side. Like Croagh Patrick, *Mámean* was a pre-Christian shrine to Crum Dubh (part of the Celtic Deity). It consisted of two stations (i.e. circles of stones), a holy well and a bed, i.e. a ledge of rock on which St Patrick was supposed to have slept when he visited the Shrine in AD 441. He Christianised the shrine as he did on Croagh Patrick during the same year.

The decline of the *Mámean* pilgrimage (until its recent revival in 1979) is difficult to explain. Certainly, the archbishops and the priests did not seem to support it. Was this due to the attitudes of Cardinal Cullen and his supporters in the ranks of the bishops and the clergy? Cullen seemed to discourage the popular devotions of the people because of his strong commitment to total orthodoxy and explicit loyalty to Rome. Did he see the people's behaviour a threat to that orthodoxy? Also, the missionaries from the various religious congregations and orders never, in my hearing, encouraged participation in pilgrimage to *Mámean*. As an Irish Language shrine, it would have been culturally remote from the predominantly English-speaking and Anglo-Roman-oriented Church leaders. Local folklore also referred to the switch to Croagh Patrick at the beginning of the twentieth century, marked by the building of the chapel on the summit in 1905. This was accompanied by the growth in popularity of the pedal bicycle, which reduced the significance of distance. And then there was the clergy's opposition to the availability of *poitín* as part of the annual pilgrimage celebrations. The rise of popularity of Our Lady's shrine at *Cnoc Mhuire*, which was different from the traditionally Irish type of pilgrimage (and might have fitted in better with the prevailing European pilgrimages at Lourdes and Fatima), continued to grow in the 1940s. In the light of all of these opposing and competing factors, we were lucky that the *Turas go Mámean* (pilgrimage to *Mámean*) survived at all. My mother's people kept *Mámean* very much alive in my little world, *buíochas le Dia*.

Looking back at the religious practices and socialisation of the 1930s and 1940s, the family played a central role in the transmission of the faith. The 'penny' and 'sixpenny' catechisms were basic sources of doctrine. While we read the Gospels when in secondary school, we were not very conversant with the Bible. This was in contrast to the approach of our Protestant brothers and sisters. Very few Catholics had copies of the Bible in their homes at the time. My father read the Bible from cover to cover in later years, when he was in his late sixties. He found some of the stories difficult to comprehend, since he read from the perspective of a solid understanding of the teachings of Christ. My own study of the Old Testament was also from a New Testament perspective. I felt that such an approach helped to avoid biblical fundamentalism. Christ, in my opinion, was a 'scriptural revolutionary', i.e. He carried out a radical and rapid change of spiritual values and norms which upset so many people reared on the Old Testament. Many of the continuities were broken, for example, Christ's teaching on the universality of the neighbour, the imperative demand for forgiveness, the end of the 'chosen race', the equality of women and men, etc. Granted, these themes were anticipated by the prophets and teachers of the Old Testament, if one reads them from Christ's perspective.

The relationship between the people and the parish clergy was one of respect and a distant friendship. There were exceptions. The priests seemed to get a little closer after Vatican Two in the 1960s. Seán, Austin and I never served Mass because we were too far from the Church. I had no regrets for not being able to serve at the time. The priests' houses were, as noted earlier, between middle- and upper-middle class in standard. They had motor cars and took holidays, which the rural or urban peasants would not even dream of in those days. This difference of social class position was a further barrier to true, non-patronising relationships with the people I grew up with in the 1930s and 1940s. By the end of the 1940s one would hear elements of dissent, especially among those who would come home from England to visit their families. There was a strong degree of consensus in the mass media in relation to the teaching and preaching of the Catholic Church. *The Irish Times* was rarely, if ever, read in our village, since it was perceived as a non-Catholic and non-nationalist paper. *The Irish Press* and the *Irish Independent* were the two national newspapers; the former was *Fianna Fáil* while the latter was *Fine Gael* in ideology. These were both favourably disposed to the Catholic clergy, especially the *Irish Independent*.

The public status of a bishop was very high and was recognised by the State in so far as a new bishop is given a 'Guard of Honour' by the Defence Forces. (In 1954, Our Lady was formally acknowledged as 'Patroness of the Irish Defence Forces'.) Fasting and abstinence were widely practised. We never ate meat on a Friday and we fasted during the forty days of Lent. Also, during Lent there was a legal ban on public dancing. Pubs were closed on St Patrick's Day. All in all, the bishops exercised a fairly tight control over the social life of the people. The people accepted those curtailments without much protest at the time. In 1930, censorship was introduced under statute. This led to an unhealthy lack of freedom of creative expression. In our village the 'blockbuster', *Gone With the Wind*, was going the rounds. It had a brown paper cover on it. I think it was banned. I am sure there were copies of other 'banned books' also in circulation. The fact that every family had so many relatives working in England and America made it easy to smuggle in the 'spicy' books. The fear of decadence, which would weaken the moral strength of the people, may have made 'our benevolent minders' overprotective. Really, I do not think it affected us that much as we struggled with poverty and material hardship! The legacy of Protestant Puritanism and Catholic Jansenism in Irish morality seemed to dominate and suppress the mercy of God at times. I never agreed with this attitude down the years.

5. Education in Post-Colonial Ireland

The transition from colonial dominance by Britain and her agents (Protestant and Catholic) in Ireland was still in the early stages of adaptation during the 1930s. The effects of the Civil War in the 1920s were very serious. The conflict was caused by the 1922 Treaty, which was seen to be defective by many and divided our country and subjected a large minority of Catholics and Nationalist citizens in the Six Counties to a regime of formal discrimination and the occasional purge to remind the minority of their inferiority, politically and religiously. The legacy of this dysfunctional arrangement is still with us today. During the 1940s we were still trying to assert the distinctive Irish cultural ethos of the Irish as different from other nationalities. The new political leaders made attempts to support the national (cultural) traits. The coming together during the 'Emergency' helped to reunite those who opposed each other in the Civil War of the early 1920s.

The political and 'republican' undertones of the revival of Irish culture met with very articulate opposition, sometimes with understandable cause. Nevertheless, a period of exaggerated assertion was inevitable to enable a downtrodden people to gain self-identity and throw off the sense of 'inferiority' *vis-à-vis* our recent masters. By the end of the 1940s I had become more conscious of the need to enculturate more into the Gaelic tradition. In 1947, I joined an Irish dancing (i.e. group dancing) class in the Vocational School in Westport. On the night I joined the *Céilí* Dancing class I also signed up for *Conradh na Gaeilge* (the Gaelic League). This marked the beginning of a lifelong involvement with the Irish language movement. Most of us were strongly supportive of *Cumann Lúth-Chleas Gael* (the *Gaelic Athletic Association* or *GAA*). We would not attend or support 'foreign games', i.e. soccer, rugby, cricket or hockey. This ban on foreign games survived until the late 1960s in *Conradh na Gaeilge* and the 1970s in the case of *Cumann Luth-Chleas Gael*. In addition to the banning of foreign games, members of the RUC and of the British security forces were banned from playing or being members of the GAA

Mayo had a very good county football team at the end of the 1940s and during the second half of the 1930s when they won the All-Ireland in 1936 against County Laois (my county of birth). County Mayo won many National League titles at this time. Despite being born in County Laois, my first loyalty has always been to the County Mayo football team. Westport always had a good soccer team. We would have little or no contact with Westport Soccer or Rugby at the time. Later when the 'ban' was relaxed some players played both games, i.e. Gaelic and Soccer.

Rugby was an upper-middle-class game and was played only by those who attended the private colleges, i.e. Clongowes, Blackrock, Rockwell, *et cetera*. The fact that these upper-class colleges with notable exceptions did not play Gaelic Games was quite serious and was a major contributory factor to the continuing of social-class-position divisions (in the informal sense) in Irish society down to the present day. Of course, it enabled a certain 'garden party ecumenism' between Catholic and Protestant social elites and even provided some cross-border favourable contact between the sons of the higher professional classes. This was maintained in the one Irish Rugby Team. Unfortunately, it did not seem to ameliorate the condition of the Catholic minority in Northern Ireland/ the Six Counties over the years.

The great thing about Gaelic football in the 1940s, was its strictly amateur and voluntary nature. Later it was to become over-skilled and too dependent on extensive training, which ruled out the ordinary young lad in remote areas being able to qualify for county teams, *et cetera*. Managers and coaches were to become more important than team captains! In fact, it was to become quasi-professional, especially the dominant county teams.

Second-level education in the 1940s was provided at a low symbolic cost by the Christian Brothers and the Sisters. The country's debt to the voluntary and dedicated work of Irish Brothers and Sisters is inestimable. Without them, only an elite of wealthy sons and daughters would have been educated. Another service which has been unfairly overlooked as 'builders of the new Ireland' were the local vocational school teachers, who were the backbone of our skilled tradespeople and also important general educators of the children of the working class. Because of the unjust snobbery of Irish society, which did not give the appropriate status to manual skills, the work of the vocational schools or technical schools (as they were often called), was grossly under-appreciated by our biased social commentators.

Our religious Brothers and Sisters have been much maligned in recent times by people who have almost defined them by the misdemeanours of a minority of unsuitable staff in under-resourced (and under-supervised by the State) reformatories, industrial schools and orphanages and such places. This negative stereotyping is appalling and unjust. Of course, those individuals who abused young people in their care have been totally wrong and the victims of their abuse deserve whatever help they require. For some unbalanced Irish commentators it seems to be another sad expression of the 'apostate complex', i.e. a compulsive alienation/ hostility towards their own socio-religious roots! Few journalists, political leaders or social commentators seem to have the courage to stand for public fair play!

Third-level education was a mix of 'meritocracy' and 'aristocracy', i.e. scholarship students and those graduating from the private second-level schools. There were two major universities in the Republic of Ireland (so declared in 1949), i.e. the National University of Ireland and the University of Dublin. The former NUI consisted of those constituent colleges in Dublin, Cork and Galway with a recognised college in St Patrick's College, Maynooth. The University of Dublin, more popularly known as Trinity College of Dublin (TCD), was not attended by Catholics because of the Bishop's perception of its Protestant ethos and of a history of neglect of Irish Catholics' educational rights. Irish was an essential subject for matriculation to the NUI, but not required for entry into TCD. During the 1940s in Westport those keen on going to the university would (generally) attend private boarding schools run by the dioceses or the religious orders or congregations. Aspirants for teaching in national schools would do their second-level schooling in the *Coláistí Ullmhúcháin* (preparatory colleges) before qualifying for the Teacher Training College in Drumcondra, Carysfort, Limerick and elsewhere. Places in the *Coláiste Ullmhúcháin* were filled by competitive entry examinations. It meant, therefore, that entry was by means of a scholarship system, which attracted students of high academic ability.

Competence in the Irish language was a central aim of the *Coláistí Ullmhúcháin*.

The Government of the 1920s, 1930s, 1940s and 1950s appeared to be more genuine in their efforts to restore the native language to its proper place. The colonial authorities, aided and abetted by the local establishment, had almost succeeded in eradicating the Irish language, especially through the national school system. In the nineteenth century the traumatic effect of the Great Famine also resulted in massive 'migration' of the native Irish-speaking population to the United States and elsewhere abroad. I entered for a scholarship to a *Coláistí Ullmhucháin* in 1944/5 but was not successful because I failed the music examination. My overall mark would have made me eligible. At that time I was very interested in study and found it easy.

The cultural idealism of the leaders of the Independence Movement (1916-21) had a positive influence on education up until the end of the 1950s. *After that a more pragmatic cultural policy towards education seems to have begun to hold sway.* The influence of support from the World Bank in the 1960s had a culturally de-radicalising effect. Even the ideal of a holistic education became watered down in the last quarter of the twentieth century. Many attempts have been made to promote science and technology and applied skills at the expense of the classics and the humanities. This was a retrograde trend, in my opinion. It was understandable because of the pressures from industry and other employers.

We were fortunate in the early and middle twentieth century that religious orders and congregations were in a position to influence the curriculum and try to educate the whole person. Also, the pressures for examination results were less intrusive, when compared with recent decades. Of course, educational participation was far too low in the 1940s, and completing secondary school would be as rare as getting an MA in Ireland today. What we then needed was more education while today we need better education, to quote a visiting American professor of mine! By better education I mean a balanced curriculum, which has much greater emphasis on the humanities, i.e. literature, theology, philosophy, history, geography, the human sciences, art, *et cetera*, as well as transmitting the social, domestic and occupational skills.

Critics of the curriculum of the 1940s can justly point out that the career relevance of our secondary education was weak. Perhaps the universal curriculum lacked relevance for the needs of small farmers in the West of Ireland. Educationalists seemed to ignore the needs of local communities such as area needs like fishing, forestry, peat production, tourism, mountain sheep farming, etc. It never seemed right to me that a curriculum was the same in suburban or urban Dublin and in Achill Island or Loughloon! When challenged, senior education officials would say that they focused on the individual rather than the local community. What a narrow view! The failure to develop the West of Ireland was in part due to our 'universal curriculum', which siphoned out the talented young people for jobs in the bureaucracies, industries, professions, etc., located in the cities (at home or abroad).

6. DEATH OF A NEIGHBOUR

A townsland (village) in the hill country of the West of Ireland was really like an extended family. This was brought home to me on the sad death of a neighbour to whom I referred already, the late Mr Pat Walsh, on the eve of 8th December 1942 (the feast of the Immaculate Conception) and the birth (at home) of my youngest brother, Pádraig, during the early morning of the feast day. He was christened Pádraig Noel Mary. Pádraig was after Pat Walsh, who had died the previous evening. Noel, or *Nollaig*, was to signify the feast of Christmas (which is *Nollaig* in Irish), which was very close. Mary was in honour of the Blessed Virgin whose Immaculate Conception was being celebrated. As the fifth son, our parents were free to select a name outside the parents' and grandparents' names. In fact, our family followed the naming custom of the Irish tradition, i.e.

First Son   Father's father's Christian name, i.e. Seán;
First Daughter   Mother's mother's Christian name, i.e. Mary;
Second Son   Mother's father's Christian name, i.e. Micheál;
Second Daughter   Father's mother's Christian name
                    (would be Catherine);
Third Son   Father's Christian name, i.e. Austin;
Third Daughter   Mother's Christian name
                    (name already given to Mary).

In our family this tradition was followed for the first three sons and the one daughter. The fourth son was called after my mother's grandfather,

Owen. In the case of the third son or daughter there would be a variation of the parent's name, i.e. my brother Austin (the third) was always called Austie so as not to confuse his name with my father's. My mother's name was Máire, the same as that of her own mother and grandmother. She was always called Molly/Mollie and her mother was called Méiní. That meant that my sister could be called Mary. There were quite a number of variations of the common Christian names, e.g.:

John   i.e. Johnnie, Jack, Seán, Shane, Eoin, etc.

Michael   i.e. Micheál, Haulie, Mick, Mike, Micil, Micky, etc.

Mary   i.e. Méiní, Máire, Maureen, May, Molly, etc.

Also in parts of the west of Ireland, surnames were rarely used. For instance, in Connemara my name would be Micheál, Mollie, Mike, Micil Coyne. If such a tradition were still operating in Loughloon my name would be Micheál, Austin, John, Padney McGreal. This system of naming people was very useful in districts when there would be many families of the same surname, e.g. the McGreals around *Taobh na Cruaiche* (Owenwee) / Loughloon, the Coynes in Curr / Maam / *Bun na gCnoc*; the O'Malleys in the parish of Louisburgh; the Joyces in 'Joyce Country' (*Dúiche Seoighe*); to name but a few of the more popular surnames close to my family.

Returning to the sad death of Pat Walsh (a next-door neighbour in Loughloon) it was for me my first real experience of the passing of a living person I knew and was very close to. He was the father of a large family (eight living at the time) between the ages of eight and twenty-one years. He was very hard-working and during the last year of his life when his health was failing I would spend much time with him in the fields looking after the sheep and harvesting the crops. He was suffering from cancer and he kept going until the evening he died, when he collapsed on a seat in the kitchen of his house, and passed away peacefully. A few weeks before he died I brought him the sad news that a neighbour of his in Faughburren (Prospect) had passed away. We were in *Garra Glas* (a field) at the time. Pat then said to me, '*I will be next to die.*' I sensed he was serious and meant what he said. It rocked me. I came home to my mother very upset and told her that Pat Walsh was going to die. She tried to persuade me it was not true. Then, a short time later, Pat's prediction came true.

I was eleven and a half years old when Pat Walsh died and I do not remember ever being so upset in my life before that time. Despite the excitement in our house at the birth of Pádraig, which we were all delighted with, my attention was occupied by going over-and-back and back-and-over to Walsh's during the two days Pat was over-board. I still recall every detail. His remains were carried in a coffin on the well of a sidecar. One of his teenage sons was hanging on to the coffin in desperate grief. All the family and close friends of Pat (including me) were crying as the cortège left for Aughaval Graveyard about a mile and a half from the house. Most of the mourners walked behind the coffin. His widow, Katie (née Duffy), and other older relatives sat on the sidecar each side of the coffin. We children were not allowed to go to the funeral but we observed it from the top of our hill as it wound its way to the graveyard. It was a very maturing experience for me and it raised questions in my mind about the passing nature of this life and the reality of life after death. My mother was able to answer my major queries. She was really quite a wise spiritual director. She had been in attendance (as a retired nurse) at most of the cases of serious illness and death in the neighbourhood. Coming to grips with the death of a close relative or neighbour was very difficult for us young people. The saying that: '*Old people go to death but death comes to young people*' is very true in my experience. Eternal rest to Pat Walsh! I will never forget him.

During the early 1940s, the two nights' wake was still the norm with most remains going directly from the home to the graveyard. Such was the case of the late Pat Walsh. (I was not allowed to go to Pat's wake as I was too young.) The wake was an all-night affair. The congregation at the wake was offered clay pipes and tobacco or cigarettes, snuff and tea and sandwiches. The rosary was recited at midnight. As I noted elsewhere, the age and circumstances of the deceased's death would determine the mood of the wake. At times, it would appear more a celebration of the dead person's long life than an occasion of lamentation, although there would be a sense of general sadness for the loss or break experienced by the bereaved. All in all, I believe the wake in the home of the deceased was and is a most positive institution. A wake enabled the family, friends and neighbours of the deceased to come to grips with the reality of death in a most intimate way. Also, the filling-in of the grave while the mourners were assembled was an experience of finality. The rosary would be recited while neighbours would take turns to shovel the earth on top of the coffin. All these gestures were very precious.

Unfortunately, we have made death and burial less personal and less 'real' today. This must cause unnecessary psychological problems for the bereaved. An eminent psychiatrist once remarked that some people, who had lost 'loved ones', tended to go into denial about their death and had to be enabled to relive the experience (of the death) on his couch, before therapy would be successfully applied. *We must always respect the wisdom of cultural tradition.* Rituals like wakes have many latent functions, which commercialised burial does not have. It is very healthy in the psychological sense to see the recent revival of the wake, so long as it is kept simple and personal and not artificial or too generous with alcoholic drink! Unfortunately, the decline of the importance of 'kinship' and of community makes the restoration of the traditional wake practically impossible in some cases.

Commercialisation, in my opinion, is basically impersonal and no amount of soft music or conventional politeness can replace the personal and voluntary manner of relating to death and bereavement. The current trend of the mass media to probe into the most personal aspect of life, including death and burial rituals can undermine the rituals. Social scientists, especially a certain brand of anthropologists appear to have become cultural voyeurists. Their intrusion has tended to objectivise what is exclusively subjective, personal and confidential. Because of this I have certain reservations in breaking confidence (in this text) with my ancestors and my neighbours of so many years ago. I intend only to reveal what is sufficient to enable the modern reader to understand the cultural and social customs which made our lives meaningful and satisfying, despite enormous difficulties, material deprivation and a sense of powerlessness against an inadequate social system. This was due to factors largely outside our control.

7. The Emergency

One such factor was the Second World War, which caused *Ireland's State of Emergency*, between 1939 and 1945. When one realises the series of misfortunes confronted by our young State, i.e. the Civil War of the 1920s, the Economic War of the 1930s and now the Second World War of the 1940s, it seems miraculous that we survived as a society at all.

The trials of trying to keep going without trade with Britain during the 1930s caused us to become more self-reliant economically. This stood to us in the 1940s and enabled us to defend a neutral and non-aligned stand. Despite the anger of Britain at our neutrality, we were kind to their cause by exporting food to the British people and permitting Irish workers and volunteer soldiers and airmen to help the war effort. My later enlisting as a Cadet (1950-52) and as a Commissioned Officer (1952-59) enabled me to look at the Emergency years from a vantage point of military science. I must admit that the curriculum of the Cadet School did not dwell much on the *State of Emergency* or even on the *War of Independence* and the *Civil War*. There may have been wise political reasons for avoiding too much explicit reference to the latter because of the fact that the senior officers had been engaged on both sides of the conflict. My main source of information about the Emergency came from colleagues and Reserve Officers who would join our Battalion summer exercises.

Before attempting a broader analysis of the Emergency and the War, I would like to first of all share my memories of what it was like to grow up in those troubled times. The news reports and the daily casualty tables read out on the wireless were literally horrific. One local family (the Simmons Family from Kildangan) sadly lost two sons (Alfred and George) in the British Navy on board the HMS Gloucester at the Battle of Crete in 1941. May they rest in peace. The accounts of the bombings in Britain and in Northern Ireland were reported regularly on nightly bulletins. The old men would discuss the progress of the War and most would be quite ambivalent towards Germany's progress and Britain's difficulties. At school the master would point out on the map the countries overrun by the Nazis. The name Rommel featured often as a 'hero figure'.

When the United States entered the War on the side of Britain, there was a slight change in the attitudes. Anti-British dispositions (because of the partition of Ireland and the legacy of maltreatment of our ancestors) could not be applied to the 'Yanks', who would rank as an 'in-group' in most families. There was great excitement one evening when a 'pilotless' large, British/ American bomber almost crashed into the side of the Reek on its way out to the Atlantic Ocean where it duly blew up on hitting the water. On another occasion, a British bomber (which had unloaded its deadly cargo out at sea) made an emergency landing behind

Louisburgh in a flat stretch of bogland. The aircraft was dismembered by the air mechanics and the 'carcass' was carried on heavy loaders through Westport *en route* to Northern Ireland. Sure, it would not be that useful to the Irish Defence Forces!!! The United States were involved in the war at the time! Was this an example of qualified neutrality?

All captured members of the security forces of Britain and of Germany were in two 'prisoner-of-war camps' on the Curragh of Kildare. A third prison on the Curragh was for IRA suspects and Republican sympathisers. It was known as the 'Hare Park Internment Camp'. It was feared that the IRA would try to facilitate and negotiate an invasion of Northern Ireland with the Germans to expel the British from Northern Ireland. This was strongly opposed by *An Taoiseach*, Éamon de Valera.

The Curragh Training Camp was a fascinating place during *the Emergency*. At Army officers' social functions, British and German officers were given parole passes to attend, i.e. one group for the first half of the function and the other group for the second half. This rotation would alternate from function to function. IRA officers did not enjoy such privileges, although they used their time 'inside' to study and improve themselves academically and culturally. It was a very disturbing time for Ireland, but we succeeded in getting through. The experience did much for the Defence Forces, in that it helped to unite former enemies (in the Civil War). It also proved to our own people that we were an Independent State.

The question is often raised now in public debate on the level of the Irish people's awareness at the time of the abominable racist and anti-Semitic policies and actions of Hitler's regime. I have to admit that it was never discussed but we had a very sinister opinion of the excesses of the Gestapo and their means of torture. As I said earlier, we used to play prisoner-of-war games wherein we would devise weird methods of torturing when acting the role of a Gestapo officer. It was amazing how little credibility the British anti-German propaganda had at the time in rural West of Ireland. Yet, the callous cruelty of the bombing of civilian populations in England really upset us. A neighbour and relative, the late Johnnie McGreal, had experienced the bombing of Coventry and gave a graphic account of the tragic event. Our ambivalence towards the war was best summed up by Yeats' poem, 'An Irish Airman Foresees His Death':

> *I know that I shall meet my fate*
> *Somewhere among the clouds above;*
> *Those that I fight I do not hate,*
> *Those that I guard, I do not love ...*

The slaughter in Russia also failed to arouse our anger or adequate sympathy. This may in part be due to the 'demonisation' and 'criminalisation' of Communism, which was aided and abetted by Catholic teaching on Communism at the time. How the slaughter of the Russian people would bring about the conversion of Russia from its 'evil socialist' and communist ways, I now find difficult to understand. The Nazi regime exploited the anti-communist feelings of the extreme Flemish Catholic Movement, AVV – VVK (all for Flanders – Flanders for Christ) (*Alles Voor Vlanderen – Vlanderen Voor Kristus*), and recruited a regiment of volunteer soldiers to join the German invading army in Russia. Once again, the power of the Russian winter and the strength of the Soviet Army stopped the Germans in their tracks and began the reversal of fortunes for the Nazi expansionism. Other turning points took place elsewhere, e.g., the military brilliance of Marshal Tito and extraordinary courage of the Serbs in standing up to Hitler in Yugoslavia and the defeat of Field Marshal Rommel's army at *El Alamein* by Field Marshal Montgomery should be recorded as turning points. The Normandy Invasion and the march through occupied Europe consolidated earlier progress. The 'blanket-bombing' by the Allies of European cities occupied by the Germans was to me outrageous, i.e. the destruction of Dresden and other cities.

The savage war in the Far East was brought to our awareness indirectly through many missionaries as well as from Irish-American sources. The reports on the media were, naturally, quite slanted in favour of the Allies. The scale of the Japanese expansionism was not fully comprehended by our friends and neighbours. We were led to admire the heroic achievements of the American GIs (many Irish-Americans fought in both the European and the Far Eastern theatres of war).

As we discovered later, the Second World War began with the violent excesses of the Germans and the Japanese, i.e. bombing of cities, sinking of merchant shipping, etc. These Axis excesses were to continue (unknown to most of us) in the concentration camps, mistreatment of prisoners, etc. Hindsight and the occasional media reports at the time began to question the overkill by the Allies, i.e. in the bombing of civilian populations in German and Japanese cities, largely by US bombers and bombs. The most horrific incidents of all this was the wilful use of the Atomic Bomb in Hiroshima and Nagasaki. This manifested a total demise of ethical standards and its substitution of excessive expedience.

I had noted that in every major conflict in which the United States has been involved, since General T Sherman's march through Georgia in the 1860s, in the American Civil War, *'the tactic of overkill'* has been used. *Enemy lives were not as valuable as our own*! A moral military leadership should be concerned about the lives of the enemy's population as much as it is concerned about its own people's lives, in my opinion. For that reason, the US military strategy seemed to rely totally on the almost indiscriminate use of conventional and nuclear weapons of mass-destruction in its defence or in the pursuit of its 'legitimate' interests. If this is true, then, God help the human race! Of course, a similar policy was adopted by Britain in her day of superpowerhood. The only difference is 'the curse of technological advances', which have multiplied the death-inflicting power in the hands of today's superpowers. Our scientists bear a big responsibility for all this excessive destruction of mostly innocent human life and the fabric of the natural environment.

In my view, military technology has dehumanised war still further and the licence to kill the civilian population in the pursuit of military goals has made it very difficult, if not impossible, for a true Christian to participate. Vatican Two (in the 1960s) had only two *'anathema sits'* (absolute condemnations). One was the deliberate termination of life in the womb and the other was that *'any act of war aimed indiscriminately at the destruction of entire cities or extensive areas along with their population is a crime against God and man himself. It merits unrequited and unhesitating condemnation'*. (*The Church Today*, Par. 80.) Could the Church be clearer in condemning acts of population destruction in the Second World War on both sides? I always thought that there was something very cowardly about the use of guided missiles and high-flying bombers pouring out their containers of incendiary and explosive devices (including cluster bombs) on unarmed men, women and children of all ages. How un-chivalrous? How immoral?

During the *Emergency*, Ireland built up a credible defence of its neutrality – sufficient to prevent either side from invading us without serious loss as they might have done with their superior weaponry and demographic advantage. The Army increased to over 40,000 with a very strong part-time Reserve Force made up of the LSF (Local Security Force) and the LDF (Local Defence Force). The latter were trained in matters military while the former would deal with civilian needs in the event of the outbreak of hostilities. In the end there was a soldier in practically every house, which meant that an external enemy would find it very difficult to occupy Ireland, unless they were prepared to institute a 'reign of terror'. Of course, the strong presence of people of Irish descent in the US and in Britain would also deter Churchill or Roosevelt from contemplating an invasion of our country. Post-war records of diplomatic exchanges revealed that such an operation was recommended. Also, there was a plan for the invasion of Ireland in the records of the Third Reich, on the likelihood of the IRA being willing and able to muster popular support, which was preposterous at the time. Should such an event as a German invasion/ occupation have taken place, Britain and the US would have entered on the side of Ireland to ensure that it would not succeed.

The strange thing about our policy of neutrality was the almost unanimous support for it in the population. I do not remember anyone who challenged it in our neighbourhood during the war years. Lord Haw Haw, William Joyce from Galway, was the English-speaking announcer and propagandist on the German radio station, *Germany Calling*. We would listen to his nightly bulletins on the wireless at home. This was the practice in other homes with wirelesses as well and may have contributed to our ambivalence towards Germany as England's enemy. *Raidió Éireann* was more objective in its daily bulletins. Some people who would visit our home would question the right of Germany to imperial aspirations. That would have been answered by questioning Britain's right to imperial aspirations in Ireland and elsewhere. Before the War more than half the world seemed to be 'painted red' on the world map – indicating the extent of the British Empire. This was to contract after the war during the 'decolonisation years'!

As the war wore on we began to feel the pinch in regard to rationing. All consumables were rationed. Money was of little use at the time unless one was able to buy things on the 'black market'. There were a number of cases of merchants being caught for smuggling goods across the Border (each way). Tea was the item getting more attention. Our friends in the United States (especially my late aunt Catherine) were most generous in sending us tea and some items of scarce clothing. Even then, the amounts received were limited. Tillage greatly increased and the Government imposed a compulsory tillage order, i.e. a certain percentage of all arable land had to be tilled. My father took conacre, i.e. a few acres of arable land for the sowing of grain and root crops. We had little or no arable land in Loughloon, although we had quite an amount of tillage in the rocky fields and gardens. All this meant we were practically self-sufficient in basic food needs. All items of footwear and clothing were mended when need be. It was a 'million miles away' from the 'throwaway' consumer society of the 'Celtic Tiger', which was leading people to be improvident. Recycling was, in effect, reusing. Nothing was wasted. A few years ago, my uncle-in-law, the late PJ McMenamin, told me (shortly before he died in 1996) that: '*This country will never be right until the ration book comes back again!*' It was his wise way of making a point in favour of the virtue of frugality.

8. AFTER THE WAR

Despite the heroic efforts of the people, we still endured deprivation. My grand-aunt, Bridget McGreal (née Moran), widow of my late grand-uncle, Austin McGreal, who had a pub and grocery shop on the Quay Road (now Quay Street) in Westport, would also refer to the 'hard times' of the late 1940s. Her son, Michael, was the local doctor, and both he and she would always give priority to the Travellers and to the very poor. It was from the late Bridget McGreal that I first felt an awareness of the social-class injustices in Irish society. She almost made a socialist radical out of me! She gave preference to the poor and the down and out. She called the Travellers her 'cousins' and she did not treat them in a patronising way. Of course, she paid the price for serving the Travellers. Many of her customers in the Settled Community withdrew their custom and went elsewhere. I learned then that trying to be just in a small town could make one unpopular with so-called '*bona fide*' citizens. Things have not changed that much since, in my experience.

After the War ended with the decimation of German cities, the occupation of countries and of large parts of Japan, Ireland's neutrality elicited a very trenchant criticism from Winston Churchill. This was eloquently replied to by *An Taoiseach*, Éamon de Valera, who did not fail to point out the reasons why Ireland could not see its way into entering the War formally. Britain's occupation of Ireland made it inconceivable that we could become an ally in war. Fortunately for Ireland, Churchill was replaced as Prime Minster by Mr Clement Atlee, a friend of Ireland. I remember seeing him walking around the streets of Westport when he was on his annual holidays in Newport, County Mayo. Ireland retained its rationing and continued exporting food to Britain. Also, after the War there was great demand for workers in Britain to carry out the reconstruction of the cities. Irish labourers and those from the British Commonwealth were invited in to do the work. This led to a growing emigration from Ireland to England. The loss of so many young British men in the War (through death and injury) left their country in a demographic deficiency, which the Irish and other foreigners helped to fill.

Emigration and immigration are always a 'push-pull' issue. Poor economic conditions at home provide the 'push-factor' while attractive demands abroad creates a 'pull-factor'. The combination of relatively poor economic circumstances in Ireland after the three Wars (Civil, Economic and World) and the very weak industrial base we inherited from British rule in Ireland meant that the country was not in a position to employ a large portion of its workforce. The post-war reconstruction of Britain, coupled with aid from the Marshall Plan, resulted in a 'pull-factor', i.e. a demand for able-bodied workers, male and female. The only good thing about emigration to Britain was its proximity to Ireland and the fact that most emigrants returned home a few times a year. A considerable minority of the young people who stayed at home contracted tuberculosis and many died in their late teens and early twenties. As I already stated, the arrival of a cure for this deadly disease and the development of a vaccine to prevent its spreading in 1948/ 1949 was such a life-giving relief.

Shortly after the War, in 1946, things began to become normal again. Oranges and bananas were available again in the shops. Women rejoiced on the return of silk stockings and, by degree, the severity of the rationing declined. Petrol was once again available and my father's motor car, a Vauxhall Ten (IZ 3816), was back on the road again (although its engine block was cracked because some water was left in its sump and the winter's frost did the rest). As noted above, emigration became really bad and an air of depression seemed to fall upon our neighbourhood. There was a very wet harvest in 1946, followed by one of the most severe snowfalls in the spring of 1947.

9. MOVING FROM LOUGHLOON TO DRUMMINDOO

In the summer of 1946 (the year Seán and I did our Intermediate Certificate examination) the family moved from Loughloon (almost four miles west of Westport) to Drummindoo (one mile and a quarter east of Westport in the direction of Castlebar). As I said earlier I was heartbroken leaving Loughloon, but in time, new friendships grew in the new neighbourhood. We were well received by our next-door neighbours, although I learned later that some local farmer(s) must have felt that the land we bought (forty-two acres in all) should have been divided (freely) among the local farmers by the Land Commission. We did not sense this resentment. My father bought the two smallholdings of land 'fair and square'! It is very sad later to see land losing its agricultural or horticultural purpose and good arable fields being consumed voraciously by motorways, bypasses and golf clubs. This appears almost sinful to me. The primary purpose of land must be the production of wholesome organic food for humans and wildlife.

Although Drummindoo was only one-and-a-quarter miles from Westport, it was very much a rural farming village with very few, if any, non-farming rural residents. The Bugler family in Monamore was the only exception. Mr Bugler was a 'weights-and-measures' sergeant in the *Garda Síochána* in Westport.

One of our fields, 'the bog', was where the local camogie team (a girls' hurling team) would train. It was great to see so many young athletic girls assemble (the Derrygorman Camogie Team) to learn the skills of the *camáin*. Quite a number of young lads would also come to cheer them on. So much laughter and fun would stir the heart. It also enabled us lads to relate naturally with girls and have a healthy outlook on life. In the house of a local single man, Mr Ned Geraghty of upper Drummindoo, the Camogie Club would organise house dances/*céilís* (only half-sets) to collect funding for the camogie players. These dances were very well patronised and supervised. Again, it afforded a wholesome and reasonably structured peer-environment for the development of boy-girl relationships. The music was usually supplied by a local melodeon player. When he was absent somebody would lilt jigs, reels and hornpipes. They would also tap their feet on a small sheet of galvanized iron. The entry fee was sixpence.

All went well until on a fateful night we got a visit from a local curate who held strict views on courting couples, and so forth. About half-way through the dance somebody said that the local curate was coming. Then the strong voice of the priest asked, *'Are there any girls in here under eighteen years of age?'* *'Oh no, Father,'* we responded in chorus. Then there was silence. The music and dancing had stopped. Up stepped a young woman and said, *'Indeed, there are two girls in here under eighteen years,'* and she proceeded to name them. *'Bring them out here,'* said the priest. The two sixteen or seventeen year-old girls timidly came forward. One of them was a niece of the woman who told the priest about their presence. The priest then advised that these two girls were to go home immediately and they had to be escorted by two older girls/ women. He then left and immediately we all asked the woman who named them why she had done so. She replied that *it would not be right to tell a lie to a priest*! Shortly after this unfortunate encounter our regular house dances stopped, to be replaced by the more anonymous ballrooms and the showbands in a few years. In this new social evirnoment, the strict surveillance by the clergy was no longer possible!

I have often reflected on this sad experience of the very protective role of the priest. He did not realise he was killing a very innocent (relatively speaking) form of local fun and aesthetic pleasure. It did not enhance my affection for the clergy. They were acting from quite a genuine Jansenist perspective, I would say. I always realised they were doing it for what they believed to be our moral protection. Some priests later would take a different attitude. For example, Fr James Horan, CC, in Toureen, Aughamore, built a massive dance hall for the purpose of providing enjoyable and healthy entertainment for the young people. The sixpenny dances in Ned Geraghty's would probably have ended in a short time anyhow. It was very sad that the local priest found it necessary to intervene. He probably went there at the request of some 'concerned' neighbour or 'worried' Catholic. In my opinion, then and now, it was a great pity that he felt it necessary to act in the way he did. He was a very genuine and much liked priest and a very close friend of the people.

In 1947 we got rural electrification of the houses in our area. I had learned my electricity so well in class that I was able to wire a house (for lights only) on the loop system. It passed the ESB officer's test. Rural electrification was a product of the Marshall Plan for Ireland, I learned later. It meant much for the people. It was great for doing our homework at night. Most people in the beginning only saw it as 'getting in the light'. Of course, it was much more than that and it changed the nature of domestic chores at the time. Eventually, it meant a universal distribution of 'power' to the people and raised their material standards of accommodation and living. It was delivered practically free of charge. As a public service scheme, it was in the same league as the renewal of rural housing before the War. I would hate to guess how much rural electrification would cost the State and the customer today!

By 1947 all the six siblings of our family were going to school. Austin got his Primary Certificate in Brackloon School in 1946 and enrolled in first year in the CBS Secondary School. Owen entered sixth class that year while Mary went into fourth class in the local Mercy Convent National School. Pádraig was just entering lower infants in the Convent School also. My father had returned to work for a few years after the motor car came back. Every year now made great changes as all our worlds opened up. Seán and I got the Leaving Certificate in 1948 and Seán successfully got the Cadet's Examination later that year. I was considered too young for a career and I was persuaded to do a second Leaving Certificate in 1949, in which I attempted honours mathematics and honours agricultural science. I did reasonably well in both new subjects, i.e. 58% in honours mathematics and something similar in agricultural science. My educational motivation left much to be desired but I did succeed in getting a second Leaving Certificate after a very difficult year of cramming two years' syllabuses into one. (This was something I did much more successfully in Leuven sixteen years later.)

After completing second-level my next task was to seek out an occupation. I worked on the land for about a period of eight months. It was not suggested to me that I stay on the land. I was unsuccessful in getting the Cadets' in 1949 partly because only sixteen new Cadets were admitted. At the beginning of 1950 Mr Tim Hastings, a garage owner in Westport and a lifelong friend of my father, offered me a training apprenticeship in Stores Management in Joseph Lucas Limited, North Portland Street, Dublin, and McCairns Motors Limited, in Tara Street, Dublin. (I will comment on those experiences and my diagnosis of Dublin City in the next chapter.)

One of the difficulties that Seán and I experienced in our time in Drummindoo, was the fact that we were still going to school, with only something like two shillings a week for pocket money. We were allowed to go to wakes, the local 'twenty-five' or 'one hundred and ten' card schools, and the cinema once a week (after our parents were satisfied we had all of our homework done and had performed the usual chores on the land including milking cows, etc). The vast majority of our peers had stayed at home from school at fourteen or fifteen years of age. They were earning money and they were going to dances and attracting beautiful girlfriends. What girl would be interested in a penniless schoolboy? I remember a conversation between my father and a fellow hill-farmer at the pattern/ fair of Leenane (15th August in 1947, I think) and the conversation went something like this.

> Farmer: *Austin McGreal, you are a foolish man, killing yourself working and slaving while those big 'stacks' of sons of yours are going to school and them well able to work. You should send them out to work and earn a few shillings. Why don't you bring them with you into the timber business?*
>
> My Father: *Paddy (not his real name), education is no load, even if they are only 'breaking stones' on the side of the road. I will support them until they get the Leaving Certificate and then it will be up to them after that. In your and my time we could get on without much education but that is not going to be the way in the future.*
>
> The Farmer: *I still think you are a foolish man but I wish you and them all the best.*

This may not be the exact sequence of words. I did not write them down on the spot. I did not appreciate my father's sacrifices at the time as my educational motivation had been distracted by the draw of the land and other teenage tensions, which every one of us had to go through. Looking back now I am extremely grateful to my parents' enlightened approach. My low ebb in educational motivation and performance was driven home to me by an encounter I had with a most genuine teacher,

Brother Irwin, in fifth year. He was giving out to me over my failure to complete an exercise. Then, after about ten minutes, I put up my hand and I said, '*Sir, I am finished.*' (Meaning I had finished the exercise.) He replied, '*Micheál, I think you're finished in more ways than one.*' I realised exactly what he meant. It was a clear warning to me to 'pull up my socks' and renew my commitment to school work, which I belatedly began to do. I am ever grateful to Brother Irwin for his warning to me on that memorable day as a sixteen-year-old confused adolescent. This experience has since been very central in my understanding of young people (when lecturing in the University) who may not be able to apply their great ability to the task in hand. It is rarely too late to recover. Leaving Certificate results do not tell us everything about students' academic ability. Hence, the limitations of the so-called 'points' system' determining too much of a young person's career in education!

It is difficult to imagine today the heroic commitment of our teachers (Brothers and lay) who had to teach us a prescribed course with hardly any resources. For instance in our senior cycle, we were all together in the one classroom and the one master would be going back and over from sixth year to fifth year. Honours and pass mathematics to two years would be taught by the one teacher in the same classroom and many of us not properly motivated or possessing sufficient confidence. No wonder, some of our teachers would 'lose the rag' and become too rough, at times. I know that some of my classmates have never forgiven their teachers because of the rough manner. I have come to understand both teacher and student - both were right and both were wrong! Of course, some teachers were better than others, as were the students.

All in all, we owe an extraordinary debt of gratitude to our dedicated teachers operating under unbearable limitations in the context of modern pedagogical resources. Maybe our Leaving Certificate results were unimpressive (in our case we all opted for Pass papers on the day of the examination in 1948, having been prepared for Honours). But I found out when I would later compete with very high Leaving Certificate performers from boarding schools and elsewhere in the most privileged areas, I was well fit to perform as well, if not better, than most of them. I do not say this in a boastful manner, as I feel I have very little to boast about. Rather, I say this as thanks to my teachers in the Westport Christian Brothers' School, which my father believed was the 'best school in Ireland' with my mother's enlightened support. Maybe my parents were right? At least I can say with confidence that the Westport Christian Brothers School was the best for me.

If only the Department of Education had the wisdom to question the value of the 'universal curriculum' and include subjects which would enable us to address the social and economic problems of local communities! It would have made second-level education more relevant for the people of western communities. The Leaving Certificate was to become *a passport for work outside my local community,* which needed my services more than even the Defence Forces or the other professions. At least, in my time, most of those who stayed at home were intelligent enough to 'keep the home fires burning'. I often thought that the real heroes of the West of Ireland were those who waited behind, married and raised a family in lean times. Later, they would get 'the farmers' dole' which was the least the State could do to supplement the income of those who kept our local communities and parishes alive. Maybe we should erect a monument to 'the unknown doler' in the rural parishes, who kept 'the home fires burning' in the rural communities of the West of Ireland! It always annoyed me to listen to politicians (of the right-wing type) criticising the small farmers drawing a meagre enough dole. One eminent politician compared those on the dole to 'piglets sucking on the sow of Ireland'. What insulting rubbish! It was very clear that he did not understand the socio-economic conditions of the times.

10. INTEREST IN POLITICS

Politics always interested me. In a democracy it is very important for political parties to involve committed young people and provide good representation for the people. At one stage my neighbour, the late Johnnie Reynolds, brought me to a meeting of the local *Cumann* of *Fianna Fáil* in 1949. That party was quite radical (socially) in the thirties and forties. Its leaders worked for justice and promoted the Irish language and the reunification of Ireland (by peaceful means). I agreed strongly with these aims and would probably have continued in the party were it not for the fact that I became interested in seeking a Cadetship in the Defence Forces. Also, my mother, who was involved in the War of Independence and on the Republican side in the Civil War, supported the founding of

Fianna Fáil in the 1920s. The *Fianna Fáil* Party had been defeated in the 1948 General Election and this afforded it a chance to renew itself after sixteen years in Government.

The new inter-party Government (1948-51) under John A Costello TD as *Taoiseach*, declared the Republic of Ireland in 1949. Mr de Valera had refrained from such a declaration so as to make it easier for people of a Unionist persuasion in the 'Six Counties' to work with the Government of the Twenty-Six Counties. Also, I do not think he favoured the use of the term Republic unless it covered the whole thirty-two counties. Nevertheless, our legitimate Government declared and enacted our new status and that was that!

Politics in Europe developed fairly rapidly after the end of the war. There was no repeat of the disastrous Treaty of Versailles (after the First World War). Reconstruction was the immediate task and the Marshall Plan was a very enlightened programme devised by the United States to help in the reconstruction. The United Nations was set up in 1948. While it had serious structural limitations in that it only represented the victors of war, its Charter was highly commendable. The most serious consequences of the outcome of the victory were the division of continental Europe between the Eastern bloc and the Western bloc. The former were under the influence of the USSR while the western states were under Anglo-French-American control. In time, France, West Germany and Italy would become major players in the Western European bloc. We in Ireland would wait on the wings of the Western group of nations although we did not become formally linked to NATO (North Atlantic Treaty Organisation) or seek membership of the United Nations (until the mid-1950s). In West Germany an elected government was established under a pre-Nazi Mayor of Cologne, Mr Konrad Adenauer. He was supported by the Allies.

After a bloody guerrilla war against the authorities in Palestine, the State of Israel was set up with the support of the United States in 1947. The public sympathy towards the Jews after the 'holocaust' under the Nazis, as revealed in the Nuremberg trials after the war, contributed to the international support for the State of Israel, and did not rally behind the mass of Palestinians, who were 'ethnically cleansed' to make place for the Israelis. History has shown since how inadequate this solution was and could well eventually lead to a Third World War if the problems of the dispossessed are not fairly dealt with. The people most to benefit from a just solution would be the Jews. At present, the crisis is likely to aggravate anti-Semitic extremists and destroy the goodwill towards Jews generated after Nuremberg. I would rate the Israeli-Palestinian problem among the most important challenges facing our world leadership today. There is an urgent need for pluralist, ecumenical dialogue between Jews and Muslims to establish cooperative coexistence in this area of the Middle East. An exclusively secular solution to the Middle East problem does not seem viable.

The full recognition of Israel and Palestine as autonomous states is a *sine-qua-non* for a viable and just solution. The granting of citizenship to Palestinians within Israel and to Israeli within Palestine is also necessary to ensure mutual equality. The potential of such a solution, based on mutual respect and maximum cooperation, would be a major step towards a peaceful and prosperous Middle East – '*A land of milk and honey*'.

Chapter Three

THE 1950S
THE WORLD THROUGH THE SIGHTS OF A SOLDIER

1. IN SEARCH OF A JOB

As already stated, I began the 1950s in the motor trade. By special arrangement with Mr Tim Hastings, the Fairgreen, Westport, and my father, I was sent to Dublin for a period of six months to study the stores' system for electrical and mechanical parts of motor cars and lorries. *A motor vehicle is an elaborate assemblage of parts and gadgets.* The aim of this brief apprenticeship was to enable me to establish a genuine parts' stores in Hastings Garage in Westport. My allowance while in Dublin was ten shillings a week plus my board and laundry. The first three months were spent in Joseph Lucas Limited, North Portland Street, Dublin 1, manufacturers and providers of all electrical parts for motor vehicles produced in Britain. The boss was Mr Maguire (who also had an interest in Irish singing and dancing in Dolphin's Barn). He and all the staff at Lucas's were very helpful. Mr Murphy in the Sales Department was from County Mayo. Mr Kinane (father of a Jesuit scholastic, John Kinane) was working in the car batteries' department.

My first major problem in Lucas's was accent. I found it hard at first to understand the Dublin accent on the telephone from the storemen in garages around the city and they, in turn, missed some of my pronunciations. In a short time we could communicate. The system of storage was known as 'the punch-card system'. There would be a punch-card in the shelf for each item in stock. On selling an item its punch-card was withdrawn from the shelf and sent into the office. At the end of the month all the punch- cards sent into the ordering office would be mailed to the head office in Birmingham and a replacement item would be returned for each card returned. This operated also as a quasi-rationing system.

During the second phase of my apprenticeship, I studied the methodology used in McCairns Motors Limited, Tara Street, Dublin. McCairns Motors assembled Vauxhall cars and Bedford trucks in their plant in Alexander Basin. The stores in Tara Street supplied parts to all agents of Vauxhall and Bedford throughout the country. Tim Hastings was a main Vauxhall and Bedford dealer. The stores manager was a Mr Biggar, who operated a different dual-card system, i.e. one card in the shelf with the items and one card in the office. (This was the system I would introduce in Tim Hastings Garage in Westport on return there in July.)

This was my first experience of work outside the farm. It was quite strange. My weekly income of ten shillings a week (with lodgings and laundry paid for) ensured that I lived sparingly within my means. I tried to send some of it home. It was an accepted custom that we would give a portion of our income to our parents. In Dublin I visited every place that was free, i.e. churches, national art galleries, the natural museum, the zoological gardens (through peepholes in the fence), etc. I went to the cheapest places in the cinema and theatre ('the gods'). In the course of my stay in Dublin I got a good overall view of urban life (from the outside) in 1950. This included the very many tenement blocks in Gardiner Street and elsewhere. People showed signs of severe poverty. They did not look as healthy or robust as the people at home. I became homesick at times. The devotion in the churches was most impressive. Living in a lodging house in Belvedere Road (off the North Circular Road), I would go to Mass nearly every morning in the Jesuit Church, Gardiner Street. It was a 'warm' and devotional church. The ushers were dressed in magnificent robes. Confessions in Gardiner Street were special and, I thought, mature (so much so, that whenever I had a problem later in the Army, I would go to confession in Gardiner Street to straighten it out). I stayed very much in the background and did not make any contact with the priests. This was my first contact with the Jesuits!

In 1950, they had just closed down the tram system in Dublin, which in hindsight was a mistaken. They were lucky to have trams working during the Emergency years. There was still a wide use of horses by CIE, Dublin Dairies and the Bakeries. One would hear the regular click-clacks of the horses on the streets and pavements early in the morning. The buses were great. For a few pennies it was possible to cross the city. Dublin was still quite small in area. It was surrounded by green fields and tillage land. Some post-war housing estates were being built on the Southside (south of the Canal, e.g. Crumlin, Walkinstown, etc.). There were very few houses north or west of Collins Avenue. Finglas was expanding. Alexander Basin was a hive of industry. The Port was still very busy. Frequently cattle would be driven down the North Circular Road by professional drovers from the Cattle Market to the cattle boats. The Liverpool boat from the North Wall would carry livestock and passengers.

Dublin was a very safe city and serious crime was rare. A murder would occupy the headlines for days. Ireland had fewer than ten murders a year in the early 1950s. We were all warned about a rough gang who operated around the Amiens Street Railway Station (now called Connolly Station). There was a strong following of soccer in Dublin, but I, as a loyal GAA man, never attended a soccer match. I would attend Croke Park every Sunday that there were matches. It was a good place to meet other migrants from the West. A number of us (country lads) would meet regularly in a milk bar at the corner of Parnell Square and North Great Denmark Street. I did not make close friends with many Dublin people – apart from those with whom I was working. I do not remember going to one dance in Dublin while working there. Anyhow, I only knew how to dance 'half-sets' and a few Irish group dances. I was very much a loner. Mayo and Meath were the top football teams that I was interested in at the time. Mayo won the All-Ireland final that year. I remember coming up from Westport on the turf train for the match.

On returning to Westport I set about establishing a 'genuine parts' stores in Hastings. To do that I introduced the dual-card system and everything was up and running in a short time. My weekly wage package was thirty shillings a week (one pound and ten shillings). At the beginning of September I told Mr Hastings I was intent on applying for the Cadets in the Defence Forces. He was very annoyed and tried to persuade me not to go ahead with it. This was understandable and must have seemed ungrateful on my part. I offered to train in an understudy, but he did not agree. Eventually, he let me off to do the Cadet's interview and I returned to work after it. I felt the two interviews and the medical examination went well. I understood why Tim Hastings would feel annoyed at my trying to go elsewhere so soon, but I would have been too old for the Cadets if I had not succeeded in 1950.

Some time in October word came from the Army to say that David Regan, the son of the local Garda Sergeant, and I were successful in our application for the Cadets and we were to report to the Military College

(Cadet School) on 24th October 1950. Tim Hastings, while congratulating me, again tried to persuade me to decline the offer and stay with him. My decision to go to the Curragh Camp was very definite, although I was sorry to leave the Garage and Westport. Only God knows if I made the best decision! Thank God, my replacement in Hastings Garage was better than me and under him and his assistant the Stores went from strength to strength. I was very sorry at having to leave Hastings Garage.

It was a very opportune time to enter the motor trade. Knowing the workers and the customers was a very rich experience for me. The work ethic in Hastings and in Lucas's and McCairns was commendable. For all their sweat and labour, salaries in 1950 were very low. Apprenticeships to the fitter/mechanic trade were hard to come by and took a number of years to learn-on-the-job. The work was, of its nature, quite dirty and greasy. The men seemed to enjoy it.

There were interesting developments in the car engine. The magneto was being totally replaced by the coil [which I learned later was invented by Professor (Fr) Callan of St Patrick's College, Maynooth]. The growth of the diesel engine was also new. In Lucas's, the CAV injector was being developed. The B90 scheme was introduced whereby a defective generator or starter would no longer be repaired in the garage but rather replaced by a fully repaired generator or starter supplied by Lucas Limited, i.e. with the armature rewound and bushes replaced in the factory. This system was introduced in 1950 and is still in operation today. It was not unlike the reconditioned engine, which was also repaired in the factory. When working on the coil, the experts were more interested in the engine's capacity to generate revolutions per second than a vehicle's miles per hour performance. It proved to me that the experts' understanding of engine performance was far more sophisticated than that of the ordinary 'lay' car owner-driver. Every generation of cars has its own advantages and driving today is made easier. The mechanic today is dependent on new computer technology to carry out the various tests. In 1950 the brain of the mechanic was the only computer available!

2. THE CADET SCHOOL: A NEW ADVENTURE

I was very excited and a little unsure of the new world facing me when I arrived at the Curragh Camp on that cold, grey-blue October day in

1950. We all met in the billiard room in the Cadet School and waited our turn to be sworn in as Cadets. The Cadet's military status was as stated by a bouncing Corporal Hartley – '*Members of the Forces with none of their privileges!*' We were assigned to eight-man billets according to height. Institutional living was totally new to me. I must have appeared very raw on arrival. Luckily, I had David O'Regan, as a fellow Westport man. Also, my brother Seán was nearing the end of his cadetship and would shortly be ready for commissioning. I learned early on 'to give everyone my ear and few my voice', (the advice of Polonius to Laertes in Shakespeare's *Hamlet*). Our first meeting in the refectory was some experience. The former boarding-school boys knew how to grab the best food, while those of us who were less 'streetwise' would have to do with the leavings. In a short time we learned the norms of communal dining.

The Cadet course was divided into a number of areas, i.e. normal recruit training, including learning the skills of firing infantry weaponry, drill and ceremonial skills, physical training, endurance training, battle drill, academic study, the study of leadership, military history, etc. Physical fitness and discipline trials were quite challenging. We were also encouraged to develop our cultural and aesthetic tastes. I, and a number of others, became accomplished amateur photographers. Also, I began to enjoy listening to classical music in the evening time and developed a greater appreciation of music in general. The programme was exhausting at times. We were expected to write term papers and do examinations in many subjects. My two major papers were on *General Tecumseh Sherman* (Genius of the American Civil War) and *The Leadership of Napoleon.* Our Cadet Master, Lieutenant Colonel Seán McKeown, gave us lectures on leadership, which were like inquisition sessions on our reading norms.

Our Class Officer was a famous Antrim Gaelic footballer, Captain Seán Gallagher, and our Class Sergeant was Sergeant Matthew Roche. Other officers and NCOs who were designated to our formation included the famous all-Army champion marksman, Company Sergeant Peter O'Connor, who kept a 'paternal' eye on our progress and was very approachable. Sgt Tommie Lydon from the Maam Valley was on the administrative staff of the Cadet School, which eased my burden. There were forty-four Cadets in our class in the beginning. After the completion of our two years, we still had forty-four commissioned. This was an extraordinary achievement for the diligent class captain, Seán Gallagher, who was affectionately nicknamed 'Gildy', and his efficient staff. Two years previously there was a very high number of Cadets who were not allowed to continue.

Most of our class were Pioneers and a high proportion of us got up very early and went to Mass every morning. This was taken for granted and was not restricted to 'holy Joes'. The three local towns, i.e. Droichead Nua, Kildare and Kilcullen, were out of bounds to Cadets, as were the public houses in Brownstown. The absence of young girls deemed suitable for potential officers was a felt deprivation. It would be frowned upon by the authorities if a cadet or an officer were to fall in love with the daughter of an NCO (Non-Commissioned Officer) or private soldier. (I rebelled against this restriction of choice of girlfriend later, as a Second Lieutenant when I dated the daughter of a NCO after a dance in the CYMS Hall in Kildare town.)

The general ethos cultivated in the Cadet School was one of honour and a keen appreciation of art and culture. I was very impressed by the balanced interest in politics in general (rather than party politics) and in current affairs. I remember a visit of the United States aircraft carrier, *The Saipan*, during my time in the College. United States Naval Cadets were on board and they invited us to visit the carrier. We paired off with the US Cadets. One member of the group told me that the Captain of *The Saipan* briefed them on their way into Dublin. He encouraged them to discuss any topic but 'religion' and 'politics' with us. Of course, we spent a most stimulating afternoon discussing the affairs of Church and State. (In my opinion, religion and politics are probably the most suitable topics for adult discussion, i.e. God and humankind.) Sport, and particularly athletics, was important in the Cadet School. We got a good training in the gymnasium. We became very fit, physically. We were also trained to be referees in a number of sports.

Of course, not everything was 'rosy' in our Cadet School. There was an element of bullying between staff and Cadets and among Cadets at times. Viewed from today's perspective, pressures were put on us to test our level of endurance and to push us in order to find out if we would respond in an insubordinate manner. I remember a very determined Cadet being forced to 'double around the square' for a long time carrying a 'sand pack' to test his subordination. They were not able to 'break him'! As a result, we developed an 'us and them' attitude and we were determined that they would not overcome us. We also cooperated in adversity, which was a contributory factor to all of us getting through. We 'carried' each other and would encourage the 'slaggers' and restrain the 'eager beavers'. I agree very much with Lieutenant Colonel Seán McKeown when he said to us (later on the Youghal Exercise in 1955) that comradeship was the most important feature of an army. It was the basis of *esprit de corps*.

We certainly developed a level of comradeship in the Cadet School that I had not witnessed before or since. For example, our year still comes together regularly to renew our comradeship. At the time of writing some twenty of our fellow-cadets have passed on. *Ar dheis Dé go raibh a n-anamacha*.

Living conditions were all right for the period. Food was limited by Army rations but it was good and wholesome food. I do not remember many 'going sick' with stomach ulcers! In the end, we were much disciplined. One day, C/S Peter O'Connor said to me: '*Cadet Mac Gréil, you are over-disciplined. You should go up to Dublin for one of 'them weekends' and 'let your hair down'.*' I just smiled and tried to relax and went to the pictures in the Curragh cinema, where we had to go upstairs to the more expensive seats. The one thing I always strove to protect was personal privacy, which can be undermined in an over-institutionalised environment such as a Cadet School, an army barracks, a novitiate, a seminary and other similarly structured environments.

For a long time the regime in the military barracks throughout the world did not fully respect (sufficiently in my view) the personal privacy of individual soldiers. Such basic human virtues as 'modesty' and 'confidentiality' should not be rudely intruded upon in the name of macho group control. The current spate of interpersonal violent behavioural incidents in various armies raises serious questions relating to the insensitive training being promoted by certain policies, and, possibly, resulting in the violation of personal privacy and true respect for fellow human beings.

The brutality experienced in the recent Iraq invasion, for instance, is also another example of this phenomenon, some of this 'macho-type training' tends to desensitise and dehumanise the soldier. I also have great problems with the effort to cultivate a feeling of hatred towards the enemy. This raises real difficulties for me about some forms of military training of soldiers to motivate them for combat. Many of these questions have come to me over the years. *In case there may be any misunderstanding, our training was not based on hatred of the enemy.* We, in the Defence Forces, were more focused on the defence of our people and their institutions. We did not envisage ourselves as an 'offensive army' at all. At least I did not see myself doing anything but defending the State from enemies from without and from within. The 'peace-keeping' role under the United Nations would be an acceptable mission for me. The 'peace-enforcement' role would raise serious problems for me, and people like me.

Let me return to the Cadet School and note some interesting happenings. (I will avoid all military secrets.) The academic work was very interesting and helped to broaden our understanding. One example of this was our project on other countries. I was given Portugal as my project. I had to write to the Portuguese Embassy for information on the State's institutions, etc. This was a gentle introduction to a simple research methodology (using secondary analysis). I do not think my paper was that brilliant, but it was a start. Perhaps the most valuable benefit which I derived from my Cadet training was learning how to instruct and to teach others. An officer who was not able to train the soldiers and NCOs under his command would be less effective. At that time, the level of education achieved by recruits before joining was not very high. So we had to train in the simplest and clearest way. More than that, we would have to supervise our NCOs as they transmitted the basic skills to the 'raw recruit'. In other words, a good field officer had to be a very good trainer and supervisor of soldiers and NCOs. The Military College was first-class in transmitting the necessary pedagogical skills. Years later, when lecturing in the University I just adapted what I learned in the Military College with reasonable success. The only test of teaching skills is the response from the learner. I always questioned myself as a lecturer, if a student was not able to perform well in his or her examinations. *The cost of failure in training soldiers correctly could be measured in the loss of life.* Hence, the importance of being a good trainer or supervisor.

Getting used to the glamour and status that accompanied the rank of Army Officer was not that easy to adjust to outside the barracks. For instance, we were supposed to go to the best seats in cinemas and theatres.

We could dance only in tennis clubs and such places in Dublin. Once commissioned, we could not fraternise with private soldiers or NCOs and we were obliged to travel first-class on the train. We wore kid gloves to indicate that we did not engage in menial manual work. We were aspiring 'officers and gentlemen'! As someone wrote somewhere, certain rules 'were for the guidance of the wise and the (literal) observance of fools'! I must admit that wise officers tried to avoid being 'prisoners of protocol'.

The army was a three-tier social structure, i.e. officers, NCOs and private soldiers. In the 1950s, these tiers reflected a type of 'class structure'. Those of us who did not approve (personally) of this social class structure were reluctantly resigned to go along with it only as far as it was deemed necessary and avoid hassle or bother. One of the great scandals of the 1950s was the absence of the sons of NCOs and privates in the ranks of the cadets. I would now classify this form of discrimination as segregation, since it was backed by accepted custom. Thank goodness this situation has changed and the sons and daughters of NCOs and private soldiers are welcome to become cadets if they have the necessary qualifications. I am not sure of the level of progress achieved in relation to the regimental social class structure referred to earlier. It would appear to me that more could be done to integrate the officers and the NCOs, at least. Also, in areas not required by 'good order and military discipline', fully qualified (three-star) private soldiers should be socially integrated more. Maybe the authorities could begin with the Mess structures? An army of a democracy should strive for maximum egalitarianism among all ranks, while admitting functional hierarchy of command.

3. THE LIFE OF AN ARMY OFFICER IN THE THIRD BATTALION

In 1951, the first Inter-Party Government under *An Taoiseach*, John A Costello, was forced to go to the people and a *Fianna Fáil* Government under *Taoiseach* Éamon de Valera TD, was returned with a very slender majority. Two of the significant achievements of the 1948-51 Government were the curing of tuberculosis and the implementation of a long-overdue programme of reafforestation. The latter made a great difference to the West of Ireland. The minister responsible for this progressive programme was a Mayo man from Belcarra, Mr Joseph Blowick TD (*Clan na Talún*). (His brother, Fr Patrick Blowick, was one of the founders of the

Dalgan Missions to China.) The Minister who led the vigorous attack on tuberculosis was Dr Noel Browne TD (*Clann na Poblachta*). The country owes much to Minister Browne and his Department. In 1951, all of the Cadets were inoculated against tuberculosis. Minister Browne's Mother and Child Scheme was to lead to the fall of the Inter-Party Government because of disagreement between himself and the Catholic Bishops over certain aspects of the proposal. Minister Browne also fell out with the leader of his party, Mr Seán MacBride TD, over the same controversy.

In November 1952, I was commissioned as a Second Lieutenant by the Minister for Defence, Mr Oscar Traynor TD. The Minister's speech was brief and to the point. It went something like this: '*Congratulations, gentlemen. You now have weight. Pull it and don't throw it around. You have ten days' leave.*' My new number was O7545. Among the officers (not directly involved in my class) who impressed me during my time in the Cadet School were Captains Bill Doheny and Denis Quinn.

On commissioning I was posted to the Third Curragh Infantry Battalion (popularly known as '*The Bloods*') where I was to spend my seven years as an officer. It was not my first choice as I had applied for the Cavalry Corps. I had not been very successful in my choices within the Cadet School. Shortly after arriving in the College I applied for the Navy but did not get the appointment, although I passed the colour test. My next choice was to become a pilot in the Air Corps. Up to that year, pilots were selected from the Cadet class on commissioning. Unfortunately, for our year, a new programme of recruiting officers (pilots) for the Air Corps in conjunction with *Aer Lingus* (the Irish State airline) was introduced. So all my preferences were unsuccessful, but I did not let it get me down, despite my disappointment.

As things worked out, the Army's decision was the best choice for me! The 'Bloods' were a tremendous group of comrades. The Third Battalion was older than the Army itself. It was the surviving unit of the Third Northern Division of the Old IRA, which could not continue because of the partition of Ireland. The Battalion had a certain 'hard man' reputation. It would be difficult to find a unit with so many colourful characters in the ranks of its officers, NCOs and men (there were no women in the army in the 1950s).

Shortly after my posting to the Third Battalion, one of the great characters of this unit passed away, Lieutenant Colonel Charlie O'Doherty,

Commanding Officer (RIP). He died shortly after my commissioning. I met him at the pre-commissioning dinner in the Military College. Before going to our different units, we were assigned to the Artillery Barracks in Kildare Town to complete an *A and Q Course* in simple accountancy, under the 'famous' Captain Larry Furlong. What we learned was very practical and most relevant in later years. We were taught how to do such things as audits of messes and other organisations, operating accounts. It was, in fact, a mini Quartermaster's course. It also gave the 1950-1952 Class graduates a pleasant six weeks together enjoying the privileges of living in an Officers' Mess as officers for the first time. It gave us a new freedom, which we enjoyed. I was later to serve as Assistant Quartermaster of the General Training Depot (on detachment) for a number of months with responsibility 'to feed and clothe' over 600 soldiers. I also served as Assistant Quartermaster of the Third Curragh Battalion for a period.

When the course in Kildare was finished, we all reported to our respective units. Three officers of our year were sent to the Third Curragh Battalion in Connolly Barracks, i.e. Second Lieutenant Johnnie Heaslip, Second Lieutenant Gerry Manning and myself. We were very well received. Lieutenant Colonel Jack Lewis (a well-known member of the Army Equestrian Jumping Team) was the new Commanding Officer. It took some time before we were fully integrated, getting to know 'who's who' and 'what's what' and, for me, to 'know the ropes'. One old officer called me aside and told me that '*one did not learn everything in the Cadet School or from books and manuals*'. Common sense would always be a necessary ingredient in 'this man's army'! Of course, we had to take the regulations seriously, but we should never forget that we were '*dealing with people*'. I must have been very strict as a young officer!

I tried very hard to carry out my duties but I soon discovered that I also needed to relax. A popular method of relaxation within the Mess was the bar. In fact, our Mess was a very attractive one for sociable drinking of alcohol and a wide circle of officers from around the Curragh Training Camp would drop in for a chat and a drink. But I was a Pioneer and, while enjoying the company of those who took a drink, still, I would not hang around the bar too much. This resulted in my getting involved in a number of voluntary groups – i.e. music society (in a passive role), Irish language groups, the Curragh historic society, etc. I tried golf but I felt that it was too obsessive a hobby. In time, I would develop a fairly active 'spare-time' life. In the area of sport, running (one mile) and basketball would become my choices. I loved Gaelic football, but was not skilled enough in it. During the 1950s, religion on the Curragh was accepted as a serious part of one's life and young people in their early twenties would not find it strange to participate beyond the 'call of duty'. I got involved in two lay groups, i.e. *An Réalt* (The Irish language Legion of Mary) and in the Patricians (a movement set up by Fr PJ Brophy of Carlow which provided a forum for the serious discussion of matters affecting the 'meaning of life').

We were very fortunate in the Curragh Training Camp that we had seven autonomous military units with seven Officers' Messes, i.e. Connolly, Plunkett, Kent, Clarke, McDermott, McDonagh and MacPiarais. In the 1950s, 'garrison life' for a young officer was considered very important, that is, we were expected to live in for at least four years after commissioning and would not be entitled to marriage allowances until after that time. Also, there were a number of officers' quarters in the Barrack vicinity. The Curragh Military Hospital was also an important unit, both medically and socially. The Officers' Mess Dances (Balls) were features of our 'high' social life and I enjoyed them immensely. Dance is the most aesthetically enjoyable experience of all. When I went to the Curragh I could dance only the 'half set' and other Irish group dances. I had to learn how to waltz, foxtrot, etc. in the Cadet school. Some of the more 'with it' and sophisticated cadets taught us how to waltz with chairs as partners!

The early 1950s was a period of a very low crime rate in the Republic of Ireland. I remember that the circuit court judge in Naas was once presented with 'white gloves' to indicate no indictable case being presented to his session. The homicide rate (nationally) was annually in lower teens or even single figures. There were relatively few in prison (and many of those were there for trivial offences, e.g. Traveller women stealing a half-a-crown). Suicide was extremely low (even if one were to add 'death by misadventure') and family stability was very high, despite the difficulties of seasonal emigration, unemployment, larger families, etc.

There were little or no 'hang ups' about religion. Most people accepted that God's existence was as real as the air that they breathed. That did not mean that we would not question Church teaching and argue religious issues. We were aware of some of the inadequacies of some authoritarian clergy but as Christ said: '*They were in the seat of Moses and, therefore, merited our attention.*' Courting was preferred to sex before marriage. This situation was more conducive to the building of good relationships (than the reverse order) apart from the moral and ethical questions. The mass media were more respectful of the privacy of people's lives, which was also conducive to a better quality of life. Much of the media (print and electronic) today, in my opinion, have become vulgar, tasteless, prying, obscene and feeding on the hidden faults of the people (which should be kept confidential unless they intrude on the rights of others) and tend to trivialise interpersonal social norms and morality.

Among the greatest tragedies of the 1950s was the haemorrhage of emigration of Ireland's young men and women, due to weak economic conditions at home and a strong pull from abroad to get workers to reconstruct battered Britain after the War. This was an extraordinarily valuable contribution of Ireland to the restoration of Britain in the 1950s. Also, some of our finest young people (my brother Austin among them) went to the United States of America and helped to make up for their young GIs whose lives were tragically ended in the World War. *Emigration nearly always helps the host nation and weakens the country of origin.* It is much better for Ireland when those leaving the country are balanced by those coming into Ireland to work and settle. In the 1950s, it was all one-way traffic out of the country. With such a 'brawn and brain drain' it was almost impossible for the Irish State to do much about it. Once Britain was rebuilt there was a lowering of the 'pull-factor' and also conditions at home began to improve somewhat (during the following decades) and the Government was in a position to put together national recovery plans. These plans would not have been possible in the early 1950s, in my opinion, because of structural economic forces outside our control. The Irish who emigrated to the United States during the early- and mid-twentieth century worked in business and in the professions. Some were to become leaders in the building trade.

In 1954 the de Valera (*Fianna Fáil*) Government fell and the Costello Inter-Party Government returned to office. General Seán Mac Eóin (the 'Blacksmith from Ballinalee', County Longford) was the new Minister for Defence. He, like his predecessor, Oscar Traynor, was a leader in the War of Independence 1919-21. He was quite a religious man and declared Our Lady as Patroness of the Defence Forces, in 1954, the Marian Year. It was reported that he believed that Our Lady saved his life when he was shot by the British during the independence struggle. Later in the early 1970s I visited him when he was ill in St Bricin's Hospital, Dublin. I found him to be very spiritual and most friendly. During my visit we were discussing the 'conversion of St Paul' as reported in the *Acts of the Apostles*. He told me that he saw Saul as a 'Black-and-Tan' in search of 'the lads' when he was struck by lightning and fell from his horse! He was then converted to supporting the true cause! What an 'application of the senses' (in the Ignatian sense)! My mother (who was on the other side during the Civil War) often talked about Seán Mac Eóin and his wife. She knew them during the War of Independence. She spoke of them with admiration. There is another story told about the General during the Black-and-Tan campaign. He was once driving down from Dublin to Longford dressed as a priest. Going through Maynooth he got a puncture. He knocked up this house in the village looking for help. The man of the house suggested he might seek assistance in the College from one of his colleagues (as a number of them had cars). Mac Eóin replied that his Latin had gone a bit rusty and he could not approach them in an ordinary way. '*I understand your position very well, Father*' said the man. '*Come in for something to eat and we will get your puncture repaired.*' So everything ended up well and the General in disguise gave his blessing (in words) to those good Samaritans who helped him.

I had the privilege of meeting Minister Seán Mac Eóin one day when I was in charge of the Garrison in Devoy Barracks, Naas. He was on his way home from Punchestown Races and dropped in unannounced. I was in the Curragh Camp collecting rations for the Garrison. As I arrived (back in Naas) at the gate of the Barracks, whom do I see but the Minister for Defence, and the corporal (Orderly Sergeant) coming down towards the gate. All excited, I marched up to him and presented myself as the officer in charge. He told me to relax as he was on an informal visit. He had just dropped in on his way home from the races. He said that his cabinet colleague, Minister Bill Norton TD, was telling him all about the Barracks, and he wanted to see it for himself. I told him that if I had known he was coming, I would have informed the Officer Commanding the Curragh Camp, Colonel AT Lawlor. '*And then,*' said the Minister, *'the Barracks would be all done up for my inspection. The fire buckets would be all painted red*!' No, he wanted to see it as it was and the Corporal gave him all the information he required. (I said to myself this is a real old soldier who could not be bluffed!) I rang the Command OC, Colonel Tony Lawlor, and he seemed not too worried by the visit of his old comrade in the War of Independence and in the Civil War.

The real purpose of the Minister's visit to Naas Barracks that day was to prepare it for the new Army Apprentice School, which, in my opinion, was a most worthwhile development. It was, in effect, an adult technical boarding school, which produced a wide range of skilled workers for the Defence Forces and later for Irish society. The decision to close this valuable school in 1998 was one of the most short-sighted decisions carried out by the Minister for Defence and his Defence Force's planners. I, and all the trade union leaders in County Kildare, appealed to the Government not to go ahead with their ill-advised decision. It seemed to me that the closing of the Apprentice School was part of the snobbery in attitudes towards manual skills. The Army Apprentice School had become a 'showpiece unit' of the Defence Forces. I remember in 1958 or early 1959 presenting a high percentage of the apprentices with *An Fáinne*, a badge expressing competence in and willingness to speak Irish. The graduates from Naas went to the various units and corps of the Forces.

It is very difficult now to visualise how underdeveloped the living conditions of soldiers, NCOs and officers were during the lean 1950s. Rooms were all heated with turf of mixed quality. Billets were little, if at all, changed since the time of the British. Cookhouses and dining halls for soldiers were rough and ready. In Connolly Barracks the old stables near the cookhouse were used as dining halls. Indoor toilets were only being built in the passages between the billets in the 1950s. The living conditions of the soldier were really primitive. Officers' messes were damp and very inadequately heated. The menu was quite basic, but wholesome.

My job as Mess Caterer was to keep the cost of food to a minimum. I achieved my target at three shillings and seven pence a day in the Mess. One senior married officer told me one day that I would charge him for *hanging his coat in the hallway!* Another said he was afraid that his ears were becoming like rabbits ears because of the amount of lettuce on the menu. I did not mind this friendly banter, so long as the single living-in officers were getting cheap Mess bills, because our salaries were quite small, around fifty pounds per month. As I wrote in an article later in *An Cosantóir*, junior officers were 'gentlemen of little material substance'.

We certainly were not in the Defence Forces for the money. Neither were the NCOs and the men. But there were 'hard times' throughout the country and we in the Army certainly shared much hardship. Very few officers and other ranks had private motor cars or motor cycles. Even pedal cycles were not that plentiful. We depended almost totally on public transport, Army bicycles or on walking. Nobody wondered that much about walking to *Droichead Nua* or to Kildare Town. I remember doing a line with a girl who lived three miles south-east of Kildare town. I would walk the twelve miles regularly in the evenings and thought nothing of it. I would drop in to the Barracks' Mess in Kildare on the way back for a cup of tea.

The Curragh Camp was a very large town in its own right with over fifteen hundred children at school at different levels. They were mainly children of soldiers living in married quarters. It appeared to me at the time that families tended to be very large. One would know that on payday, because the married soldier's pay increased accordingly as his family size would grow. Despite its density of youth population there was relatively little juvenile delinquency on the Camp. Youth clubs could have received more support from the State, but things were not that progressive at the time. For older teenagers and young adults, a number of us, mainly NCOs and men, organised weekly dances and weekly *céilís* in McDermott Hall. These events were very well attended and the young people and those not so young were very well behaved. Occasionally, during the 'gentleman's excuse me'; a dispute might break out between soldiers from different units. Those with signs of alcohol on them would not be permitted to enter. At certain times during the year (during the month of May, I think) there would be a pause at half-time for the public recitation of the rosary. Voluntary Church groups would support the weekly dances and *céilís*.

There was another excellent recreational place on the Curragh Camp – Sandes' Home. This was run by a Protestant benevolent group who provided non-alcoholic recreation for soldiers. But there was a certain bias or opposition to Catholics taking part in events at Sandes' Home by some Catholic clergy and others. I once organised an Irish play, *Íosagán*, in Sandes' for young people to promote the Irish language. The hall filled with soldiers in support of the young people. It was a great night. As a result, I was reported to the Camp Adjutant by a member of the Catholic clergy for organising an Irish play in Sandes' Home. But common sense prevailed, and I was not 'put on the mat'! These were not very ecumenical times! The Curragh cinema was very well patronised by those of us who did not drink regularly. The selection of movies was quite good and the admission charge was very reasonable.

As I noted earlier, I deliberately avoid any reference to matters specifically military as they are in the realm of professional confidentiality. Some duties demanded long hours (without overtime) and at short notice. We were on duty from reveille to sundown and on call from sundown to reveille. We were soldiers-in-defence. Our training (and that of those under the officers' care) was oriented to the needs and equipment of the day. In addition to strictly military duties, we had administrative and ceremonial responsibilities as well. In fact, our Battalion was given the task of revising the *military funeral ceremony*, under the colourful guidance of Lieutenant Colonel Con John Burke, our commanding officer. We used a steel wardrobe as a coffin working out the different drills. In the end, we worked out a very good ceremonial.

Taking part in major ceremonial events required much preparation and precision. Guards of Honour were quite difficult for the officer in breeches because one was out in front and on display. Presidential Guards outside the General Post Office (GPO) in Dublin were special. We would rehearse during the night-time when there would be little or no traffic. While the old tramlines were there we would get the soldiers to put their toes on the line to ensure the line was dead straight. *A Shoillse* Seán T Ó Ceallaigh was *Uachtarán na hÉireann* from 1945 to 1959. He was small in stature but mighty in character. I felt privileged to be on his Guard of Honour. We used to provide guards of honour for *An Taoiseach*, for Ministers of Government, for Ambassadors, for Bishops and Papal Nuncios, and for visiting Heads of State. Military and State funerals were also occasions for ceremonial participation, which we took in our stride. We in the Curragh Camp did not have as many guards to do as did our colleagues in Cathal Brugha and the other Dublin barracks.

Among the military funerals that left a lasting impression on me were those of the late Commandant John Joe O'Reilly (Cavan), the late Sergeant Hughie McCabe (Cavan) and that of the late Lieutenant Andy Moore (*Droichead Nua*). I was a Cadet (Second Year) when the late John Joe died in the Curragh hospital after an operation. I was speaking to him shortly before he died after he recovered from his operation. It must have been a clot that caused his death in the end. John Joe was a much admired officer and a great County Cavan footballer. My brother Seán was one of John Joe's assistants in the NCOs Training Course in the General Training Depot in McDonagh Barracks. While I was visiting my brother one evening in McDonagh officers' Mess, John Joe came in with an army football team (returning from a match). He entertained them all in the Officers' Mess to a meal and refreshments. The team was made up of officers, NCOs and men. This example of fusion between the ranks really impressed me at the time. The funeral of John Joe left the Curragh Hospital for his native parish in County Cavan. It was most impressive and truly the funeral of a hero. *Ar dheis Dé go raibh a anam uasal.*

The burial of the late Lieutenant Andy Moore (father of the singer Christy Moore) is big in my memory because I was the officer-in-charge. Andy was a reserve officer of the Third Battalion. We buried him with military honours in Milltown Cemetery. He died unexpectedly in the Jockey Hospital, the Curragh, where he was undergoing a minor operation. Andy was a great character and his wife, Nancy, supplied groceries to the Mess later. *Solas na bhFlaitheas dá anam uasal.*

The death of Sergeant Hughie McCabe, who was in charge of the Third Battalion Officers' Mess, was one of the saddest events in the Battalion in my time. He was one of nature's gentlemen. He looked after the best interests of the officers, some of whom were wayward, wild and impulsive at times. He was always loyal to the officers who occasionally were in danger of taking one too many. During the Emergency he organised a 'field officers' Mess' when on exercises. His wine cellar was locked in famous 'green boxes'. As Mess Caterer and Bar Officer, Hughie and I spent much time together. During our time together working on the books, checking stock, etc. he taught me much more than I learned from the manuals! Hughie was quite a religious man and never indulged in drinking or gambling. Gambling on horses was quite widespread on the Curragh Training Camp at the time. He was very proud of the Third Battalion and its officers. He was a very quiet type of man who always had a smile and a word of encouragement for those he would meet or deal with. He was a very effective Mess manager, in my opinion. His sudden death cast a cloud of heavy sorrow over us all. His funeral was attended by very many officers and was very poignant as his coffin was carried to his grave in a lonely valley in County Cavan. The Third Battalion pipe band, with its drums wrapped in black cloth, played the dead march in such a way that it was impossible for us grown men to hold back the tears. Hughie taught me something about life, which helped me later. *Sonas na síochána air go deo i bhfochair na naomh ar Neamh.*

4. THE IRISH LANGUAGE AND THE 1950S IRA CAMPAIGN

The Costello Inter-Party Government fell in 1957 and Éamon de Valera returned as *Taoiseach* with an overall majority. One of the issues that led to the loss of popular confidence in the Inter-Party Government (which, in my opinion, made worthwhile contributions including bringing Ireland into the United Nations) was the devastating effect of mass emigration. The new de Valera Government was to initiate a more rational process of economic planning under the Minister for Finance, Dr Jim Ryan TD, and the Minister for Industry and Commerce, Mr Seán Lemass TD, who was also appointed *Tánaiste* (or deputy Prime Minster). I believe great credit is due to the Minister for Finance, Dr Jim Ryan, for encouraging and permitting Mr TK Whitaker, Secretary of the Department of Finance, to prepare and publish an economic development programme. (They were too wary to call it a plan because of antipathy to socialism and State plans.) The Whitaker Programme was accepted as Government Policy and had a very positive effect on the Irish economy over the following five years, when it would be replaced by an even more ambitious and comprehensive plan. The effects of the Marshall Plan on the continent of Europe were beginning to show significant economic growth.

The new Minister for Defence was Caoimhín Ó Beoláin TD, (Mr Kevin Boland TD), who was, in my opinion, underrated by the critics among the officers. An t-Uas Ó Beoláin was more a soldiers' than an officers' Minister. It was pointed out to me by an observant commentator that he listened to the members of the working class as much, if not more, than he did to the middle- and upper-middle classes. He was consciously nationalist and very genuinely interested in the promotion of the Irish language in the Defence Forces. At the same time, he defended the 'institutions of the State' against a perceived threat from Republicans, who would not recognise the State or would be prepared to engage in an armed intervention in Northern Ireland. The internment of the Irish Republican Army leaders and sympathisers took place under his regime as Minister for Defence. This added greatly to our security duties, especially those of us stationed in the Curragh Camp units. Again, as loyal servants of the State, we all responded without a murmur. It was not a pleasant time, although I had no difficulty in obeying legitimate orders in relation to security of the people. Of course, I had personal reservations about 'internment without trial'. At the same time, it was a great relief when Hare Park (the Internment camp) closed and things returned to 'normal'. A new area of service began in 1958, namely, Irish members of the Defence Forces serving abroad with the United Nations as peace-keepers.

Much of my spare time during the middle and late 1950s was involved in the promotion of the Irish Language. I was convinced that Irish was a necessary part of the culture of our people. Later, when studying anthropology, my conviction was to be confirmed by such scholars as Edward Sapir, Mandelbaum and others[2]. The Irish language was the uniquely Irish nuance on reality over the centuries since the Celts occupied the country around 300BC. It would, in my opinion, be an unforgivable tragedy for our generation to lose this cultural heritage. Those who tried to underplay the importance of the language tended to use two plausible arguments, i.e. that it lacked material utility and the point that it was just part of late nineteenth-century nationalist romanticism! So what? 'Man does not live on bread alone.' Also, the revival of our native language was the most realistic factor in the manifestos of our nationalist philosophy. It should not be confused with the more superficial elements of that historic movement.

My personal support for the universal revival of the Irish language as the authentic cultural bond between all of the Irish people and of those living in Ireland (even on a temporary basis) has never weakened.

---

2 *Selected Writings of Edward Sapir in Language, Culture and Personality*, University of California Press, 1949, 1958.

If anything, the case for Irish has got much stronger. The campaign to restore Irish in our more materialistic and consumerist society today is inevitably more difficult. In the words of the anthropologist, Piritin Sorokin, Ireland and other so-called 'developed societies' are going through a spiritually stifling sensate era, which no doubt, we will evolve out of, when the people will join together in the pursuit of meaning, which materialism fails to provide. How long this will take will depend on the extent to which material forces can succeed in wooing the young away from what is spiritual and meaningful. So long as there is a significant minority of committed people willing to work for the Irish language and keep it alive culturally, the cause is not lost and when a more favourable cultural climate emerges, as I believe it will, the people will opt for their own 'symbolic meaningful system', i.e. the Irish language.

Shortly after my posting to the Third Curragh Battalion, I joined *Cumann na nOifigeach*, an Officer's Irish Language Club. I was elected *Rúnaí* (secretary) and the Curragh Camp Adjutant, *an Ceannfort* Brian MacGuirc, was elected *Cathaoirleach*. Captain Breandán Ó hUallacháin was our literary adviser. Quite a number of officers of all ranks joined and we had a most creative programme of educational and recreational events. We invited well-known speakers to address our meetings, i.e. *An Fear Mór, An t-Ath.* Seosamh Ó Muirthile SJ, Earnán de Blaghad, *An t-Ath.* Aibhistín Valkenburg, OP, *An t-Ath.* Tomás Ó Fiaich, *An t-Ath.* Diarmaid Ó Laoghaire SJ, and many others.

After some time, we expanded to become *Cumann Gaelach an Churraigh,* which organised *Feis an Churraigh* for a number of years on the Feast of Corpus Christi. The *Feis* became very big and had over a thousand competitions. We also organised scholarships to *An Ghaeltacht*, under Seán Ó Maoláin Scheme, for children from the Curragh Camp National Schools. *An Fáinne* was promoted, thanks to the support of Seosamh Uasal Ó Cadhain (brother of the well-known language activist, Máirtín Ó Cadhain), *Rúnaí an Fháinne*. In all, over four hundred people qualified for the *Fáinne* in my time, thanks to the promotional work of the *Cumann Gaelach*. Every week we sponsored a *céilí* in McDermott Hall and often had the services of the Gallowglass Céilí Band, a very popular local group of traditional musicians. As was noted already we produced Irish language plays. Much of this voluntary activity was happening before the appointment of An tUas C Ó Beoláin TD, as Minister for Defence. We also had the full support of the officer commanding at the Curragh Camp, Colonel Tony Lawlor. We had our own monthly bulletin, *Claidheamh Soluis an Churraigh*.

The Minister's new pro-Irish policy was welcomed by many of the Cumann's committee. We may have had some reservations about some senior officers' use of 'strong-arm' tactics to promote Irish officially. We wanted to do it in a sensitive manner and tried to cultivate positive motivation for such a radical (and welcome) change. A number of genuine Irish enthusiasts felt that the latent motive of pushing Irish insensitively would be its failure in the end. Of course, a number of people may have gone on the 'Irish bandwagon' as an aid to promotion. At the time such aids to promotion were limited because of a fairly strict adherence to seniority. Despite all the shortcomings, the campaign to promote the Irish language throughout the Defence Forces was very timely. It appeared to me, as stated already, that patriotism was an essential trait of a good soldier or officer who was dedicated to defend the people and their democratically-based institutions. This level of patriotism was implicit in most of my colleagues and enabled us to be loyal to our oath at all times, even when we were faced with the task of keeping people in prison who were explicitly dedicated to pursue the Republican ideal outside the confines of *Bunreacht na hÉireann* (The Irish Constitution) and who saw themselves as committed to the aims of the struggle for full Irish independence. The Democratic State needs a Defence Force while it cannot always depend on professional mercenaries. A true soldier cannot be bought!

Our work for the Irish language and for what was richest in the Irish culture, i.e. drama, music, dance, etc. was a source of national pride. We were true to the ideals of Hyde, MacPiarais and Connolly and others, and we did not have to apologise to those who would question the nature of our loyalty to Ireland. The State, since its foundation, was able to rely on the members of the Defence Forces to defend the Constitution. This was especially commendable of the officers, NCOs and men who had fought on both sides during the Civil War, who were willing to serve side by side in the interest of the common good of our country. Patriotism also was the motivation that enabled the State to create such large voluntary Defence Forces (on wages of less than one pound a week) during the Emergency (1939-45). In this context, the association of the Irish Defence Forces with Irish language and culture was a very positive thing, in my opinion.

5. SOCIAL AND PERSONAL LIFE AT HOME AND IN THE CURRAGH

During the 1950s, my family continued to live in Drummindoo. They were lean times for sheep farmers who had lost stock during and after the 1947 great snow. My father worked very hard to keep everything going. Three of the siblings were about to leave for work and training. My brother, Austin, went to the United States of America, where he worked as a joiner, then volunteered for the US Army and served in the Far East. On return to Philadelphia, where he stayed with my Aunt Mary and the McDonnell cousins, he went to the University. In time, he graduated and went on for legal studies in Maryland Law School and qualified as an attorney. He married an Irish-American secondary teacher, Margie Bennett, whose family came from Newry, County Down. My brother Owen joined the Oblate Fathers (OMI) and went to their novitiate in Cahermoyle, County Limerick, and later to the OMI Seminary in Piltown, County Kilkenny. He was ordained a priest on 30th May 1959. My sister, Mary, entered the St Louis Order in Monaghan in 1955 and was professed later and took the religious name Sr Mary Gregory, which was also the religious name of my Aunt Annie in the St Louis Order, who died, before her time, in the St Louis Convent in Ballymena, a seventy-seven per cent loyalist town in County Antrim. The only sibling remaining at home with my parents was my youngest brother, Pádraig (who was born in Loughloon on 8th December 1942).

The sad death of Onnie Conway (née Coyne from Kimeen, Lanmore), an elderly widow neighbour from Loughloon (where she was married to the late Willie Conway) took place in 1952, when I was in the Cadet School. She had been living with our family after her late husband died in 1932. Willie Conway was a first cousin of my grandfather, John McGreal. She was in effect, a living-in adopted granny for us and we were very sad when she died at the age of eighty-three years in 1952. Onnie Conway had a very positive influence on my sister and brothers. She was a valuable companion for my mother. She knew Irish and would converse in that language on private family matters. My curiosity to know what they were talking about was an incentive for me to perfect my Irish. A strange phenomenon happened to me. I was a senior Cadet in Pearse Barracks in the Curragh Training Camp at the time and I had a very vivid dream about Onnie on the night she died - although I had not heard of her final illness. She was very kind to us and we were very attached to her. She was quite witty and had her own views about people she knew. She could 'see through people' who were haughty. *Go ndéanaidh Dia trocaire ar a hanam uasal.*

My only surviving grandmother Méiní Eoghain (my mother's mother whom we knew as *Máimeó*) died on the 3ʳᵈ of October 1956 at the age of eighty-six years. She was a very elegant and beautiful woman. *Solas na bhflaitheas ar a h-anam.* Méiní had not an easy life with her husband, Mike, away during the week building houses, schools and churches. Our *Máimeó* was a very 'dignified lady' who had the highest ideals for us. Her two sisters, Mrs Maggie Butler and Mrs Julia Keane, were national teachers in *Tír na Cille* and *Seanafarachán* respectively.

Social, personal and recreational life in the 1950s was enjoyable and, when compared with later decades, relatively simple. Ballroom dancing (in addition to the formal dances in the Officers' Mess) was very popular. We had a number of very well-known 'showbands' who provided lively dance music. The dances would go on until two or three in the morning. There was no alcoholic drink on sale at the dances. We had, however, well stocked mineral bars, which couples would frequent for refreshments. The young men would line up on one side of the hall and the young women on the other side. Unescorted patrons would enjoy the dancing partnership of many partners. In the case of a young man finding a particular girl attractive he would ask her out to dance once or twice. Then, when a 'ladies' choice' was called, if the girl would ask him out to dance (and they both were unattached) things were looking up. The gentleman would then invite the young woman to the 'mineral bar' for refreshments and a chat. Depending on how they were relating, the visit to the mineral bar would be followed by a few more dances together. The next move would be to ask to walk the girl home. A few kisses might be exchanged at the end of the journey, before saying goodnight and, maybe, making a 'date' for the following week's dance.

This could be the beginning of a long 'line' and, in some cases, end up with a proposal to marry (after a few years going out together). That was how many 'love stories' began and developed in the 1950s. We enjoyed courting and did not consider more intimate relationships until we would get married. We did not feel deprived or sexually repressed, although we would be erotically attracted to each other. It was a most human way of premarital relationships in my experience although I did not have the privilege of getting married because I opted to pursue a celibate vocation. Relationship norms today for many seem to miss out on the joys of courtship without sexual intimacy.

During the 1950s I became a regular patron of the Abbey Theatre and tried not to miss any play put on the stage. I still remember attending the old Abbey before the tragic fire in 1952. I used to get a ticket for 'the gods' and found it very sophisticated. The little orchestra played before the drama and during the interval and this added to the atmosphere. After the fire, performances were put on in the Queen's Theatre in Pearse Street. I enjoyed Seán O'Casey's plays, although later I was not that happy with the revisionism of the *Plough and the Stars*. Walter Macken's plays were very good, I thought, especially *Home is the Hero*. Later, I was to enjoy Brian Friel's *Philadelphia, Here I Come*. John B Keane's original *Big Maggie* was an excellent play. My visits to the Gate Theatre to see Micheál Mac Liammóir play Shakespeare, Wilde and others were occasions of creative entertainment. Beckett's, Miller's and Chekhov's plays were feasts to my expanding mind. The live theatre was my choice of entertainment.

Every year the Curragh Musical Society, under the baton of Lieutenant Denis Mellerick, B Mus, would produce a light opera. My brother Seán (an officer) would be on the organising committee and I would also volunteer to help out in an administrative capacity. When Lieutenant Colonel Bill O'Kelly succeeded Lieutenant Colonel Jack Lewis as Commanding Officer of the Third Battalion, we became more musical. Bill O'Kelly was Chairperson of the *Dublin Grand Opera Society*. He was affectionately known as 'the fixer', i.e. he had the art of dealing with the highly sensitive 'musical prima donnas'. I remember one famous incident when his services as 'the fixer' were called into action. The musical director, Denis Mellerick, had a disagreement with the lead soprano at a rehearsal and, as a result, she went off the stage in a huff, and said she was withdrawing from the show on the night before the first public performance. The musical director would not compromise. We had to send for Lieutenant Colonel Bill O'Kelly, who, with great tact and adroitness, pacified the pair and persuaded them to cooperate in the interests of the show. The outcome was brilliant performances all round to the joy of 'full houses' of audiences who came from the Curragh Camp and the towns around – Droichead Nua, Naas, Kilcullen, Kildare and Monasterevin.

One of the great latent effects of the Bishops' ban on dancing during Lent was the many amateur drama and musical societies who spent long evenings rehearsing for their plays and shows. The Curragh Dramatic Society produced some high-class productions under the skilful direction of Captain Aidan Watson (known widely as 'the Wat'). Because of the absence of fusion between the officers and their wives and the other ranks and their wives, nearly all the amateur performances were of the officer class. This division was a real pity and was something we tried to avoid in the more broadly based *Cumann Gaelach an Churraigh.* Golf was another officer-class recreation on the Curragh Camp in the 1950s, and this was one of its unattractive features for me personally. Maybe the 'peasant' in me was always too strong for my acceptance of class distinction. (This was something I have had to struggle with in my future career as a Jesuit priest and as a University lecturer!) The weekly dances and *céilís* in McDermott Hall did not, unfortunately, attract many patrons of the officer class. This was the reverse situation to that of the Curragh Musical and the Curragh Dramatic Society.

Our interest in classical music was cultivated by a small group under the leadership of Lieutenant Connie Costello. We were trained to listen to records of operas and follow the score and a translation of the arias. We also listened to records of symphonies and other pieces of classical music. I had already developed a taste for classical music while I was a Cadet and found great relaxation in listening to Mozart, Bach, Beethoven and others. This enjoyment was enhanced by the Connie Costello sessions. There was a corporal in the Third Battalion, Danny Carlton, who used to entertain the soldiers to records of Caruso, Gigli, Burke-Sheridan, McCormack, McEwen and others on his manually operated gramophone. During the fine weather he would gather an audience outside at the corner of the barrack square. He was a great character with a musical mission. Later when he became Mess Sergeant in Connolly Officer's Mess he would render arias and ballads himself to entertain the regular patrons. He loved to be asked to sing!

The Christmas Dinner was an all-male function, until Colonel Tony Lawlor (General Officer Commanding the Curragh Command) tried to 'lift the lid on things'. He encouraged more mixed functions, but not with that much success for Christmas Dinners. At other times in the year, Dinner Dances were to be organised to which officers were expected to bring their wives and (those not married) their girlfriends. The dress dances were magnificently romantic and elegant occasions. Senior and Junior Officers would mix in a relatively free and easy manner. Of course, we junior officers would never address a senior officer on a first-name basis, but as *'a dhuine uasail'*, or 'sir'. Not infrequently, our girlfriends were the charming daughters of senior officers, as it was in my case for over two years. Even in such cases we would never presume to neglect our subaltern status. It did not affect our relationship with the daughters apart from being careful to behave always as 'gentlemen'. It was part of the 'code of honour' to treat women as 'ladies' (not in the pejorative sense, as in the Deep South white subculture of the nineteenth century). 'Falling in love' was the most ecstatic of all experiences to a young adult in late teens and early twenties!

Club na hOifigeach parties introduced traditional music and Irish group dancing. For a decade (the 1950s) which is now being portrayed as dull and grey by many modern commentators, I would say it was the very opposite for my colleagues and me. We may not have had much money or luxuries in the material sense (compared with modern young adults) but what we had was a most satisfying time aesthetically and culturally. I hope that every generation of young adults enjoys life as much as we did (in our relative poverty). I believe that my being a Pioneer (total abstainer) enabled me to experience a very high quality of life as a young officer. Our lack of luxury in the material comforts probably made us more sporting in lifestyle. Also, the level of material poverty experienced by most of the citizens of Ireland made our conditions relatively less severe. As I said before, when everybody is poor, nobody feels it that severely.

6. ADULT EDUCATION AND COURT-MARTIAL DEFENCE

Two areas of service, in addition to the normal call of duty, which appealed to me was *Court-Martial Defence work* and the *improvement of the educational standards of NCOs and men.* These two areas of involvement were to occupy much of my spare time as a junior officer in the Third Battalion. One night I was Orderly Officer in Connolly Barracks and I called to supervise the closing of the NCOs' Mess as part of my duty. Sergeant Maurice Sheehan, was acting Mess Sergeant. He was privately engaged in solving mathematical problems involving 'repeating decimals'. He was very interested in mathematics. When I asked him how far he had continued at school, he told me that he had finished at the age of fourteen years and he was self-educated since he joined the Army. We discussed the position of numerous NCOs and men, whose schooling was minimal but would benefit from adult learning. Maurice had also been my platoon sergeant in A Company. We got together and planned an evening course (for the *Second Class Certificate*, which would be the equivalent of at least the Intermediate Certificate in the Secondary system). Commandant Con John Burke, who was second-in-command of the Battalion at the time, and responsible for training and education, approved a 'pilot' night-school.

Word was sent around about the special night course and, to our pleasant surprise, a full classroom of enthusiastic students turned up on the opening night. They were mainly NCOs from the Battalion and from neighbouring units on the Curragh Camp. We had about sixteen students. The subjects taught were *Gaeilge* (Irish), English, Mathematics, History, Geography and 'Civics'. Captain Breandán Ó hUallacháin, Curragh Command Education Officer, and other officers chipped in to give us a hand. The course lasted for one term of between four and five months. It proved to be a great success and the students performed very well in their final examinations. The demand increased and we organised a course each winter for a number of years. A number of the NCO graduates later were successful in becoming Commissioned Officers under a scheme introduced to give 'other ranks' a chance to get a Commission. This was an excellent move, which was in line with the policy of Minister Caoimhín Ó Beoláin TD, for a more egalitarian army.

Most of my fellow officers were supportive of the night-school project although some thought that it was not part of an officer's duties to 'be teaching school'. It was, nevertheless, a response to a need that had been there since the foundation of the army. Many, if not most of the army other ranks' personnel, did not get the opportunity to complete their education, despite their good intellectual talent. It was typical of a class-based structure to maintain the educational demarcation between the officers and the 'other ranks'. A similarly institutionalised system operated with religious orders, i.e. between the lay brothers and the priests or teachers, and between the 'lay sister' and the 'choir sister'. How far removed we had become from the Christian ideal of equality!

On reflection, I see that the class dimension of the army educational hierarchy was being unwittingly operated. There was also the fear that an educated and articulate 'other ranks' would be a challenge to the officer leadership. I remember an officer giving character evidence at a court martial once in favour of a defendant, who was found guilty of technical desertion, i.e. AWOL of over 180 days. The officer said: *'Private X was a decent type of a soldier who would do anything you asked him to do without asking questions. It was a pity that there were not more like him'.* When asked if he would welcome Private X back to his Company, he replied that of course he would. (As things worked out this was a most supportive piece of evidence, which resulted in a reasonably moderate punishment. Private X was duly allowed to return to his original Company.) The attitude expressed by the officer, in his evidence, reflected a paternalistic outlook towards soldiers, which many would agree with at the time and even today, in my opinion. I would be uneasy with such a view. A similarly patronising attitude was held towards women (in a totally different context) i.e. the concept of lady. In a class-structured society it was and is generally expected that those at various levels 'know their place'. In a liberated republic, I would have expected such benevolent class distinction to be removed. The only type of hierarchy would be functional hierarchy, i.e. the senior surgeon calls the tune during the operation and in determining the caring routine, which would follow it. But such hierarchy should not extend beyond the medical operation! Of course, income differential, which is rarely questioned today, reinforces informal class distinction.

My experience as a 'Court-Martial Defence Officer' began on quite a low scale. The Camp Legal Officer organised a special course for young officers interested in acting as defence officers for soldiers and NCOs appearing before court martial. It was mainly concerned with procedure and the law. It was a very interesting course and I took it seriously. After the course, I was asked by defendants from a number of units on the Curragh Camp to be their Defence Officer, which I accepted. Some cases were relatively serious while others were less so. In the more serious cases I was obliged to trace back the criminal court precedents, in order to argue the case and refute the prosecution whenever possible. This was not always easy as the prosecuting officer was always a trained lawyer and officer. On the other hand, the court was made up of fellow serving officers. We would say of a court martial that it 'had more justice than law'. After the verdict of the court was communicated and the punishment handed down, the convicted were entitled to appeal a verdict or sentence to a Senior General Officer, which I recommended on a number of occasions. Because of the many cases that I was asked to defend, I was never available to be a member of the Court Martial. A Defence Officer could not serve on a court martial trying his clients. I do not think I regretted this deprivation, as I did not wish to judge others.

7. ÉAMON DE VALERA RETIRES AS TAOISEACH (1959)

In 1959 Éamon de Valera TD, (elected for County Clare) resigned as *Taoiseach,* having served in the position for twenty-one years since 1932, i.e. 1932-48, 1951-54 and 1957-59. Earlier he had been President of the first *Dáil* from 1918 to 1922. For me, personally, Éamon de Valera was one of the real 'Fathers of the Irish State' under whom consensus prevailed. The first decade of the Irish Free State, because of the tragic and cruel Civil War, lacked the same level of consensus. Nevertheless, the Government of the 1920s, William T Cosgrave TD, did essential work in establishing an executive responsible to the *Dáil* and also ensured continuity in administration, under 'native' control. It also facilitated the withdrawal of imperial security forces from the twenty-six counties and appointed a local judiciary. The Inter-Party Governments, under John A Costello TD, served the country well for six of the nine years I spent in the Defence Forces, i.e. 1950-51 and 1954-57. Despite my admiration for Éamon de Valera TD, I was very honoured to serve under the Costello administration during its time in office.

The final rally before a General Election was always held in Dublin
City – *Fine Gael* assembling on O'Connell Street (outside the GPO)
and *Fianna Fáil* on College Green (outside the Bank of Ireland). I was
present in the wings (in civilian attire) for de Valera's last great General
Election Rally in College Green in 1957. *'Bhí an domhan agus a mháthair
i láthair'*. ('The world and its mother were present.') I remember a whole
company of old *Fianna Fáil* veterans marching on to College Green from
Suffolk Street. They were singing the Republican Civil War Anthem:
'Soldiers of the Legion of the Rearguard'. The congregation gathered
was very large and there was thunderous applause when the man himself,
Dev, arrived on the platform. The old hero rose to speak and you could
hear a pin drop. He must have been seventy-six years of age at the time
and his eyesight was weakening, despite the treatment he received from
medical experts. One of the criticisms that were being levelled against
de Valera and his Front Bench was that they were old and the country
needed young energetic leadership. I still remember him addressing this
criticism. It went something like this:

> De Valera: *They tell me that the outgoing Government Parties
> are critical of my age and the seniority of the Fianna Fáil Front
> Bench! Well, I say to the people of Ireland - if you want greyhounds
> to run the Government of your country, do not elect Fianna Fáil.
> But if you want to elect wise and experienced ministers then, you
> should vote for Fianna Fáil...*

This was the gist of his rebuttal of the age criticism. Mr Seán Lemass,
Dr Jim Ryan, Mr Erskine Childers and, of course, Mr Frank Aiken, were
among those lined up beside de Valera on the platform. The mood on
the night was special. In a sense it was de Valera's *'last hurrah'* after
such long and distinguished service in Irish politics to date. There was
a genuine mystique about the man. He was not arrogant. Some might
accuse him of being a 'benevolent despot'. But that would be unfair.
He always honoured the ballot box since the founding of *Fianna Fáil*
and, as I said earlier, had he been hungry for total power, he might
well have abused his charismatic appeal and become a despot. In the
Irish Constitution (*Bunreacht na hÉireann*) he set out to curb such a
possibility in the 1930s, when we had Hitler, Mussolini, Franco, Salazar
and others, all over the Continent of Europe. In Éamon de Valera, prestige
(of office) and esteem (of personality) came together for his most loyal

110

followers. This was a powerful combination in a national leader. Another factor which saved de Valera was his strong Front Bench and Cabinet. They were never 'yes men'. He had his shortcomings and would admit as many failures as successes in his term in office. He was jealous of political power, in the sense that he would not agree to concede it to any political group operating outside the Constitution. In a Republic, formal political power was the preserve of the elected representatives. Of course, he would consult non-political bodies when devising policies and procedures.

I felt that he did not give sufficient authority or power to elected local government bodies. There seemed to have been a tendency after the War of Independence to concentrate all power in the hands of central government. A classic example of this was the disbandment of the Prisons' Board in the 1920s and the absorption of the total running of prisons in Ireland under the direct control of the Department of Justice. Changes in Governments did little to decentralise executive power. Mr de Valera has to take his share of blame for this state of affairs. Another example of this over-centralisation of executive powers is evident in the 'County Managers' Act' which, in effect, gives more say to Managers than to the County Councils in a number of important issues. Of course, the real boss was the County Manager who was under the Minister for Local Government (or under whatever other title he or she travels from time-to-time).

In assessing de Valera's contribution to the administration of the Irish State, a very deep and broad analysis would be required. So far, I have not read such a critical or objective appraisal. He was in charge through relatively tough times in Ireland. Most of our major difficulties were not of our own making. In the first instance, we were a post-colonial society, which was not well served by our former 'masters'. *Our depopulation of the rural countryside was not balanced by industrial development in the provincial towns. The urban areas to benefit from Irish rural depopulation were the cities of Britain, the United States, Australia and others.*

Mr de Valera and other leaders tried seriously to curtail the expansionist policies of Adolf Hitler's Third Reich through the weak League of Nations. The flawed *Treaty of Versailles* indirectly strengthened Hitler's hand. The Second World War had become inevitable in the end. Ireland's stand of neutrality under de Valera was probably the only honourable one due to the unsatisfactory solution to the ending of British rule in Ireland. We have suffered the consequences of this politically unsatisfactory situation for over ninety years – at a serious cost of life and limb, not to mention poorer than possible economic and social growth. The 'Economic War' of the 1930s, which was precipitated by de Valera's insistence on halving the annuities paid to Britain to compensate the 'bought out' landlords under Prime Minister Asquith at the beginning of the twentieth century, was another legacy of British-Irish history.

Mr de Valera's support for Irish Language and Culture was something I totally agreed with and my only regret was that he did not succeed even more in encouraging public servants to use the language more frequently. Following on the positive policy of Ministers Earnán de Blaghad TD, and Dick Mulcahy TD, in the *Cumann na nGael* Government, he made significant progress in improving the teaching of Irish. No other *Taoiseach* so far seems to have had the same idealism in relation to the Irish language and culture.

Support for the family and, indirectly, for the local community were priorities for de Valera, in my opinion. The destructive forces of the so-called industrial revolution, which crowded so many people into the one relatively small space, i.e. factory, office block or large commercial establishment (resulting in the individualisation of the workforce), had not, as yet, fully infiltrated the Irish social fabric. But, it was only a matter of time until market forces would dethrone 'the family' as the 'pivotal institution' in Ireland. The 'family' and 'religion' would be replaced by the 'economic institution'. In Mr de Valera's time, 'family' and 'religion', as meaning-giving institutions were still quite pivotal. Education was not only in the service of industry and commerce. De Valera favoured liberal arts and languages (including Irish and the classics). By 1959 participation in second-level education was relatively low, largely due to lack of resources and limited demand. It was not easy to convince the majority of my contemporaries of the value of going on to the Leaving Certificate. In the context of all this we should evaluate de Valera's ideal of village life. He was addressing what was best in the quality of life in Ireland of his time. It was more a counsel of perfection than a realisable goal, in the light of the assault that was to descend upon us from the raw materialism, which would make us wealthier but socially more dysfunctional, i.e. until the 'culture lag' following material change has been adjusted!

8. GOODBYE TO ARMS FOR ME

The year 1959 was to be very significant for me personally. On the 30th May 1959, my brother Owen was ordained a priest in Kilkenny in the Oblates of Mary Immaculate (OMI). I had been visiting him regularly in the Oblate seminary (philosophate and theologate) at Piltown in south Kilkenny. His study had broadened his range of wisdom and understanding and our extended discussions on philosophical and religious topics began to open my mind to the notion that meaning was to be found in the spiritual and religious dimension of life. By the time of Owen's ordination I was reaching a 'crisis of meaning' in my own life. I had been deeply involved in spiritual reading and, as noted already, I was active in *An Réalt* (the Irish language section of the Legion of Mary) and in the Patrician movement (a discussion group set up by the late Father PJ Brophy of St Patrick's College, Carlow). I had become friends with the three Army chaplains on the Curragh Training Camp, Father Patrick Boylan, Father Seán Hayden and Father Gaspar Rugouet. All three men were very fine spiritual leaders, each in his own way. They were most mature and respectful of one's 'path to God'. Their personal humility also impressed me very much.

I was also, because of my involvement in the Irish language movement on the Curragh Training Camp, in touch with a number of priests who were keen on the Irish language. They included *an t-Ath* Seosamh Ó Muirthile SJ, (Rahan, County Offaly), *An t-Ath* Ailbhistín Valkenburg, OP (Droichead Nua College), *An t-Ath* Tomás Ó Fiaich (St Patrick's College, Maynooth) and *An t-Ath* Diarmuid Ó Laoghaire SJ (Rathfarnham Castle, Dublin). These priests would attend Irish functions on the Curragh Camp and would write articles in *Claidheamh Soluis an Churraigh*. *An t-Ath* Valkenburg, OP, wrote articles on the medieval theologian, St Thomas Aquinas, which I found most interesting. *An t-Ath* Seosamh Ó Muirthile SJ, would give talks on the 1798 Rising in *Contae Chill Dara* and elsewhere. While I was not explicitly aware of it, these contacts helped to develop in me a great taste for things spiritual and a respect for priests and religious.

Every year I would religiously go on a pilgrimage to Croagh Patrick and visit other shrines as well. My involvement in the Pioneer Total Abstinence Association was also a partially religious experience.

Attendance at the 1949 Rally in Croke Park (fiftieth anniversary of the PTAA); in the 1956 Father Theobald Mathew Rally in Cork City and in the 1959 Monster Rally in Croke Park (sixtieth anniversary of the PTAA) were milestone experiences.

My close relationship with my late aunt, Annie Coyne, Sr Mary Gregory SSL, who died in the St Louis Convent in Ballymena, County Antrim on 22nd March 1956, was deeper than I realised. Her sanctity and humility were so transparent to me and the manner in which she endured her final illness (at the age of forty-four years) without a trace of self-pity was nothing short of saintly. She left a lasting impression on me. Aunt Annie died while my sister, Mary, was a novice in the same Order in the St Louis Convent in Monaghan. As noted earlier, the authorities gave her Aunt Annie's name in religion. In other words, she became the second Sr Mary Gregory in our family. As in the case of my brother, Owen, I would visit my sister, Mary, regularly in the St Louis Convent, Monaghan, and got to know very eminent religious women, such as Mother Dominica Hughes, the Mistress of Novices, Mother John Regis, the Order's treasurer, and others. What impressed me about these religious women and other nuns like Sister Philomena of the Presentation Sisters in Kildare Town was the high level of human civilisation and culture they had reached. It appeared to me that their lives were most meaningful and were like a leaven in society. The convents were like 'oases' in their local communities, which enabled the 'people of God' to aspire to higher things. Their status in Irish society at the time manifested the reality of the faith. It was clear to those of us who knew brothers, nuns and priests living in convents and monasteries at the time that members lived hard lives of poverty, chastity and obedience, for the glory of God and the service of the people. My first cousin in Philadelphia, USA, Fr James McDonnell, was respected in my family (he was later a Senior Chaplain in the US Eighth Fleet).

Leading up to May 1959 I had another side to my life, which was also very satisfying and attractive. My career as an Army Officer worked out fairly well. I was happy in my work and I was afforded ample opportunity to live a full social and cultural life. I was personally keen to marry and settle down. I had been fortunate in meeting a girl I would be happy to marry. (We first met at a Legion of Mary meeting in the Cathedral in Carlow.) Earlier I had been going out with other beautiful girls. But things did not work out, more because of cultural preferences than any lack in personal affection.

It was very difficult for me to leave the Army and my friends, especially my girlfriend, when I was making up my mind to change career and direction towards a more exclusive commitment to the spiritual, priestly and pastoral life at the age of twenty-eight, back in 1959. It was one of those great crises of life in pursuit of greater meaning. This was not unique to me. We all have/had to make significant decisions to go in one direction which deciding means not to go (or to turn away from going) in another direction. As the Irish proverb puts it: '*Ní féidir an dá thrá a fhreastal*' ('it is not possible to serve two strands in the same tide'). It is even more difficult when both routes are desirable.

Shortly after my brother Owen's ordination, when alone one day on the road (outside Tunney's old house) in Drummindoo, Westport, the question of meaning came up again and the possibility of my pursuing a vocation for the priesthood became more explicit. This was the first time I asked myself the question for real, although it may have come up earlier as a remote option when I was in my late teens. I tried to let it pass, but, as days went on, it would not 'lie down'. A week later I discussed this 'wild question' with the late *Ath* Diarmaid Ó Laoghaire SJ. He advised me to pray about it for a month and see what would happen. I also consulted the chaplains on the Curragh Training Camp. They told me that they saw the question coming for some time. Apart from that I kept quiet about it and I read three significant books, i.e., Ronald Knox's *Translation of the Letters of Saint Paul*, Dom Boylan's *The Tremendous Lover*, and Ronald Knox's *Translation of the Diary of Saint Thérèse of Lisieux*. After one month's praying about it, I decided I would pursue a vocation to the priesthood and resign my Commission as an officer in the Defence Forces. To be precise, my decision was taken while on a one-day retreat in the Dominican Priory, Tallaght, Dublin, on 4th July 1959 at 6.00pm. I had written the question in my diary some weeks before. Once the decision was made to pursue a vocation as a priest, my immediate task was threefold, i.e. to get some superior to accept me as a candidate, to resign my commission, and to end my relationship with my girlfriend. With regard to selecting a religious group to join, I sent away for information (catalogues) from a wide range of Orders/Congregations.

After serious reflection, I decided to apply to the Jesuits, and, thank

God, I was accepted for admission to the Noviceship on 7th September 1959. My reason for opting for the Jesuits was influenced by the positive experience my brother Austin had of the Jesuits in the United States, and by the esteem I had for *An t-Ath* Seosamh Ó Muirthile SJ, and for *An t-Ath* Diarmuid Ó Laoghaire SJ. I was not that enamoured by their reputation in Ireland for playing 'foreign games' and educating the sons of the elite. To my pleasant surprise, my initial interview with Father Provincial, Luigi Ó Grádaigh SJ, was all in the Irish language. My application for resignation of my commission was accepted. Should I not succeed in the pursuit of my vocation to the priesthood, I would be readmitted to my career as a commissioned officer. This was a general regulation. The ending of my relationship with my girlfriend was most painful but she was very generous and understanding. I told her that I would go out of her life completely so that she could make a new relationship. I was happy to learn that she met a better man some time later. The break was very painful for both of us.

The reaction of my parents and family to my decision was most supportive if a little surprised. When I wrote to my parents (some time before I decided to join the Jesuits) asking them for their prayers for a decision I planned to make. My father remarked to my younger brother, Pádraig: '*He might at least have sent us her photograph before proposing marriage!*' When I told him of my decision, he just said one thing to me, namely, advising me not to hesitate to return home should my vocation not work out. This was a most noble reassurance that I would not feel any moral pressure to stay on in the Jesuits, if I learned that I did not have a vocation. There was a time in Ireland when a seminarian would be very embarrassed to return home. A 'spoiled priest' was unwelcome in a family, in Irish society during my youth. My father's more enlightened attitude was representative of a growing maturity in relation to those who wished to pursue a vocation. My mother's reaction was happy and sad. She worried for me and felt that I would find the long formation quite difficult. She had a very realistic view of the situation. My brothers and sister were also supportive, if a little surprised by the news.

For me it became much easier once the decision was made. From then on, I focused on the requirements involved in the pursuit of my new vocation. Thank God, on reflection at this stage, I am happy at having addressed the 'crisis of meaning' in the way I did. Of course, my response to the rich range of opportunities that were to come my way has been far greater than I expected or deserved. But, the good Lord and my fellow-Jesuits have borne with me with forbearance! It sometimes arose in conversation that had I continued my career in the Defence Forces would I have been able to meet the challenges? That is now mere speculation. I have never lost contact with my esteemed former colleagues. My friends in the Irish Language movement had mixed reactions. Some feared that I would be posted to the 'foreign missions' to ensure I would not be a nuisance – promoting the revival of the Irish language and culture. As things worked out the foreboding was not true. In fact, being a Jesuit enabled me to work for the Irish language and culture quite effectively.

9. Pius XII Succeeded by John XXIII (1958)

I remember the morning the news came that His Holiness, Pope Pius XII had died. The Orderly Sergeant in my unit, the Third Curragh Battalion, knocked on my door at 7.00am (on 9th October 1958) to tell me that the Pope was dead. We were all very saddened, as Pope Pius XII had endeared himself to the faithful as a saintly and austere priest. His writings were very spiritual and full of meaning and helped me in taking life more seriously. He was criticised for not taking a public stand against Hitler and the Third Reich. In his judgement, such a line of action would have resulted in even greater suffering. It seems he strove night and day to ameliorate the persecution and evils caused by that deranged regime. It was also very obvious that he suffered within himself because of the 'diabolical' reign of terror, which had enveloped continental Europe.

Pope Pius XII's public opposition to the gross excesses of Joseph Stalin throughout the Soviet Union before and after the Second World War in the countries of Eastern Europe was frequently stated. The fact that Joseph Stalin was on the side of the Allies during the war must have created another problem for the Pope. It would mean that public statements would have to be equally condemnatory of both totalitarian regimes that had total disregard for human rights. He lived in one of the most horrific periods in world history. The overuse of weapons of mass destruction (including the atomic bomb) by the Allies, also deserved public papal condemnation. I suppose it is easy to criticise the Holy Father in hindsight when in possession of more information than was clear at the time of the heinous crimes performed by military and security machines.

The successor to Pius XII was Archbishop/Cardinal Roncalli from the small northern Italian town of Bergamo. He was like a rotund farmer with an open heart and a most attractive personality. He was very unlike the austere Roman nobility-class pope, Pius XII. He took the name John XXIII, and was seventy-six years of age when he became Pope. Commentators said he was a 'stop-gap' Pope, as the Church waited for Archbishop Montini to assume the high office. I remember a comment of a refined middle-class woman on the bus from the Curragh Camp to Dublin saying to me that it was so strange to have a Pope with such 'big hands', like those of a farm worker! She, apparently, was expecting a more sophisticated urbane man to be Pope. Pope John XXIII was soon to win the hearts of most people, including the disaffected faithful. In the five years of his Papacy, he was to initiate an '*aggiornamento*' which was to bring the Catholic Church into dialogue with modern society. What a stop-gap Pope! More than that, Cardinal Roncalli is now Saint John XXIII.

10. THE WINDS OF CHANGE ARE RISING

In 1959, Éamon de Valera resigned as *Taoiseach* and won the election for *Uachtarán na hÉireann*, a post he was to hold for the next fourteen years. He was succeeded as *Taoiseach* by Seán Lemass TD, who initiated a more economically developmental policy and seemed to adopt a more pragmatic approach to socio-political issues. He was not so strong in support of the Irish language and culture as was his predecessor Éamon de Valera. Gradually, the economic institution became more pivotal with liberal capitalism becoming the dominant ideology. Socio-economic conditions at home in Ireland were to 'rise on the rising tide'. The distribution of the labour force was to change, i.e. there was a reduction in the percentage working in agriculture and an increase of proportion in industry and in the services. 'Efficiency' and 'rationalisation' were soon to become key terms. This trend was to continue over the following decades. With the rise in the workforce in industry and the services, the trade union movement was soon to become more pro-active in securing a fairer return to the worker and this was to cause serious industrial conflict during the 1960s, which Dr Charles McCarthy defined as the *Decade of Discontent*, i.e. the title of a small book on the decade (1960-1970). For the first time, it would appear Ireland was becoming an industrial society. We were not that well equipped to cope with the growing demands of such radical social change.

The changes resulting from the rise of the pivotal role of the economic institution operated along capitalist lines, despite the continued role of semi-State industries, e.g. *Bord na Móna*, the Irish Sugar Company, Irish Shipping, Aer Lingus, Electricity Supply Board, *Coras Iompar Éireann*, Irish Steel, etc. The process was eventually to lead to the growing dominance of the free market, which would end up some decades later with the privatisation of most of the semi-state companies, aided and abetted by the EU 'capitalist-driven juggernaut'. The seeds of change were being sown at the end of the 1950s and, in a sense, 'Irish family and community-based Ireland' was on the wane as de Valera moved to the Park and handed over the reins of Government to a new breed of more culturally detached political leaders under the leadership of Seán Lemass TD, whose commitment to Ireland was very sincere and most noteworthy.

A new era was being born in Ireland which was to bring forth great advantages but which also was to undermine the position of the family and local community as previously pivotal institutions. It was also to herald a level of materialism and consumerism, which would be a serious challenge to spiritual values and religion, in my opinion. The ascetic and aesthetic would be challenged by the self-indulgent and the vulgar destruction of the environment to satisfy the insatiable demands of material progress. Among the advantages brought about by the new wealth and prosperity was greater participation in education, better health services for the people, better (domestic) material standards of living for the majority, improvements in communications and a higher level of social mobility. Just as the 'brave new world' was about to dawn, I turned away from it and withdrew into the Jesuit monastery in Emo Park, to be cut off from 'the world' literally for two solitary years!

Because of my decision to enter the Society of Jesus, I was to leave behind for the next six years, at least, the exciting beginning of the 'new era' in Irish society under Sean Lemass. The two years in the Novitiate in Emo Park, Portarlington, *Contae na Laoise*, was a period of withdrawal into a monastic regime. Contact with the 'outside world' was strictly controlled by a set of rules, which would do justice to any 'total institution'. In other words, we lived (happily for the most part) within the novitiate's institutional and physical boundaries. The change from a very active life on the Curragh Training Camp to the restrictive life of a Jesuit novitiate was akin to my going back to the Cadet School all over again. It took a while to adjust to the very strict regime. A further difficulty was the 'ten years' gap between my age and that of the fellow novices. And yet, I liked the life from the first day. My noviceship is best described as a two-year vacation, which enabled me to taste and experience the depth of Christian spirituality. Meditation and spiritual reflection were to constitute my full-time job for two years. The hardest task of all was the discovery of my personal self, warts and all. The mystical wisdom of Saint Ignatius gradually sunk in. I found the Master of Novices, the late Fr Paddy Cusack SJ, to be holy, mature and extremely tolerant and helpful. The socius, the late Fr Brendan Brennan SJ, was shy, saintly and most caring for our needs. His shyness made him appear to be a little eccentric. Are we not all eccentric? So what? Novices helped and 'corrected' each other and this was not easy to take at first. The level of openness between us was very great. We trusted each other.

In that environment, I said goodbye to the 1950s. My world was about to expand spiritually and contract physically and socially behind the walls of the Jesuit Noviceship! Looking back on the decade in my life just ending, I notice one thing, namely, that the 'twenties and late teens' were a period of energy, impatience and a degree of arrogance about issues affecting personal and social affairs. Age and the broader experience of life would make me more tolerant of the ambiguity of the world around me, while not diminishing my commitment to the common good. Is this not a common feature of young adult and late adolescent years?

Chapter Four

THE 1960S
THE HEADY DECADE

1. CALM BEFORE THE STORM

The seeds of change in Ireland and, for that matter, in the whole world were sown in the late 1950s. This was influenced greatly by the recovery of Continental Europe and Britain and the questioning of the adequacy of political, religious and social norms and values that had failed the people in the two World Wars, which ravaged much of the 'developed' world. The gradual emancipation of colonised countries in Africa and Asia resulted in a degree of optimism that, regretfully, was not to be realised, owing largely (in my opinion) to the 'racist' regimes of their former colonial masters and their failure to prepare newly emancipated peoples for the norms of participative self-government. Third-level education, which transmitted the people's cultures, had been denied to indigenous people, with rare exceptions. Because of the Cold War, i.e. between the USSR-dominated Eastern Europe and the USA-dominated Western Europe, support for the emerging independent States was to be influenced by East-West political interests.

The Christian Churches had largely failed the people of Nazi-dominated Europe in the early decades of the 20th century. This was not only in their failure to stand up to the German regime, but in their failure to remove the injustices on which the Third Reich and other totalitarian regimes were able to exploit and achieve political power. In my opinion, the Christian Churches did not translate the liberating message of the Gospel into solving the concrete plight of the people. We had not grasped that peace, love, equality and true faith were only possible when there was social justice. Again, in my view, there cannot be true Christian evangelisation without the effective promotion of social justice. The distribution of wealth is more important, from the Christian (Catholic) point of view, than is its production. One of the greatest single achievements of the 1960s has been the acceptance by the Christian Churches of the integral place of 'social justice' as part of the full message of Christ for his people. Morality was seen as social as well as personal. If one were to define revolution as *'a radical and rapid change of social values and norms'*, then the acceptance of social justice as an integral part of the Christian values and norms in the nineteen-sixties was the beginning of a contribution to the social and religious revolution. Unfortunately, we have not succeeded so far in achieving or realising on the ground what we gave assent to at the time. [It will be shown that we (in the Christian Churches) have back-pedalled and withdrawn our real commitment to social justice since the 1970s.]

Vatican Two (1963-65) and the Thirty-First Congregation of the Society of Jesus (1965-66) were, for me, the forums that brought Christianity into social relevance in the promotion of justice in the service of the faith and provided a sound basis for effective pastoral (social) action. It reawakened the 'prophetic' role of the Christian Gospel in the Catholic Church as it emerged from centuries of 'priestly' dominance. Vatican Two and the Thirty-First General Congregation were key Church events in the 1960s. Naturally, the follow-up has had its problems but we can never 'turn' back the clock nor put 'the genie back into the bottle'. On reflection, one can see the positive influence of writers like Teilhard de Chardin SJ, who released Church thinking from the trap of *'semper idem'* (always the same). The idea of development in the Church's understanding of the Gospel message was a vital ingredient of the Council and of the Congregation. With such an understanding of cultural evolution in the Church's understanding of itself, there was need to examine 'the signs of the times'. This gave the pastoral programme flexibility and a capacity to be wholly relevant.

Like every other significant and radical advance in history, it seemed to me there were two extreme responses, namely, the denial of what had been decreed as valid, on the one hand, and a 'gung-ho' response, on the other hand. The former was reactionary while the latter failed to bring the 'people of God' along with it. During and after Vatican Two, religious journalists did perform a valuable job of communicating to the faithful what was taking place in Rome. At the same time, many fell into the trap of 'paperback theology', i.e. theological reflection that was quite superficial. Unqualified (in theology or the study of Scripture) writers, and commentators began to hold forth on the mysteries and teachings of the Church, without the level of study such expertise would require. This inadequate level of commentary has continued even in the sophisticated broadsheets and discursive

programmes until today. One would not, for example, place authoritative credence on matters pertaining to history, literary criticism and economic theories without consulting trained historians, recognised academics or qualified economists.

This is not to say that every person who prays and reflects seriously on divine mysteries has not a valid point of view. Rather, it points to the need to take theology and Sacred Scripture studies as serious and difficult areas of academic endeavour. On the one hand, we must avoid 'the tyranny of superior knowledge' which would silence all lay opinion and dismiss the people's point of view. On the other hand, it is only just that persons, who take it upon themselves the role of religious commentators, should make known their credentials to authenticate such public pedagogy. Religious fundamentalism is also enhanced by a low level of academic formation among those who take it upon themselves to espouse the cause of interpreting Sacred Scripture and Church teaching. It would be ideal if the overall level of religious (academic) awareness were raised among the faithful so that they could discern the quality of commentary and debate. Unfortunately, not that many young intelligent people seek to become informed in Scriptural and theological matters. It is tragic that the level of religious education in the population is not commensurate with their general education.

The above remarks are not intended to give the impression that theologians and Sacred Scripture scholars have not continued to serve the Church/'People of God' well since Vatican Two. They have. But in my opinion, discursive theology has taken a back seat in recent decades. Auto-censorship may also be a fact in the case of theologians and Scripture scholars who would like to revive a healthy level of speculative theology. At times, we 'theologians' – lay, clerical and religious – are rarely prepared to open up questions publicly that some magisterial authorities would discourage. This can lead to intellectual dishonesty and can stifle the keener academic and pastorally committed believers from serving the Church in an enlightened way. Of course, discursive theological debate cannot and should not change the 'deposit of faith' as revealed by Jesus Christ. Rather, it should adapt the 'deposit' more adequately and intelligently to meet the needs of our time. Dogma is very important, but if it becomes merely 'institutionalised truth' it will lack the credibility it requires from a more academically enlightened 'People of God'. Let us not forget that today in Ireland some forty-two per cent of the young age cohort (eighteen to twenty-five years of age) has some higher third-level education and this percentage is rising. What a challenge this is to the Church of tomorrow and today! We can no longer be satisfied with teaching the faith in a manner adequate for twelve-year-olds!

2. JESUIT FORMATION

Returning to my formation as a Jesuit Scholastic, at the end of my first year in the Novitiate the Master of Novices gave me permission to take the Jesuit Vows privately. This was most reassuring for me personally. At the end of the second year, on the 8th September 1961, I was allowed to take the Jesuit Vows formally and publicly. It was an important incorporation ritual into the Order. It was a pity that our parents or family were not invited to the vows. It was a very private and 'low-key' event.

My next posting was to the Jesuit Philosophate in Rahan (Tullabeg) near Tullamore. I was delivered to the railway station in Portarlington and took the train to Tullamore, where I was met by Brother Pat Guidera SJ and Fr Kieran Hanley SJ, in the house car from Rahan. The College at Rahan (Tullabeg) had a distinguished history in the Irish Province. From the late 1860s until 1886 it was one of Ireland's leading Catholic Boarding Schools for boys. In 1886 the College of Rahan merged with Clongowes Wood College and Tullabeg became the Jesuit Novitiate until 1931 when Emo Park took over that role. From 1931 until 1962 it was to be one of the main Irish Philosophates.

I was fortunate to have been able to spend one year in this historic college as a philosophy student. Many scholastics were very critical of Tullabeg, but I was not among them. I liked its austere conditions. Real philosophical questions were discussed and the mind was opened to the provocative reasoning of the Hellenists and the Medieval Philosophers, as well as the ideas of the Renaissance, modern and contemporary philosophers. To me it was sheer pleasure to ponder deeply the philosophical questions. The relationships between scholastics and staff were excellent. Living conditions were a little primitive but liveable. I could not see what the criticism of Tullabeg was all about at the time. One member of the staff whom I got to meet often was *An t-Ath* Seán de hÍde SJ, a wise philosopher and a gifted theologian. He used to ask me to give him a haircut regularly. We spoke Irish and I enjoyed his subtle sense of humour. One of my biggest difficulties in the philosophy examinations was my rusty and poor Latin. It was an encumbrance for scholastics like me. Yet, I was fairly lucky and survived the end-of-the-year examinations.

3. INTERVIEWS WITH PRESIDENT DE VALERA

While I was in Tullabeg, I got the idea of writing a brief popular biography of *An Uachtaráin*, Éamon de Valera. The book would be in Irish and would give a summary of his long public life as well as an insight into his personality. My friend, *An Ceannfort*, Breandán Ó hUallacháin, ADC to the President, arranged that I meet the President for a number of interviews (six in all) at Áras an Uachtaráin in Dublin. This was before the decision of the Visitor, Fr John McMahon SJ, to close Tullabeg and send us all to the four winds. I did, however, succeed in having two one-hour interviews (in Irish) with the great man before abandoning the project and going on the *exodus*. With all the going and coming, I mislaid my notes of the interviews.

Nonetheless, a number of facts from the interviews have remained in my memory. The first was Breandán Ó h-Ullacháin's description of the lifestyle of Éamon de Valera and his wife, Sinéad (Ní Fhlanagáin). He said that they lived with the simplicity of an old couple in the *Gaeltacht*. This did not surprise me when I began to listen to him. Despite his high office and such a long time in power, he was very much a 'grass roots' person. He was deeply religious, without being over-pious. He was highly intelligent and very well educated.

During his youth he told me that he considered becoming a priest and even thought of joining the Jesuits. After recalling this early attraction to the priesthood, he then put the rhetorical question to me: *'I wonder if I had been right in not going for that direction?'* (or words to that effect). I tried to reassure him that in my opinion, it was quite clear that he was called to follow a vocation in Irish public life. In so doing, he and his colleagues enabled the Irish people to be free to pursue their vocations, including those leading to the priesthood and religious life. I tried to point out that God's call was to a very varied and wide range of careers and ways of life. It was quite humbling for me to enter into this in-depth dialogue with the President, but that was the way he addressed those he met. He seemed to place me on a plane higher than I thought I deserved. He treated me as an equal. (I learned so much from this privileged experience.)

I asked him (in the course of my two interviews) how he arrived at major decisions affecting the affairs of State and what decisions or situations worried him most. He replied that in political life most decisions are forced on the leader, i.e. situations would arise requiring a decision. If he had the opportunity he would consult those whose honest advice he would trust. After the consultation he would make his decision and live with it thereafter. With regard to decisions that worried or upset him most, he mentioned the execution of a convicted murderer. He admitted that he felt intuitively that capital punishment was wrong, but it was legal and acceptable at the time. The Cabinet always had the power to commute the death sentence to life imprisonment, but it rarely did so. The days of execution were never easy for him as *Taoiseach*. He was pleased that capital punishment had been abolished.

In response to a question on his relationship with the Anglo-Irish Ascendancy, I well remember his reply. He told me a story about the visit of a new friend to his office in Government Buildings shortly after the outbreak of the Second World War in 1939. This friend, who was a leader of the Anglo-Irish Ascendancy, asked to meet him. The President related their conversation as follows: the young Lord said that the people he represented and those *An Taoiseach* represented did not see 'eye to eye' in the past. However, from then (1939) on he assured Mr de Valera that they would cooperate in every way possible for the benefit of Ireland. In reply, *An Taoiseach* shook the hand of the leader of the Anglo-Irish Ascendancy and that, in the memory of President de Valera, marked an important stage in the ending of animosity and in the strengthening of solidarity in Irish society. The young Lord promised that when he completed his service in the Royal Air Force, he would seek ways and means of instituting greater cooperation. Sadly, the noble Lord was killed in action in the early years of the War, RIP. This was a source of great sadness for President de Valera. I feel that such a story should be recorded to the credit of both leaders.

De Valera's views on the revival of the Irish language were of particular interest to me. My first question to him referred to what, in his view, caused the slow progress in the revival of Irish? He said that after the *1916 Rising* and the *War of Independence* (1919-22) there was tremendous good will towards Irish, and readiness to learn and speak the language. We had failed to harness the positive willingness of the people. One factor, in his opinion, which could have made a difference, was the attitude of the prestige colleges. They did not throw sufficient weight behind the revival and were in a position to do so. The President said that he regretted their failure to grasp the cultural significance of the Irish language for the Irish people. I also asked him if he could single out the most important development that he succeeded in implementing for the Irish language. His reply was the *caighdeánú* or standardisation of Irish. He said that it took much time and effort to bring it about, but time would show it was worth it. President de Valera never lost hope in the revival of the language, which, in his view, contained the people's memory. It was a real privilege to speak to him (in Irish) and I regret that my interviews had to come to an abrupt end as I had to set sail for Heverlee, Leuven in Belgium, in August 1962.

4. POSTED TO HEVERLEE, LEUVEN, IN BELGIUM

In January of 1962, a Visitor from Father General Jansens SJ, was sent to the Irish Province. His name was Fr John McMahon SJ, an American Jesuit. He was given the nicknames 'Megaton Mac' and 'Mac-the-Knife'. After less than six months he began to change things in the Province. He closed the Philosophate in Tullabeg and forced us scholastics to become migrant scholars throughout the European Philosophates in Belgium, France, Germany, Italy and Spain. In September 1962 I was sent to Heverlee Scholasticate in the Flemish-speaking Belgian Province of the Society of Jesus. I appealed to be sent to an English-speaking Scholasticate but my request was rejected. Another fellow-scholastic, the late Mr John Kinane (with whose father I worked when in Lucas Limited in 1950) was also posted to Heverlee. This unexpected move had good and not-so-good consequences. The Visitor made a number of other changes within the Province, which met with a mixed reception.

In my opinion and that of many others, he should have carried out more consultation before putting 'the axe to the tree'. For instance, none of us scholastics were consulted about our future destiny. Participative decision-making was not practised at the time.

It was indeed quite an exciting experience for John Kinane and me to arrive in Heverlee, Leuven, in August 1962. We were to spend the next two years completing our degrees in Philosophy, i.e. B Phil in 1963 and a Licence in Philosophy in 1964. Within a relatively short time we acquired sufficient Flemish or Nederlandish to follow the lectures. In the beginning we probably missed some of the finer nuances. Since philosophy is very much concerned with nuances of meaning this was problematic. The Flemish scholastics and staff were fluent in four languages, i.e. Flemish, French, English and German. They were extremely hospitable to us, although the regime in Heverlee was fairly strict, under Rector Father Jan Van der Linden SJ, and an ebullient Minister. Academically, the approach of the professors was different to that in Tullabeg. One of the professors said '*we Irish had to be de-Hellenised*'. The major school of philosophy to impress me in Heverlee was 'existential phenomenology' which had its roots in the Danish philosopher, Søren Kierkegaard, and in the German thinker, who lived in Leuven, Edmund Husserl. Other writers whom we tried to study were Martin Heidegger, Jean-Paul Sartre and Maurice Merleau-Ponty. We also studied the writings of Teilhard de Chardin SJ, who had been given acceptable status by Pope John XXIII after the intervention of Fr Henri de Lubac SJ.

In our final year we were asked to do a dissertation. My thesis was on the philosophy of Jacques Maritain, the eminent French 'Neo-Thomist', who luckily escaped the Nazi Gestapo, by being in the US when the Germans occupied Paris at the beginning of the War. This was a very fortunate choice for me in that it brought me into contact with a very important thinker and leader in post-War Europe. He was one of the drafters of the original *United Nations' Charter of Human Rights* in 1948. It also made it clear to me that 'Thomism', although not the 'flavour of the month' in Heverlee by some professors, had much to offer the searching mind. It was very much one of the foundation stones of Christian Humanism. I certainly found it to be so. My thesis director was Professor Jan Kerkhofs SJ, who would be influential in my pursuing the serious study of social sciences later in the Catholic

University of Leuven and elsewhere. The whole Heverlee experience was very difficult because of the cultural and study challenges. Nevertheless, John Kinane and I survived. We got our degrees and our minds were opened to the views of a wide range of diverse philosophers. We left Heverlee in 1964. John Kinane went on to the missions to Zambia and I was admitted to study Social and Political Sciences in the Catholic University of Leuven. I changed residence to the Jesuit House of Studies in Minderbroederstraat in downtown Leuven. Because of the influence of Professor Jan Kerkhoffs SJ, I decided to concentrate on the academic study of *intergroup prejudice and tolerance*. Through contact with fellow-Jesuits, John Kinane and I were made aware of the Nazi persecution of Jews, Gypsies, homosexuals and others. During 1963 we visited the German Concentration Camp in Dachau. It was a traumatic experience.

Because of previous accredited studies it was possible to complete the two years' undergraduate course in Leuven University in one year. This demanded a very hard programme of study for me. It meant working day and night and over weekends. Two other Flemish Jesuit Scholastics, Guido Diereeckx and Erik Van Hove joined me on the course in the Catholic University of Leuven. We were in the Flemish language part of the bi-lingual university. Both of my Jesuit colleagues would become professors in Sociology in the Universities of Antwerpen. Erik resigned from the Jesuits before ordination. During my year in the University the students organised regular protests against the French-speaking section of the University being located in a Flemish-speaking community. Eventually, they won the case and a new campus was built for the French-speaking departments south of Brussels. Within the Social Science Department we had a student body called Politika and the students elected me on to its committee. It was an invigorating experience to be active in this student body. I felt very much at home in the University and developed a taste for the academic life, (which was later to become my career). While there I met Karl Dobbleaere, one of the young lecturers who would later become a distinguished Professor of the Sociology of Religion. We have kept up contact down through the years. We three Jesuit scholastics did relatively well in the examinations at the end of a hectic year. *Deo gratias*.

5. VATICAN TWO

On the 25th January 1959 Pope John XXIII made his first unexpected announcement that he planned to convoke the Church's twenty-first Ecumenical Council. On the 11th October 1962 the Second Vatican Council opened in Rome. Pope John XXIII, then four-score years, in the fourth year of his most distinguished papacy, addressed the assembled bishops and gave pastoral impetus at the first meeting of the first session which lasted until 8th December 1962. By then the health of the Holy Father was deteriorating and he passed on to his reward in the summer of 1963, having awakened the Catholic Church to a new vision of its mission. It was to clarify the Church's definition as the 'People of God'. The charisma and transparent honesty of Pope John XXIII were most appealing to believer and non-believer alike. The almost four years of preparation between January 1959 and October 1962 were to generate a new vibrancy in the Catholic Church. This old 'stop-gap' Pope, as some described him, was to enable the Church across the world to re-examine itself 'root and branch' through his prophetic convocation of the *Twenty-First Ecumenical Council of the Catholic Church*. For us Jesuit scholastics in Heverlee, Leuven, it was a most inspiring time. Various prelates and theologians would bring us up to date on the progress of the Vatican Council. It was a great time to be studying for the priesthood. Leuven was a crossroads and many subcommittees of the Council would consult with the Jesuit theologians.

After the sad death of Pope John XXIII (now Saint John XXIII) Cardinal Montini was elected Pope Paul VI on the 21st June 1963. He convoked the Second Session of the Vatican Council on the 29th September 1963. This session ended on 4th December 1963, while the final session of this most significant Ecumenical Council was at work from 14th September until 8th December 1965. It meant that during my year in the Catholic University in Leuven, the Council was well into its work and the shape of the findings was becoming very clear. Our Belgian Primate, Cardinal Suenens, was on the drafting committee of the decree on *the Church in the Modern World, Gaudium et Spes*, as was the late Bishop James Corboy SJ, of Monze in Zambia. He was a native of Limerick. Theologians such as Karl Rahner SJ, Edward Schillebeeckx, OP, (from Antwerp), Joseph Ratzinger (Germany, later to become Pope

Benedict XVI) and Henri de Lubac SJ (France), were very significant advisers to the Bishops and were household names in Leuven at the time of the Council. Back in Ireland, Fr Tim Hamilton SJ, would discuss the deliberations with Bishop James Corboy SJ, during his visits to Milltown Park, where he was once a professor.

The Second Vatican Council ended on 8th December 1965, and Pope Paul VI promulgated its many decrees. An era of optimism had emerged in the Catholic Church, which bordered on the unrealistic. This coincided with a mini-revolution in the youth culture in the US and in Western Europe. Elvis Presley (USA), The Beatles (England) and other 'pop stars' were giving expression in song and dance of a 'heady' cultural rebellion, for many young people to become 'rebels without a cause'. The authority and guidance of parents, teachers, the Church and even the State, was challenged. Youth as a subculture had become a more powerful cohort in society and market forces began to adjust to them. It was inevitable that the relatively recent phenomenon of prolonged adolescence (created by the demands of the economy and the expansion of the middle classes) was going to assert itself in this manner, i.e. without accepting self-responsibility that characterised adult status. In the wake of this 'licence to be irresponsible', we have had the growth of very serious social problems among teenagers and those in their early twenties, expressed in excessive use of alcohol, drug abuse, sexual promiscuity and their consequences by a minority. This cultural isolation (or insulation) of teenagers and young adults from continuously real contact with older generations could lead to the undesirable situation of a new one-generation culture weak in relation to values, norms and convictions, which provided the human basis of family and community. This, of course, produced a socio-cultural condition conducive to greater geographic and social mobility, which was very functional for industrial and commercial society. On the positive side, the 'emancipation' of the post-war youth gave a new energy and honesty, which expressed itself in movements such as anti-war campaigns in the US and the 'civil rights' movement' in Northern Ireland.

The Second Vatican Council made a most welcome contribution to the ministry of Christian ecumenism. People could hardly believe the change. What had been a 'reserved sin' in my youth, i.e. Catholics attending a Protestant funeral service, had become 'an act of charity'.

Dialogue between the Churches at all levels from the local Church to the Vatican and the *World Council of Churches* became the norm. Pope Paul VI had a special relationship with Archbishop Ramsay of Canterbury. At home in Ireland, the *Irish School of Ecumenics* was established by Father Michael Hurley SJ, in the late 1960s. I had the privilege of being one of the original staff members of the school. Some of us had hoped that mutual recognition of Orders and intercommunion were only a matter of a short time. I was involved for two years (1969-70) in a discussion group of ten priests (Protestant and Roman Catholic), known as *decem viri*, who met monthly in Dublin to discuss matters of mutual (ecumenical) interest. The Greenhills (near Drogheda) Annual Ecumenical Conference was also a very important and well-attended event. The Vatican Two *Decree on Ecumenism* had enabled us to work hard for the bringing about of Christian Church Unity. Of course, we were also keen to see the reunion of the Orthodox Churches with our Church, i.e. the Roman Catholic Church.

I suppose it was inevitable that there would be resistance to ecumenical unity within the Catholic clergy and laity. It amazed me at the time that, otherwise good priests, would not row-in behind the *Decree on Ecumenism* of the Vatican Council, which was the most authoritative voice of the Church. While they did not oppose the ecumenical movement publicly, they used more subtle means such as lip-service and tokenism. This was to delay any substantial development on intercommunion and mutual recognition of Orders. But, as in so many other areas of radical change in the Church, it appears that we are often forced to move at the pace of the slowest culture. This is the nature of a universal Church. We in Ireland would benefit from ecumenism receiving a higher priority on all sides, including the Catholic leadership.

Pope Paul VI's visit to the Medelin CELAM Conference (1968) in Latin America gave us all great hope for the emergence of the Church's identifying with the plight of the poor and oppressed. It was an expression of solidarity from one of the greatest Popes in the twentieth century. On his return to Rome he tried to strip the papacy of the symbols of power and pomp. His visit to South America was a tremendous boost to the work of the basic Christian Communities, inspired by the growing interest in 'liberation theology', which identified with the poor and recognised the great impediment to their emancipation was the dominant power of the rich and privileged, who would resort to the most savage measures to maintain and protect their interests and unjust privileges. Repressive regimes persecuted those people who would constitute a threat to the privileged classes or spoke out on their behalf. Right through the 1960s, 1970s and 1980s there were reports of the persecution and martyrdom of committed Catholics and others who dared to stand up against or even threaten repressive regimes. *The solidarity of Pope Paul VI with the poor and the conscious involvement of religious and clergy in the pastoral pursuit of social justice in the service of the Faith brought the Church closer to the suffering People of God.* Later, among the most notable (publicised) martyrs of Latin America would be the late Bishop Romero (1980) and the six members of the Jesuit Community of El Salvador (1989).

The Civil Rights Movement in the United States and the anti-war outrage against brutalities in Vietnam during the late 1960s and early 1970s were inspired by the Christian Churches. The martyrdom of Reverend Martin Luther King bore witness to the Christian commitment to social justice in the service of the Faith. In my opinion, the late Pope Paul VI was a most significant source of inspiration for this new pastoral reawakening of the Christian Churches as defenders of basic human rights. For us at the time, who were seriously committed to the Church, we could no longer escape into personal piety and become detached from the suffering of fellow human beings. This misery was caused by unfair structures, by vested industrial, commercial and politico-military interests as well as by repressive leaders, who backed the interests of the powerful against those of their poor and downtrodden. The globalisation of capitalist interest led to weakening further the state of the poor. The 'world' was still moving away from Christ!

Two theological/spiritual camps or schools of thought emerged in relation to that pastoral involvement of the Church. One was in a collectively pro-active manner on the side of the poor and the weak and in opposition to the superfluity of wealth, influence and power of the privileged classes. A re-examination of the Gospels and the prophets pointed to the connection between sanctification and liberation. The call to social justice was seen as an integral part of the Judaic-Christian vocation. This understanding of the call of the Bible was to divide the Church, as an inspiration to Christians to become involved in socio-political action.

This collectivist response led to a strong counter-movement, i.e. the revival of a more private vocation to personal holiness with an accompanying *detachment* from the structural evils. Prayer (personal), piety and austerity were promoted among the faithful. This personal piety movement was very strong in the United States and became an important bulwark against the evils of abortion, euthanasia, spreading secularism, sexual promiscuity, violation of the Sabbath and other expressions of personal immorality. It was also attempting to attract people away from the liberation movement and weakening its positive effects on structural change in Latin America and elsewhere throughout the world in favour of social justice.

It would take great pastoral skill to keep both 'wings' of the committed Church united. Christians, who advocated a purely spiritual personal piety without collective involvement in liberating the poor and downtrodden, were viewed with greater favour by the rich and the powerful and their evangelising programmes were welcomed in Latin America as a counter-force to those who supported the 'liberation' approach. In fact, around the time of the martyrdom of the Jesuits of El Salvador, it would be reported that a special meeting of the 'personal piety' Christian leaders was held in Santa Fe in the United States (in the late 1980s) to promote a counter-liberation missionary campaign throughout Latin America and elsewhere in the Developing World. Most of the personal piety evangelists tended to be Protestant in their Christian denomination.

Catholics tended to be more open to the collectivist pastoral approach. This may explain the collectivist political approach of Karl Marx, who was reared in the early 19th century in the strongly Roman Catholic environment of Trier in Westphalia, although he was personally a Jew (but not a particularly religious member of the Jewish Faith). His raising of the public consciousness of widespread social inequality was quite scriptural in the Old Testament prophetic tradition and in the clear call to social justice in the preaching of Jesus Christ. While rejecting atheistic and materialistic Marxism, it is possible to understand Marx's condemnation of Christian religion as 'opium' for the masses. This was mistaken, although one could see some grounds for this impression in the failure of the Churches to lead the people in revolt against so many historic cases of gross social injustice. The incident in Irish history that disappointed me most was the relative absence of 'liberation theology' during and before the Great Famine in Ireland of the 1840s. This happened at a time when the Protestant Church was still a powerful force and the Roman Catholic Church was regaining popular strength. Both churches failed the people, with the notable exception in the case of individual members of the clergy. Of course, there were expressions of grave concern and public condemnation, but these were not enough. There was a minimum of solidarity for effective action against the more privileged classes, at the time, in support of the starving peasantry, whose very poor existence was a scandal for Churches called to stand by the poor. The Third World in our time is akin to Ireland in the time of the Great Famine. At least, some saintly Catholics have proven their commitment to their faith by their courage and suffering on behalf of the deprived. The Christian Churches have failed to qualify private property rights in the interests of the poor.

6. KENT STATE UNIVERSITY

I will return to the theme of polarisation within and between the Christian Churches in relation to their pastoral mission to the People of God at a later stage. While an undergraduate student in the Catholic University of Leuven in 1964-65 we had a Fulbright Scholar from *Kent State University* (KSU), Ohio, in the USA, i.e. Professor Larry Kaplan, a Professor of American Political History, who was a distinguished scholar. The two courses he taught were on *'The History of the United States Government'* and a special course on *'American Foreign Policy'*. I took both courses and found them most rewarding. As a service to the students, a translation of the lecture notes into Flemish was provided by Politika. Professor Kaplan lectured in English. My task was to retranslate the Flemish version of his notes 'at sight' into English for the Professor before publishing them. This meant that I got to know Larry Kaplan fairly well. He was also very interested in the history of the Irish relations with the USA. As the academic year drew to a close Larry asked me about my personal plans for the future. I had not thought that much about them, as I understood my Jesuit superiors would direct me where they thought best. He suggested that I should think of spending some time in one of the Jesuit universities in the United States, as they had a good academic reputation.

I wrote a letter to one of the Jesuit Universities. After some time I got a reply from the Jesuit Dean suggesting that I wait until I was ordained a priest and then apply for courses. I would be able to finance myself by carrying out 'supply ministry' in a local parish. I reported this to Professor Kaplan, who was disappointed that I did not receive more encouragement. Then he asked if I would be willing to spend five terms, i.e. three 'trimesters' and two summer terms, in his own *Kent State University in Kent, Ohio,* (KSU**)**, a city some thirty miles south of Cleveland, Ohio. I immediately said yes and I wrote to my Provincial who kindly gave me permission to apply. Larry Kaplan wrote, on my behalf, to Professor Laing, Head of the Department of Sociology and Anthropology in Kent State University. I was accepted for a Masters' Course in Sociology and Anthropology in Kent State, and, thanks to Professor Kaplan's recommendation, I was given a 'Graduate Assistantship' worth $3,000 and was provided with free accommodation in the Newman Centre on campus. I would help the Catholic chaplain with a few pastoral jobs.

This proved to be a most satisfactory arrangement and, in terms of money, I received more than I spent for the five terms from September 1965 until September 1966. It was to be one of the best academic years of my life to date having received the fairly rare distinction of getting a 'straight A' grade in all the courses, and winning the *Fleming Award* for the best postgraduate dissertation (MA) of 1965-66. Both of these academic achievements surprised me as I judged myself as a fairly average graduate student. The KSU experience was unique in my mixed range of examination results.

More than these academic distinctions, my mind was 'blown open' to the nasty side of society and the need to question conventional wisdom without being presumptuous. I was challenged to become an intellectual in Karl Mannheim's meaning of the concept, i.e. *one who was capable of being critical of one's own culture and, at the same time, being loyal to it.* This was much greater than being a mere academic, i.e. one who has the capacity to accumulate a great deal of accurate scientific knowledge. Being an academic did not automatically mean that one was an intellectual and being an intellectual did not necessarily mean one was an academic also. Of course, it was possible and even desirable, to strive for both personal qualities. The 'intellectual' required wisdom and commitment as well as knowledge and experience. *It became very clear to me that one of the latent functions, i.e. objective consequences, of the broad Jesuit training in spirituality, humanities and natural sciences, philosophy and theology, was the enabling of formed Jesuits to become intellectuals.* It was during my graduate studies in Kent State University that I realised that St Ignatius was shaping my world view and enabling me to stand back and cast a cold eye on it all. I developed, I hope, a greater tolerance of cognitive ambiguity and saw the injustice caused by closed-mindedness and authoritarianism in many organisations and systems. There was no correlation between authoritarianism and human intelligence.

All this strengthened my desire to examine, to the best of my ability, the destructive power of social prejudice. But I had to avoid allowing my normative commitment to expose social prejudice (in the hope of undermining it) to intrude on my strictly non-normative scientific research on the subject. This internal tension between the objective restrictions of scientific research and the almost messianic mission of the researcher to expose the debilitating consequences of prejudice for society must be kept in check! Hence, the importance of very strict academic standards when enquiring into the whole area of intergroup relations, which I had now begun in earnest in KSU.

On arrival in Kent State University (KSU) I selected a 'menu' of postgraduate courses covering all aspects, i.e. psychological, sociological and anthropological, dealing with intergroup relations. Under the general title of 'intergroup relations' were issues or topics such as racism, ethnocentrism, anti-Semitism and the nature of social prejudice in general. Ethnography and ethnology were also important subjects as were the sociology and anthropology of religion. We were all compelled to study general social theory and research methodology. With the obligation to carry out a Master's dissertation, in addition to the coursework, it meant that we had a very heavy academic programme, involving many hours of private study. At one stage, I remember working into the night and, for a short time, consuming up to thirteen cups of coffee a day/night to prevent my dozing off to sleep. The chaplain advised me that my health was more important than study, at the end of the day. I took his advice and scaled down my excesses.

As graduate assistants we had to work as tutors and help with correcting of examinations. One professor asked me to give a few lectures to undergraduates. It was a real challenge to lecture to American students. Their accent was strange to me and, of course, they found my 'brogue' different. Irish idioms (in English) were new to most of the class. Sometimes students would challenge the lecturer. The weather in Kent was hot and humid in the summer and cold and humid in the winter. Autumn and spring were very pleasant seasons. In Cleveland there was a strong Irish settlement with a number of families from Kilmeena (between Westport and Newport).

The pastoral work I was asked to do in the Newman Centre at KSU was quite minimal. It involved helping those students who were preparing to become Roman Catholics. I also helped out at the liturgies. I enjoyed helping at some of the student weddings. While I was in KSU the question of the Catholic Church's attitude towards the use of contraception was in the news and a special committee in the Vatican was reviewing it. Pope Paul VI's encyclical, *Humanae Vitae*, was to decide the issue later. One day a gentleman asked to see me. His only concern was whether contraceptives would be permitted. I told him that I did not know and that such decisions were to be taken at the highest level of the Church. He was not pleased. I asked him why he was so interested and he told me that his family had a commercial interest in the manufacture and sale of condoms! I did not think that the ethical question was that central to his concern about contraception. Apart from this exceptional enquiry, my work in the Newman Centre was worthwhile. The chaplain and his team were very friendly.

I was formally attached to Walsh Jesuit High School, a short distance from the University. It was in the Detroit Province of the Jesuits. Fr Paul Besanceny SJ, Professor of Sociology from the Jesuit University in Cleveland, was most helpful to me when doing my research survey for the MA thesis. As I said already, my academic work was so intense that I had little or no time for extra-curricular activities. I was very conscious of the need to use every waking hour for work because of the relatively short time limit available.

The academic staff in KSU were most friendly and pedagogically competent. The standard was high and demanding. The person with whom I worked most closely was Professor Chuck Hildebrandt, who taught 'ethnic and racial relations'. Professor Clarke was also a most stimulating lecturer in Social Anthropology, which became my second major subject. (Later, I was to lecture in Industrial Anthropology in the College of Industrial Relations, Dublin, and I introduced a basic course in Cultural Anthropology in 1971 in St Patrick's College, Maynooth.) Chuck Hildebrandt directed my MA thesis: *A Psycho-Socio-Cultural Theory of Prejudice*, confirmed by the findings of a survey of intergroup attitudes among evening students attending St Joseph's University in Philadelphia and the University of Cleveland. My studies gave me a conceptual framework by which it was possible to diagnose those racial and ethnic relations in Cleveland and in Philadelphia. Many respondents were of Irish origin and were most willing to cooperate.

During Christmas and Easter vacation time I stayed with my brother Austin, and his wife, Margie, in Philadelphia. At Easter, I carried out the survey (in St Joseph's University) of a sample of adult undergraduate students. Professor Michael Smith SJ, of St Joseph's (with family connections in Caracastle, County Mayo) helped me get a very good spread of respondents for my sample. The questionnaire measured social distance in relation to a range of ethnic, religious and racial categories, i.e. people were asked how close they would be prepared to admit members of the various categories: kinship, friendship, next-door neighbour, co-worker, fellow-citizen, visitor only or would deny citizenship. This seven-point social distance scale was originally devised by the sociologist, Emory Bogardus, in 1925, in the United States, and had been used with high 'validity' and 'reliability' to measure social prejudice many times since the 1920s. (In my subsequent research work I have used the *'Bogardus Social Distance Scale'* with successful results.)

During my stay in Philadelphia on New Year's night 1966, I was permitted to accompany a police patrol throughout the city of Philadelphia to witness first-hand the policing of the mixed racial and ethnic communities. I accompanied the leader of a section dealing with 'gang-related criminal activity'. I was a passenger in his patrol car. We were on patrol from 10pm to 2.30am. From what I could witness, the police were even-handed, but a high proportion of the criminal activity, reported and pursued was in the more deprived black quarters of the city. In the course of the night those arrested were on charges including homicide, drug-related crimes, public disorder, robbery, arson, etc. To my pleasant surprise the senior police officer whom I accompanied said he had never taken human life in the course of his policing duties. His manner of confronting gangs was in no way aggressive. In fact, I saw him persuade potential trouble-makers to disperse and desist from inter-gang violent contact. It was not like what one would see on television or in the 'Cops movies'. What amazed me was the willingness of agitated young male gangs to follow the advice of the police officer. Incidentally, the reason why I was on the patrol at all was the outcome of an interview I had had with the Chief of the Police in Philadelphia on the question of racial prejudice and the police. The Chief said to me: *'the best way for you to answer that question is to see for yourself and accompany the police on patrol. Would you be willing to do that?'* I answered, *'Of course, I would.'* Then he said he would arrange it. I could pick my area of patrol. Since the head of the 'gang section' covered the whole city of Philadelphia, I opted for that division. It was an eye-opening experience, which helped to give me a new perspective on social deviance (a topic I would lecture on later in my career).

Spending Christmas and Easter with my brother Austin and his wife Margie in their home in Philadelphia in 1965 was a most pleasant experience. I discovered that the extended family was still very important and the level of religious practice was very high among both Catholics and Protestants. The Irish and even County Mayo connections thrived. Home dining and family and friend visitation were not that dissimilar from what I had experienced back home in County Mayo. The parties were very enjoyable and the singing of emigrant ballads was of a very high quality. The people were very optimistic in outlook and the laughter was hearty. The cloud of 'hard times', which seemed to prevail in Ireland at time was absent. The people seemed to look at the more positive side of life. The glass was perceived to be 'half full' rather than 'half empty'. I would say that this sense of perpetual optimism was an American trait, at least among the people I met in Philadelphia and elsewhere. The sociologist, Robert K Merton, noted in his writing about 'reference groups' that Americans rarely accept 'failure'. They saw it more as 'deferred success'!

An internal revolt was underway in the United States against the deadlocked war in Vietnam, and also against the socially unjust position of the black people, many of whom were on subsistence level in ugly ghettos in the major Northern industrial cities. I witnessed the Hough riot in Cleveland where a whole slum neighbourhood was destroyed by arson. Other riots happened elsewhere in the United States in 1966. Martin Luther King was our 'greatest inspiration'. Bobby Kennedy was the 'heir apparent' to Lyndon Johnson after the assassination of President John F Kennedy. My brother, Austin, was a strong supporter of Bobby Kennedy for president in 1968. There was an air of excitement. The momentum for greater civil rights was gaining ground. *In Kent State University we had a strong anti-war and pro-rights ethos.* (This was later to lead to the killing of white students by members of the National Guard in 1969, which was a key tragic event that contributed to the withdrawal of US troops from Vietnam.) In my opinion, the presence of US troops in Vietnam was quasi-messianic, i.e. the United States wanted to protect the Vietnamese from 'the evils' of Communism and promote their (US) way of life, behind the 'barrel of a gun'. Of course, vested industrial-military interests were quite happy to supply endless amounts of conventional weapons of mass destruction. One could see trains, over a mile long, carrying new armoured vehicles from Detroit to the West Coast of the US for shipment to the Far East. Also, there was a danger of allowing the 'red flag' to come too close to the United States! The delicate balance of power between the West and the East had to be maintained!

It was a really great time to be in the United States and to witness the nobility of the sons and daughters of white privileged citizens joining in solidarity with their black brothers and sisters within the US and in genuine sympathy with the unfortunate poor of Vietnam, whose country was being destroyed by war. Around this time, I received a small book from Chuck Hildebrandt entitled *The Dagger and the Cross*, by Dr Albert G Rutenber, which pointed to the way the Christian Churches had betrayed the pacifism of Jesus Christ over the centuries. We had turned the Cross into a dagger! I believe that this was the final 'straw' that converted me into a Christian pacifist. My new state was not to be confused with that of a Christian passivist. My role model would be the Reverend Martin Luther King. I still admired the Reverend Dietrich Bonhoeffer, although he was prepared to support violent action against Adolf Hitler, in defence of the innocent people of Germany and elsewhere. In my opinion, Martin Luther King and Dietrich Bonhoeffer were two of the great Christian saints of the twentieth century.

I realise now, in hindsight, there were many excesses committed by the so-called 'liberated generation' (as distinct from liberation theologians) of post-Vatican Two of the 1960s and 1970s in the United States and elsewhere in Europe (including Ireland). Many times they 'threw the baby out with the bathwater'. Nevertheless, that generation was necessary for the future health of Western civilisation.

We had to challenge an accepted system of basic social injustice. The old order had failed the people. We had acquiesced in racialism, imperialism (under different guises), elitism, authoritarianism, despotism (sometimes benevolent but often malevolent), sexism, pre-emptive offensive action and the 'rule of might' rather than the 'rule of right'. It was good to see that the young people of a 'superpower' were to play a leadership role in the 1960s in exposing the human misery caused by the acceptable 'rule of might'. It was very self-therapeutic for me to be at the heart of this pacifist revolution in KSU during 1965 and 1966. Providence dealt me a good hand of cards! The Berrigan brothers, two well-known anti-war American priests (one of them a Jesuit, Fr Dan Berrigan SJ) were later to fall foul of the US war machine and its backers in the Pentagon and in the White House. They helped to restore confidence in the Catholic Church. Priests, brothers and nuns were to unite with Protestant ministers and committed laity in the common cause of peace and justice. This was, for me, the seedbed of true Christian ecumenism. We all became rebels with real causes.

My personal involvement in the civil rights and peace movements was limited by the pressure of study and by my status as a foreign student on a special visa. I attended the meetings organised by the student bodies at KSU. One most memorable meeting was held in a large meeting room at the cellar level of the Sociology and Anthropology Department. I remember the floor was cold concrete. The guest speaker was the *leader of the Communist Political Party in the United States*. There was a very good audience. Some were hostile but they were very much in the minority. I wore my Roman collar and this drew a certain amount of whispering attention. His speech was very reasonable and he took all questions 'head-on'. There were many things done in the name of Communism that he did not agree with, such as the Russian invasion of Hungary. He was opposed to the US involvement in the Vietnam War and was fully supportive of the civil rights movement for racial and ethnic equality. At the end of his speech a large glass bottle was passed around into which we all put a subscription to cover our guest's costs. As it was reaching the end of the round, this rude, rabid anti-Communist took the bottle and smashed it on the concrete floor! Very many American and Western Europeans were paranoid about Communism at the time. Communists were seen as 'public enemy, number one'.

When one listens today, some forty-eight years later (in 2014), to popular US politicians, that use of Communists as a negative out-group is still paraded to cultivate 'in-group cohesion' through 'out-group hostility', to use George Sumner's famous theory. Unfortunately, our opposition to the common enemy can be contrived and manipulated by the authoritarian establishment to solidify the resulting cohesion within our otherwise diverse and divided society. We also tend to compound all evil with the out-group and all good with the in-group. The role of the intellectual is to counter such irrational simplification. Of course, there is a need for those who defend civil rights and social justice for all to avoid slipping into the simplification trap and seeing no good in the views and endeavours of the perceived right-wingers. We must be clear that *what we oppose is not 'them' but certain policies, systems and behaviour*, which they hold and enforce. With such a balanced attitude a degree of dialogue is possible which can lead to positive change.

During the 1950s in the United States, under the Presidency of General Dwight Eisenhower, the level of anti-communism and anti-intellectualism reached an appalling level. Senator McCarthy carried out a witch-hunt, which, in my opinion, was a disgrace to any enlightened democracy. What we were experiencing in the 1960s was a return of self-confidence, which gave the people a chance to express their true feelings without fear or favour. It was like a 'breath of fresh air'. A similar sense of liberty was felt in the Catholic Church after Vatican Two, as it emerged from a period of well-intended and benevolent clerical dominance.

7. THEOLOGY IN MILLTOWN PARK AND VISIT OF FR ARRUPE SJ

On completion of my studies in Kent State University, I qualified for a general scholarship to Ohio State University to study for a doctorate in sociology (of Race Relations) under Professor Brewton Berry. I sought permission from my Provincial. He thought it would be better if I returned to Ireland and commenced theology. By September 1966 I was back in Ireland to begin my studies in Theology at Milltown Park, Dublin. The course would last four years. At the time there were over one hundred (114) Jesuit scholastics studying philosophy and theology in Milltown. The decrees of Vatican Two were being studied as major texts. One school of thought was given sway at the time, namely, the writings of a Canadian Jesuit philosopher, Fr Bernard Lonergan SJ. His views influenced both philosophy and theology. Not every lecturer or student was convinced of the superiority of the Lonergan School. I was respectful of his wisdom but not convinced of his superiority over other profound thinkers. This was to have an influence on whether I would be chosen to continue lecturing in Milltown on completion of my theology. There was a certain tension between the 'neo-Lonergonians' and the others. The former were perceived by some as the 'elite school' within the theologate and philosophate. The most prominent advocate of the Lonergan School was Fr Philip McShane SJ, who was a genius in his own right.

Some years later (in the early 1970s) I met the great philosopher, Fr Bernard Lonergan. He was staying in the College of Industrial Relations at the time. We were on our own in the recreation room. In order to sound intelligent I asked Bernard, what, in his view, was the cause of pollution? I had to wait a few minutes for his answer, which was as follows:

Pollution is basically an epistemological problem. It is the result of specialisation where scientists "look at the sun" through their tunnel vision. They do not examine the lateral damage of their new inventions or discoveries.

On reflection, I found this reply the most satisfactory explanation of pollution that I had heard or read about before or since. It raised the standing of Professor Bernard Lonergan in my estimation.

In 1967, the Milltown Institute of Theology and Philosophy was formed. It represented a number of religious (male) orders and congregations and was divided into two faculties, i.e. theology and philosophy, and a school of human sciences. I was asked to lecture in sociology and was appointed Head of the School of Human Sciences. This gave me a position on the Council of the Institute. The Provincials of the religious orders/congregations (with staff and students in the Institute) constituted the Trustees. The Jesuit Provincial was the Vice-Chancellor while the Jesuit General was the Institute's Chancellor. Our first President of the Institute was Father James Healy SJ, who was Professor of Moral Theology. I felt that the 'Lonergan School' had not that much time for the Human Sciences, which were seen as 'minor' subjects in both philosophy and theology. I did not mind the 'humiliation' deriving from the perceived lower status of the human sciences. After all the human sciences were relatively young subjects and were still not accepted by the 'superior' disciplines!

I regretted at the time, and I still do regret, that the Institute did not use the human sciences more so as to equip the students with a greater capacity to diagnose and explain important socio-psychological, sociological and anthropological phenomena, and thereby, enable them to read the 'signs of the times' more accurately. More specifically, a serious study of the empirically measurable dimensions of religion and its effects, as conditioned by the human personality, society and human culture, would enable priests and other graduates to enter into dialogue with, and even challenge, some of the dismissive conclusions of psychologists, sociologists and anthropologists in relation to religion. Human scientists are, in a sense, very often the contemporary 'prophets of secularism', despite their claim to be 'non-normative'.

There is a very wide gulf between the deliberations of many human scientists and theologians. In fact, one could go so far as to say that some of the human scientists appear to be 'metaphysical agnostics'. The Church, in the post-Vatican Two era, did not address this epistemological problem adequately, in my view. We had an opportunity then to free ourselves from the 'anti-modernist cul-de-sac' and to enter into real dialogue with our human science academic colleagues. Vatican Two had recognised the rightful 'autonomy of the secular', which human scientists appreciated. It did not, unfortunately, move beyond mutual recognition to the creation of a co-existence of the physical and the metaphysical, which would end the fruitless dualism, which impoverished (and still impoverishes) both the believer and the non-believer in the modern world.

The Thirty-First General Congregation of the Society of Jesus was convened after the sad death of Father General John Baptist Jansens SJ, (on 5th October 1964) by the Vice-General of the Order, Father John L Swain SJ. The first session of the Congregation met in Rome on 7th May 1965 and elected Father Pedro Arrupe SJ, a Basque Jesuit (on the third count) on 22nd May 1965. The first session ended on 15th July 1965 and the second session began on the 6th September 1966 and ended on 17th November that same year. The new Father General, Pedro Arrupe SJ, had been Provincial of Japan and earlier Master of Novices in that province. He had trained in medicine before entering the Jesuits. The Novitiate was on the outskirts of Hiroshima, one of the Japanese cities destroyed by the American atomic bomb. Father Arrupe was one of the first to come to the assistance of the injured victims of this horrific act of human cruelty, which was to become a blight on Western civilisation. Since the Thirty-First General Congregation coincided with the end of Vatican Two, it provided a comprehensive set of Decrees aimed at the renewal of the Society of Jesus for the contemporary situation in the world. By the time the Thirty-Second General Congregation of the Society of Jesus was convened on 2nd December 1974, the impact of Vatican Two was more fully realised in the Church and the Jesuits made a more definite option for the poor. The commitment to the promotion of justice in the service of the faith was spelled out in the Decrees by the General Congregation of the Society of Jesus:

The mission of the Society of Jesus today is the service of faith, of which the promotion of justice is an absolute requirement. For reconciliation with God demands the reconciliation of people with one another. (Article 48 of the Thirty-Second General Congregation Decrees).

Much of this radical orientation had been anticipated in Vatican Two and in the Thirty-First General Congregation. (I will refer to this commitment to the poor and underprivileged when commenting on the developments of the 1970s.)

Shortly after his election as the new General, Father Pedro Arrupe SJ, visited the Irish Province (in the summer of 1968). I was appointed his *aide-de-camp*, which meant I had the privilege of accompanying him everywhere he went. Fr Eddie Kent SJ, Director of the College of Industrial Relations, was in charge of the organisation of the visit, which was planned down to the very last detail. My major responsibility was to ensure that the General was on time arriving at the designated venue and leaving on time for the next place. The visit generated a great buzz among the Jesuits. He met all members of the Province and their close families who could travel. The visit worked like clockwork. Father Arrupe was a most inspiring man whose wisdom and sanctity were remarkable. He was an *alter-Ignatius*! He was very much aware of the strengths and weaknesses of the Church and of the Society in his time. He was also courageous and was willing to take risks for the Kingdom. He won the hearts of nearly all of the people (Jesuits and their families). He seemed to remove the repressive dimension of Jesuit life – real or imagined. We could breathe more freely. In the view of many, he was a second St Ignatius.

Looking back now at the changes taking place at the time of the General's visit, it is possible to detect the peaking of public practice and vocations in the Catholic Church in Ireland in the 1960s. The new youth subculture was beginning to attract young people and young adults away from traditional austerity. The student revolt in Earlsfort Terrace (UCD) of 1968 was a symptom of a sense of emancipation. This rebellion against traditional authority in Ireland was echoed all around the Western campuses and cities, i.e. London, Paris, Los Angeles, New York, Amsterdam, Berlin, etc. Accompanying the revolt was a move towards hedonism and sexual permissiveness (if not promiscuity). Patriarchy and matriarchy, i.e. the dominance of parents, were to be replaced in Western society by a new sociological phenomenon, filiarchy, i.e. the dominance of youth. This coincided with the substantial extension of adolescence brought about by an expansion of second- and third-level education and the demands of the post-industrial society. There was a clear culture-lag (see Ogburn) emerging as a result of the decline of parental influence over the teenagers. Later, in Ireland and elsewhere, these changes were to accelerate and become even more serious, according as the adolescent cohort began to earn more money and indulge their recreational appetites with even greater vigour, e.g. the growth of the disco-cum-nightclub! The Catholic Church was (apparently) unsuccessful in maintaining an influence or even a presence in the new youth subculture, which became seemingly secular. Holidays were no longer holy days, for the most part.

Vocations to the priesthood and religious life, which had peaked (in the late 1960s in Ireland) after the Second World War, had begun to decline much more rapidly than did Church attendance, although the latter had also slipped in the surveys. The Trojan effect of the Church's Fathers in Vatican Two and the very serious attempts of Father Arrupe and the Jesuit leadership to fill the culture-gap of the 1960s and 1970s were not enough to maintain meaningful contact with the newly emancipated youth going through their extended adolescence. Maturation (the physiological development of the body) and socialisation (the transmission of the convictions, values, norms and symbolic systems of the people, which results in the development of the human personality to cope with adult life's requirements) seemed to go 'out of kilter'. The religious socialisation of adolescents and young adults seems to be the major challenge facing the Christian Churches in the so-called 'developed world' today. The understandable resistance of a proportion of clergy, religious and laity to follow the Vatican Council and leaders such as Father Pedro Arrupe SJ, may have meant that the 'new youth subculture' was not given the pastoral and evangelising priority required. In the words of St Ignatius Loyola, *'we must attempt to go in their door to try to bring them out ours'* (i.e. the Pauline approach). Greater dialogue and understanding would be necessary before the religiously detached (from the Church) youth could be served. This is not a reason for not commending the 'breakthrough' of Vatican Two, Thirty-First and Thirty-Second General Congregations of the Society of Jesus and tireless efforts of the late Father Pedro Arrupe SJ, our esteemed Father General.

The current state of religion in the Western World is bad enough but it would have been much worse without the 'breakthrough' noted above. The growth of the genuine feminist movement, i.e. seeking the emancipation of women to a status of equality with men, has added a further dimension to the challenges facing Church leaders today. The apparent patriarchal structure of the hierarchy of the Roman Catholic Church had become a topic of criticism throughout the West, just as male dominance in political, industrial, commercial and recreational bodies was also under the feminist spotlight. We have not seen the end of this evolution towards gender equality yet! If I may repeat the words of the late Professor John Jackson (Professor of Sociology in Trinity College, Dublin), i.e. the *'dynamic conservatism of the institutions is a reality which makes radical change very difficult, but not impossible'*. Also, we have to acknowledge the universal nature of the Roman Catholicism, which seems to restrain the rate of change to that of the slowest culture. When the Church was conterminous with the Roman Empire even universal change would have been more feasible. Cultural pluralism raises problems for the Church in its efforts to adapt to cultural change in diverse cultures. It is a real pity that Vatican Two did not address the challenge of regional and cultural pluralism!

A global assimilation of all diverse cultures into one dominant culture would be the reduction of the human race to a restricted nuance on reality. When that global culture emanates from one superpower, e.g. Anglo-American, or some other power-group with global ambitions, the situation of cultural colonisation emerges. Universal languages would tend to result in universal value systems, e.g. the current spreading of liberal-capitalist values around the globe on the coat-tails of dominant languages. These values do not necessarily harmonise with Christian Gospel values. The enculturation of Christianity into the liberal-capitalist, Anglo-American 'world' culture would be an extraordinary challenge, because of the basic contradictions between a predominantly competitive, individualistic and materialistic culture and that of the Catholic Church, which is a cooperative, collectivist (family and community) and spiritual culture. Where can real compromise be reached? Of course, Anglo-American culture is not all negative. The promotion of such concepts as individual rights, gender and ethnic and racial equality, as well as universal franchise have been nurtured within the Anglo-American culture group, but not exclusively so. Some would see aspects of the Catholic Church's hierarchical structure out of line with the latter so-called 'liberal values and norms'. Maybe, some degree of enculturation could bring about some desirable changes in both the Catholic Church culture and in the liberal-capitalist Anglo-American culture? It is at this level I see the real challenge facing the Christian Churches in Western culture over the next decades.

There was a real buzz in Milltown Park during the second half of the 1960s, under the wise and open leadership of our Rector, Father Cecil McGarry SJ, who became Provincial at the end of the decade. He was later elected as Assistant to the Father General Pedro Arrupe SJ, following the Thirty-Second General Congregation of the Society of Jesus. The Irish Province carried out an overall review of its areas of ministry and a serious examination of the 'signs of the times'. I was appointed to write one of the reports on the signs of the times. It was entitled, *The Economic Basis of Industrial Relations in Ireland*, under the general guidance of Father Tim Hamilton SJ of the College of Industrial Relations (where I had been a part-time lecturer since 1966). In researching this report I had to interview a number of important leaders in the Trade Unions and management in Dublin, Shannon Industrial Estate and elsewhere. I also took as my dissertation topic (for the *STL), The Theological Basis for the Church's Involvement in the Social Apostolate.* These two academic projects enabled me to acquire a first-hand familiarity with the central social, industrial and pastoral landscape of the post-Vatican Two Church and the developments in the emerging industrial culture in Lemass's Irish Republic. This made my theology and sociology relevant and Ireland-centred. In the course of my work for the Irish Province in the area of industrial relations, I was introduced to some of the trade union, farming, industrial, commercial and public service leaders. Both Ireland and the Catholic Church were enjoying a real sense of optimism. The vulgarity of excessive wealth and superfluity had not yet arrived in Ireland to make our people selfish and self-indulgent. The mid-1960s were heady years!

8. Clouds of Unrest Gathering in the North

The conflict within industry in the 1960s was inevitable because of the demands of industrial workers to get adequate pay and conditions. Standards of living were rising and a new order was being created. There was a decline in the number (proportion) of workers engaged in agriculture, where mechanisation was reducing the labour force drastically. The Trade Unions were becoming a major social partner throughout the country. Some multinational companies from the United States were finding it difficult to retain a 'non-union policy', e.g. EI Company in Shannon Free Airport Industrial Estate. The conflict and tension that was occurring was 'constructive conflict', which was a mature form of industrial peace. Of course, the intransigence of some managements as well as the occasional Trade Union militant leader did lead to unnecessary loss of workdays due to industrial strikes. I was never alarmist about an energetic industrial encounter between workers and management.

The gradual demise of the 'owner manager' and the emergence of the 'corporation' with its professional managers created an ideological dilemma for the bureaucratic boss without an ownership stake in the company, which was basically owned by the anonymous investor on the stock market. This is still a problematic situation, where management and workers are both employees! Demographic changes in Ireland were beginning to reflect the rise of the industrial and services sectors and the decline of the agriculture proportion of workers. Ironically, the Whitaker proposals resulted in a very significant increase in farm productivity, without a commensurate increase in farm employment. Were we witnessing the first steps towards 'industrial farming in Ireland'?

It should be remembered that the above changes had all taken place outside the EEC, although it was Government policy to seek membership. This pending possibility of membership of the Common Market probably motivated some of the foreign multinational corporations to invest in factories in Ireland at the time. The whole style and demeanour of politicians changed from the simple rural, urban working-class, to ideological representatives of the more sophisticated, fast-moving, pin-striped, 'with-it', pragmatic, bureaucratic-oriented type of TD and Minister. Of course, there were exceptions. By the mid-1960s the economic institution was becoming more pivotal.

In 1968 the twentieth anniversary of the *United Nations Charter of Human Rights* was being celebrated in Ireland. Copies of the Charter were circulated to schools. This helped to raise the level of consciousness of the lack of basic civil rights in local communities. Voluntary, peaceful campaigns were being organised throughout communities, where obvious rights had been denied. The area in Ireland where Civil Rights' Campaign gained most momentum was in Northern Ireland (the Six Counties). There had been a more relaxed relationship developing between the Sean Lemass's Government and Terence O'Neill's Stormont Government. The *Taoiseach* and the Northern Prime Minister had met publicly. The Labour Party Government in Britain, under Harold Wilson MP, was also favourably disposed to better North-South relations in Ireland.

This background facilitated a more effective civil rights campaign. I remember being invited to the Queen's University, Belfast, to read a paper on 'Prejudice and Civil Rights' in 1968. There I met some leaders, i.e. Paddy Devlin, Gerry Fitt, Professor Scott, David Bleakley, Ruth Patterson and others. Areas of discrimination included employment opportunities, housing, education and political gerrymandering. The manipulation of job opportunities resulted in a sinister system of population control. The Catholic populations with their higher birth-rate were forced to emigrate to 'mainland Britain' and elsewhere for employment, while the concentration of work opportunities was in Protestant-populated areas. It was a subtle form of 'ethnic cleansing' in favour of the reigning dominant group. Informal 'apartheid' was also widely practised. All of this was becoming clear in 1968 and there was pressure on the British Government and on the exclusively Unionist Stormont Administration to dismantle the unjust system. In 1968, Fr Bernard McGuckian SJ, Professor Chuck Hildebrandt (of Kent State University, who was on a visit to Ireland) and I walked in a major *12th July Orange Parade*. We disguised our identities. It was more like a carnival than anything else.

For whatever reason, the British Government and the Stormont Administration 'dragged their heels'. Instead of granting 'one-person-one-vote', fairer distribution of jobs, equal housing and educational opportunities, the Stormont Minister for Home Affairs and the Royal Ulster Constabulary (aided by the B-Special Auxiliary Force) approved and engaged in counter conflict against the Civil Rights Activists. In 1969 there was a mini-pogrom of a Catholic-cum-Nationalist urban neighbourhood in Belfast with widespread arson of the poor (Catholic) people's homes. A Civil Rights march from Antrim to Derry was organised to expose the counter-violence of the security forces of the State and attract them away from Belfast. In order to remove the pressure from the suffering citizens of Belfast the marchers hoped to attract the police out of the city. Again, the Civil Rights march was attacked as it approached Derry City and more mayhem ensued.

The Irish Government in Dublin reacted in an ambiguous manner, under the *Taoiseach*, Jack Lynch TD, (who had succeeded Sean Lemass whose health had failed). It made a request to the United Nations to intervene, but this was blocked by the United Kingdom Government. In such a chaotic and desperate situation, what was to become the Provisional IRA was born as a nationalist Citizens' Defence Organisation and adopted paramilitary means to respond to the obvious offensive assault on residents and on their civil rights' defenders. *Thus, was born a quarter-of-a-century of incredible violence in the relatively small community of Northern Ireland.*

In my opinion, this twenty-five years plus of paramilitary violence could have been avoided had the British and Irish Governments insisted on the granting of their basic rights to the Catholic Nationalist minority, as soon as it was made clear that there was discrimination against the minority. Decades of blatant injustices were allowed to fester under the very nose of Westminster and in the name of the King/Queen of England. I have often asked myself, 'Where were the judges and the influential Church leaders, especially those with influence in Stormont and Westminster, all this time?' The situation was somewhat akin to the apartheid system in South Africa. Once again, in 1969, the 'genie was out of the bottle'.

The real tragedy of Northern Ireland, as I have just said, was the failure of the different establishments to eliminate the gross and festering injustices which plagued the Six Counties for so many miserable years (1922-69) without effective intervention. The fault must lie, primarily with the dominant groups in the United Kingdom and in Ireland. But what is new about this? Let us look around us today. *If the 'constitutional authorities' fail to act, paramilitary action will inevitably and eventually follow.* When superpowers are in control, that paramilitary action is of a guerrilla or 'terrorist' nature. These are the facts of modern history throughout our unjust globe. There are none so insecure as those who are over-secure! Sooner or later chickens come home to roost!

9. ORDINATION: A GATEWAY TO MINISTRY

On 31ˢᵗ July 1969 (Feast of Saint Ignatius of Loyola) I was ordained a priest in the Society of Jesus by the late Archbishop Joseph Walsh DD, of Tuam (who had handed over the Archdiocese to the late Archbishop Joseph Cunnane DD, after being thirty years in charge) in my home parish of Westport (Aughaval), County Mayo. It was a most memorable event. Father Cecil McGarry SJ, preached the homily and the late Canon Tom Cummins, Adm. Westport, was Master of Ceremonies.

My parents and all my family including first and second cousins were in attendance. The local Church of Ireland Rector, Archdeacon Duggan took part in the ceremony. Among the guests were Jesuits, local clergy, army colleagues (including Generals Dan McKenna and Seán McKeown, [my former Cadet Master]), neighbours and friends from the parish and elsewhere. The reception was held in Belclare House Hotel. The general consensus was that all went very well. I was very tired after the whole event.

My first Mass was offered in Westport while my second Mass was offered in Kilkenny for the Travelling People with whom I had spent some time the previous year living in a caravan (accompanied by Father Des O'Brien SJ) on the Kilkenny circuit. I was to repeat this experience later in 1969 on the Kilkenny-Carlow circuit. The late Bishop of Ossory, Dr Peter Birch, approved our staying with the Travellers. The time I spent living in disguise on the roadside was very important for me and greatly influenced my positive attitude towards Travellers. I found them to be a wonderful people who were seen as a 'lower caste' in Irish society.

On return to Milltown Park in October 1969, we newly ordained Jesuits started our final year. We were awarded the BD (Bachelor of Divinity) in June of that year. On weekdays we offered Mass in houses of the Irish Christian Brothers in St Helen's, Oatlands and Bray. On Sundays we offered Mass in neighbouring parishes of the Dublin archdiocese (although we were not invited to preach any sermons). While in Milltown, I helped Father Michael Hurley SJ to run the Milltown Public Lectures. These attracted very large crowds during Lent and were dealing with post-Vatican Two topics. The Archbishop of Dublin, Most Reverend Dr John Charles McQuaid, kept a very firm hand on the public lectures and statements issued by clergy. Every summary statement sent to the media had to be censored by the archdiocese. There was only limited freedom of expression in the Catholic Church in Ireland at the time, especially, for clergy and religious orders and congregations. There was a ban on Catholic students attending courses in Trinity College, Dublin. For priests to encourage Catholics to do so would result in an *ipso facto* loss of faculties to hear confession in the archdiocese.

This ban on TCD was all to change when the Minister for Education, Mr Donagh O'Malley TD, announced a proposed merging of TCD and UCD in 1969. It is hard to realise the extent of control exercised by the bishops over priests, religious and the faithful up to this time. It has had to relax a great deal since.

While much criticism of Archbishop McQuaid was reported in some of the print media, it had to be admitted that he was a most effective administrator in that schools, hospitals, social services centres and new churches were provided to meet the needs of a growing archdiocese. Also, the age profile of clergy and clerical students in the archdiocese was the healthiest of all the dioceses researched in the early 1970s. In addition, the chaplaincy support of VEC schools was highly praised by many commentators. A further compliment was paid to the archbishop and his archdiocesan top management team for the enlightened manner in which he released priests for special studies in mass communications, social work studies and other areas of potential pastoral use. These positive aspects of the very controversial Archbishop were rarely noted. On a personal level, John Charles (as he was affectionately known) was most supportive of clergy and laity in need of help. It was a pity that, at times, he appeared to have been 'a prisoner of clerical protocol'. All things considered, I found the late Archbishop McQuaid was a very complex personality. He merits a prominent place in the gallery of Ireland's most distinguished leaders over the past decades. He was a good friend of the late Monaghan poet, Patrick Kavanagh. Archbishop McQuaid was once asked if public criticism upset him. He was supposed to have answered that, like the Lord, the bishop would appear to be 'a sign and a contradiction'. *Ar dheis Dé go raibh a anam dílis.*

During the time I spent in Milltown Park, the Irish author, Seán de Fréine, who was a lecturer colleague of mine in the *College of Industrial Relations* (*CIR*), invited me to become a member of a small (sociological) research team to carry out a study of the development of *Conradh na Gaeilge* (the Gaelic League) as a social movement. I agreed and had the privilege of meeting the young and dynamic *Uachtarán of Chonradh na Gaeilge,* Maolsheachlainn Uasal Ó Caollaí, who briefed us on the work that *An Choiste Ghnó* (the Board) would like us to do. A fourth member of the team was *An t-Ath* Séamus Caomhánach, Professor of Social Sciences, in University College Dublin. We worked well together as a research team and produced an interim report for *An Choiste Ghnó* in a few months. This was the beginning of a long and chequered relationship with the headquarters of *Conradh na Gaeilge* over the next two decades. Uachtarán Ó Caollaí, made a valiant and intelligent effort to breathe new life into an organisation on the eve of its centenary. He saw *An Conradh* as a socio-cultural movement, which was, hopefully, to enter a new and more dynamic cycle. He drew heavily on the human sciences to guide his strategy. Unfortunately, not all of the members or leaders fully understood his aims or supported his efforts. Nevertheless, he did equip the organisation to play a positive role in the eventual procurement of Irish language radio, *Raidio na Gaeltachta*, and television services.

The President also saw the importance of Irish language *Naíscoileanna* (preschools), as they had proven to be very effective in Wales for the

155

preservation and promotion of the Welsh language. Another development (which I had the privilege of proposing at a meeting of *An Choiste Ghnó*) was the setting up of a *Coiste Chearta* or a language rights committee (sometime in the early 1970s). As an active movement, *Conradh na Gaeilge* was to receive a higher profile and was not afraid to take part in public protest. Maolsheachlainn Ó Caollaí was very much opposed to Ireland entering the Common Market. I, and others, did not agree with him at the time, but now, in hindsight, many of his negative predictions have been borne out. (My current position is in favour of Ireland joining, but opposed to subsequent treaties, which have centralised major powers in Brussels, and emasculated the power of our national parliament in a wide range of social and political areas.)

Before leaving the research subcommittee I feel that I must recall a meeting I had with Professor Séamus Caomhánach (later Bishop James Kavanagh) outside Westland Row Parish church as we were going home from an Irish language meeting. Fr Séamus asked me what I planned on doing after I finished my theology course (for the STL) in June 1970. In reply I said that I might revive my attempt to do a PhD in race relations in Ohio State University in the United States, under Professor Brewton Berry. Fr Séamus suggested that I might consider doing a PhD in Sociology on *Intergroup Relations in Ireland* and he would be willing to direct me in the Social Science Department of University College Dublin. He felt that, to date, nobody had carried out a proper study of social prejudice in Ireland. I immediately warmed to the idea and discussed it later that week with my Jesuit superiors, who also agreed that it would be a very worthwhile academic project.

On that fateful night, under a lamppost outside the Church of St Andrew, Westland Row, Dublin, the focus and direction of my academic and research career were determined. What followed was but the filling out of an inspired suggestion of one of my best friends and colleagues, the late Professor/Bishop Séamus Caomhánach, whose academic integrity, Christian kindness, rich personality, and tireless support would enable me to contribute more than I ever dreamed of to the Irish people's self-understanding in regard to intergroup relations. More than that, he would become a role model for me as a priest, and in my respect for students and colleagues in my thirty years of lecturing since 1969. (I had already been lecturing some three years.) I always felt that the Catholic Church should have made Fr Séamus the Archbishop of Dublin. He had so many of the qualities of Saint (Pope) John XXIII.

During the years 1968 to 1970, Ms Dorothy Dalton, a senior civil servant, introduced the theologians in Milltown Park to *Pax Christi,* the Catholic Peace Movement. This movement had its origins in the Nazi Concentration Camps where a number of French and German Roman Catholic prisoners agreed that if they survived the war, they would come together to reconcile the enemies of the Second World War. His Eminence, Cardinal Alfrink, of Holland, was its International President. The annual Mass of *Pax Christi* was offered in the convent of the Loreto Sisters on St Stephen's Green. I attended these Masses and revived my interest in more active pacifist campaigning for peace based on justice in Ireland. In 1970, I was appointed the first *Irish National Chaplain of Pax Christi,* a position I held until 1974. This inevitably resulted in my becoming involved (privately and publicly) in the Northern Troubles. *My original dream for the movement was to have an active branch of Pax Christi in every parish, whose mission would be the promotion of justice and peace within the local area.* For some reason, there was reluctance among other leaders to build such a strong and rooted pacifist movement. Was it that we feared it would become too radical and, as a result, challenge some aspects of the politico-religious *status quo?* In the light of my pending studies, and most academic and other experiences, this more explicit entry into the peace movement was providential for me.

The United States of America experienced a turbulent decade during the 1960s. The election of John F Kennedy, as the first Catholic President, was greeted in Ireland as very hopeful. His Irish (post-Famine) ancestors identified him with our country. He was charismatic, intelligent and sensitive to the rights of black people. During his relatively short period in office (1961-63) he won the respect of many throughout the world. I had been a student in Belgium at the time of his assassination in November 1963 and experienced the personal sense of loss among nearly all the people. Nikita Khrushchev (USSR), John XXIII (Pope) and JF Kennedy (USA) were three major world leaders with a popular appeal which made the world feel a sense of reconciliation. This added to the tragedy of the sudden victory of 'evil over good' in Kennedy's assassination (according to one of our professors in Leuven, Belgium). We were celebrating the Feast of St Cecilia (22nd November 1963) at the end of a special dinner when the tragic news was announced.

President Kennedy's Vice-President, Lyndon B Johnson, succeeded him as President and ratified JFK's civil rights legislation. The former Attorney General, Robert Kennedy, was later assassinated while campaigning to succeed President Johnson in 1968. This double cross for the Kennedy family was also traumatic for the American people. When one adds to this the assassination of Martin Luther King around the same time, there must be a *prima facie* case for an anti-civil rights conspiracy in the US during the 1960s. The 'forces of evil' cannot coexist with those who promote the good and seem compelled to destroy them! This futile brutality leads to martyrdom, which, in turn, strengthens the mission of those martyred!

10. THE GROWTH OF THE PROPHETIC CHURCH

A most welcome change was taking place within the Jesuit Order after the Thirty-First General Congregation in relation to a more structural level of social justice between the grades of Jesuits. A welcome challenge was proposed to the unacceptable elitism between the professed fathers, spiritual coadjutors and temporal coadjutors. The final vows of the three grades were permanent. The professed fathers were chosen mainly according to their academic achievements in philosophy (LPh) and in theology (STL). They were invited to profess solemn vows and make a solemn promise of obedience to the Pope. The spiritual coadjutors were fathers, who qualified in philosophy and theology at the undergraduate level. They were invited to make lifelong simple vows. Temporal coadjutors were Jesuit brothers who were also given permanent simple vows. Members were not encouraged to seek to improve their status.

After the Thirty-First Congregation, spiritual coadjutors were welcome to apply for Professed Father Status and brothers were invited to pursue studies so as to improve their education and skills. They were also to be treated on an equal status with priests in regards to dining, living quarters and recreational facilities. There was a formal end to all symbols of 'second-class citizenship' within the Order. Attempts by later congregations to do away with formal profession for priests only were prevented by the Vatican. The pejorative concept of 'lay' brother and 'lay' sister was to disappear throughout religious orders and congregations.

Such a 'class structure' was, in my view, totally contrary to the spirit of the '*Man from Nazareth*' and I welcomed the first formal steps towards its ending. The Church was inching its way forward from the straightjacket of the medieval feudal structures, which was in harmony with that of the secular Roman Empire.

This new sense of social equality within the Jesuit Order soon spread to the pay and conditions of those lay people who worked for us in our various works, especially the men and women engaged in the unskilled and semi-skilled grades. In Milltown Park, for instance, Brother Anthony McSherry SJ, got union recognition for commis chefs in the kitchen, while Brother Hughie Monaghan SJ, organised a special school for the improvement of the level of ordinary education for younger teenagers engaged as unskilled workers. We scholastics helped out as teachers and directors of curriculum. Most of us had had valuable experience in teaching and lecturing. The special staff school idea was also started in Tullabeg in 1961-1962, by Brother Hughie Monaghan SJ. All houses of the Irish Province had to review the relatively poor pay and conditions for lay staff in operation. The ethos of equality was breaking through. It was a case of justice and charity beginning at home! But, I must admit that the process was very slow to reach any realistic level of comparative equality.

The *Donagh O'Malley Scheme* (1967) of free second-level school education for all was a source of great joy to many, but it had some disturbing repercussions for those engaged in the provision of private secondary education for Ireland's children of the elite. Of the six secondary colleges run by the Jesuits, two entered the O'Malley Scheme, i.e. *Coláiste Iognáid* in Galway and the Crescent (Comprehensive) School in Limerick. Three of the other four, i.e. Clongowes Wood College in County Kildare and Belvedere College and Gonzaga College in Dublin remained private and fee-paying. The fourth private college, i.e. Mungret, was to close in a few years. Both Clongowes Wood and Mungret were boarding schools. I was among those Jesuits, who regretted the closing of Mungret because of its very good Apostolic School and its service of the needs of those families with modest incomes and living in relative isolation in relation to secondary schools. The continuity of our private schools/colleges was a topic of discussion among members of the Order. A significant minority felt that they were difficult to justify in the context of our call to 'promote justice in the service of the faith'. I would identify with this minority. This is not to deny the very excellent work our private colleges do for their students and I respect them for it. *My real complaint with elitism in education is its contribution to the continuity of the class structure and the unfair advantage of members of the old boys' network.* According to sociologist, Talcott Parsons, the great 'structural functionalist', the function of education in society is pattern-maintenance, i.e. facilitating the rotation of elites in society. The O'Malley Scheme, which was backed by the World Bank, supported the philosophy of pragmatism in education in the interests of the economy. This inevitably led to a weakening of the transmission of culture and personal development as a primary function of education.

My relations with the College of Industrial Relations began when I started lecturing there in 1966 on a part-time basis. This college was founded by the Jesuits in 1951 to provide education in Industrial Relations to workers (Trade Unionists), supervisors and lower and middle management. It was supported by some of the Trade Unions and by members of the Employers' Organisations. It was 'radical' for its time and contributed to the new industrial culture, which emerged in the 1950s and 1960s. Father Eddie Kent SJ, and a small number of committed Jesuits and lay friends, i.e. Frs Bill McKenna SJ, Tim Hamilton SJ, Kevin Quinn SJ, Mr Andrew Ryan, BL, Mrs Pauline Connolly and others, built up the College's reputation over the years. The original founders' and supporters' main mission was to enable the workers, supervisors and lower and middle managers to articulate their needs and seek to improve the work environment as a place where the human dignity of all workers was recognised in their relationships on the job and in their pay and conditions. The Catholic Church's strong tradition in the area of work and justice was also transmitted to the students in a non-proselytising manner. Long before the rise of the new feminist movement, courses were provided for women trade-unionists. Later female workers would enrol in the mixed courses.

As the 1960s (a decade of change and optimism) drew to a close, the clouds were gathering. Student revolt in the universities did bring about a certain degree of improvement but the counterchange forces of the long-established structures were coming down on the reformers. Some of the protests turned nasty and even violent. Probably the most worrying

160

aspect of the failure of the advocates of change and the custodians of the established order to arrive at an ordered transition were social divisions and anomie or a growing sense of normlessness. Within the Catholic Church we were to witness a mini-schism, i.e. the refusal of a group of traditionalist Catholics under the leadership of Archbishop Lefebvre to accept the legitimacy of the changes brought about by Vatican Two. Some went even further and did not accept the validity of the papacy of Pope Paul VI or his successors. The year 1968 was seen as a year of revolt across the Western World.

At the other end of the ideological-cum-religious spectrum were those who wished to challenge all moral and conventional restraints – 'love and do what you will'. This wing did not become a schismatic group. Rather, they seemed to opt out altogether. Of course, this deprived their followers of the support of basic Christian morality to guide their lives in a meaningful manner. We were soon to witness an appalling rise in abortion rates, in the liberal abuse of drugs and a growth in sexual promiscuity with its devastating effects for stable human relationships and on monogamous, indissoluble marriage. Sentiment and expedience seemed to replace reason and morality in the advocacy of some who promoted this new age of unrestrained liberty. Unfortunately, much of the extreme promotion of the 'love-and-do-what-you-will' camp was almost exclusively individualistic in their understanding of the 'good life'. It was in this that they lost me because I believed, and still do, that life is social. I am an *'other-than-the-other's-otherness-with-the-other's-otherness-in-the-world'*. My identity, welfare, development, achievement, comfort, fulfilment and understanding of life are all dependent on others as well as myself. As I have noted earlier, Roman Catholicism is basically collectivist in its understanding of the human condition. I have found that a degree of asceticism is essential for a good life.

The positive thing about another category, the so-called 'left wing' of the Catholic Church, was this greater commitment to the collectivist view. The 'left wing' constituted a broad collectivity, and was to come into conflict with some authorities, but was, for most part, able to keep in union with the Church. In fact, quite a number of bishops (such as Bishop Helder Camara from South America) and religious superiors supported those more radical advocates of social justice. Their place within the Church would be defined as more diverse than divisive. I would see myself in this 'camp' for most of my active ministry. To commit oneself to this more radical stance implied that one would be unlikely to ascend the ladder of ecclesial or other preferment. I would agree with the view that: *You cannot be a radical above the rank of lieutenant!* It was a real skill to be active within the establishment, without compromise of one's principles. It was necessary to be in at the 'lieutenant rank' in order to have sufficient influence and credibility (in respect of criticism) to promote necessary change. If a person of this 'left wing' were to be promoted, there would always be a danger of his or her becoming a defender of the *status quo,* thus, dampening the desire to work for necessary change of it. Of course, some one-time radicals opted to accept promotion in the belief that it enabled them to be more effective. I am happy now not to have been given promotion above the rank of lieutenant! In some instances in history, the establishments seem to have promoted 'Radicals' in order to routinise and, thereby, de-radicalise them.

During the months of September 1968 and 1969, I had the privilege of living on the roadside as a Traveller in disguise. In 1968, Fr Des O'Brien SJ, and I (as a scholastic at the time) were invited by the Travellers and their friends in Kilkenny to spend a month on the roadside in a caravan at various sites with a number of families. We spent the days 'hanging around' and offered Mass in the caravan at nightfall. Afterwards, we had refreshments around the campfire. We got to know the families and to experience the joys and challenges of living on the roadside. The Travellers taught us so much about life, about ourselves and about Irish settled society. The following year, 1969, I repeated the experience (without Jesuit companions for the most part) and was able to learn much more about the social, personal and cultural aspects of the life of the Travelling People in Ireland and the overwhelming impact of social change of Irish society on this relatively small (0.5%) cultural minority where their social status was that of 'Lower Caste'. Despite their humiliating deprivation, I found the Travellers to be wonderful human beings with rich and colourful personalities. I felt 'bored' when I returned to the 'comforts' of bourgeois living!

One of the consequences of the changes brought about in the devotional life of the Church after Vatican Two was an almost perceptible *rejection by some Church Authorities of popular devotions,* which had played a very important part in the spiritual life of the people for generations.

The Catholic Church in a sense, changed from being 'high Church' to becoming 'low Church' with bare simple *décor*. Devotions such as Benediction of the Blessed Sacrament, Stations of the Cross, Sodalities, Novenas, etc. were gradually being phased out in favour of more participation in the Mass. New churches were stark and void of statues, shrines and a cosy, maybe cluttered, ambience with the flickering of rows of 'penny candles', all of which made Church visitation a rewarding and warm experience. Why was it necessary to get rid of the past popular practices in order to introduce the welcome changes in the liturgy? It may have been aesthetically more acceptable to the sophisticated and appear less anthropomorphic? But, it stripped Mass and devotions of the human 'feeling' dimension for many devout people.

The domestic church, i.e. family prayer, especially, the rosary, was also to become a post-Vatican Two casualty as was the playing-down of regular sacramental confession. Of course, the intrusion of television helped to push it out also. There was yet another change in the Church's message to the people, namely, the downplaying of reparation and atonement and the value of penance, fasting and abstinence. This change was expressed in the removal of abstinence on Friday and the dropping of fasting during Lent. The Pioneer Total Abstinence Association of the Sacred Heart was lucky to survive because of its spiritual link with the concept of reparation to Christ 'for the sins of intemperance'! I believe we must re-evaluate the spirituality of asceticism and reparation. Many of the new changes were unnecessary and were not required by the welcome new vision of Vatican Two. We must never forget the priority of the 'People of God'. If the Church does not satisfy their need for devotional expression, either they will seek it in more fundamentalist religious groups outside the Roman Catholic Church or they will gradually withdraw from worship, which is a necessary expression of our faith in a Personal God.

Chapter Five

THE 1970S
THE DECADE AFTER OPTIMISM

1. PREPARATION FOR AN ACADEMIC CAREER
AND ACTIVE MINISTRY

The 1960s ended on a high note with a series of revolts by youth and civil rights' groups right across the Western World. These were active expressions of dissent against an establishment, which was perceived as unjust and discriminating against minorities, i.e. racial, ethnic, gender and youth itself (or should I say those experiencing the restrictions of an extended adolescence). In Germany and in Italy the revolt turned nasty with paramilitary expressions of discontent. In Northern Ireland, 'the fat was in the fire' and an almost all-out war was about to be waged by Republicans against the Security Forces of the Crown. The anti-war campaign in the United States was in full swing and a 'sympathetic' movement was being organised in solidarity with American protestors throughout Europe. In June 1970, the Wilson Labour Government in London was defeated and a Conservative administration replaced it under the premiership of Mr Edward Heath MP. Ireland's decision to join the European Common Market in 1972 was to be given a very short honeymoon because of the rise in oil prices in 1974, which led to, or coincided with, a degree of economic depression.

The violent struggle in Northern Ireland and offshoots of it in the Republic and in Britain were, in a way, displacing the short-lived pivotal position of the economic institution and replacing it by the centrality of the political institution, which was to dominate much of our energies for over two decades. With part of Ireland at war, we in the Republic could no longer suppress the need to get involved in changing the intolerable situation north of the border!

On completion of my fourth year theology in June 1970, I was assigned to live with the Jesuit Community attached to the College of Industrial Relations, i.e. at Sandford Road, Ranelagh, Dublin 6. I was lucky to pass my STL examination as I was up all night before listening to the results of the British General Election, which led to the defeat of Harold Wilson and the Labour Party! (I would stay with CIR for the next twenty-eight years, until September 1998, when I would be transferred to the Jesuit Community of Upper Gardiner Street, Dublin 1.) I became involved in the College Faculty and joined in the work for the renewal of the courses.

Earlier every ministry had been asked by Father Provincial to review its work and structures in the light of Vatican Two, the General Congregation 31 and the series of reports that the Province had carried out on different areas of work. I had, two years earlier, the temerity to propose a comprehensive suggestion of setting up a humanities third-level college, centred around Milltown Institute of Theology and Philosophy, the College of Industrial Relations, Gonzaga Secondary School and the Sisters of Charity in Mount Saint Anne's next door. I entitled the proposal *'The Milltown Complex'*. I circulated the proposal but, I regret, it did not enter the Province's grand plans! What a missed opportunity!

My personal academic plans were already drawing me towards University College, Dublin, and the task of carrying out a major survey of prejudice and tolerance in Ireland as a PhD research project. Father Eddie Kent SJ, Director of the College of Industrial Relations, had hoped that I would have focused on the sociology of industrial relations and become involved full-time in the College. Around this time Father Kent retired from the CIR and was replaced by a fellow-founder, Father Kevin Quinn SJ, as Director. Father Quinn had worked in Zambia and in the Gregorian University in Rome as a professor of economics. He was a man from whom I learned much.

In 1970 the Irish Conference of Bishops set up a Research and Development Unit (R & D Unit), attached to the Catholic Communications Unit, located at the south end of Booterstown Avenue near Stillorgan in Dublin. Father Joe Dunne, of '*Radharc*' fame, was asked to set up the unit. I was invited to become one of a three-person team, i.e. Professor Liam Ryan, Maynooth, Father James Lennon (later appointed Auxiliary Bishop of Armagh to Cardinal Tomás Ó Fiaich) and myself. Among the early projects, which the unit was asked to research and present reports to the Irish Bishops, were: vocations to the priesthood and religious life in Ireland, and a survey of second-level schools in Ireland (Republic and Northern Ireland). Father James Lennon was the full-time director of the Research and Development Unit. Father Liam Ryan and I were 'sociological consultants'. In fact, I was assigned the task of compiling the demographic profile of priests and religious. I had also worked with James Lennon to get the facts about second-level schools. Later, Dr Máire Nic Ghiolla-Phádraig would direct the fieldwork for the unit.

In October 1970 I registered for a PhD in Sociology in University College Dublin and was given a lecturing position there, i.e. teaching Durkheim and Weber to second year students and also giving a course on intergroup relations to third years. At the same time, I continued lecturing in the College of Industrial Relations, Milltown Institute and in Kimmage Manor. I found lecturing and tutoring quite exciting. Third-level students were generally very interested in seeking a better understanding of society. I tried my best to be non-normative. One of the most stimulating aspects of lecturing at the time (it was to change somewhat later) was the dynamic company of colleagues. At first, they were trying to 'weigh me up', I felt. Under the kindly leadership of Professor James Kavanagh, and Doctor Conor Ward, the team seemed to be like a family. I was the newly adopted member. In a short time I got to 'know the ropes'.

My PhD proposal was *'to describe, explore and explain' the level of intergroup prejudice in Ireland.* I would use a large random sample of the people of Greater Urban and Suburban Dublin as my respondents. A comprehensive survey questionnaire was to be prepared. A special section on religious attitudes and practices was added to the questions measuring social prejudices. The Research and Development Unit (of the Bishops' Conference) provided the necessary finance to carry out an interview-questionnaire survey of some 2,311 respondents in Greater Dublin. The 'field headquarters' was in *Veritas* offices, Lower Abbey Street, Dublin 1. In return for the Research and Development Unit's support, I later presented (published) reports on *Religious Attitudes and Practices* and on *Educational Participation in Dublin.* The interviews were carried out (under my supervision) between September 1972 and March 1973.

2. Joining Maynooth Staff

During the summer of 1971 Professor Liam Ryan invited me to apply for the position of Junior Lecturer in Sociology in the NUI part of St Patrick's College, Maynooth, County Kildare. St Patrick's also had a Pontifical University College as well as Ireland's National Catholic Seminary. The NUI 'Recognised College' was in the process of opening up to lay students and some lay academic staff were appointed at this time. It would mean that I would commute from the CIR to Maynooth each day (a round trip of approximately thirty-five miles). I discussed the invitation with Father Provincial, Cecil McGarry SJ, who thought it was a very good opportunity for me. He was also happy that by teaching in Maynooth I would be able to get to know diocesan clergy and be in a position to help out in whatever way possible. The President of St Patrick's College, Maynooth at the time was Monsignor Jeremiah Newman, who was also a previous professor of sociology. My Jesuit Superior in CIR was Father Tony Baggot SJ, who also supported the idea of my joining the Maynooth staff.

In September 1971 I took up the position of Junior Lecturer in Sociology in Maynooth at the annual salary of £1,400 a year or slightly less than £27 a week. Even allowing for inflation, this was a relatively small salary. We definitely did not work for the money only! It was one of the first tasks of IFUT (Irish Federation of University Teachers) to equalise salaries in Maynooth and those in University College Dublin. We were also on probation for three years, at the end of which we would be promoted to the grade of Lecturer. One would have to await promotion to the grade of Senior Lecturer before becoming a 'statutory lecturer' within the NUI system. All very feudal! I continued lecturing (part-time) in UCD until the mid-1980s.

Initially, the first group of external staff was invited to share some meals with the 'internal professors' (all of whom were priests) in their handsome dining room. This gave us the impression that we would be integrated into the College staff. Regretfully, that was not to be. In a short time, 'external academic staff' and all college administrative (white-collar) staff were assigned their own dining room – at first in a temporary location near the bursar's quarters and later in a room above the college kitchen. The 'internal academic staff' was akin to the

'Fellows of Maynooth'. Despite the separation of dining facilities a good proportion of the 'internal academic staff' were quite keen to integrate us (new external members) into a common *Academic Staff Association*, which would later become a strong branch of IFUT (the Irish Federation of University Teachers). This was later registered with the *Irish Congress of Trade Unions (ICTU)*.

The Academic Staff Association was very busy during the early 1970s drafting rules and procedures for the expanding NUI Recognised College. Professor Enda McDonagh (Moral Theology), Professor Patrick McGrath (Philosophy) and others, including Father Malachy O'Rourke (French), were very articulate in framing an endless stream of documents. One of the most admired leaders was Professor Gerry Meagher (Sacred Scripture) who saw the value to Maynooth of having an effective staff Trade Union. Professor Enda McDonagh was elected President of IFUT, which was an indication of the national standing of Maynooth at the time among the academics from the other universities, i.e. University College Dublin, Trinity College Dublin, University College Cork and University College Galway. IFUT did not join ICTU (Irish Congress of Trade Unions) until the mid-seventies. Professor McDonagh was President of IFUT in the pre-Congress stage.

On reflection later, some of the external 'junior staff' were to discover that the rules proposed by the Maynooth ASA in the early 1970s were quite restrictive for us at the bottom of the academic staff ladder. They copper-fastened quite a rigid system of promotion and salary differential. What they really did was to adapt the UCD structures to the emerging and expanding NUI Recognised College. Some of us 'young rebels' at the time felt it was more an association of professors and heads of departments, keen on keeping obsolete distinctions, such as restricting the title 'professor' to heads of departments, which was out of date in the United States and in most of the Continental universities. I personally found the dressing-up in ornate gowns, etc. a little bit medieval. Unfortunately, these rituals and rubrics were later being indulged in by most third-level colleges and institutes offering qualifications, i.e. certificates, diplomas and degrees. Degree and diploma-awarding ceremonies were not that much different from some of the more colourful 'high church' religious ceremonies. It would be unreasonable to expect it not to seek to follow the example of UCD! The Jesuit tradition was less ornate!

The role and status of a priest on the full-time staff of Maynooth College was later to become an issue of national controversy. On arrival at the College in 1971, the President, Monsignor Jeremiah Newman, greeted me and wished me well. He reminded me of two things, i.e. priests on the staff always wore their Roman collars during duty hours, and lecturers were expected to wear their academic gowns while lecturing. As a good and obedient private I said '*Yes, Sir*' and honoured my commitment to the 'collar' and the 'gown' (as long as it was required)!

One thing needs to be said about President Newman, namely, he was the founding father of the new Maynooth, especially in sowing the seeds from which the current NUI Maynooth has emerged. It is to be regretted that this fact has not been formally recognised. Organisations have no memory! Once a person's usefulness is gone, the focus is on the current regime. I make these complimentary remarks about Monsignor Jeremiah Newman as one who gave me a hard time later, for whatever reason.

3. The Peace Movement: *Pax Christi*

During the early 1970s I was deeply involved in many movements and action groups, i.e. the peace movement (*Pax Christi*), the Irish language campaign, the promotion of equality of opportunity, participation and achievement in education in Ireland, the defence of Travellers' rights, and the ecumenical movement. Academic staff and students were seriously involved in these movements and many of us were willing to march through Dublin and address mass gatherings in public, even near the Kildare Street gate of Leinster House! All this must have shocked some of the more conservative professors, senior lecturers and administrators. Maybe we, at times, went 'over the top' in expressing our outrage at the ineptitude of the establishment(s) to provide for basic human equality and a precondition of social justice, which, also was a prerequisite of Christian charity! For my fellow protestors and I, people's rights took precedence over cosy systems.

The globalisation of the civil rights movement created a threat to many administrative political, religious, social, economic and cultural systems. The threat to the dominant structures was soon to arouse counter-action against those who would articulate the cause and raise the public awareness of the blatant injustices in Ireland and throughout the world. In the early seventies in Maynooth, the students, and some of the staff, developed a solidarity, centred on campaigning for social justice and peace, as well as the protection of the natural environment. My own research and study of prejudice enabled me to take a hard look at ethnocentrism (prejudice based on nationality and culture), at racism (prejudice based on physical difference), at anti-Semitism (i.e. against the Jews), at sexism (largely prejudice against females), at social-class prejudice (i.e. in Ireland contributing to anti-Traveller attitudes), at homophobia (prejudice against homosexuals), and at other groups and categories who were victims of prejudice and discrimination. It was not surprising that there would be definite reactions by the authorities who had integrated informal discrimination into their systems, e.g. social-class hierarchies, etc. The revolt in Northern Ireland against decades of formal segregation and informal discrimination had repercussions in the Republic as well. Unfortunately, the Northern scene had become very violent and elicited a violently repressive counteraction from the authorities and those paramilitary groups who identified with British rule in Ireland.

It would be arrogant and unjust for the civil rights protesters not to appreciate the concerns of the senior staff in Maynooth who disapproved of our pacifist activism. Their fears were genuine and their tradition was that of respectable restraint, except when taking on the unjust system through their clever use of the pen. In fact, it required great discipline on the part of the activists to resist serious confrontation with authorities. The march in Dublin after Bloody Sunday in 1972 (organised by the Irish Trade Unions) was a case in point, which ended up with violence and arson, i.e. the burning of the British Embassy on Merrion Square, Dublin 2. I was on that march and I tried to intervene outside the Embassy when I saw what was being attempted. I remember standing on the steps of the next house to the Embassy and pointing out (aloud) *'we came to protest and not to burn'*. I was shouted down by a raging and angry crowd. Thank God it rained heavily that afternoon and the damage of the fire was minimal. My fear had been the danger of a person being trapped in the buildings. There was a strong element of 'social contagion' present. It appeared that a scapegoat was necessary and the burning of the British Embassy in Dublin let off steam as a result of the Irish people's anger and frustration at what appeared to be an act of public persecution of innocent marching citizens in the City of Derry on Bloody Sunday. Thank God, the fire had the benefit of calming the people's anger and nobody was injured. Earlier that week nearly every able-bodied student and members of the academic staff marched the fifteen miles from Maynooth to O'Connell Street, Dublin, to voice and demonstrate our collective outrage at the Derry slaughter at the hands of the so-called disciplined British soldiers.

To continue on the post-Bloody Sunday reaction, a massive protest march was organised for Newry, County Down on a Sunday after the massacre. There must have been over three hundred thousand on the march. A large contingent of staff went there from Maynooth. Our contingent began in the *Doirí Beaga* estate and marched down to the centre of Newry. The police warned us that we were breaking the law. We told them to arrest us and find prison places to hold us. The march went off without any violence at all. Unfortunately, the British authorities failed to respond in a just way to the Derry cold-blooded slaughter. This led to a loss of confidence in the British Government and in the authorities in Northern Ireland and swelled the ranks of the Provisional IRA. This, in turn, was to result in acts of violence, which escalated out of control. Northern Ireland became a 'police state' for the next twenty-five years. Over three thousand lives were lost in a relatively small population, while thousands were wounded, imprisoned and intimidated (on all sides) between 1969 and 1994. We soon seemed to become accustomed to the daily slaughter and destruction. A number of abortive efforts were made to intervene, but to little avail. Interest in the Republic was surprisingly less than one would have expected!

In 1970 there was a crisis in Jack Lynch's Government over the support offered in 1969 by a number of Ministers to the beleaguered nationalists, who were being attacked in Belfast by the security forces and other elements. Three senior cabinet ministers were sacked by *An Taoiseach*, Mr Jack Lynch TD, for acting outside cabinet authorisation. The three ministers were Mr Neil Blaney TD (Donegal), Mr Charles Haughey TD (Dublin) and Mr Micheál Ó Móráin TD (Mayo). A fourth minister, Caoimhín Uas Ó Beoláin TD (Dublin), resigned on principle. Messrs Blaney and Haughey were charged before the courts but were not convicted of criminal activity. The mix-up has never been fully clarified and probably never will be. It was a matter of interpretation of what was meant by the Cabinet's decision to assist the victims of violence in Belfast and elsewhere. It was a terrible pity that the United Nations did not intervene when requested by the Government in Dublin. The British Government failed over the years to grasp the 'nettle' that had been stinging the Catholic/Nationalist minority for so long. The people were to pay a terrible price for this failure and the refusal by Britain to admit the United Nations, on the grounds that it was an 'internal matter' (which they could not control). *Bhíomar go léir thíos leis.* (We were all down because of it.)

4. SOCIAL STUDIES AT MAYNOOTH

When the academic year opened in St Patrick's College Maynooth in October 1971 there were only two full-time members on the academic staff to teach sociology – Professor Liam Ryan and myself. We had well over one hundred undergraduate students taking sociology as an arts subject. I was given two courses in first year, *Introduction to Social Psychology* and *Introduction to Cultural Anthropology*. In second and third year I taught courses in *Crime and Deviance, Social Survey Techniques* (including social statistics) and *Social Institutions*. Later I would add courses in *Classical Theory, Sociology of Knowledge* and *Intergroup Relations*. Professor Liam Ryan taught courses in *Introduction to Sociology, Irish Society, Rural and Urban Sociology, Sociology of Religion* and other more specific modules. This heavy load of lecturing put big demands on me, as I was preparing my own research into prejudice and tolerance in Greater Dublin. In UCD I also lectured twice weekly and kept up courses in the College of Industrial Relations. I used to work night and day with great satisfaction. One friend said to me that I was a living example of the 'Protestant ethic', while another detected the makings of a 'workaholic' in me. So be it. It did not worry me. By the following year we would get additional staff, first on a part-time basis. The atmosphere in the Maynooth campus was energisingly informal and most supportive. All lecture halls and offices were in the old campus. Plans for building a new Arts Building in a new Campus were well underway. An over-road pedestrian bridge was to be erected with a floodlight, which the wits called 'Newman *gentium*' (a parody on *Lumen Gentium*). Things were happening still! There was a great spirit on the campus as we set out to expand our university!

In 1972, Mr Richard Nixon was re-elected as President of the United States of America. His second term was to end in disgrace in 1974, because of irregularities associated with unlawful entry to the Democratic Party's Headquarters. The incident became known as 'Watergate'. He permitted atrocities in the use of conventional weapons of mass destruction against the Vietnamese and the Cambodians during his six years in office. He was, however, instrumental in developing dialogue with 'Communist' China, which was generally accepted as a positive move.

May I repeat my reflection on the way our world was developing? We had a major global injustice problem. The so-called Western 'developed' countries were moving towards material standards of living which were wasteful and superfluous. At the same time, the 'developing world' was forced to live on a level of subsistence or at a standard below that. The relatively wealthy countries were to become part of a superpower club, which defended such blatant privileges by means of conventional and (the threat of) nuclear weapons of mass destruction to prevent the weaker peoples from access to wealth. These poorer people, for instance, would resort to non-conventional paramilitary actions, which we call 'terrorism'. The United States was fast becoming leader of the privileged world and this position seemed to have strengthened more during Republican administrations than during Democratic ones – allowing for notable exceptions. (I hope to return to this scenario as the scene unfolds right up to the present day.) To the individual, a privilege becomes a right in a short time!

In the General Election of 1973, the *Fianna Fáil* Government of Mr Jack Lynch TD, was defeated after having negotiated the Republic of Ireland's entry to the *European Economic Community* in 1972. The new inter-party Government of *Fine Gael* and the *Labour Party* was formed under *An Taoiseach*, Mr Liam Cosgrave TD, and *An Tánaiste*, Mr Michael O'Leary TD. During the period in office of the new Government, new regulations were put into Irish law as part of our EEC membership.

The early 1970s were interesting in Ireland, economically, politically and culturally. The economy continued to grow right up to the 'oil crisis' of 1974. There was great euphoria on our joining the Common Market – the EEC (EU) – in 1973. It provided a bonanza for some sectors but hastened the decline of traditional manufacturing and manual work. Our infrastructure (roads especially) benefited, as did the larger farmers.

There was a growth of participation in second-level education following the radical decision of Minister Donagh O'Malley, despite the failure of the move to the provision of 'community schools/colleges' to reach its full potential. There was a marked shift to a more technical curriculum and a decrease in the prominence of the humanities. There was the unfortunate demise of Greek and Latin, partially due to the Church's vernacularisation in its liturgy. The Irish language was also losing its rightful status in the curriculum. Also, competence in the first language would be no longer necessary for Civil Servants serving the people!

In all, we were entering the new era of educational pragmatism. This was to reap benefits later for the growth of the so-called 'Celtic Tiger' in the late 1990s. Such growth was to be weakened later by the drastic reduction in the fertility rate, leaving this country short of future 'Celtic Cubs'. Is the seed of its own demise in a society's materialist success? We were to become very dependent on the immigration of blue-collar workers. (The collapse of 2008 was to expose, once again, the vulnerability of the neo-liberal 'free market' system at a catastrophic cost to the people.)

5. WAR IN NORTHERN IRELAND

The political situation in the North of Ireland continued to enter more deeply into the quagmire of guerrilla war and unimaginative State response. Atrocities filled the print and electronic media headlines and attracted attention from around the globe. Northern Ireland was almost in a state of martial law. Normal life was impossible in certain areas. The Dublin bombings in December 1972 enabled the Lynch Government to pass through very tough emergency legislation, which was later to be enforced by the Coalition Government under Liam Cosgrave TD, (son of the late William T Cosgrave TD, who was head of the Free State Government from 1922-32). Some of the legislation in the Republic appeared over-restrictive to me at the time. The Christian Churches did make a number of efforts to end the paramilitary violence. Two efforts were noteworthy, namely, the Feakle Meeting, and the joint *Inter-Church Working Group on Violence in Ireland*. I was a member of the latter group with Professor Kevin McNamara, Maynooth (who was to become Bishop of Kerry and Archbishop of Dublin later). My involvement in *Pax Christi* kept me in touch with what was going on in the 'peace and justice world'. We hosted a very successful International *Pax Christi* Peace Walk in 1972. It converged on Kilkenny.

The overall effect of the 'Northern Troubles' was not only political. As I said earlier, it reduced the dominant position of the economic institution and restored the political institution to a more pivotal position in Irish society. It also affected normal life in Britain. Economic progress was rendered almost impossible in Northern Ireland in the 1970s. The normalisation of its conflict (i.e. accepting ongoing violence and intimidation as normal) was something that surprised us all. In a sense this proved the resilience of the people to survive in the midst of constant and ongoing violence. Public sympathy in the mass media was very much against the IRA. The media rarely tried to expose the root causes of the problem, i.e. the refusal of the British Government and the Stormont administration to address the injustices and decades of segregation. Once the British Army failed to establish order in an even-handed manner, as exemplified by Bloody Sunday, its credibility was weakened in the view of the minority community. The Royal Ulster Constabulary was seen by many nationalists and Roman Catholics as a Protestant-Unionist Police for a Protestant people. Their failure to protect the minority in Belfast in 1969 only confirmed that widely held view. The reputation of the auxiliary police force, known as 'B Specials', elicited more fear than confidence in certain Catholic communities. The refusal of the United Kingdom Government to admit the *United Nations Peace Force* left prospects bare.

The condition that, in my opinion, would describe best the minority community was that of widespread alienation, that is, a sense of powerlessness. They were 'foreigners' in their own land. The superstructure was so arranged as to prevent Catholics from public positions of effective influence. In a sense, it was not a democratic society, which treated all its citizens as equal. It was to a degree 'majority supremacy' based on an erroneous idea that democracy was the equivalent of exclusive majority rule. A society that denies its minority its right to participate is not democratic. We should always be wary of a society that plays '*the majority card*' to the detriment of members of the minority. This situation exists to a greater or lesser extent in many societies. The original determination of the boundary of Northern Ireland to that of six of the nine counties in Ulster was an attempt to ensure that a majority of the population would be Protestant and Unionist in religious belief and in political allegiance. Many genuine Protestants were convinced that their majority status gave them the right to exercise their authority without sharing power with nearly forty percent of their fellow citizens. This was done in a mistaken interpretation of democracy. I hope that when or if the Catholic nationalists achieve the numerical majority, a reverse situation will not occur. We must never allow the 'tyranny of numerical majority' to happen again in the name of democracy. Democracy must strive to ensure consensus more than majority rule!

The rise of the Nationalist and Loyalist paramilitary wings was inevitable when the relevant authorities were either unable or unwilling to satisfy the needs of and provide protection for the vulnerable communities throughout Northern Ireland. The Republican paramilitaries filled the gap that had been created by the pacifist Civil Rights movement's demise after the outbreak of violence in 1969. To their credit, elected politicians such as John Hume, Gerry Fitt, Paddy Devlin, Austin Currie, Ivan Cooper, Séamus Mallon and other nationalist and alliance politicians, tried valiantly to keep the case for the rights of the minority before the public in an exclusively non-violent manner. Unfortunately, the British Government underestimated the depth of resentment that was pent-up in the minority over the decades. The military and security issues were given priority by the authorities, and repressive measures only added to the problem. The treatment of suspect insurgents in Castlereagh and in Armagh Barracks was to cause grave concern about the standards operated by the security forces. The introduction of *internment without trial* in 1972 was to worsen the situation further and resulted in strengthening the support for the Republican paramilitary groups in the minority communities. The vast majority of the Roman Catholic and Protestant populations in Northern Ireland always favoured the pacifist approach but that was rendered ineffective by the treatment the Civil Rights movement received from the Stormont Administration in 1968-69 and, thereafter, by the predominance of the paramilitary and security force's continuous destructive engagement.

The reaction of the Republic of Ireland to the Troubles in Northern Ireland in the 1970s is quite difficult to appraise in hindsight. Two incidents that raised serious questions in relation to manipulation of Irish public opinion were the bombings in Dublin in 1972 and in 1974 (bombing in Dublin and in Monaghan) carried out by Northern paramilitaries with suspected collaboration of the British and other intelligence services. The 1972 bombing coincided with the voting on special powers' legislation in *Dáil Éireann* and the 1974 massacre also had an ulterior political motive that seemed to involve the State agencies in line with the policies of the perpetrators of these abject actions. With regard to the latter our Gardaí failed to discover who was behind the bombings. We still await the answers from the Northern and British authorities in relation to possible links between their Security Forces and the Loyalist paramilitaries suspected to have been involved in the 1974 bombings.

The (Irish) State opened a number of military barracks on the Republic side of the border. The Army and the Gardaí carried out joint-patrols along the border. The prison in Portlaoise was upgraded to that of a top-security detention place. Military and Gardaí units were to accompany transfer security vans when distributing and collecting cash to and from banks and post offices. All these security measures were to cost the taxpayer a considerable amount of money and, tragically, the life and limb of Gardaí in the exercise of their duty.

In my survey of 1972-73, the attitudes of respondents pointed to a certain 'distancing from the Northern Troubles'. For instance, some 55% of the sample felt that Northerners on both sides were unreasonable. You would almost think that the majority of people had repressed their solidarity with their fellow Irish men and women in Northern Ireland. There was evidence in a later survey in 1988-89 that the Border had succeeded to a degree in creating two different Irish societies in the North and in the Republic, i.e. the emergence of separate but related sub-ethnic societies. (The *two-nations' position* weakened in the findings of the 2007-08 national survey.)

Of course, conditions in the Six Counties had discouraged substantial visitation by people from the Republic. Also, every effort was being made by Stormont to create as much insulation as possible around the six counties, e.g. failure to improve communications between the two parts of the island. This inevitably led to the economic and commercial decline of the local communities each side of the border. The closing of the rail link between Enniskillen and Collooney was an obvious example of such reinforcement of north-south insulation leading to social isolation over the years. Hence, the resultant distancing of the two populations, which enabled authorities in the Republic to 'keep their distance' when the minority in the North were being denied their rights.

We were soon to pay dearly (especially within Northern Ireland) for decades of neglect and Unionist consolidation of power and privilege at the expense of the Nationalist (Catholic) minority. The Unionist argument was that they could not share power with Nationalists, whose political aim was the integration of the six counties into the thirty-two counties. The genius of the *Good Friday Agreement* (1998) was the development of an administration based on consensus rather than on 'majority' democracy. *If the day should come (or when the day comes) that we will have an All-Ireland Dáil and Government it will be essential to ensure mechanisms of consensus be put in place to ensure that a Loyalist minority will not be treated like the Nationalists, who were forced to live in a state of permanent opposition without any say in their own affairs.* The closing of the Stormont administration in 1972, while understandable, was regrettable.

The *Sunningdale Agreement* in 1973 was a serious effort made by the British Government to set up a local administration with power-sharing between Nationalists and Unionists. It shared power between the Social Democratic and Labour Party (SDLP) and the Unionist Party in a devolved Northern Ireland Government. This was an extraordinary breakthrough by the constitutional political forces but it was brought down by the destructive action of extreme loyalist protesting forces. The British Government failed to enforce its own legislation. What a pity! But it did something that would be a model for a future solution to the crisis over twenty years later. John Hume MP was on the ascent to become a competent and courageous Irish leader who was to keep the cause of Northern Ireland before the world. I had the privilege of being a visitor to his family in their home in Derry during the time he was Minister in the power-sharing Government. I learned much from

John Hume in my understanding of the Northern problem. One thing I admired about him was his refusal to carry a firearm while a minister. At the time of my visit to him I was beginning to find out much about the prejudices of the Irish as part of the problem. Prejudice was identified by John Hume as one of 'the most lethal forces', which had poisoned intergroup relations in Northern Ireland. We met later on numerous occasions. He had been a student at St Patrick's College, Maynooth in the late 1950s and early 1960s. From John Hume I got an insight into the material and political damage that paramilitary violence was doing to the economic and community life of the North. It reduced inter-community trust and delayed an acceptable solution. Despite all this he was convinced that a solution was possible and would be realised some day!

6. IRELAND JOINS THE EEC

From 1973 until 1977 a Coalition Government under *An Taoiseach*, Mr Liam Cosgrave TD, was in power in the Republic. During that period there were a number of significant adjustments due to our membership of the EEC. Workers' Rights' legislation, in line with European Community practice, was introduced into Irish legislation. One of the characteristic changes imposed on Ireland was in relation to the watering down of our 'common law tradition' and the enormous increase in European 'codified' laws and regulations. The European system is so cumbersome and bureaucratic that it is likely to elicit a serious backlash in Ireland and the United Kingdom sooner or later. And yet, such European over-codification did not save people from the excesses of dictatorships over the past two hundred years! That being said, some of the new regulations were to be welcomed, such as equality legislation with regard to gender – but, alas, not with regard to social class. It was equality within the classes that the European law was promoting, rather than equality between the classes. (I am very disappointed that the countries of the 'common-law' tradition have allowed the 'over-codified' Roman and Napoleonic tradition to dominate the European Union with the over-regulation of people's lives – to the point that we are no longer free!)

The predominant socio-economic-political ideology of the European

Economic Community has been from the start liberal capitalism based on the ('sacred') free market. Soon, State-sponsored industries would be trimmed of taxpayers' support, and a fertile playing field was provided for multinational manufacturing, distributing and servicing corporations. Collective ownership would not be welcome in such an environment, apart from that of the stock market, with its overriding power of systems and tycoons. The ordinary individual workers would be more powerless (i.e. alienated) in relation to company policy.

Asset-stripping and transfer of productive activity to places where labour and raw materials would be cheapest would become quite normal. In the course of the 1970s we were to witness examples of such turnover but, since Ireland was for the initial decade or so, a country of relatively-speaking low wages and therefore enjoying the 'blessed status' of being 'competitive', we would experience a decade or two of growing manufacturing employment. The Trade Unions were not going to have workers on low wages while companies were enjoying super profits, and pressure for more realistic incomes was growing. The power and influence of multinational ('globalised') companies and the rise of multinational financial and administrative superstructures was an ever-growing expensive burden on the backs of the people as the family and local community were being phased out. (This was all going to collapse in 2008 and expose the dysfunctional structural basis of the 'brave new world'.)

Another change was taking place in the 1970s in Ireland, namely, the substantial growth in participation and achievement in second level education. Immediately this happened, there was a degree of 'educational inflation' in regard to the demanded qualifications for jobs. This happened at a time of de-skilling, which was due to an increase in automation and technology. Most jobs that were classified as skilled in the old regime were now reduced to semi-skilled status, demanding much shorter apprenticeships and so forth. Elaborate mechanisms were devised for quality testing and more technological instruments were operated to produce all kinds of goods. Because of the de-skilling of our workers and, later, the demise of manufacturing jobs (to developing countries and elsewhere with lower labour and raw material costs), Ireland was to witness a steep decline in manual work (skilled, semi-skilled and unskilled) right through the 1970s, 1980s and 1990s. In my own research I found the following class changes in the Dublin samples between 1972-73, 1988-89 and 2007-08.

	1972-73	1988-89	2007-08
1. Upper Class	3.1%	6.9%	4.5%
2. Upper Middle Class	11.0%	15.0%	16.3%
3. Middle Class	19.0%	33.2%	26.9%
4. Working Class	45.8% } 66.9%	27.5% } 44.9%	42.4%*
5. Lower Class	21.1% }	17.4% }	9.9% 52.3%
	(100.0%)	(100.0%)	(100.0%)

* *Note*: The impact of the arrival of foreign migrant workers contributed to some of the changes in the 2007-08 distribution.

This table tells the tale of what had happened in Ireland in the first sixteen years (1973-89) of our membership of the EEC/EU. It really shows the extent of the *embourgeoisment* of the Dublin population. *The continuation of this process would lead inevitably to Irish families seeking only middle-class, non-manual employment for their children and educating them out of the manual occupations.* But, since a basic number of manual labour tasks continue, migrants from the developing countries were recruited to do the jobs that the Irish middle class refused to do. I personally found the decline of manual workers among the Irish to be undesirable.

Loss of the manual skills is not good for the quality of life of the community. *We are told that up to one-third of the human brain is devoted to manual dexterity, etc.* The stage may well be reached when all we will do with our hands will be to operate a computer-related keyboard, to play golf, tennis, etc. Also, we will not have the capacity to create monuments and the crafts of building and other forms of manual activity – apart from the odd artist, who would represent only a very small percentage of the population. One of the ways to restore equality to the skills would be to upgrade them higher than the technological semi-skills. I know this concern about the decline of the blue-collar worker may be considered nostalgic. I assure the reader that it is not a form of romantic nostalgia! All young persons should be encouraged to develop to the full their manual skills, whether they are in instrumental music, in farming, in building, in fitting, in plastering, or in fishing, etc. The 'white-collar' generation, which we are now helping to create, will not know what they are missing! Of course, within the 'professional' occupations we have some requiring manual skills, e.g. medical surgeons, etc.

The decline of traditional industries and commercial services has had serious consequences for communities. It has made life miserable for many, especially at the local community level. The decline of the rural community has been most destructive of the fabric of Irish society, i.e. out-migration of youth, closing of schools, decline of parish clubs and pubs, ageing population, deterioration of postal and commercial services, withdrawal of public transport, increase of loneliness and depression, and so forth, have continued in Ireland since our entry into the EEC and despite of, at times, our (until recently) staggering increase in macro-wealth. I believe that the increase in concentrated urban communities experiencing rapid socio-economic growth with their so-called 'critical masses of population' are also suffering from the reverse ills of the communities which many of the new urban citizens had left behind. The in-migrants to the cities and suburbia did not receive the same support of kinship and rooted neighbourhoods.

7. SOCIAL AND RELIGIOUS CHANGE

Overall in Ireland I have observed a serious increase (since the 1970s) in the four major statistics that signify sociocultural disintegration most eloquently, namely, the homicide rate, the suicide rate, the proportion of the population in prison and domestic break-up. These negative statistics have all increased in the Republic of Ireland since our entry into the EEC. Of course, *post hoc non est propter hoc* (after the event is not necessarily because of the event). One clear cause, in my opinion, has been the decline of the local community with its central unit being the family. The individualism of the new situation was most functional for the social and geographic mobility required by the market-driven new socio-economic order, which has transformed the face of Ireland since we joined the EEC and followed its regulations religiously! The many material benefits, which came to Ireland in the form of the upgrading of the infrastructure and assistance to modernise our schools and hospitals, were badly needed. The people seemed to have been blind to the social and cultural consequences, which our people were paying for material gain. Material gain seemed to be the most important advantage in the minds of our political leaders, irrespective of the price that had to be paid in terms of family and local community decline and the destruction of the physical environment. Social planners seemed to have neglected to a large extent the non-material consequences in their 'development planning'!

The extension of the commercialisation of life, which had already begun with the commercialisation of work, was another change that took place during the last three decades of the twentieth century in Ireland. This was seen most clearly in relation to leisure. Informal self-entertainment was greatly reduced. The practice of family and neighbourly visitation had become less regular. People were to find their entertainment in hotels, clubs, pubs, restaurants, theatres, concerts, etc. The home was to become more private. The arrival of multichannel television made domestic recreation more passive and less creative. It has also urbanised our cultural values and norms. The irony of the improvement of recreational facilities in new houses has been a significant decrease in home entertainment compared with the time when it all happened in the one kitchen-cum-living room!

The change in collective religious practice at home meant the decline of the 'family rosary' or any other form of family prayer. Irish traditional music shifted from the family or the neighbours' houses to the local lounge bar, where it became associated with the drinking of alcohol, thereby increasing further the commercialisation of leisure. Celebration of the main rituals in the life of the person, i.e. baptism, first holy communion, confirmation, marriage and death, were also to shift from the home to the commercialised settings of hotels, clubs and public houses. The celebration of the sacraments was to become more social than religious. These events gradually became more and more expensive and peer pressure forced people even to incur serious debt to keep up with the accepted commercial standards of these ritual observances. The bulk of a couple's wedding gifts went to pay hotels and other professionals, rather than to support the building and furnishing of the newly weds' new home. The self-generating drive to spend even on unnecessary goods and services opened the floodgates of the growing 'credit machine'!

Another area to experience a most striking rate of change was to do with the public collective expression of people's religion. Observance of the Sabbath, which was acknowledged in Europe for more than two thousand years, by 'abstaining from unnecessary servile work' and commercial activity, was to be changed beyond recognition. Megastores and supermarkets were to become more and more the new 'synagogues, temples and cathedrals' of modern Ireland, occupying the fervour of the new worshipping consumer! All forms of sport (amateur and professional) were to occupy the free time of the consumer on the Sabbath. Amateur sports had been part of Sunday recreation for Roman Catholics in Ireland, since the emergence of group sports in the last quarter of the nineteenth century. Many of the Protestant communities did not support even amateur sports on Sundays. To facilitate a Sunday free from the constraints of worship, parishes introduced Saturday evening Masses. Weekly Mass still provided the functions of assembling the local people together to some extent, but to a lesser extent as a pedagogical weekly experience, through which the congregation could deepen its understanding of the 'Word of God'. For many believers weekly Mass was the only opportunity they had to deepen their faith. Very committed believers would seek help in personal prayer, study, pilgrimages, retreats, etc. But for the ordinary conventional Catholic, his or her opportunity for deepening the understanding of the faith was quite limited and dubiously adequate, in my opinion.

Returning to my experience as a junior lecturer and social researcher in the NUI section of St Patrick's College, Maynooth, I found the work very challenging. The students were very easy to work with and they had a good relationship with Professor Liam Ryan and me. We had quite an exhausting schedule. At the same time, Liam and I were working with Father James Lennon of the Research and Development Unit (attached to the Catholic Communications Institute). We carried out a comprehensive *Survey of Catholic Clergy and Religious Personnel 1970* (report published in *Social Studies*, March 1972). The report on this survey must now be one of the key benchmarks, in that it gave the accurate figures for vocations and strength of clergy and religious in Ireland at the time. The beginning of the serious decline in vocations was clearly indicated in the published findings. Unfortunately, follow-up research into the causes of changes in the minds of persons eligible for the priesthood and religious life was not carried out. In the light of the changes in the cultural ethos of the new Ireland, with its rise in materialism, the collapse of vocations by the end of the 1990s and early 2000s seemed almost impossible to prevent, unless the Church was prepared to adapt its requirements to attract young men and women of the new era. Such adaptations have yet to happen. Rereading the report on the 1970 survey must be of great interest to anybody seriously interested in Irish priestly and religious life up to 1970. Our contribution to the Missions was incredibly great and helped to spread the light of the Gospel to all points of the globe.

The 1960s marked the beginning of the decline of this extraordinary witness of total generosity for the love of God and the welfare of the neighbour by Irish religious men and women. In 1970, 19% of the 18,662 Irish Sisters were on Missions abroad, while 49% of the 7,946 Irish male religious were in foreign lands. Of the total of 7,891 Irish priests and religious who were overseas at the time, 55% were in developing countries, while 45% were in developed countries. In the light of what happened in the 1990s to the standing of the clergy and religious (owing to the misbehaviour of a minority), it is good to have on record the level of contribution of dedicated men and women (priests and religious) in the pastoral, medical, educational and social welfare service of the Irish people and of so many communities and parishes abroad. We should also add to that the number of lay missionaries who accompanied the priests, nuns and brothers in far foreign fields for Christ and the love of the neighbour.

Without our priests and religious at home in Ireland, we would not have had schools or hospitals or welfare services to meet the needs of most of the people throughout the first half of the twentieth century. The State gradually took over responsibility for the provision of these needs – it had done so at a great cost to the taxpayer. That is as it should be now. Such resources were not available in earlier decades of this State. Most community services were to depend on the generosity of men and women of dedicated religious orders. Reading commentators in today's media bears out the proverb: '*Eaten bread is soon forgotten!*'

8. THE 1972-73 SURVEY OF INTERGROUP ATTITUDES

From October 1972 until September 1973, I was acting Head of the Department of Social Studies in Maynooth, during Professor Ryan's sabbatical in St Louis University in the United States of America. During that year three new members of staff were to join the Department, initially on a part-time basis, i.e. Eileen Kane (Anthropology), Michel Peillon (Sociology) and Séamus Ó Síocháin (Anthropology). They were to become full-time pillars of our department during the following year. It was also during 1972-73 that I directed the major survey of Intergroup Attitudes in Dublin. The project was sponsored by the Research and Development Unit (CCI) and by the Irish Jesuit Province. The research team consisted of fourteen interviewers, two research assistants, Diane Lonergan and Micheál Ó Gliasáin, and two administrative assistants, Eoin Garrett and Raymond O'Hanlon. Mrs Maria Woulfe was secretary of the survey and continued working in that capacity until the publication of *Prejudice and Tolerance in Ireland* in 1977. The experience of directing this research team was very invigorating.

The 2,311 respondents interviewed were the real contributors to the findings. It was an extraordinary collective act of generosity by so many people of all ages, educational standards, occupational status, social class positions, residential areas, places of origin, religious denominations, marital status, genders, ethnic backgrounds and racial groups. This social survey was, in effect, a consultation of the population of Greater Dublin – urban and suburban areas. The average duration of the interview was fifty minutes. The skill of the interviewers was most impressive. The fieldwork, i.e. interviews, was carried out between 28th August 1972 and 3rd April 1973. During the period from April 1973 and July 1974, research assistant Micheál Ó Gliasáin and myself worked on coding and transferring the data onto punch cards (with eleven cards of data) for each questionnaire. This meant that there were 25,421 punch cards of data in the pack or almost two megabytes, i.e. two million plus bytes of data.

Two Reports from the findings were published in 1974, i.e. *Church Attendance and Religious Practice of Dublin Adults*, and *Educational Opportunities in Dublin*. The former Report was presented to a special meeting of the Irish Hierarchy held in Mulranny, County Mayo, in the spring of 1974, and received much praise. The Report on Education participation was widely commented on in the national media and raised awareness of educational inequality in Dublin City (between residents of the different city postal areas and the suburban and exurban areas).

In March of 1974 I applied for one year's leave of absence without pay, from October 1974 until September 1975, to avail of a Ford

Foundation Scholarship in the University of Michigan, Ann Arbor, in the United States (i.e. two terms studying social survey research data analysis) and time to complete the analysis of the Dublin Survey. My PhD Thesis was based on the findings. To my utter dismay my application was not granted. Instead, the Trustees gave me permission to resign my position as a junior lecturer in the College and to 'feel free to apply' for such a job in Maynooth on completion of my research. They also intimated that I should have had their permission before applying for the Ford Foundation Scholarship. My reaction was one of incredulity that the same Bishops, who had already praised my work in the *Church Attendance Report*, could refuse my application for a year's leave of absence without pay.

My reply was to say that I would inform the Ford Foundation of my inability to get a year's leave of absence and decline its offer to me. I did not want to lose my position as a 'lecturer' in Maynooth. The reason given by the Secretary of the Trustees was that since I was still on probation, i.e. a year-to-year basis, it was not legally possible to give me a year's leave of absence. I offered to reduce the year to eleven months but this did not make any difference. I felt, at the time, that I was seen by some of the authorities to be too outspoken on social issues. My Provincial, Father Cecil McGarry SJ, wrote to Cardinal William Conway, Chairperson of the Trustees, seeking an explanation. Also, Father James Lennon, Director of the Research and Development Unit, made enquiries on my behalf – all to no avail. My union (IFUT) Maynooth, offered to fight my forced resignation. It was a most stressful time for me.

In April 1974, the President, Monsignor Jeremiah Newman, was appointed Bishop of Limerick and he was succeeded by Monsignor Tomás Ó Fiaich, who had been Professor of Modern History in Maynooth. The new President advised me not to cancel my plans to complete my research. At their June 1974 meeting of the Trustees, the March meeting minutes were amended to read that I would be guaranteed appointment as a junior lecturer in Sociology at the end of my year's research 'in the normal course of events'. When I asked the President what was meant by the 'normal course of events', he said that it meant that 'the person who left would be the person returning'. And *'What would make me different?'* I asked. The President suggested that *if I married in the meantime I would be different.* He then laughed heartily! He also said I would continue my membership of the special joint-committee on the future of Maynooth during 1974 to 1975.

Because I trusted Monsignor Tomás Ó Fiaich, I accepted having to surrender to a break in my employment and deferring my promotion to lecturer, which I was entitled to in 1974 after completing three years' probation as a junior lecturer. This experience once again highlighted the feudal structure of a university, which made a negative decision in my regard without even giving me the reasons for their refusal of my application. The Trustees' decision was within their legal rights, no doubt, but it was a severe blow for me who had always respected the bishops and still do. In all my time after that on the lecturing staff, I never applied for sabbatical or leave of absence again. I refused to apply on principle. Was I 'cutting off my nose to spite my face'?

The reason why I include this unpleasant episode in my early academic (staff) years is to highlight how difficult it must have been for the college to adapt to change and cope with employees' rights not in its control. The seminary-cum-university had been run for almost two hundred years (since 1795) by a strict Church hierarchy. The arrival of lay staff and active trade unionists required a new industrial relations structure and procedures. Dialogue between unions and management had to be worked out. My case highlighted the slow transition from the old regime to the new! Therefore, I understand what happened to me without necessarily condoning it. Despite having to operate under such a regime, an atmosphere of genuine friendliness was maintained on the ground under the bishops.

With the Ó Fiaich compromise in my pocket, I tried to put Maynooth behind me and concentrate my mind on the analysis of my huge basket of social research data. It was one of the biggest surveys of Irish inter-group attitudes ever carried out in Ireland. I remember the great sense of thrill when the first findings were 'coughed out' by the noisy computer. It was like observing 'a child being born out of the womb of the computer'. My hypotheses had anticipated many of the findings. This was a requirement in any true research that would have scientific standing. The Director of the CIR, Fr John Brady SJ, gave me an office for the purpose of processing and analysing the data. Micheál Ó Gliasáin and Maria Woulfe continued working as research assistant and secretary. Despite the usual difficulties, the research went according to plan.

The experience in Ann Arbor (University of Michigan) during the summer of 1974 was most valuable from many points of view. The campus was so large that it had an internal shuttle-bus service. The quality of the courses was very good and most useful to me in my data-analysis work. The Ann Arbor software programme OISIRIS was also suitable for some of my scale analysis. University College Dublin at the time had the OISIRIS and the SPSS programmes.

Before going to Ann Arbor I had a keen interest in the renowned cultural anthropologist, Leslie White, who was a professor in the University of Michigan for years. When I made enquiries about him on arrival, I was told that he had just retired to a town in California. Leslie White was quite agnostic if not atheistic, in his approach to religion and many were surprised that I had such an interest in his work. His religious views were his own affair. After all, we believe faith is a gift. Therefore, why should we blame people for not having it? White's sociocultural determinism irked many 'psychologistic thinkers', who seemed to see all explanation in the personality. Of course, it could have been argued that White also erred, when neglecting the unique role of the individual person in the life and development of his or her society. White also was a macro-anthropologist and was one of the great cultural evolutionists, which would also make him an 'adversary' of those who refused to accept even the possibility of the evolution hypothesis. It was said that his classes in Ann Arbor were often stirring affairs, with anti-evolutionists and keen believers raising their voices in opposition to his eloquent teaching. It was a disappointment for me not to have met Leslie White, whose writings I had studied and taught.

While at Ann Arbor, the impeachment hearings against President Richard Nixon were being publicly transmitted on the television news channels. It was in a way a little sad to see the Head of State being tried by his parliament in public. Eventually, he was forced to resign and an Ann Arbor alumnus, President Gerald Ford, succeeded him. It was during President Ford's 'reign' that the United States withdrew from Vietnam in April 1975, after failing to win a war that was really unwinnable. The lessons learned by the defeat of the US in Vietnam and its decision to withdraw were noteworthy. It showed the power that the pacifists and intellectuals within the US had to persuade their Government to listen to the voice of reason. By losing the war in Vietnam, the people of the

United States won the peace at home and restored international respect abroad for their moral courage.

Unfortunately, subsequent events would show that the lessons of Vietnam had a limited 'sell by' time. The American sociologist, C Wright Mills, in his famous book, *The Power Elite* (New York, Oxford University Press, 1956), would seem to indicate that the real movers behind public administrative decisions, often resulting in war-like and other forms of pre-emptive interventions, were the military-industrial-commercial power elites, who invariably got their representatives into Washington DC to legitimise their vested interests. It would be quite rare for the non-aligned citizens to muster and maintain support against the interests of those most powerful elites. If that was so, real democracy has limited effective power. Modern corporations, many of them multinational, are also 'plugged into' the power-elites' network! The mystery of 1975 was the temporary defeat of the power-elite network in the US and the rise of the 'student and worker peasantry' if I may speak allegorically!

A movement that was to influence the revival of devotion in the Catholic Church had been promoted on the Ann Arbor campus by two Jesuit scholastics and others sometime before I arrived there. It was to be known as the Catholic Charismatic Renewal Movement. To my shame I did not even attend a meeting of the movement during my time on the campus I was so preoccupied with study and research. Also, I was not very keen on the 'charismatic expression' of personal devotion, as it appeared too emotional for me. That was not to say that it did not help others who were feeling empty as a result of some of the post-Vatican Two austere forms of devotion. In the late 1970s and 1980s the Charismatic Renewal Movement spread throughout the Catholic world. It also gained a very large following in Ireland and throughout Europe. But it was very much a spiritually 'expressive' movement rather than a pastorally 'instrumental' one. The latter was more to my liking.

The status and condition of the Native American People, (i.e. the American Indians), many of whom had been insulated in the reservations, had begun to arouse the conscience of the Civil Rights' supporters. While in Ann Arbor I joined the *Wounded-Knee Society*, a movement, which had tried to win justice and recognition for the wrongs done to the Sioux and other Tribes in the nineteenth and early-twentieth centuries. My earlier experience of interviewing Native American young people on a special 're-location course' in Detroit back in 1966 had alerted me to the tragic plight of these noble people, whose ancestors were victims of a form of genocide by the European invaders of their land. The more I got to know the situation the more I felt drawn to their cause.

Later (in the 1990s) when I was appointed to the position of Chairperson of the PTAA, I proposed that we should promote the association among the Native American tribes, many of whose members were being destroyed by addiction to alcohol. (Unfortunately, I have not been able to generate sufficient interest so far among our American Pioneers to spread the movement beyond the Irish-American community.) I often felt a sense of collective guilt and sadness because of the way in which the Irish-Americans (as part of the European colonisers of the United States territories) treated the Native Americans over the centuries. While in Ann Arbor I read about the adventures of General Wild Anthony Wayne (after whom Wayne County was named) and how he mistreated tribes on the Michigan Peninsula. President Jackson, 1767-1845, (of Irish origin) in the early nineteenth century treated the Native Americans with callous cruelty and expelled them from their lands in the eastern States to reservations near the Rocky Mountains. Alcohol was used by the colonisers to weaken the spirit of the people. The PTAA could help to restore their strength and freedom. Anthropologists have pointed out that the Native Americans had given much, in the area of vegetables, fruit and medicines, to the Europeans, who occupied their lands. We in Europe have benefited enormously from the food and medicines developed by the Native Americans.

During my time in Ann Arbor, I also attended the *Annual Conference of the American Sociological Society Association*, which was held in Toronto, Canada, in 1974. It was a massive meeting and the mood was dynamic. It was good to listen to some of the great American sociologists of the time including Talcott Parsons, Joseph Fichter SJ, Robert K Merton, Harry Johnson, Harold Garfinkel, Neil Smelser and others. Toronto was a city with a different ethos from the cities of the mid-west of the USA. At the Conference I joined the company of my old friends from Kent State University, Professor Chuck Hildebrandt and his wife, Judy. The conversation was of high quality and we were entertained to rich comments on the weaknesses and strengths of current society from the sociological perspective. It impressed me how critical some of the authors were of the cultural patterns and values of the US and Canada. In general, sociologists are very much focussed on the patterns of social behaviour, with a 'weather eye' on the causes and effects of social and cultural change. After attending a major conference one returns with new ideas, new questions and renewal of personal contact with colleagues. As one wise professor told me – *'A well prepared and clearly delivered lecture is as good as a book.'* That is, to the perceptive student or listener.

I returned to Dublin (College of Industrial Relations, Ranelagh) in October 1974 and spent the next year working on the data and findings of the Greater Dublin social survey of intergroup attitudes. The period in Ann Arbor was most useful, if not essential, for the applications of proper data-analysis technique. The testing of hypotheses was the main scientific task. I adapted the *psycho-socio-cultural theoretical approach* to the findings in order to reach some level of explanation of the variations between the scale-scores of different samples, i.e. age, gender, education, marital status, area of residence, place of origin, occupational status, social class position, religious affiliation, religious practice, political affiliation (or support), level of authoritarianism, etc. There was one independent variable that I had neglected to measure during the fieldwork, namely, the level of anomie (or normlessness), which I also found out later was significantly correlated to social prejudice. It is by our omissions and mistakes we learn! Mr Micheál Ó Glaisáin and Mrs Maria Woulfe were part of my reduced research team. We worked very well together.

By December 1975 I was ready to submit my PhD Research Thesis, entitled *Intergroup Attitudes in Ireland,* based on a survey of the attitudes of a random sample of Greater Urban and Suburban Dublin and other published reports. It was a very large typed document, i.e. over 1,100 pages in two volumes. At this stage, Rev Dr Conor Ward had become professor of Social Science in UCD after the appointment of Professor James Kavanagh as an Auxiliary Bishop of Dublin archdiocese. That meant that Conor Ward would be my new official thesis adviser, although Bishop James Kavanagh continued to advise and assist me in the preparation of the final text. Professor Ward discussed with me my choice of external examiner. I suggested that he ask the most qualified and established sociologist available. I felt if I was going to be awarded the PhD or rejected because of the inadequacy of my work, it would have to be by one whose standing and ability I respected most. He invited Professor Robert K Merton of Colombia University, New York, who ranked among the leading sociologists at the time. His text, *Social Theory and Social Structure*, was widely recognised in English-speaking universities around the world. I came across his work in Leuven (Belgium), in Kent State University (USA), and in University College Dublin (Ireland), and I was impressed by his interpretation of structural functionalism as a theory. I had not known him personally although I attended two conferences where he spoke.

Letting Professor Robert K Merton decide on my work was a risk I was prepared to take. In fact, I felt humbled that the great professor agreed to become the external examiner and was willing to 'plough through' over eleven hundred pages of text and tables. The 'die was cast' and I had to wait fourteen weeks before I was given a most positive result, which recommended that the thesis be 'published in full'. This was the highest award! Professor Merton added the further comment (as told to me by Professor Ward) that in his opinion, the text was a 'benchmark' in inter-group attitudes research in Ireland. All this information came to me on the telephone in the spring of 1976. It was a most satisfactory result, which made all the hassle and years of 'academic slavery' worthwhile. I was very honoured that my parents and family were able to attend the relatively simple graduation ceremony. Dr Joyce O'Connor was conferred on the same day. We were the first two graduates to be awarded a PhD in Sociology in the National University of Ireland (as far as I know).

Before leaving the early 1970s, I would like to reflect on two interesting visits abroad, i.e. one to Geneva in Switzerland and another to Stockholm and Uppsala in Sweden. Both occasions were related to lecturing on prejudice and tolerance. The visit to Geneva (summer 1972) was on invitation from the *United Nations Association (UNA),* which represented non-governmental organisations throughout the world. I was asked to lecture at a special summer school on the topic of racial and ethnic prejudice. The students were mainly from Western 'developed' countries, with a minority from the 'developing world'. The chief executive of the UNA was a Mr Perrera from Ceylon and I had a number of conversations with him. Mr Perrera's daughter was secretary of the Research and Development Unit in Dublin. He noted the great tension and mutual distrust between the West and the East in Europe.

Also, Switzerland was very well policed and 'big brother' had nearly everybody in his sights – especially, foreigners like us on the course. The members of the international student body were very tolerant and friendly. Questions relating to decolonisation and desegregation were openly discussed. I learned as much as I taught. My visit to Geneva was prior to Ireland's entry into the EEC.

In November 1973, I was invited to give a lecture on Social Prejudice in the chamber of the Old House of Parliament in Stockholm, which had been vacated by the members for a more modern building. (Since that time the MPs have returned to their Old House of Parliament.) The lecture was under the auspices of UNESCO. It was quite challenging but I did not feel intimidated. The questions were most probing. One could capture the liberated ethos of the Swedish activists. Their commitment to civil rights was very genuine.

My second lecture was in the University of Uppsala on the theme of Christian Pacifism. It was organised by the 'pacifist Trotskyites'. Their philosophy was centred on 'ongoing social revolution' in a strictly pacifist manner. While in Uppsala, I visited the tomb of the late Dag Hammarskjöld, the Secretary General of the United Nations, who was killed in a suspicious plane crash in Northern Zambia during the troubles in the Congo at the end of the 1950s and beginning of the 1960s. (When in Zambia later, i.e. 2004, I passed by the spot where the Secretary General's plane crashed.) Dag Hammarskjöld was a very sincere Christian and was most spiritual in his writings. The real value to me of these two visits was that it enabled me to get to know the open outlook of intelligent and enlightened people (mostly young) who were committed to a better world. The ethos of the young population was temporarily liberal and affectionate! Ms Ulla Gudmundson organised my programme during the Swedish visit.

9. *BÁS* ÉAMON DE VALERA (1882-1975)

On Friday 29th August 1975, Éamon Uasal de Valera died in Linden House Nursing Home in Dublin, after a short illness, RIP He was ninety-three years of age. In 1973, he had retired from the office of *Uachtarán na hÉireann* after completing two seven-year terms. He was the last surviving leader of the 1916 Rising. I had always promised I would take a day off work for his funeral, which I duly did. I was among the many concelebrants in the Pro-Cathedral, Marlborough Street, Dublin, for his requiem Mass, which was attended by Heads of State and many eminent Irish people. After the Mass I went to Glasnevin Cemetery, where his remains were laid to rest in the Republican Plot. Priests had a special corral assigned to them near the grave. His Mass and burial was in Irish and Latin (with not a word of English). His grandson, *An t-Ath* Seán Ó Cuív CC, was the chief celebrant. The full *Stabat Mater* was sung in Gregorian chant. It was a most fitting Christian farewell for a man who was 'larger than life' and had been one of the great architects of the young Irish State.

Mr de Valera had the courage and humility to become a 'bridge-builder' after the unfortunate Civil War. During his twenty-four years as Head of Government he had to steer Ireland through very hard times – mostly caused by circumstances outside the country's control. At a time in the 1930s when fascism was popular in Europe, de Valera desisted from assuming non-democratic power and strove to prevent others from doing so. The *Bunreacht* (Constitution), which he brought before the people in 1937, enshrined the basis of democracy and the rule of law. He was also positive, when in opposition. Of course, he had limitations, and was a man of his times, having to operate within the social, economic and cultural constraints of his generation. At times he did not win total consensus. His stand on Irish neutrality during the Second World War had almost full support in the *Dáil*.

Éamon de Valera was not a *'polaiteoir arún'* (i.e. a universally popular politician). While he generated great loyalty from his followers, few people were neutral in relation to Mr de Valera. He benefited from his opposition, in my opinion. The fact that he had to contest the office of *Uachtarán na hÉireann* each time (in 1959 and again in 1966) bore out his controversial status and the enduring contention in relation to this great Irish hero. I believe that de Valera would have wished it to be no other way. For him, a fair opposition was an essential dimension of democracy. He never sought, nor did he receive, 'fear, favour or affection' in the inequitable sense. Of course, for me, he was a great role model. His deep Christian faith and his generous patriotism were examples to be followed. Also, he was a good family man and, despite his high office and length of time in the most powerful office in the State, he tried to keep his lifestyle modest. In the 1930s he believed in a 'maximum income policy', i.e. a salary above which nobody would be entitled. He is reported to have said in the late 1930s that *nobody was worth more than one thousand pounds a year to the State*. This would also be a position I would agree with totally. *Ar dheis Dé go raibh a anam uasal.*

10. PUBLICATION OF *PREJUDICE AND TOLERANCE IN IRELAND*

Once I completed my one-year's retirement from my job as junior lecturer in sociology in the NUI Section of St Patrick's College, Maynooth, I returned to the College, where I was once again appointed a junior lecturer. President Tomás Ó Fiaich offered to put me on the fourth years' junior lecturer's scale, which I accepted. The question of my promotion to the lecturer grade was to be deferred for another year. The net position now meant that I had lost two years' seniority, as well as a break in service, which were hard to take. But I was not in Maynooth for the money. Still, it vexed me to be denied what I considered to be my rights. In St Ignatius' ideal of 'the third degree of humility', which each good Jesuit should aspire to, we should welcome failure rather than success, if it be for the betterment of our souls!

On reflection, this negative encounter with the Maynooth bureaucracy was very good for me and strengthened me morally to face other occasions of humiliation. I tried to avoid the martyr's complex and worked even harder for the welfare of the College in the Academic Staff Association and in the Department of Social Studies, where our full-time staff increased to five and the subject of sociology had become very popular. We offered a very rich curriculum of sociology with supportive courses in social psychology and cultural anthropology. The Department adopted a more 'theoretical' approach to the subject rather than an 'applied' one.

Once I learned that my PhD thesis had been accepted and that it was a 'publish-in-full' verdict, I immediately set out to prepare the text for publication as a book. This required a small amount of editing and translating some of the 'jargon' into readable English, without watering down or popularising the contents. My aim was to produce a precise but readable college textbook that would also have a broader appeal. Journalist John Armstrong (*The Irish Times*) was an enormous help to me in proof-reading and editing the text. Since the project did not qualify for any major research grant, the text was published by the (Jesuit) College of Industrial Relations (CIR). The Jesuit Provincial gave me permission to proceed and advised that the published text should be priced within the reach of students. Profit was not to be an issue. In fact, the Jesuits subsidised the text to the tune of one pound per copy for the 2,500 copies sold in Ireland. The *Leinster Leader Limited,* Naas, County Kildare, agreed to print the text and did so at a reasonable price and at a high standard. It was to become one of the last books printed with lead type.

The title of the published text was: *Prejudice and Tolerance in Ireland (based on a Survey of Intergroup Attitudes of a Sample of the Greater Dublin Urban and Suburban Population).* It was published in 1977 and aroused great interest. One of the most significant reviews was written by the then Minister for Post and Telegraph, Mr Conor Cruise O'Brien TD. His review took half a page in *The Irish Times.* While he did question some specific findings, his overall judgement was that the book was an important contribution to Irish self-awareness. The editor of the *Irish Press,* Mr Tim Pat Coogan, also praised the contribution of the book as providing material that would enter into the consciousness of Irish society. Mr Frank Delaney of the BBC reviewed *Prejudice and Tolerance in Ireland* most positively, and interviewed me in Maynooth. A relatively new reporter in RTÉ, and former lecturer in Bolton Street College of Technology, displayed an impressive familiarity with the findings in his review of the text on *Radio One.* The reporter/commentator was Mr Pat Kenny. While most reviews were very positive and even flattering, there were some who did not show such praise of the text. One commentator wrote that some of what I put down as prejudices were more often principles! The most serious criticism came from a particular sociologist who seemed to question the value of the social survey (questionnaire/ interview) methodology. She also implied that I displayed a structural-functional theoretical bias. She seemed to conclude that of its kind, *Prejudice and Tolerance in Ireland* was good and true to its quantitative methodology and sociological theory, but she questioned both the theory and the method used in the arrival at the findings. I accepted her criticism as valid, but, of course, I disagreed with it. Sociologist Professor Paul Besanceny SJ, (of Detroit, USA) wrote a most positive review of the book and pointed out a number of marginal errors. Professor Liam Ryan of Maynooth was very supportive of the work. Putting everything together, I was very pleased with the public reception the text received. The hardback edition of a thousand copies sold out in a relatively short time, which was considered very good for a work of its kind.

In the late summer of 1977, I was invited to take part in the British-Irish Conference in Oxford University, at which Dr Conor Cruise O'Brien (the former Minister for Post and Telegraph) was a key speaker. I brought a car-boot load of my books and all of them were sold. The British-Irish Conference was an occasion when political leaders from the nationalist and unionist camps would interact in a top security environment. Members of the Irish and British governments and opposition political parties also took part. It was my first encounter with a number of political personalities from Britain and Northern Ireland who were featured regularly in the Irish and British media. Among the politicians I met there were Terence O'Neill (Lord), former Prime Minister of Northern Ireland, Paddy Devlin of the SDLP and others. Lord Longford chaired my brief intervention. I would later encounter his brilliant daughter, Antonia Fraser. It felt a little unreal for me to be asked to autograph my book for some fairly 'hardline' Unionists. Unfortunately, neither the Democratic Unionist nor the *Sinn Féin* leaders were present to share their ideas. What the British-Irish Conference in Oxford taught me was the genuine desire (or at least willingness) on the part of the Unionists and Nationalists; Tories, British Labourites and Liberals; and *Fianna Fáil, Fine Gael* and Irish Labourites, to come together 'in conclave' to exchange views on the 'Irish problem'.

In November of 1977, I received a telephone call one evening from Mrs Jane Ewart-Biggs, widow of the assassinated British Ambassador to Ireland, the late Christopher Ewart-Biggs, to inform me that my book had been read by a panel of six international assessors, who recommended that I should be a joint awardee of the first *Christopher Ewart-Biggs Memorial Peace Prize*. She asked me if I would be willing to accept the prize. I said, without any hesitation, that I would be honoured to do so.

Christopher Ewart-Biggs was assassinated on his way to work in the British Embassy from his home on 6th July 1976. I found the assassination to be outrageous and against the basic principles and practices of international mutual recognition of a State's autonomy. The Ambassador to Ireland from the United Kingdom was a concrete witness to the independence of the Republic of Ireland in the judgement and opinion of the former coloniser. A date was fixed for the award ceremony, which I willingly attended in London with the other joint-recipient, the Unionist historian, Dr ATQ Stewart of the Queen's University, Belfast. After the award we were entertained to dinner at the Garrick Club by the panel of assessors who included Graham Greene (the novelist), Antonia Fraser, Máire Cruise O'Brien, and representatives from France and Belgium. I was seated with Graham Greene, who was a most 'ordinary man' to meet. We discussed some of his work and his views of the Catholic Church, which he felt had lost some of its character after the liturgical changes brought about by Vatican Two. In reply to my question on why he had not written a novel involving the Church's ethos in Ireland, he said that it would take too much time and detailed research to do such a work – although it might be of great interest. He impressed me as a man who thought seriously about life. I had always admired his writing skills.

On my return to Ireland, after receiving the *Christopher Ewart-Biggs Memorial Peace Prize*, a storm was breaking out in *Conradh na Gaeilge*. A distinguished veteran Irish Republican (whose name I was not told at the time) had written to *Conradh na Gaeilge* objecting to my receiving the prize in honour of the assassinated British Ambassador, since I was a member of *Coiste an Airgid* (The Executive Committee of *Conradh na Gaeilge*). By so doing (according to the complainant) I was in violation of the objective/aim of *Conradh na Gaeilge*, namely *'Éire Saor Gaolach'* (a Free Irish Ireland). On the Saturday after my return from London, I attended a meeting of *An Coiste Gnó* (the Board of the *Conradh*). The question was raised by a person, who was not a member of *Coiste an Airgid*, asking about *'an litir'* (the letter). It was clear to me that there was some sort of a conspiracy being 'churned up'. When asked, I answered that I willingly accepted the honour of the *Christopher Ewart-Biggs Memorial Peace Prize*, as a way of promoting *'peace and understanding between the peoples of Ireland and between the peoples of Europe'*. I claimed that I had the right to serve my country as best I could. I did not expect others to agree with my way of doing so. It was a matter of principle, i.e. the principle of my freedom. I was informed by a member of the *Coiste Gnó*, that membership of an organisation limited that freedom. But I did not see my action in accepting the prize as contravening the aims of *Conradh na Gaeilge.* Incidentally, I had not applied for the *Christopher Ewart-Biggs Memorial Peace Prize.*

The row over the Ewart-Biggs Prize soon hit the national media headlines. I was interviewed on the telephone by the *Evening Press* one morning at breakfast time and asked if I would return the prize, because of the objections within *An Chonradh.* I said that I felt honoured by being nominated for the prize and had no intention of returning it. Soon, letters poured in from all over the country. I received some sixty-four letters of support from branches (*Craobhacha*) of *An Chonradh.*

It finally came to a head at the meeting of *An Choiste Gnó* on the 12th December 1977. For me this was the 'meeting of the long knives'. A motion was before the meeting offering me three choices:

(1) to give back the Ewart-Biggs prize;

(2) failing that, resign from the *Conradh*, etc.;

(3) failing these two options, face expulsion.

This motion came from *Coiste Chathair Bhaile Átha Cliath* (the Dublin District Committee). I refused to give back the prize or to resign my position in *Conradh na Gaeilge* and said I would fight option number three. After a lengthy debate, the President proposed a compromise motion not necessarily agreeing with my accepting the Ewart-Biggs prize but asserting my right to do so. This compromise motion was carried by over two to one (with seven votes against). I suppose I had no option but to accept the compromise.

The whole episode was unfortunate and reflected the re-entry of the influence of strong Republican sentiments into the *Conradh.* The 'troubles' in the North of Ireland in the late 1970s were very nasty and a certain spin-off south of the Border was also inevitable. I understood perfectly the interpretation certain Republican sympathisers would put on my action of accepting the Christopher Ewart-Biggs prize. But, where they were wrong was in trying to impose that interpretation on me or on anybody else. This, in my opinion, contradicted the aim of Irish freedom, which meant nothing if it did not respect the person's right to promote his or her community in a different manner. That would be intolerable, in my view. The aftermath of this crisis continued for some time to polarise positions throughout the organisation. I was shunted into the media and my privacy was invaded. A series of feature articles in *An Phoblacht* tried to denigrate me for accepting the prize. At one stage, I felt things were getting out-of-hand, and I said so to the then President of *Sinn Féin,* Ruairí Ó Brádaigh. After that the abusive articles seemed to cool down a little. I am glad to say that despite the crisis, I remained on good terms with most of the members of *Conradh na Gaeilge* who took a stand against me.

11. DEATH OF MY FATHER, AUSTIN (1893 – 1976)

On 24th December 1976 (Christmas Eve), after three weeks' illness, my father, Austin, died at the age of eighty-three-and-a-half years, RIP. I felt very empty on his departure. The death of one's parent is a very traumatic experience. It makes brothers and sisters of us all. My mother decided not to remove the remains from the Sacred Heart Home, Castlebar, until St Stephen's Day, with burial on the following day in Aughaval Cemetery. He was buried in the traditional way (at his request), i.e. the grave was filled in by his neighbours while the rosary was recited. The Irish greeting on the death of a loved one – *'Is oth liom do bhris'* (I regret your break) – grasped very accurately the feeling of parting, i.e. the break.

It took me some eighteen months to get over the loss of my father. Acceptance came in a meditation on death. St Ignatius advised that we imagine our death in a very real way by imagining our corpse in the coffin as it was being lowered into the grave. While trying to do the Ignatian meditation on death I drifted into a daydream. I thought I was in my coffin, which was very well lit up, velvety, etc. on the inside, as it was resting beside my father's coffin in the family grave. In my (very realistic) dream, I heard a knock on the side board of my coffin and I opened it to find my father reaching over his hand to me from his coffin and saying: *'Micheál, you're welcome'*. I immediately woke from my daydream with a totally new disposition towards my father's death. I would no longer look back to his illness and death, but, rather, look forward to meeting in that beautiful place! It made heaven more real and personal for me. This is not to underrate the pain of the break but it ended it with a longing to meet again. *Ar dheis Dé go raibh a anam dílis.* (For me, death is the incarnation in reverse, i.e. we go from our current state of becoming to sharing in the fullness of being in the company of God and all the family of Heaven [including my parents].)

After my father's death in 1976, my mother was left on her own. She also took nearly eighteen months to adjust fully to his leaving us. When the change came, she would love to talk about the wonderful times they had together. She even told me that they met for the first time 'on the train from Maam Cross to Galway'. The following Christmas when I was putting the memorial notice in the *Mayo News*, she asked me to add this statement: *'Memories are something that even death cannot destroy'*. I have noted this power of memories at work in the lives of many bereaved people ever since. But it is not possible to part with a loved one without feeling the painful sense of emptiness and loss. It takes time before we can begin to relive our memories and look forward to joining them in the company of God and the saints. This looking back at happy memories and looking forward to the final reunion are totally compatible ways of coping with the sad loss of a parent, spouse, child or other loved one. Following the death of my father on Christmas Eve, the celebration of the season of Christ's birth has been richer for our family. It also sharpened my understanding of Christmas as also a celebration of Christ's second coming in death. The death of each of us is a unique type of Christmas celebration, i.e. when we experience Christ's second coming to us personally. For that reason, death at Christmas time is spiritually appropriate. Those of us who live in the northern hemisphere experience the winter season during Christmas, which is also the most natural time to die!

After the death of my father, my mother lived on her own in our home in Drummindoo, Westport. To live alone was the destiny of quite a number of widows living in our parish. Members of the family strove to visit my mother regularly and we arranged to rotate our stays at home and stagger our holidays accordingly. My mother's next-door neighbours were very supportive. My brother Pádraig and his family, who lived in Westport, were a great support. She had a great rapport with teenagers and young adults. The neighbours, Anne and Michael Murphy, Johnnie and Ellen Reynolds, and Bridie and John Geraghty were better than any of us could have been to my late mother.

Still, I worried about her being on her own, within a mile and a quarter from the town of Westport. One day I asked her if she felt lonely living on her own. *'Where is your faith?'* she replied. *'I am never on my own, because I believe that the Lord is always present with me.'* That put me in my place! Only then did I discover the depth of my mother's faith having reached the mystical stage of living in the continuous conscious presence of Our Lord. I later discovered that she had a rosary hidden under the rug she had around her knees when sitting by the fire. She would be very annoyed if she thought I should praise her deep religious life. She was most discreet about her personal devotions. She did not wear her religion on her sleeve. Another day she said to me that she wished to remain in her own home as long as she had her senses. If it should happen that she were to suffer from serious dementia or Alzheimer's disease, we were to find a place for her in a nursing home. She would not wish to be at home when she was not able to grasp what was going on. (Thank God, it was not necessary to find a home for her outside her 'own corner'.)

The lot of parents spending their final years on their own was a relatively new phenomenon in Irish society. It was due to two changes in family life. The first of these was the practice of neolocality, i.e. almost all newly-weds building, purchasing or renting a house for their new family and the decline of the practice of patrilocality or matrilocality, namely, the son or daughter (getting the place) living in the parents' home. This has had serious consequences for the expansion of housing needs and also, for the caring of the elderly in their own homes. Éamon de Valera's idea of the building of a second home on the farm made great sense if the people's concern was the support of a higher quality of life for the family. It is still not too late to revive that housing policy.

A second social change which has led to the isolation of older parents in the West of Ireland was the desire of parents to encourage their children to pursue white-collar professions, rather than occupations that would enable them to find work near home, at least, for one member of the family. My family was a classic example of a professional family, i.e. one nun-teacher, an attorney (in the US), two senior army officers (in Galway and Athlone) and two priests (parish priest in Wales and a Jesuit lecturer in St Patrick's College, Maynooth). We were very fortunate that one of my brothers, Pádraig, and his wife Jackie, opted to live in Westport within one and a half miles of my mother's home and was happy to commute to Athlone. This gave my mother the reassurance of having her son's family so close to her home. I raise all of these points to highlight the ever-growing isolation of our senior citizens because of the family-unfriendly changes, which have been taking place in Irish society since the 1960s. Of course, when emigration was very high in Ireland, the old also suffered from the severe separation when all their children were forced to emigrate as economic migrants. The tragedy today is that even during the welcome improvement in economic conditions, the plight of the old is even more serious because of the structural changes in society which are driving us towards individualism, with the resultant neglect of the family and of the local neighbourhood and community. Most housing development in Ireland today is more developer-led than community determined.

12. RETURN TO LOUGHLOON

As I stated earlier in this text, I spent the most formative years of my life from 1936-46 (between the ages of five and fifteen years) in the home and farm of my father's ancestors in Loughloon. The house we were living in was built by my great-grandfather, Padney McGreal, who married a next-door neighbour, Kitty Conway, on the 3rd April 1847. The McGreals and the Conways occupied two 'half-holdings' with every second field divided between the families and each family had a quarter of a 320-acre mountain commonage, which was separated from the two half-holdings (each around twenty-six acres in area). When the family moved to Drummindoo in 1946, the two houses in Loughloon were unoccupied. Conway's was already a stable, and McGreal's was to be used as a store for fodder and later to be converted into a stable. Around 1958, my father took the corrugated roof from the old homestead in order to re-roof a hayshed in Drummindoo.

The roofless house continued to be used as a sheep pen in Loughloon by my father. One day, in 1973, I was 'pulling sheep' for my father, who was busily shearing them (at the age of eighty years). I examined the walls of the house and found them to be in relatively good condition. I suggested to my father that I would rebuild and re-roof the old house. His reply was interesting. He said: '*That's in your imagination!*' In response, I said: '*Sure is it not in our imagination that most things begin?*' He agreed then with the idea and offered to pay for the materials. This meant the 'go ahead' for a project, which was to be very successful. By the end of the summer 1975, with the voluntary help of friends and neighbours, we re-roofed and restored the house. The house, which went back on the rates in 1976, was formally blessed with a Mass concelebrated by Fr Éamonn O'Malley, Administrator, Westport, my brother Fr Owen and myself in the summer of 1976. A great gathering of family, neighbours and friends constituted the congregation. It is hard to believe now that the cost of the materials came to the princely sum of £400 (with voluntary labour)!

Apart from the therapy, which the Loughloon project gave me, the restoration of the old house had a much greater significance for me. It was an attempt to react to the demise of our ancestors' homesteads at a time when we were quite happy to preserve the homes of the gentry and the former landlords. The houses of the 'peasant' tenant farmers were not being preserved save in 'museum' or 'touristy' settings. My aim was to relive the conditions of living of my ancestors. For the first twenty-one years, i.e. up until 1997, I did not have electricity in the house. The double-wick paraffin-oil lamps provided adequate light and the open fire heated the house. In the 1980s we were connected with the local public water scheme. It was to become my research and writing office as well.

After my father died in 1976, my late uncle, John (the 'Major'), looked after the house and the land. He cut the bracken every year and reared mountain sheep on the farm. His son, Pádraig, used his plastering and other skills to make the restored cottage structurally sound and suitable for human habitation. Pádraig sadly passed away (in November 2007) as a result of a severe brain-haemorrhage, RIP Together, we restored some of the out-offices. My brother, Seán, was owner of the house and the land and he was quite happy that Uncle John and I looked after the place, as he pursued his career in the Army in Ireland and overseas with the United Nations in the Lebanon. During the weekends I would stay in the house and be available to do supply work for the local parishes, especially if the local priests were unable to offer Mass either due to illness or to being on holidays or on retreat. This pastoral experience reminded me of my primary duties as a priest and also helped me to get to know the great characters who were the pastoral leaders of the parishes of West Mayo. The house in Loughloon was ideal for my writing.

Once a year during the late 1970s, 1980s and early 1990s, we organised a Mass and dinner for the Tuam clerical students in Loughloon. The menu was 'bacon and cabbage'! The students really enjoyed this annual coming together in an informal manner.

13. INDUSTRIAL RELATIONS CRISIS IN MAYNOOTH

Back in St Patrick's College, Maynooth, staff conditions were improving. The Academic Staff Association opted to register as a branch of the Irish Federation of University Teachers (IFUT). The attempt to entice us to constitute a branch of the Teachers' Union of Ireland (TUI) failed to get sufficient support, although I voted in favour of the TUI, as I thought it would be a stronger trade union in favour of the rights of the junior and part-time academic staff. The vote was overwhelmingly in favour of IFUT and, as a democrat, I threw my support in favour with that union. IFUT registered and was accepted as a member-union of the Irish Congress of Trade Unions (ICTU). Because I had been lecturing on industrial sociology in the College of Industrial Relations since 1966, I was very familiar with the structures and functions of the Trade Unions in Ireland.

A major industrial-relations crisis emerged in Maynooth in the mid-seventies, to be known as the *McGrath-O'Rourke Case*, which had very serious and divisive implications for staff relations and for the operation of procedures between the ASA (the local branch of IFUT) and the management. Professor Patrick McGrath was a Professor of Philosophy in both the NUI Section and in the Pontifical University. Fr Malachy O'Rourke was a lecturer in French in the NUI Section. They were priests of the diocese of Kildare and Leighlin, and the archdiocese of Armagh respectively who were leaving the clerical state. The dissatisfaction of the Trustees related to the clerical status of the two members of the staff, Fathers Patrick McGrath and Malachy O'Rourke, and had nothing to do with their work as academics. For personal reasons they were retiring from the priesthood and this would, in the view of Trustees, necessitate their resignation from the Academic Staff of St Patrick's College – NUI Section and Pontifical University. The two members refused to resign their academic posts in the NUI Section, and the Trustees proceeded with their formal dismissal.

The local ASA and IFUT opposed the forced dismissal of the two members from their academic posts, because of issues not related to their academic work. The Minister for Labour, Mr Michael O'Leary TD, signed into action the recently enacted *Unfair Dismissals' Act* at this time. This enabled IFUT to take the Trustees to court claiming that the dismissal of McGrath and O'Rourke contravened that Act. The High Court supported the IFUT case. The Trustees appealed the decision to the Supreme Court, which reversed the judgement of the High Court on the grounds that the Statutes of Maynooth (which were approved prior to the opening up of the College) were *de facto* and *de jure* binding on ordained academic staff. The Supreme Court ruled in favour of the Trustees.

IFUT was forced to impose a special levy on all members to pay for Court costs. The Union was very displeased with the judgement of the Supreme Court and 'blacked' the two positions from which its two members were being dismissed. Members of the Union, who refused to pay the levy, would automatically lose their membership of IFUT. As a President of IFUT said at a Union meeting some years later, when commenting on the McGrath/O'Rourke case, '*it might have been wiser for the Union to have opposed the dismissals by means of industrial action rather than through the Courts*'. The industrial action approach would address the *de facto* situation while the Courts focussed on the *de jure* dimension.

The outcome of the dispute did serious damage, in my opinion, to the ethos and reputation of St Patrick's College in the Irish academic world. The support of IFUT was a source of consolation to the disillusioned members of the Maynooth ASA. It was a difficult time for the Chairperson of the ASA and the staff members, because of the emotional, political and ecclesial fall out. My position was made more difficult by my friendship with staff members on both sides of the division. I stood firmly behind our Union at all times, but I felt sorry that the management could not arrive at a more conciliatory solution. It would take time to recover, but I felt that with goodwill on both sides we could put even this crisis behind us. Unfortunately, the public scandal of the event throughout university staff in Ireland and abroad reflected badly on our College's management structure and procedures. But what was done was done and we had to live with it! It was feared that staff who were publicly on the side of Frs McGrath and O'Rourke would be unlikely to get preferment in the College for some time. This was talked about among the staff. On the side of the Trustees, one could see their concern about the need to clarify their expectations from ordained members of the College staff. At this time, a number of eminent priest-professors were applying for laicisation and the Trustees must have been very worried about the effects of such an exodus on clerical students. Nevertheless, it appeared to me that the McGrath and O'Rourke dismissals were unjust.

The whole ethos of the mid-1970s was one of almost uncontrollable social and religious change within the Church. That was true also of the staff of Maynooth College, where there were two camps, i.e. those who were afraid of where the Church was going after Vatican Two and wished to 'batten down the hatches', and those who were frustrated by the slow pace of change which they had anticipated after Vatican Two. Many of the latter group left the priesthood and a few became hostile towards the Church's leadership. For both sides, it was a 'time after optimism', which we know from history, is the most vulnerable time in the life of an organisation. Happily, both of the dismissed members of staff got good jobs. Patrick McGrath was appointed Lecturer in Philosophy in University College, Cork, and Malachy O'Rourke was given a responsible position in the languages office of the EEC in Brussels, Belgium.

14. Mgr Tomás Ó Fiaich Becomes Archbishop of Armagh

In 1977, President Monsignor Tomás Ó Fiaich, was appointed Archbishop of Armagh. Monsignor Michael Olden (Waterford and Lismore Diocese) was appointed President of St Patrick's College in succession to Monsignor Tomás. While I welcomed Monsignor Olden's appointment, I was very sorry to see *An t-Ath* Tomás leave Maynooth. He had made a great contribution to the life of the college by his genuinely friendly approach to the students. In his early days as a clerical student he had suffered from bad health but his recovery had enabled him to profess Irish history with a certain aplomb, which won the interest of the student and listener. His work for the Irish language was very noteworthy. He became the founder-president of *Glór na nGael* (the Pride of the Irish), a movement which invited communities and parishes to seek recognition for the use and promotion of the Irish language throughout their community. He was also one of the founders of *Cumann na Sagart*, an association of Irish-speaking priests. I was later to become its *Runaí* (secretary) under *An tAth* Pádraig Ó Fiannachta, as Chairman.

Monsignor Tomás had a good reputation for being a patriotic Irish man. His native parish of Crossmaglen in South Armagh was kept under close vigilance by the crown security forces, because of its reputation for being republican. His good friend, Father James Lennon, my boss in the Research and Development Unit, was to be his auxiliary Bishop of Armagh and parish priest of St Peter's, Drogheda. They were to prove a great combination in the very troubled times ahead. Monsignor Tomás' elevation to Armagh meant that I would lose regular and close contact with a friend of many years, to whom I felt deeply indebted. I wrote him a long letter of farewell into the lofty and lonely highlands of the Primacy of All Ireland. He often told me afterwards that he reread my epistle of farewell on a number of occasions. No doubt, Maynooth's loss was to become All Ireland's gain. In my opinion, his choice as Primate-Archbishop was excellent in order to give a Christian Pacifist leadership to a suppressed people in Northern Ireland. He was also genuinely ecumenical and very open to the cause of women in the Church. He was always friendly and jovial. As Archbishop of Armagh, Tomás would become chairperson of the Trustees of Maynooth and President of the Irish Episcopal Conference. He was neither egotistical nor pompous and he would soon win the hearts of people in Ireland and abroad.

The year 1978 was another eventful year in Ireland with continuous violence in Northern Ireland. The James Callaghan Labour Government in Britain was in a very weak position in the House of Commons with only a minimal majority. In fact, it had become a minority Government. This may have forced it to make certain concessions to the Unionist MPs. To add to our economic challenges in Ireland we had to face a second oil crisis. The previous year, Mr Jack Lynch TD, won an overall majority in a General Election. A number of tax concessions, including the *abolition of rates* and the *abolition of road tax on cars*, were introduced. These concessions did not anticipate a second oil price-hike, which led to dissatisfaction with the Government. Mr Charles J Haughey TD, was back in cabinet and becoming favoured as a new leader by a number of deputies.

My personal life was mainly preoccupied with my lecturing and correction of students' projects. I soldiered on in *Conradh na Gaeilge*, but tried to depolarise it. By letting my name go forward for the position of *Uachtarán* (President) in 1978, I was really testing the waters. In the end, I received 118 votes, just twelve votes short of the 130 received by the outgoing President. Looking back now, I am as well pleased that I was 'an also ran' (with 118 votes). The *Ardfheis* was held in the Boyne Valley Hotel, Drogheda. I was duly re-elected on to the *Coiste an Airgid* and the *Coiste Gnó* for another year. The result was reassuring in that almost half of the proactive members of *Conradh na Gaeilge* had public confidence in me despite the Ewart-Biggs affair (referred to earlier). My commitment to the revival of the Irish language never ebbed throughout my adult life.

15. A RAILWAY AND A SHRINE

Ever since the 1950s in Ireland, there had been a *policy of retrenchment* and *closure of railways* in operation in the Republic of Ireland. The closure of the railway from Collooney to Claremorris in the mid-1970s was, for me, the last straw in this short-sighted destruction of a reliable overland transport infrastructure. I wrote a letter to a local paper in late 1978 or early 1979 calling for support for the reopening of this very important cross-radial rail link between Sligo and Rosslare via Limerick. Around the same time the Chairperson of Sligo County Council, Cllr PJ Cawley of Tubbercurry, proposed the setting up of a joint RDO Railway Committee, with representatives from the *North-West* (Sligo/Leitrim), *West* (Galway/Mayo) and *Mid-West* (Clare/Limerick/Tipperary North Riding) Regional Development Organisations to work for the restoration of the rail services between Claremorris and Sligo (via Collooney).

The Committee invited me to attend a meeting of the Joint Committee and I was asked to direct a survey of the potential use of the rail services and report on the case for its reopening. I accepted the invitation and set about the long and tedious fieldwork. I got the cooperation of second-level schools along the line from Collooney to Limerick to collect information (questionnaire) on travel patterns of residents within ten miles of the track. Data was also collected on the use of the road (N17) and counts of vehicles were carried out. We also counted the number of people travelling in each car. The potential commercial and industrial use of the goods freight service was measured. Previous research reports were read and summarised, etc. I even suggested that the line from Claremorris to Kiltimagh be upgraded for the Pope's visit in September 1979. Little did we know at the time that the campaign was going to last for another thirty-five years and more before this infrastructure would be restored! Our biggest enemy to the reopening of the infrastructure was the 'dead hand' of central bureaucracy in Dublin. (More about this great project later.)

In July 1979 there was an Irish language youth camp (*Campa Samhraidh*) in Finney (near Clonbur), organised by Ógras: Óg-Ghluaiseacht Chonradh na Gaeilge. When arranging the programme, I suggested that they go on a pilgrimage to an *ancient Patrician Shrine in the parish, i.e. Mámean.* I promised to offer Mass (in Irish) at the shrine and notify the priests in Leenane, Kilmilkin and Recess churches. *Mámean* was situated on a pass (1,000 feet plus) on the Maamturk Mountains in North Connemara between the Maam Valley and Recess. The Mass was arranged for three o'clock on an afternoon in mid-July 1979. It was a warm and misty afternoon. I offered Mass on *Leaba Phádraig* (St Patrick's Bed) under a 'golf umbrella'. To my total surprise there was a congregation of up to four score pilgrims (including two score members of the Ógras *Campa Samhraidh*). At the end of the Mass the local people began putting money on the bed. I pleaded with them to take it back but they refused. They said, '*Bíodh sé agat*' (Let you have it). '*Very well*,' I said in Irish. '*With this money we will get the materials to build a Mass Rock here. We will build it together. And I promise to offer Mass here every year on Mámean Sunday, as long as God gives me the strength to do so.*' There was a *bualadh bos* (a clapping of hands) in approval. And so began the project to restore this ancient Irish language pilgrimage, which had gradually lapsed since the 1920s. A trickle of the faithful made the annual *turas* (journey) to the shrine. With the onset of the bicycle and the building of the church on Croagh Patrick (28 miles away) in 1905, many pilgrims switched to the Mayo shrine. Also, local clergy had not supported the *Turas* because of the reputation it had for celebrations (with *poitín*) in the nineteenth and early twentieth centuries.

Mámean was one of the *Crom Dubh* Celtic (pre-Christian) Shrines, which St Patrick blessed during his visit to the West in AD 441, i.e. the year he prayed on Croagh Patrick. The tradition of the *Mámean Pattern* went as far back as Medieval Times, and grew according as the population in Connemara grew. In Inglis's book on his visit to the West of Ireland in 1834 he gives a vivid account of the pattern day in *Mámean*. In 1841 Mass was offered in *Mámean*. Also, in 1932, William T Consgrave TD, Head of the Free State Government 1922-32, served Mass at the shrine with his two sons. (My grandfather, Mike Ó Cadhain, *An Cabhar, An Mám*, a stone mason, built the altar.) Ms Bina McLoughlin ('the Queen of Connemara') from Leenane was a loyal supporter of the revival of *Turas Mh*ámean from the beginning.

Coiste Tacaíochta Mhámean (*Mámean* support committee) was formed in 1979, with the local school principal, Caitlín Bean Uí Thiarnaigh, as *Rúnaí* (Secretary). People from the Maam and Recess sides joined and we decided to build the *Carraig an Aifrinn* (Mass Rock). Tomás Ó Cadhain, *Tír na Cille, An Mám*, offered to do the building and the rest of us did the unskilled work. The work would be carried out during the following summer months (1980). The Archbishop of Tuam, Most Rev Dr Joseph Cunnane, gave permission to build the Mass Rock and consecrated it on the first Sunday of August 1980. We had agreed on the Sunday after 'Croagh Patrick Sunday' to become the main (revived) national pilgrimage day to *Mámean*. The Stations of the Cross were also established.

16. THE PAPAL VISIT

In September 1979, His Holiness, Pope John Paul II, visited the Shrine of Our Lady of Knock, County Mayo, to mark the centenary of the apparition of Our Lady on the gable of the Knock Parish Church and bless and establish the new basilica (built to commemorate the hundred years of pilgrimages). The Holy Father had also visited Dublin, Drogheda, Clonmacnois, Galway, Maynooth and Limerick on his relatively brief visit to Ireland. There was an extraordinary turnout in Ireland to greet the Pope. It was very emotional and highly organised. It afforded the Catholic faithful an opportunity to celebrate (in a ritual manner) their 'coming of age' again after over four hundred years of post-Reformation religious minority status. A Maynooth professor pointed this out to me when discussing the papal visit. Of course, we were enjoying full equality *de facto* in the Republic since the foundation of the State and *de jure* since 1869, i.e. the disestablishment of the Church of Ireland. Part of Ireland (Northern Ireland) was still under a monarch, who was Head of State. During the seventeenth and eighteenth centuries, Irish Roman Catholics were persecuted for their religion (with intermittent periods of peaceful co-existence with Protestants [who were the dominant class]).

So many centuries of minority status in their own country, had, as it were, made Catholics perceive themselves subconsciously as lesser people religiously. Since the *Treaty of Westphalia in 1648*, the religion of the English king was *de jure* the religion of the Irish people. Apart from the reign of James II, the monarch was Protestant!

In the context of this long history of our being forced to play the part of religious underdog, it was only to be expected that the visit of Pope John Paul II, (the Vicar of Christ on earth to the believing Catholics), would restore our sense of religious self-respect. Of course, the faithful Catholics of Ireland or those organising the events would not be aware (explicitly) of what was happening during this self-therapeutic ritual of the Pope's visit. It was a good and necessary event. (This was the interpretation of the papal visit by a colleague.) It was a collective experience, which, for a few days, united the people in a unique manner. It must seem rather strange to the commentator that writing over thirty years after this *new emancipation of Roman Catholics in Ireland* many were not able to resist the lure of materialism and withdrew from regular collective worship in Church. This decline in religious practice and, as a result, a move away from Catholic moral norms, was in no way related to the Pope's visit or the emancipating ritual which it facilitated. *Secular norms and materialism* were part of the growing assimilation of our people into the new 'Western Culture', which was being transmitted to the people through mass media, especially television. When we return to our senses and live according to our Christian beliefs and norms, we will do so more confidently. (The recent alienation of the Roman Catholic Church, created because of an interpretation by the establishment of the handling of the clerical child-abuse scandals, has added to the secularisation agenda.)

One of the disappointments felt by many about the Pope's visit to Ireland in 1979 was the fact that he did not visit Northern Ireland. It was feared that ongoing hostilities and the negative attitudes of some Protestant groups and others would make such a visit unsafe. In parts of Northern Ireland history seemed to have stood still since 1648. Again, this pointed to the urgency (in Ireland) of an effective ecumenical movement, which would address the destructive legacy of the Reformation and the Counter Reformation in Ireland. It did little to help the restoration of better Catholic-Protestant relations since the

Nationalist-Unionist political divide in Northern Ireland had been along religious lines. As I said already, our coming together must go beyond 'garden-party ecumenism'. Providence has put us together in this one little island of Ireland. God would surely wish that we strive to live as Christian neighbours and forgive the mutual abuse of each other over the past. The sad fact that the Holy Father, Pope John Paul II, was prevented from visiting his flock in Northern Ireland in 1979 was an admission of community failure! It was, for me, the one cloud over an otherwise very wonderful papal visit to Ireland.

One message I paid special attention to from all that the Pope said while on his visit was his encouragement to the Irish to return to their traditional devotions, which gave spiritual sustenance to our ancestors. This gave us the papal 'green flag' to proceed with the revival of the *Mámean Shrine*. The evidence of the thousands who have returned to, or who have begun, coming on pilgrimage to the shrine since 1980 has proven clearly that the Lord was behind the revival of the *Turas*. Maybe, some day in the future a successor of John Paul II will join the pilgrims at the ancient shrine on the slopes of the Maamturk Mountains in North Connemara. (It was wonderful to witness the recognition of *Mámean* as a national shrine at the opening of the 50th International Eucharistic Congress in Dublin on the 10th June 2012.)

17. Major Political Changes on the Horizon

The publication of *Prejudice and Tolerance in Ireland* in 1977 was most successful and, according to many commentators, did much to make Irish people aware of their prejudices and encouraged them to be more tolerant. This self-awareness would, I believed, do much to undermine some of our more destructive prejudices and result in a better life for our minorities. At the same time, we should not be under any illusion with regard to the persistence of racism, sexism, homophobia, ethnocentrism, anti-Semitism, class or religious prejudice. Resistance to change is a characteristic of social prejudices, which are hostile, rigid and irrational. The text itself sold out in Ireland. Praeger Publishers in New York published the text in the United States, which broadened the book's circulation throughout the universities in the English-speaking academic world. In all, some 3,500 copies of the book were printed, i.e.

1,000 in original hardback issue, 1,500 in the paperback issue and 1,000 in the Praeger printing.

The award of the *Christopher Ewart-Biggs Memorial Peace Prize* won for me much more positive public reaction than the understandable, but regrettable, hostility it aroused among a substantial minority of the leaders of *Conradh na Gaeilge*. It was not that easy for me to integrate the two responses at the time. In a sense, one seemed to neutralise the other, although I never had any regrets about accepting the prize. One day, in 1978, Professor Liam Ryan told me that some people in the Maynooth College authorities were seeking a way in which to give me recognition for winning the award. I suggested to him that I might apply for *rapid promotion to senior lecturer,* which would be an appropriate form of recognition (and, I thought to myself, would give the management a chance to undo the injustice of refusing leave-of-absence and my suffering the loss of two years' seniority). The Professor supported my application and the Trustees and the Governing Body agreed to my promotion to the rank of senior lecturer. This meant that I had now reached the career grade of statutory lecturer in the NUI.

The second oil crisis near the end of the 1970s (1978) was to retard the economic growth of Ireland and of other countries that had become more and more dependent on imported oil. We were facing a mini-economic depression. Unemployment was beginning to increase and emigration of some of the most competent of our young adults to England and elsewhere abroad was to renew the haemorrhage of Irish talent. The clouds were gathering. Pressure was being put on Mr Jack Lynch TD, to step down as *Taoiseach* and two very different candidates were to contest the election of a successor within the *Fianna Fáil* party, i.e. Mr George Colley TD and Mr Charles J Haughey TD. On 11th December 1979 Charles James Haughey TD, was appointed *Taoiseach* in succession to Jack Lynch TD. A certain level of disagreement within the governing party was to cause difficulties for the new *Taoiseach* from the start, or it so appeared from the Irish media.

In the United Kingdom in 1979, James Callaghan's Labour Government was defeated in a 'vote of confidence', owing to the abstention of a Nationalist MP, Mr Jim Maguire, from Northern Ireland. After a bitterly fought general election, the Tory Party, under the leadership of Mrs Margaret Thatcher MP, assumed power in the United

215

Kingdom. This proved to be the beginning of eighteen years of Tory rule, which was not very positive for Northern Ireland and for many of the poorer communities in England, Scotland and Wales, not to mention the mining and other traditional industries. What I found most difficult to accept was the ideological rejection of the reality of the 'social' or the 'collective' in favour of undiluted individualism. It became a 'survival of the fittest' liberal capitalist regime. No one could challenge Mrs Thatcher's extraordinary moral courage and adherence to her stance on issues. These were both her strengths and weaknesses. As the 1970s ended, the political clouds were darkening in Northern Ireland, with two new energetic and strong political leaders coming to the top in the Republic of Ireland and in the United Kingdom, i.e. *An Taoiseach*, Mr Charles J Haughey TD, and Prime Minister Mrs Margaret Thatcher MP. Troublesome and challenging times awaited us all!

In the perspective of later socio-economic developments, i.e. the rise and fall of a market-driven false property prices throughout the 'Western' world (including Ireland's *Celtic Tiger*), the Reagan/Thatcher deregulation of the 'market' proved disastrous. Globalisation, which was 'unregulated' for the most part, undermined national (political) authority. I was particularly disappointed by the apparent unwillingness or inability of the EU or national Governments to intervene effectively on behalf of the people! It appeared to me, on reflection, that the EU was part of the problem rather than its prevention. I will return to this topic later.

Chapter Six

THE 1980S
THE CHICKENS COME HOME TO ROOST

1. THE TRAGEDY OF THE 'HUNGER STRIKES'

The early years of the 1980s were to be dominated by the Troubles in Northern Ireland. As far back as 1976, Republican prisoners refused to wear 'convict' clothes and, instead, they wrapped their naked bodies in blankets. This developed further into a 'no wash protest' in 1978. What the prisoners wanted was to be treated as 'prisoners of war' and not as ordinary convicted prisoners. They were, after all, in prison as a result of the sentence of a 'special court', i.e. the Diplock Court, which did not have a jury. This campaign for *special status* became very serious in the notorious Long Kesh detention centre, which was to be renamed 'The Maze'.

In October 1980 the prisoners began the first hunger strike as a further stage in their campaign for special status, as prisoners. Cardinal Tomás Ó Fiaich, Archbishop of Armagh, and Bishop Eamonn Daly, Bishop of Derry, negotiated an end to this hunger strike in December 1980, on the understanding that the prisoners would get 'special status', but the British authorities reneged on this understanding. On the 1st March 1981, the second hunger strike began for special prisoner status. *This was to be a staggered strike, i.e. as a hunger striker died, another prisoner would cease to accept food.* It became clear to the whole country that things were becoming very serious. But still, the British Government would not relent. The growth of media interest in the second hunger strike was global. The impact of *Section 31 of the Irish Broadcasting Act* of the mid-1970s in censoring reports from the Republican side in Northern Ireland had failed to let the people know of the painful campaign exercising the prisoners.

On the 5th May 1981, Bobby Sands MP, died on hunger strike after sixty days without food, RIP This made world headlines and marked a turning point in the Northern Irish struggle. His death had an effect on all of us. It aroused great sadness and great anger that, despite the efforts of the leaders like Cardinal Tomás Ó Fiaich, *An Taoiseach*, Charles J Haughey TD, and many others; the British Government, under Mrs Margaret Thatcher MP, was not prepared to make what was an honourable and reasonable concession. The giving of 'prisoner of war' status did not mean approving of the actions of the IRA – they would still be defined as 'enemies of the UK State'. It looked to me, who was not in favour of the paramilitary or armed struggle (on the grounds of my adherence to pacifism), as unreasonable arrogance.

The tragic death of *Bobby Sands MP*, was only the beginning of the self-sacrifice of nine others, i.e. *Francis Hughes*, (died 12th May 1981); *Raymond McCreesh* and *Patsy O'Hara* (died 21st May 1981); *Joe McDonnell* (died 8th July 1981); *Martin Hurson* (died 13th July 1981); *Kevin Lynch* (died 1st August 1981); *Kieran Doherty TD*, (died 3rd August 1981); *Thomas McElwee* (died 8th August 1981) and *Michael Devine* (20th August 1981) RIP It must be a record in the history of the struggle for national independence and freedom in the Western World that so many young men were prepared to sacrifice their lives in so painful and stressful a manner. We may disagree with their method of pursuing their cause and even question the moral correctness of hunger strike-to-death, but we must honour their heroic sacrifice and altruism. I record this tribute to those ten young Irish men who gave their young lives, while I prayed hard at the time that they would not have to suffer to the bitter end which they felt they had to. *Ar dheis Dé go raibh a n-anamacha uaisle.*

The *death on hunger strike of the late Bobby Sands MP, and his colleagues* forced many of us to sit up and think again about the seriousness of the struggle being waged in Northern Ireland. As I said above, *the death of the ten men on hunger strike was a turning point in the Troubles.* It became clear to many of us that military victory by the British security forces would be well-nigh impossible or be so destructive as to destroy more than it would gain. From then on two trends began to emerge, i.e. an intensification of paramilitary activity with growing community support for the IRA and the early signs of moves towards a 'political solution' within the paramilitary Republican movement. *Sinn Féin* would eventually engage in parliamentary politics in Northern Ireland and enter into dialogue with people such as John

Hume MP. Parliamentary leaders in the United States also renewed their move towards a 'political solution'. In the Republic, there were intensive negotiations behind the scenes, while in Britain public sympathy towards the nationalist cause was growing. Right across Europe and the whole world, the name 'Bobby Sands' was gaining heroic status. In time, things changed and new momentum would lead to ceasefires in the 1990s and the *Good Friday Agreement* in 1998. One could say the tragic deaths of 1981 (May to August) were to become a *felix culpa* in the cause of peace and justice. The positive influence of Monsignor Denis Faul, PP, in bringing an end to the ongoing hunger strike should be recognised.

2. THE RISE OF VOLUNTARY YOUTH ORGANISATIONS (VYOS)

The growth of voluntary youth organisations (VYOs) in the 1960s and 1970s in Ireland provided structured peer-environments for teenagers which complemented and supplemented the socialising roles of family, neighbourhood and school. VYOs also provided an element of 'emancipation' for older teenagers within the growing constraints of 'extended adolescence'. The latter was caused by the delaying of the normal adult incorporation rituals of a job and marriage, because of the needs of the post-industrial society. Adolescence is a transitional period between childhood and adulthood.

There were two kinds of voluntary youth organisations, i.e. youth work and youth affairs. Youth work organisations focused on youth services in various areas of need, i.e. athletic, educational, disability, promotion of the Irish language, religious, social welfare, Travellers, etc. Youth affairs organisations were concerned with public issues, i.e. political parties, civil rights' movements, peace and justice movements, etc. There was a wide variety of youth organisations in Ireland, including farming, trade unions, political parties, scouts, Vincent de Paul, sports, Irish language, church groups, pro-environment groups, etc. During the 1960s, a national umbrella council was established known as the National Youth Council of Ireland (NYCI).

During this time, *Conradh na Gaeilge* set up a special youth section, i.e. *Ógras: Óg-Ghluaiseacht Chonradh na Gaeilge*, which did much (and continues to do) valuable work to make Irish a living language for many young people. It affiliated with the National Youth Council of Ireland (NYCI). Máiréad Ní Chinnéide (later Máiréad Bean Uí Dhomhnaill) was Ógras's first Chairperson. Later I had the honour of becoming her successor.

By the late 1970s, there was a growing pressure within Ógras for greater autonomy from its parent organisation. This reflected the mood of the time among mid-to-late teenagers. The campaign to seek greater independence from the executive of *Conradh na Gaeilge* gained strength within a number of branches of Ógras.

A meeting was called on the 1ˢᵗ March 1980, at 11.00am, in Drogheda, County Louth, for the purpose of discussing the setting up of a new independent Irish language youth movement. At the end of the morning session, a vote was taken and a majority opted for the setting up of a new organisation/movement. Only those willing to join the new organisation would be invited to the afternoon session and this was, in effect, the inaugural meeting of the new Irish language youth movement. Some twenty-four members attended the afternoon meeting, which approved the draft constitution. The meeting also agreed to call the new movement: *Feachtas: Óg-Ghluaiseacht na Gaeilge* (*Campaign: The Irish Language Youth Movement*). The name '*Feachtas*' was the 'code name' given to the meetings held in a number of places during the lead-up to the Drogheda meeting. I supported the new independent organisation and proposed that we continue to use our 'underground' name *Feachtas* as our official one. It reminded us of our roots!

The inaugural meeting also decided that *Feachtas* would seek membership of *Comhdháil Náisiúnta na Gaeilge, Comhairle Náisiúnta na nÓg* (NYCI) and *Coiste Fhéile an Oireachtais*. We hoped some day to be able to work with members of Ógras, whose delegates were mandated to oppose *Feachtas's* membership of each organisation. Our application for membership succeeded in the case of both national organisations, i.e. National Youth Council of Ireland and *Comhdhail Náisiúnta na Gaeilge*. In time, *Feachtas* would be accepted on *Choiste Oireachtas na Gaeilge. Conradh na Gaeilge* suspended all members associated with the founding of *Feachtas* in March 1980. After some time, the suspension order against *Feachtas* members being welcome in units of *Conradh na Gaeilge* was lifted. The removal of my individual suspension was delayed for a further period because of the possibility of '*coimhlint dílseachta,* i.e. a 'conflict of loyalty'. I also had to give an assurance, in writing, that I would be loyal to the *Conradh's* constitution before my 'excommunication' could be removed. (I rejoined *An Conradh* in Castlebar in 2012.)

It took some time to be fully acceptable and I appreciated the difficulties of some of the *Conradh* leadership, who would not fully trust my interpretation of the aims of *Conradh na Gaeilge*. During all this time 'in exile' we worked together for the common cause of supporting the revival of the Irish language as an essential part of Irish culture. I am very happy today that members of *Feachtas* and of *Ógras* work side by side. The new diversity adds to the variety of the general revival movement, which enables young people to enjoy themselves as they develop through the means of the Irish language. The return to popularity of Irish-speaking schools and colleges provided good recruitment places for new leaders and members for both organisations. Unfortunately, it became more difficult to attract teachers to work voluntarily for the cause in the ordinary schools.

I would like at this stage to pay tribute to the role of the National Youth Council of Ireland (*Comhairle Náisiúnta na nÓg*), on whose Executive Committee I served as Honorary Secretary and Vice President during the late 1970s and 1980s. In fact, for a brief period I served as acting Chairperson during an *inter regnum* few months. The National Youth Council (NYCI) represented the whole spectrum of voluntary youth organisations, i.e. youth work, youth affairs and the youth sections of political parties across the ideological spectrum. Voluntary Youth Work organisations of various religious and faith-based groups were among the principal founding members.

My entry into the field was via the Irish language youth groups, *Macra na Feirme* and my association with the Travelling People. Later on the NYCI became more involved in the European and international youth confederations, including Eastern European socialist youth groups. I remember attending the International Socialist Youth Conference in Kumrovec in Yugoslavia during the reign of Marshal Tito in the 1980s. The value of such international dialogue with youth leaders from other continents and countries is a most vibrant and essential part of the process to pluralism and equality between peoples.

The links with Northern Ireland's voluntary youth groups indirectly helped our long and gradual pilgrimage to peace and reconciliation in our divided country. During my time of active involvement on the National Youth Council of Ireland, I came to appreciate the training-ground it became of public leadership in farming, politics, industry, trade unions, churches, community activities, etc. Its lobbying role has been very powerful and at times may have led to change or choice of government. The political influence and power of the National Youth Council of Ireland and its member organisation was very effective during the 1970s and the 1980s.

The role of the staff of the NYCI merits recognition as well as that of voluntary officers. Among the staff who helped me during my time as Vice-President were Mr Geoffrey Corry and Mr Tom Costello who served as chief executive officers of the Council. The expertise of the staff for the information of the honorary officers has often been under-rated. The support for the NYCI has been a worthwhile investment by the Irish State and by the voluntary contributions of communities *via* local branches of youth organisations.

3. Shop Steward in Maynooth

St Patrick's College, Maynooth, was a very dynamic place during the 1980s. The number of students was increasing in a relatively steady manner. The overall economic state of the country was not growing that well. There were constraints on the employment of extra academic staff. The level of student unrest was on the increase leading to the occupation of the college administration offices in 1982. On the serious illness of Father (Professor) Gerry Meagher, as chairperson of the Maynooth Branch of IFUT (the ASA) in 1982, I was elected to the chair and was, in effect, the 'shop steward' of the Academic and Library staff (this was a position I occupied until 1991). There was a degree of student agitation in the college during the 1980s, which involved two occupations of the administration block, i.e. 1982 and 1984.

Shortly after becoming chairperson of the union, I requested a meeting with Monsignor Michael Olden, President of Maynooth. The main item on the agenda was the renewal of normal industrial relations between the union and the management, i.e. the President and his administrative staff and the Trustees. Such relations had been practically non-existent since the unfortunate debacle of the *McGrath-O'Rourke case* in the late 1970s. I suggested that we had to *normalise the staff-management relations* and try to get over the very traumatic experience of the *McGrath-O'Rourke case* as well as working together for the common good of the college. Monsignor Michael Olden formally agreed and we both shook hands on it, to his great credit. Our relations were to be most successful.

In our meetings, the Vice-President, Rev Professor Matt O'Donnell, was a 'master negotiator' who had a most impressive 'mind for detail'. One always felt that the union had to be on its toes and know all of the necessary details. Vice-President O'Donnell could anticipate nearly every nuance that our team would bring to the meeting. Our negotiations were concerned with the conditions of employment, including promotions procedures, grievance procedures, etc. It was arranged that the union officers would meet the three representatives of the trustees on a regular basis. Such a level of serious dialogue was soon to result in the normalisation of union-management relations on a more mature and adult basis, which, in turn, facilitated a level of progress, which was to have a long-term benefit for the NUI section of St Patrick's College, Maynooth. Cardinal Tomás Ó Fiaich, Chairperson of the trustees, approved of the restoration of normal union/management relations.

During the campaign for *Seanad Éireann* in January 1983, Professor James C Dooge (1922-2010) of UCD (former Minister for Foreign Affairs) visited me to canvass for support for an NUI seat. We discussed the status of Maynooth College as a recognised college within the NUI. I asked him if he would be willing to support a campaign for Constituent College Status for Maynooth, i.e. the same as the status given to UCD, UCC and UCG. He agreed and, because of that, I would support his election within the Maynooth College. That marked the beginning of a very successful campaign, initiated by the ASA, for complete equality with the other three constituent colleges, and confirmed in law by Mrs Niamh Bhreathnach TD, Minister for Education, in October of 1997. Prior to the ASA proposal to seek Constituent College Status within the National University of Ireland for the Maynooth Recognised College, it had been decided by the Trustees to explore the possibility of seeking an Independent University College Status. Constituent status within

NUI was also supported by Mrs Mary O'Rourke TD, Opposition Spokesperson for Education and former graduate of the NUI section of St Patrick's College, Maynooth, in the 1980s.

In time, the Trustees opted for the Constituent College Status. The fact that this initiative came from the Union and succeeded in winning the support of the Academic Council, the College Executive Council (CEC) (i.e. the governing body) and the Trustees bore witness to a high degree of union-management cooperation. Much credit for this level of trust must go to Monsignor Michael Olden, President of Maynooth at the time of the initiative. Of course, the initiative had the solid support of Vice-President Matt O'Donnell. Monsignor Michael Ledwith, who succeeded Monsignor Olden as President, was also a very positive supporter for the campaign for equal status for Maynooth within the NUI.

From 1978 until 1995 I had been elected as one of the three lecturer/ senior lecturers on the College Executive Council (CEC), which greatly enhanced the communications between the union and the governing body. Looking back on my role on the CEC, I saw my function as a member of the 'loyal' opposition who raised the necessary questions to ensure transparency (*via* the circulated minutes) and to oppose policy proposals likely to penalise students or junior staff. Apart from a few tense encounters, the relationship between the management and myself was always friendly, although some seasoned academic clerics at times intimated a sense of tedium at my persistent questioning of those in authority (in the interests of staff and students). There were other elected members who were even more probing in their approach. All of this led to a more open form of government within the college, which was very good for morale. I always enjoyed encounters with the college's friendly and effective treasurer, Mr Pat Dalton. Presidents Mgr Michael Olden and his successor Mgr Michael Ledwith were efficient and courteous leaders. The Registrar, Prof Peter Carr, was a caring and genuine friend of the students.

During the occupation of the administration offices in Maynooth by the Students' Union in 1982, I, as chairperson of the Academic Staff Union, took the initiative to end the deadlock. The President of the College, Monsignor Michael Olden and the President of the Maynooth Students' Union, Mr Pat O'Doherty, agreed to a public meeting on the issues. The meeting took place in a packed Callan Hall. I had the duty of chairing the meeting and we agreed very strict rules of procedure. Among those who made significant interventions was the *President of the Union of Students in Ireland (USI)*, Mr Joe Duffy (who later became a well-known Radio broadcaster on RTÉ). The outcome of the meeting prepared the way for an honourable withdrawal from the administrative block. One of my tasks was to check an inventory of damage to the office, caused accidentally during the occupation. The issues that resulted in the surprise occupation had to do with fees and grants. It was agreed to attempt to resolve these issues through negotiation. All damage was paid for out of student funds.

In 1983, the Minister for Health, Mr Barry Desmond TD, withdrew medical cards from university students whose parents' means would not make them eligible. This led to the Maynooth Students' Union occupying the public health offices in Naas. This was part of a nationwide campaign. Because squatting had been criminalised in the 1972 legislation, the Gardaí arrested the student leaders, a number of whom ended up in Mountjoy Jail. I remember visiting them in prison in Glengariff Parade, Mountjoy. Later, in 1984, there was a second student occupation of the administrative buildings in Maynooth and, once again, I had to negotiate a peaceful solution to the *impasse*. The question of denying young adults (university students) their right to medical cards was, in my opinion, seriously unjust. It linked them to their parents' income. This was very wrong, in that it defined them as 'dependent children' although they were old enough to get married, to vote, *et cetera*. It was an ill-advised Government action, which added to the dysfunctional nature of 'extended adolescence'. But the State got away with it. Very often in life the just cause does not win out. It is a pragmatic truth and a questionable fact that 'might is right' in the long run! The withdrawal of students' (unemployed) medical cards was a classic case of might winning over justice, despite the blow to the psychological development of the young adults themselves. The 1980s were not easy years for State finances in Ireland.

The levels of inflation and of unemployment during the 1980s were very severe indeed, i.e.:

Inflation and Unemployment Rates in the 1980s

Year	Inflation Rate	Unemployment Rate
1981	20.4%	9.9%
1982	17.1%	11.4%
1983	9.2%	15.3%
1984	7.6%	16.8%
1985	4.7%	18.2%
1986	4.0%	18.2%
1987	2.6%	17.6%
1988	2.5%	17.0%
1989	3.9%	16.5%

Note: Mac Gréil, *Prejudice in Ireland Revisited*, Maynooth, 1996, p.355.

The above figures speak for themselves. A significant factor in the generation of very high unemployment was the rationalisation and automation of industry and commercial services. The computer was beginning to replace and displace workers, especially the skilled and semi-skilled and 'routine non-manual' employees. We also had a series of mergers and the closing down of such prestigious companies as Ford in Cork, Irish Shipping and others. The entry of more married women into the labour force (outside the home) also contributed to the size of the workforce and the increase in numbers unemployed. There was a fairly radical adjustment taking place in Ireland in the 1980s. Coupled with the very high level of unemployment, we witnessed the rise in emigration of semi-skilled, unskilled and skilled, as well as of highly qualified graduates (at great expense to the State). It was a sad time for university lecturers to see young people, who were needed to improve their local communities, giving the benefits of their education and training to societies and communities who were already strong (and able to pay them well). I used to tell the final year students during our final class that *it would be better for their communities if they stayed at home and went on the dole, rather than emigrate to the 'ghettoes of the strong'*. In the

1980s the County Kildare Council of Trade Unions established Resource Cetres for the Unemployed in Droichead Nua, Athy, Naas, and Leixslip. This congress-sponsored service has continued with success ever since.

4. The Death of My Mother: Máire (Ní Chadhain) 1901-1982

On 14th March 1982, my mother, Máire (Molly Ní Chadhain), died after a very brief illness, RIP. She was eighty-one years and three months old. She lived her life to the full until the weekend that she died. The death of my second parent was a traumatic break and very difficult to cope with. It brought tremendous sadness to the family and to the whole village of Drummindoo. A priest friend of mine told me that her death would bring home to me and my brother Owen and my sister Mary, the 'loneliness of celibacy'. From then on there would be 'nobody alive who would think of us around the clock'. The celibate would have very good friends but their level of closeness could not approach that of parents, spouses or children. Life since my mother's death has been truly celibate, although I have no regrets in the sense that this detachment enabled me to devote more energy and commitment to pastoral and social causes and to my professional work. The friendship of my family, and my friends (religious and lay) helped to keep me fairly normal, I hope. Celibacy is the greatest sacrifice I can offer to God out of love for Him and the good of others. It is an enduring witness of faith. This is not to say that a married person cannot be a good priest!

Belief in the 'communion of saints' was a source of great consolation in that I often prayed to God through the intercession of my deceased parents. Commitment to life after death is central to my personal belief. Because of the mercy of God and the basic goodness of people, I find it very difficult to envisage people parted from God forever. As one priest friend once said at the funeral of a person who was a cause of public scandal, '*his faults were due more to weakness than to malice*'. Also, when one appreciates the influences of social, psychological, and cultural determinants of human behaviour, only God can judge the extent of personal culpability in a bad act. Also, we have the promise of forgiveness for the repentant sinner. I am not writing all this to indicate my late mother's sinful life. In fact, she was a most conscientious and moral woman, who prayed constantly, and was very charitable towards others. And she kept her piety to herself.

My mother's wake and funeral were most memorable occasions. Because of her service in the War of Independence (1919-21) while a nurse in St Ultan's Hospital, Dublin, under Dr Kathleen Lynn, her coffin was draped in the tricolour. During her life she had refused to seek a medal or a pension. We felt that public recognition of her, at times, very brave service to her country should be given to her. At her wake in Drummindoo, the late Archbishop Joseph Cunnane, (Tuam) and the local administrator, Very Rev Tony King (who was a genuine friend of the family) called and prayed at her bedside. My mother was laid out in her 'Child of Mary' habit, which the Archbishop commented on with much approval. My mother had told me on a number of occasions that she wished to be laid out in the 'Child of Mary' habit. Her five sons and one daughter were all present as were her grandchildren and other members of the family, neighbours and friends.

It was a great wake, as she would have wished it to be. I remember her and my late father discussing their desired wakes. My father, who died in hospital, would say that he did not wish to have alcohol at his wake. My mother would reply that she would like her friends to get a 'drop of something' at her wake. We honoured her wish!

The Requiem Mass was concelebrated in St Mary's Church, Westport, with me as chief celebrant and my brother, Owen, as preacher. (I was too emotionally upset to preach either at her or my father's requiem.) At the graveyard four of her sons carried the coffin – Sean, I, Austin, and Pádraig while (Father) Owen led the cortège from the gate to the graveside. My sister, Mary (Sister M Gregory) walked behind. I realised afterwards that earlier 'Canon Law' forbade a priest to carry the coffin of a non-ordained person. So much for the narrow view of the past! I am afraid I never confessed my carrying my mother's coffin!

As we assembled in the house in Drummindoo on the day after the burial of my mother's remains, we realised that something terribly sad had happened. The heart had left the hearth! It was then that I felt profound grief. But, I remembered one thing my late mother had said to me on a number of occasions with regard to her family: '*Whatever happens I hope you will never fall out even if you disagree*'. She knew her children well. Some of us were strong-willed and quite opinionated.

She tried to teach us to be able to disagree without falling out. If only the Irish people could have had the moral strength to learn that lesson. My mother learned it the hard way during the Civil War in the early 1920s, when she had seen Dick Mulcahy putting his brother-in-law, Jim Ryan, in jail. My mother had been quite close to both the Mulcahy and Ryan families during the War of Independence. But, thank God, they made it up later. I have tried to communicate this wish of my late mother to many families. So far, thank God, we have all remained close friends. There were many other aspects about my mother's life and times, which now live on in her family, and in those who knew her well. *I bParthas na ngrás go raibh sí.* My late mother would be fascinated by the coincidence of dying on Marx Day, 14th March, 1982, the ninety-ninth anniversary of Karl Marx's death, RIP The day of my mother's first anniversary Mass was the centenary of the death of Karl Marx on the 14th March 1983. I prayed for them both.

5. CONSERVATIVE CLOUDS WERE GATHERING

Many of the social and political developments around the world were most depressing during the 1980s. The era of optimism and emancipation of the 1960s and the early 1970s was over. Still, there was a spirit of protest alive in the Trade Unions and in the University student body in Ireland. President Ronald Reagan succeeded President Jimmy Carter in the United States in 1980. This marked a radical change to the 'right' and many countries in South and Latin America, who had begun to 'breathe again' under the supportive rule of Jimmy Carter, were to meet with dictatorial repression allowed under the reign of Ronald Reagan. Also, there was a change in the commitment of the Catholic Church's support for community-based liberation movements. The heavy hand of political and ecclesial conservatism tended to dampen the hope of social justice for the 'under-class'. We thought we were on our way – that *'we would overcome'*! Within a relatively short time many supporters of the poor and the oppressed were to face persecution under the hands of leaders like General Pinochet in Chile, who had consolidated their political power positions with the supportive blessing of the Thatcher and Reagan regimes. It had become a decade of tyrants and martyrs, i.e. in the 1980s 'liberation theology' was to be discouraged and expressive religious movements were to replace instrumental (i.e. other-centred) ones. And yet, not all was lost. Catholic leaders on the ground displayed heroic courage in defending the rights of the poor. The spirit of the Jesuit General Congregations (thirty-one and thirty-two) still informed the thinking and commitment of Jesuits and their lay and religious colleagues in the campaign for justice. Some were to pay the price of martyrdom for their commitment.

The attempt to 'return religion to the prie-dieu and the presbytery' and remove it from the fight for justice was gaining ground. In the biblical sense we were moving from a dynamic 'prophetic' period of the 1960s and early 1970s inspired by leaders like Archbishop Dom Helder Camara, Archbishop of Olinda, Brazil, to a more routinised 'priestly' (as distinct from clerical) time of the 1980s and 1990s. Of course, in a prophetic era, there are real dangers to the institutional order and even to the more sophisticated, theological orthodoxy, which inevitably arouses the counteraction of those very genuine leaders who wish to restore order and routine. On the other side of the coin, in a 'priestly' dominated time, the Church's meaning and relevance will be questioned by the more committed members of the faithful. This, in my opinion, was in part the cause of the drying up of the more dynamic vocations among young people who wished to join the Church in the religious and priestly life, with the aim of restoring justice and dignity to the downtrodden. Young people who continued to be attracted to the 'priestly' Church had already flocked into the seminaries of the developing world, in order to get personal meaning in their detachment from the day-to-day affairs of men and women. A healthy dimension of the 'prophetic' continued to survive in some dioceses.

This overview of what happened to the Catholic Church during the 1980s may not find agreement among all readers. All I ask of the reader is to think about what happened. One of the most characteristic aspects of the prophetic period was the number of clergy, religious and lay men and women who proved their love of God and of their neighbour by the crown of martyrdom. A 'priestly' Church produces 'confessors', while a 'prophetic' Church produces 'martyrs'. Both are saints! I suppose only *Jesus of Nazareth* could combine perfectly the 'prophetic' and the 'priestly' in His ministry. I must admit that I feel the Catholic Church is heading for a new 'prophetic era' as we might be reaching the end of the current 'priestly' period, which began in the 1980s. It will creep up on us, as the Spirit leads on into the future and invites us to seek out the lost sheep and challenge the unjust, unsafe, unfriendly, despairing, unspirited, unecumenical, cruel and unredeemed world. I am sorry I may not be around to take part in this new prophetic era. All I can do is try to sow a few seeds here and there to encourage young men and women to consider dedicating themselves to changing our world and its structures and making it more conducive to justice, love and mutual respect. This will take courage and commitment. I believe there is a providential influence, which enables the Church to adjust to the passing challenges of history. By the Church I mean the *'corporate presence of Christ on earth'*. This includes the institutional Churches of the baptised believers and the People of God.

In a priestly decade, Pope John Paul II was strongly priestly and also prophetic in relation to Eastern Europe. His prophetic role was most clearly seen in his mission to the people of Poland and of Eastern Europe, who felt they were being repressed by the dictatorship of Centralist Communism and had experienced a ruthless ruler in Joseph Stalin and some of his successors. The Iron Curtain had fenced in and out many peoples against their collective will. But, let us not forget that this was agreed at Yalta in 1944. Pope John Paul II had grown up in Poland and had experienced the tyranny of Nazi occupation (1939-45) and of the Soviet Union after the Second World War. He witnessed the death and destruction of innocent people all around him. When he was elected Pope it was a 'providential' decision by his fellow cardinals. Within a short time, he set his sights on the plight of his native land and was a liberating influence on the whole Polish society. President Yaruzelski and he were able to communicate with each other. The leader of the Dockers' Union, Lech Walesa, was also supported by the Pope in the work of the Solidarity Movement. In Moscow a new type of more tolerant Soviet leader was also present in President Mikhail Gorbachev. This foursome of leaders with prestige and esteem were able to generate a momentum towards change, without violent counteraction from Moscow. Pope John Paul II, who luckily survived an assassination attempt in 1981, led the Church in what could be described as a non-violent revolution that ultimately resulted in the collapse of the Iron Curtain in 1989, especially in Poland. That was followed by the emancipation of Eastern European satellite states seceding from the Soviet Union, leading to the collapse of the USSR. The miracle was that this was brought about without a violent civil war as had happened in the United States when the Southern states tried to secede in 1860. The socialist and communist regime, which had already been discredited by Eastern bureaucratic centralism, also collapsed with the Berlin Wall in 1989. The Pope was not that enamoured by what replaced the collectivist socialist system, i.e. free-market capitalism, as we will see when reflecting on the 1990s.

6. Revolution in South Africa!

The plight of the majority of people in South Africa had been a matter of growing concern in Ireland and throughout Europe. As far back as the mid-sixties, street protests were being organised in Dublin and elsewhere. It was not until the late 1970s and early 1980s that sanctions and boycotts were beginning to exercise real effect on the *apartheid regime in South Africa*, when 20% of the population dominated the lives of the whole society. In Ireland we had an activist anti-apartheid movement, of which I had the honour of being a member. It was led by Kadar Asmal, a lecturer in Trinity College, his wife Louise and Reverend Terence McCaughey, also a lecturer in TCD. Kadar Asmal had been *a persona non grata* in his native South Africa. The role of the Christian Churches in South Africa in relation to apartheid was mixed. Part of the Dutch Reformed Church had for a time been supportive of many of those who backed apartheid. The Roman Catholic, the Anglican and other Christian Churches were all opposed to apartheid and took leading roles in bringing it down. Archbishop Hurley, OMI, of Durban, an Irishman, was the most eminent supporter of the oppressed for almost thirty years. Archbishop Tutu of Cape Town became a World leader in exposing the iniquities of the apartheid system.

In all my experience as a student of intergroup relations, the apartheid system in South Africa was among the most inhumane forms of stratified social segregation. *It was a crime against humanity.* On my visit to South Africa in 2004, I saw first-hand the spatial evidence of this inhumane segregation of people because of their categorisation according to their colour and racial group in a stratified manner. The collectivities in Ireland to play the most positive role in opposition to apartheid in South Africa were the trade unions and religious orders/congregations. The priests and religious who served in South Africa had experienced the evils of the system and made their friends at home aware of it. It may be too soon to do justice to these prophetic, foreign missionaries in their work for the liberation of the people of South Africa. While visiting the prison on Robin Island, where Nelson Mandela and his friends were imprisoned for over twenty years, a former prisoner told us visitors of the crafty way the Irish Catholic priest (chaplain) would keep the prisoners in touch with what was happening outside the prison by carefully leading 'Prayers of the Faithful' during Mass, which the prison guards failed to grasp. The visiting priests and ministers were very important contacts with the outside world for these isolated leaders of the struggle against apartheid.

The role of the Irish Trade Unions was also very significant, in generating solidarity with the suppressed black and colonial people of South Africa. The honourable role played by the workers in Dunnes Stores, Dublin, by refusing to handle boycotted goods won world headlines. The Irish Congress of Trade Unions established solidarity with the victims of apartheid. Many motions were passed at Union Conferences and at Trade-Council meetings and subscriptions were gathered for this great cause. We in Maynooth College were highly moved by the appalling and evil regime of apartheid in South Africa. The sports' boycott of South Africa was also effective.

At the end of the decade things were looking up. The South African cause did much to awaken solidarity between racial groups. I found in my second major survey of Irish Intergroup Attitudes carried out during 1988-89, that there was a significant and substantial decrease in racial prejudice, i.e. prejudice against a person because of membership of a group or category with different (genetically inherited) physical features, e.g. colour, size, texture of hair, shape of eyes, nose or lips, etc. This was, in my opinion, in no small part due to the quality of the ANC leader Nelson Mandela and others. The apartheid regime exposed the fallacy of racism, just as the crazy views of the Nazi Third Reich leaders did in relation to the so-called 'Aryan Super Race'. That having been said, we still have too high a level of latent racialism in Ireland, even after its reduction over the sixteen years from 1972-73 to 1988-89. This trend of a reduction in racism and ethnic prejudice was further confirmed in the findings of the 2007-08 national survey, which was published in 2011 under the title *Pluralism and Diversity in Ireland*.

7. ACADEMIC DEVELOPMENTS AT MAYNOOTH

By the end of the 1980s it was becoming very clear that the NUI Recognised College in Maynooth was expanding beyond all expectations. This was happening at a time of decline in the number of clerical students in the National Seminary in Maynooth. The Pontifical University opened up its courses in Sacred Theology to lay students and to religious. Joint degrees at undergraduate level (BA Th) were being awarded to students who 'majored' in theology and one Arts subject of their choice. This was a most positive development in that it supplied the Church and the schools with a supply of qualified lay teachers with a competent knowledge of Sacred Scripture and theology. In the light of the subsequent decline in vocations to the priesthood and religious life, the development of the Joint Theology/Arts degree was very necessary and providential.

It appears to me that the greater involvement of lay people in the pedagogical, liturgical, pastoral and administrative life of the Church (which is most welcome) requires very serious study of theology and Sacred Scripture. Liturgical and pastoral skills are necessary for those willing to be actively involved. The Maynooth course would, in time, make a significant contribution to this need. The *Mater Dei Institute* in Dublin, as well as the *Milltown Institute of Theology and Philosophy*, has also contributed to the theological education of the laity. When the ordination of deacons for pastoral ministry has been established, Maynooth and Milltown will be ideally placed to meet their training needs. Without serious training in the Sacred Sciences, there will always be a danger of a lack of self-confidence in the actively involved lay person, on the one hand, or well-intentioned fundamentalism (due to a minimum of theological and scriptural sophistication) on the other. The closure of the major seminaries in Wexford, Waterford, Carlow, Kilkenny, Thurles and, later, Clonliffe was inevitable because of the acute decline in vocations to the priesthood. During the 1970s and 1980s, it became clear to me that the Church should try to give support to particular populations, i.e. women and third-level students, and involve them more in the real life of the pastoral and liturgical ministries. I suggested this to a well-meaning bishop. He agreed with such priorities but he said he would leave it to his successor! As a Church, we have been late in identifying such priorities in time to prepare for the pending onslaught of secularisation.

In conclusion, on this topic, it could be stated that the maintenance of the Church's Pontifical Universities in Ireland and elsewhere will be very necessary to meet the demands of the people of God in the century ahead. There will be an urgent need that deacons and laity involved in the pedagogical, liturgical and pastoral service of the Church will be self-confident and equipped to respond to the challenging demands made on them. The role of the Pontifical Universities will be central in this regard. With the growing sophistication of the faithful, it will be necessary to raise the level of formation of clergy, religious and laity to respond to such a welcome social and cultural change. According as the material interests of the people are satisfied, the demands coming for the people's search for meaning will increase. I visualise a very exciting time for a more mature Church in Ireland in the decades ahead. When the appalling cases of clerical and religious child abuse have been addressed, and dealt with appropriately, and confidence is restored in the Church's teaching, a new era will come about in a more humble serving Church.

8. Northern Crisis Affects Political Life in the Republic

The political scene in Ireland was dominated right through the 1980s by the ongoing violence and mayhem in Northern Ireland and serious economic difficulties in the Republic. Mr Charles Haughey TD, was *Taoiseach* during the following years, i.e. December 1979 to June 1981; March 1982 to December 1982; March 1987 to July 1989; and July 1989 to February 1992. Dr Garret Fitzgerald TD, who had been a Minister for Foreign Affairs in the previous coalition Government led by Liam Cosgrave TD, was *Taoiseach* on two occasions during the 1980s, i.e. June 1981 to March 1982, December 1982 to March 1987. In 1982 a new political party was founded in the Republic led by the Limerick *Fianna Fáil* TD, Mr Dessie O'Malley. It was called the Progressive Democrats and was made up mainly of *Fianna Fáil* TDs who disagreed with the leadership of the *Taoiseach*, Mr Charles Haughey TD. A number of *Fine Gael* members also joined the new party. It was to join *Fianna Fáil* in a coalition Government from July 1989 until February 1992. The policies pursued by the PDs could be categorised as neo-liberal.

Despite all the difficulties and challenges, there were ongoing efforts between the Irish and United Kingdom Governments in relation to Northern Ireland. A special *Anglo-Irish Agreement* was signed by Mrs Margaret Thatcher MP, (Prime Minister) and Dr Garret Fitzgerald TD, (*Taoiseach*) in 1986. This agreement elicited public protest from the Loyalist political community, but it established a basis for ongoing dialogue and consultation between the Governments in relation to the troubled affairs of the North. It was, in my opinion, an important step on the road to peaceful coexistence in the North and Irish-British cooperation. It would take another decade before internal nationalist and republican negotiations could succeed in bringing about a ceasefire (i.e. 1994).

During this time, I was invited by a 'political' prisoner, Mr Dominic McGlinchy, in Long Kesh (renamed 'The Maze') prison to visit him as an appeals' visitor and I got permission to do so. At the time I was a member of the prisoners' group of *Pax Christi*. It was through that group I was contacted by members of his family, i.e. his wife and his sister. The prisoner was extradited to Northern Ireland from the Republic (where he was captured) on the charge of having murdered a postmistress, which he absolutely denied. His lawyer briefed me on his case before I entered the Maze. It was some experience! Visitors were mainly wives, sisters and mothers of prisoners. The armoured car in which we travelled had windows only on the roof and it drove in all directions. It stopped after about five minutes and police and military examined us. Then it toured on further before stopping near the entrance to the visitors' area. Everything was depressing – steel fencing, undecorated waiting rooms with hard seats, grey colouring and so forth. We were called out by the name of the prisoner we were to meet. Since my prisoner was fairly notorious, everyone in the waiting room looked at me as I stood up in response to my call.

The place where visitors and prisoners met was open plan, with security guards all around. They could hear our conversation. Each prisoner sat behind the middle of a long table while the visitor sat opposite. We could shake hands and I did so. Dominic spoke clearly and indicated that he felt his life might be in danger. He opened the conversation by saying: '*They're God Almighty in here*!' and then he said that he feared that he would be taken to the perimeter of the prison and shot for 'attempting to escape'. (He had been previously at the centre of an alleged 'shoot to kill' policy case in Northern Ireland.) His purpose in asking for me was to let whoever I thought had influence know that he was innocent of the particular charges that were being made against him to justify his extradition. I told him I would convey his message to the Commission for Justice and Peace (in the Catholic Church) and to others who would be interested in ensuring he received justice. He felt that his extradition to Northern Ireland at the time was to facilitate the signing of the *Anglo-Irish Agreement* of 1986.

On return to Dublin, I did as I had promised. The solicitor, who briefed me prior to my visit, told me that a leading Protestant Queen's Counsel would defend the prisoner and advocate for him in his appeal against extradition. I was not that successful in convincing the Commission, as they seemed to believe there was a *prima facie* case, which I disagreed with. I also communicated with a Senior Counsel, who I knew was familiar with cases of this nature. The outcome of Dominic McGlinchy's case was that he won his appeal in Belfast. He was returned by the RUC back across the Border to be rearrested and continue in prison in Portlaoise. Later, both he and his young wife were to be assassinated on different occasions in a most brutal and inhumane manner (before their children) by people unknown. I have not learned of any arrests or trials in relation to these two brutal murders! *Ar dheis Dé go raibh a n-anamacha uaisle.*

While in the Prisoners' Group of *Pax Christi*, I kept in touch with the plight of families and prisoners. It also made us alive to the need for political momentum in the case of Northern Ireland at the 'grass roots' level, who felt a sense of powerlessness. It was very necessary that Church-based and other groups kept their problems and views in mind and before the media. The dominant groups in society had become the most powerful lobby groups, e.g. the Trade Unions, Churches, Farmers' Associations, Industrialists, etc. They would always command a hearing. Unfortunately they did not do that much for the liberation of prisoners. *The people in prison (for whatever reason), their spouses and children, the Travellers, the homeless, and others, rarely have a voice sufficiently powerful to influence the establishment. Of all these categories, those in prison for long sentences were and are the most deprived. Society wishes to isolate the prisoner (and those with serious mental illnesses). 'Lock them up and throw away the key!'*

9. THE IRISH PRISONS

When visiting Long Kesh on that one occasion, I got to talk to some of the other visitors and began to empathise with them. I had met visitors to Mountjoy on several occasions also. When speaking at the occasion of the tenth anniversary of the founding of *Simon in Ireland* in 1979, I raised the question of the need for 'conjugal visitation' facilities for wives and husbands of prisoners serving life sentences. The strain on the prisoners' married partners to be deprived of their conjugal rights and the impediment to the conception of children seemed to me to be grossly inhumane and unjust. It must have led to marriage breakdown in many cases. It also was not conducive to the rehabilitation of the long-term prisoners. In fact, I would consider conjugal rights for married prisoners serving long sentences, without regular parole, to be a basic human right. To his credit, the late Archbishop John Charles McQuaid of Dublin also was concerned about the marital rights of long-term prisoners.

In 1980 the Report of the *MacBride Commission of Enquiry into the Irish Penal System* was published. The MacBride Commission was convened by the Prisoners' Rights Organisation (PRO) as a non-governmental Commission of concerned citizens under the joint chairmanship of Mr Seán MacBride SC, and Professor Louk Hulsman, head of the European Decriminalisation Office. The PRO leader, Joe Costello TD, who invited the Commission, was to become a Minister of State. The members included Senator Gemma Hussey, Professor Mary McAleese, Michael D Higgins TD, Paddy McEntee SC, Una Higgins-O'Malley, Muireann Ní Bhriain, BL, Matt Merrigan (Trade Unionist), Michael Keating TD and yours truly. Caitríona Lawlor was Secretary of the Commission. We began our work by inviting people who had experience of Irish prisons as former prisoners and also other people who were interested in the state of our prisons to share their views with us either in writing or orally. The Commission divided the different aspects of the Penal System among the members according to their area of competence. Experts from other countries were also consulted. The areas researched by individuals and subgroups included the causes of crime and delinquency, the history of prisons in Ireland, the Irish prison system today, the prison population, recidivism and rehabilitation. After many meetings (held in the library of Sandford Lodge, College of Industrial

Relations) a draft report was prepared and approved. I was given the task of editing and preparing the final report for publication. (It is interesting to note that two members of the MacBride Commission were later elected *Uachtaráin na hÉireann*, i.e. Professor Mary McAleese in 1997 and Mr Michael D Higgins in 2011.)

Since the MacBride Commission was not convened by the State, we did not receive the full formal cooperation of the Department of Justice. Nevertheless, we were able to get sufficient facts by circuitous routes from experienced lawyers and others, including students of crime and deviance in Ireland. Various published reports were also useful, if incomplete. I was disappointed that we did not receive the factual information we sought. The real tragedy of our penal system was the failure of successive administrations between 1881 and 1980 to have carried out an in-depth report on the prisons. *Despite all its shortcomings, the MacBride Report was the first serious report on Irish Prisons for one hundred years.* It would not have happened at all were it not for the initiative of Mr Joe Costello and the members of the *Prisoners' Rights Organisation* and the willingness of the members of the Commission to devote time and energy to the work in a totally voluntary capacity. (Mr Joe Costello TD, was a Minister of State in the *Fine Gael-Labour* Government from 2012 to 2014.)

The major recommendation of the Report was the need to set up a *Treatment of Offenders Board* to take overall responsibility for the Irish prisons. The Department of Justice would be represented on the Board and would be given responsibility for security. *The membership of the Board would be from a multidisciplinary background in law, sociology, psychology, community care, religion, etc.* The principal finding of the Report was that our prisons did not work. Recidivism rates made that fact crystal clear. As Seán MacBride told us on a number of occasions, the influence of paramilitarism in Ireland since the foundation of the State had impeded proper prison reform and resulted in the almost exclusive emphasis on security to the detriment of rehabilitation. There was very little use made of alternatives to prison, apart from fines often limited by statute (irrespective of the wealth of the convicted). We did not see much progress until a Treatment of Offenders Board took over control of Irish prisons. The Board would need to have statutory 'teeth'!

One of the most interesting features of Irish society in general is *its practically total lack of awareness of our penal system and even our criminal courts' system and procedures*. We seem to be great at turning a blind eye to that which we do not wish to see. Our fascination with crime movies and crime novels may be an escapist mechanism. It probably has also got a self-reassuring aspect, which convinces us that 'we are not like those terrible people who are so corrupt and violent, etc'! Many of us are still in the pre-liberated age, when we see the total responsibility for a criminal act in the offender. But that is just untrue! Most, if not all, crime is the product of a complex causality, i.e. medical, personal, social and cultural. Our criminal code is also very much socioculturally determined. For example, in most capitalist, free-market societies, the protection of private property rights takes precedence over basic personal and family rights. The use of our Gardaí and the time of our court officers (which is notoriously expensive) is, proportionally speaking, over-concerned with private property rights. I often ask myself, '*Are we sending the right people to jail*?' or '*Do we really allow for complex causality when the jury arrives at a verdict of guilty*?' The convicted person is often as much a victim of circumstance as a person acting out of deliberate malice. Every time we visit prison we should say, '*There go I but for the Grace of God*', which provided me with the sociocultural environment and commitment to the acceptable norms of society.

In reaction to the tendency in society to distance itself from the whole area of the treatment of offenders, I encouraged every student of First Year Sociology to spend at least two hours in the Criminal (Circuit) Courts and write a paper on the experience. In addition, thanks to the cooperation of Governor John Lonergan of Mountjoy Prison, our students were afforded an opportunity to visit the prison and see for themselves what it was like and who were incarcerated. They were not to go there as 'slummers' or seeking voyeuristic thrills! Prior to the visit to the Jail, Governor Lonergan would deliver a lecture to the class and take questions. Incidentally, one of the (minor) recommendations in the *MacBride Report* was that Judges in the Criminal system should spend at least three nights living in a prison cell. I would recommend such a treat to every Minister for Justice on assuming office!

Reflecting on the Gospel, I see now why Our Lord included visiting the prisoners as one of the criteria for entering heaven. If people visited the prisoners more regularly, we would have a better society. *In my opinion, imprisonment is necessary for convicted persons as long as they are a danger to society or to themselves.* The idea of using prisons as punishment or even as a deterrent should be questioned. Prisons as places of rehabilitation require a whole new approach, which would be the most effective way of using incarceration to the benefit of offenders and of society. These suggestions would sum up the views of the MacBride Commission. But, alas, such recommendations have not been taken seriously so far by either the Ministers for Justice or their senior officials, it would appear. To his credit, the late Charles J Haughey TD, when Minister for Justice in 1961, proposed that rehabilitation should be the main goal of imprisonment.

In 1985 the Department appointed its own Commission, under the chairmanship of Mr TK Whitaker, to enquire into the Irish penal system. Professor Liam Ryan, Department of Social Studies, Maynooth, was a member of the Whitaker Commission. In many ways it duplicated the work of the 'unofficial' *MacBride Commission*. Did this mean that the usefulness of a commission was to be determined by its official status? The advantage the second commission had over its predecessor was the availability of information from the Department's archives, which was refused to MacBride. Also, it had many more resources at its disposal. Our Commission was totally voluntary but it had the confidence of the prisoners. The findings of Whitaker were worthwhile but not as radical as MacBride. Both Reports agreed on the need to remove the exclusive control of the treatment of offenders from the Department of Justice to a more broadly-based Board. The net result of the MacBride and Whitaker Reports will be tested in the years ahead. So far, there is only limited evidence of real reform to our penal system. The number of people in prison has been on the rise until quite recently.

Over the last decade there have been calls for longer sentences and for the use of prison as a punishment, as a deterrent and as a place of detention, rather than a place for rehabilitation. The overuse of prison for petty offenders reduces its capacity to serve the needs of the serious (convicted) criminals for whom prison is necessary for their own and society's safety. With fewer prisoners, more resources would be available for their individual rehabilitation. More imaginative alternatives to imprisonment for convicted offenders are a high priority. I often wonder do the judges, Gardaí and politicians understand the gross waste of resources and of human welfare resulting from the present use of incarceration. For many prisoners they enter jail relatively innocent and leave it more hardened and skilled in professional crime, not to mention their induction into a 'community of offenders'.

10. THE DECRIMINALISATION CASE

During 1983, I was invited as a witness by Mrs Mary Robinson SC, to give evidence from my research findings, in support of Senator David Norris's Constitutional *case against the criminalisation of voluntary homosexual relations between consenting male adults*. The case brought by the Senator claimed that such criminalisation was against his right to privacy. Mrs Robinson had asked me to give evidence when I went to her for another reason altogether, i.e. in relation to the restoration of the railway services from Sligo to Limerick. My request to her was to put the Collooney to Limerick track/railway on the European Union's inventory of railways. When I asked, she said that she would be most willing to oblige and she added: '*Could I ask you a quid pro quo*?' '*Sure,*' I replied. '*What is your "quid pro quo"*?' Then she explained that she was Senator Norris's Senior Counsel in his High Court Case. She pointed to my findings in the 1972-73 survey (published in *Prejudice and Tolerance in Ireland*), which confirmed that a plurality of the Greater Dublin respondents, i.e. 45.2%, would favour decriminalisation as opposed to 39.9% against it, with 14.9% not expressing an opinion. I did not hesitate to agree to put my findings on the record of the court. I must admit that not everyone (lay or clerical) would be too happy with my going into public court to give evidence in favour of gay men's right to privacy. For me to refuse would be academically dishonourable. I found out that homophobia was one of the most invidious forms of prejudice, which was as universal as anti-Semitism. It was no accident that the Nazis' murder machine killed homosexuals as well as Jews!

When the day of my presence in the High Court arrived, I brought with me a print-out of my findings in relation to the attitudes towards the *decriminalisation of homosexual relations between consenting adult males,* i.e. by all the independent variables, such as age, gender, marital status, education, occupational status, place of residence, place of origin, religious affiliation and so forth. I was to present these findings as an 'exhibit' in the case. On my way into the courtroom, a former friend of mine asked me what I was in the Four Courts for that afternoon (2pm - 4pm). When I told him he seemed horrified and said to me, '*Surely you're not here to defend that dirt?*' I reminded him that I considered homosexuals as full human beings deserving the same respect as heterosexuals. His remarks stunned me and strengthened my resolve to defend gay people's rights before the law. The sad thing about the well-educated and highly-positioned friend of mine was the level of homophobia, which probably reflected hostility towards homosexuals in the upper echelons of our society at the time. Underpinning much of such prejudice one often finds a degree of quasi-religious self-righteousness. The encounter on the corridors of the Four Courts was not the only experience I have had of such ignorant expressions of homophobia.

The actual period in the witness stand was a very interesting experience. The Honourable Justice McWilliam presided and all court formalities had to be followed. I was nervous as I took the oath. Mrs Mary Robinson SC began by asking me to tell the court about my findings in relation to the attitudes of the Dublin sample towards decriminalisation. My prepared print-out of the findings was accepted as an 'exhibit' in the case. I answered a few technical questions by the Judge. During cross-examination, the counsel for the State, Mr O'Hanlon SC, asked me about the Catholic Church's stance on the issue of homosexual behaviour between consenting male adults.[3] In her re-examination after the cross-examination, Mrs Robinson SC, asked me if I thought that the criminalisation was discrimination? I answered, '*Yes*', and explained that criminalisation did not apply to cases of female homosexual behaviour. She also asked if I would favour decriminalisation. Again, I replied in the affirmative on the grounds that discrimination and the abuse of homosexuals by means of 'blackmail' and 'gay-bashing' had resulted in

---

3 In reply to his question – '*What was the Catholic Church's position on homosexuals?*' I replied: '*They were potential saints!*' He was then to enquire about the Catholic Church's position on consenting homosexual relations between adult males. My reply was that such behaviour was not acceptable and the Church recommended 'continence' or abstention.

the denial of their rights to this minority. Criminalisation had been used to justify 'homophobia' (in my opinion).

The outcome of the case was the refusal of the High Court to agree that Senator Norris's privacy was violated. He immediately appealed to the Supreme Court, where he was again turned down by a three-to-two verdict. The Senator then appealed to the European Court of Human Rights where his case was upheld in 1988 and, as a result, homosexual behaviour between consenting male adults was decriminalised in the Republic in 1993. I was happy with the outcome, but I would still advise continence or abstention. Promiscuous gay sex has been a factor in the spread of the HIV virus. The Church's moral teaching in relation to sexual behaviour, i.e. restricted to intercourse between consenting husbands and wives (in marriage), is to humanise it and make it an expression of truly human love. The sacrifice of continence strengthens the moral fibre of those who resolve to abstain from sexual intercourse outside of marriage. Even within marriage, love is more than 'making love'!

Unfortunately, in our modern hedonist culture, this standard is considered to be an unreasonable level of self-denial. In my view, the dropping of standards in relation to sexual intimacy in modern Western culture has been a mistake. At the same time, I would not favour a return to Puritanism and the more extreme condemnatory attitudes of pre-Vatican Two. Because of the changes in the social norms in relation to intimate relationships, we must avoid judging those who do not conform to the Church's norms without taking these changes into account. In fact, I believe that the Church needs to review its pastoral relationship with people living in 'irregular' unions. The review should take place at the highest level. This is a very serious pastoral problem, which cannot be ignored.

After my appearance in the High Court, there was an account of my evidence in the main newspapers. The reaction was, thankfully, very tolerant among my colleagues, by and large. When Mrs Robinson SC, asked me what my fee would be, I said that there would be no fee. All I was doing was my duty as a social researcher and as an advocate of minority rights. I was happy and privileged to be in a position to help. The decriminalisation of homosexual behaviour between consenting adult males repealed two Victorian pieces of criminal law (i.e. of 1850 and 1881), which reflected the puritanism of Britain during the nineteenth century. I was made familiar with both Acts of the British

Parliament when I was acting as a defence officer for the court martial of a soldier charged with a homosexual assault on another soldier in the 1950s. Even the language of the Acts sounded like the rhetoric of an old-time Puritan preacher. In my view, even then, it sounded too emotional for the objective 'rule of law'. It was quite fundamentalist.

Before leaving the topic of homophobia, it is interesting to record the change of attitudes between 1972-73, 1988-89, and 2007-08 i.e.:

	In favour of Criminalisation	Against *	Don't Know
1972-73 (Dublin)	39.9%	**45.2%**	14.9%
1988-89 (National)	35.1%	**43.9%**	20.9%
2007-08 (National)	17.5%	**64.6%**	17.9%

* Note: Percentages in favour of decriminalisation are **in bold**.

The above figures show a significant and substantial change in Irish attitudes for decriminalisation. The gap between those who favoured decriminalisation and those who were for criminalisation rose from 8.8% in 1988-89 to 47.1% in 2007-08. The worrying aspect of this result was that more than one-sixth of the national sample still favoured criminalisation in 2007-08, i.e. indicating the level of homophobia still latent in Irish society. I would find such a hard-line attitude towards fellow human beings to be less than Christian! What about loving the sinner, even if we disapprove of the sin? The reason why I emphasise these figures is to point out the danger of inflicting psychological pain on homosexuals who are still a very vulnerable minority in every society.

11. MONSIGNOR JAMES HORAN (1911 – 1986)

From 1983 until 1985 the late Monsignor James Horan had been recording his memoirs during the winter months. He was parish priest of *Cnoc Mhuire* (Knock) in County Mayo. It was on the gable of the parish church that a group of local parishioners saw an apparition of *Our Lady, St John and the Lamb of God*, in the autumn of 1879. As the Monsignor recorded in his memoirs: '*Six weeks after the apparition in Knock, Dr John McHale (Archbishop of Tuam) set up a Special Commission to examine the witnesses and to explore all possible natural causes of the phenomenon. The Commission examined fifteen witnesses and found their evidence "trustworthy and satisfactory". It carried out exhaustive research into possible natural causes and found none. Some months later in March 1880, the Commission reported to Dr McHale.'* *(Monsignor James Horan, Memoirs, 1992, p.139)* Shortly after receiving the Commission's report, the Archbishop of Tuam made the following statement to visiting pilgrims and journalists:

> *'It is a great blessing for the poor people in the West that the Blessed Virgin, Mother of God, has appeared amongst them in their wretchedness and misery and suffering.'*

This statement of Archbishop McHale was accepted as approval of Knock as a shrine and a place of public worship ever since, with around 1.5 million pilgrims praying there every year in recent times.

It was during Monsignor James Horan's tenure as parish priest of *Cnoc Mhuire* that the new basilica was built and Pope John Paul II visited the shrine (as already recorded). After the Pope's visit the noble Monsignor turned his discerning eye towards the transport infrastructure in the West of Ireland and initiated his campaign for an international airport to be located on a plateau some miles north of the shrine and within five miles of the town of Charlestown. The place was known as *Bár na Cúige* (the Top of the Province). Despite great opposition from senior civil servants and sceptical politicians in Dublin, the airport was successfully completed in 1985, one year before the Monsignor's sudden death, while on a pilgrimage in Lourdes during the last week in July. He was buried at the rear of the basilica after a solemn requiem Mass on Saturday, 2nd August 1986. His remains were flown directly from Lourdes to Knock Airport on the previous afternoon, RIP.

During his annual visit to Westport Parish at Christmas 1987, Archbishop Joseph Cassidy, gave me a 'duffel bag full of transcripts' of Monsignor Horan's tape recordings of his unfinished Memoirs. He informed me that the late Monsignor's family would like me to edit the memoirs with a view to publishing them. I agreed, having told the Archbishop of my very heavy workload at the time in St Patrick's College, Maynooth and my research programme, i.e. I had begun the preliminary work on a second major social survey (national sample) of Irish prejudices, which would be going to the field during 1988-89. The text of the transcript was most interesting but very far from being ready for publication. There were many cases of repetition and need for editing of the text, which the Monsignor would have done had he lived, to prepare it for publication.

His good friend, Chief Steward, Mr Tom Neary, had helped him with the preparation of the final manuscript. The work of preparing the text for publication took much more time than I had anticipated. It was necessary to rewrite the chapter on his early years and background, as well as writing an original epilogue to cover the Monsignor's final (and very active) year of life, i.e. 1985-86. In all the work, I received great cooperation from the Horan family, especially the Monsignor's sister, Nancy, and his brother, Bartley, and from his successor as parish priest of *Cnoc Mhuire*, Monsignor Dominic Greally, and his staff. The book, *Monsignor James Horan: Memoirs 1911-1986* (edited by Micheál Mac Gréil SJ) was published by Brandon Book Publishers Limited, Dingle, County Kerry, in 1992. It was well received.

In the six years prior to the Monsignor's death, I had got to know him fairly well and visited him fairly regularly in the presbytery in *Cnoc Mhuire*. He was always a most hospitable host and a charming conversationalist. His interest in the development of the West of Ireland was rarely far from his mind. This was very clear from his memoirs. Among the projects he pursued that made a public impact were included:

    (a) *The Dance Hall in Tooreen* (in the parish of Aghamore), which he built in 1951-52;

    (b) *The Basilica of Our Lady, Queen of Ireland, in Cnoc Mhuire* which was dedicated by Pope John Paul II on 30th September 1979; and

    (c) *The new International Airport* at *Bár na Cúige* (later known as Ireland West Airport Knock, built in 1980-85).

Like most pastorally-minded priests, Fr James Horan supported better community services in the various parishes where he served, i.e. rural electrification, community water schemes, forestry schemes, schools, community halls and centres, etc. He also took a keen interest in rural afforestation and any other scheme that would help to generate employment for local people in very hard times. He was also a good man on the media and seemed to get on very well with people like Mr Gay Byrne, presenter of the *Late Late Show*. He gave me good advice in relation to the *Sligo to Limerick Railway campaign*. He promised to come out publicly in favour of the project after he had delivered on the airport. Unfortunately, the Good Lord called him home before he could join the rail-corridor campaign publicly!

His advice on dealing with central bureaucracy (civil servants) was very fruitful. He cautioned me about the MAD file, i.e. the 'maximum-administrative-delay' file, by which authorities would hope that their repeated 'decision to defer a decision' would wear out the campaigners. He proved that he 'was wise to' this discouraging tactic – as were we in the Western Inter-County Railway Committee (where we have held out since 1979).

While a person's memoirs can give the reader a valuable insight into the life and times of the Monsignor, a critical biography would be necessary to evaluate his full contribution to the community. The latter would only be possible if sufficient archival material was available and/or relevant contemporaries were willing to be interviewed and so forth. The memoirs of Monsignor James Horan must be read within the context of such limitations. Nevertheless, much can be learned from reading the memoirs of a character like James Horan, his priorities in the communities around him and his methods of pursuing his goals with a determination which was very difficult to resist. He also displayed quite a degree of native cunning. Many said that had he not been a priest he would have been a most effective politician at ministerial level. Despite his heavy involvement in particular public projects, he always tried not to neglect his duties as a curate or as a parish priest. He found committees quite irksome and less than effective. He said, after reflecting on all the work the parish of *Cnoc Mhuire* had done (through committees) for the Papal Visit in 1979, had he to do it again, he would suggest just one overall committee and the designation of particular individuals to be responsible for the specific areas of preparation. Committees for him were better for arriving at policy rather than carrying out particular duties. I often wondered what it must have been like to work as a curate or as an assistant under such a dynamic leader. *Ar dheis Dé go raibh a anam dhíograsach.*

12. Second Major Study of Prejudice in 1988-89

When Robert K Merton, Colombia University, New York, the external examiner of my PhD thesis, *Intergroup Relations in Ireland*, reported on the work, he pointed out that it was a benchmark set of findings. The time had come at the end of the 1980s to replicate the survey in order to monitor the level of change that had taken place in the prejudices of the Irish people since the time of the original survey of 1972-73. It was decided in 1986 that a national sample of the population of the Republic of Ireland (the twenty-six counties) would be surveyed in 1988-89, which would measure the changes in ethnic prejudices in racialism, in anti-Semitism, in social class attitudes, in religious attitudes and practices, etc. The Economic and Social Research Institute (ESRI) in Dublin was commissioned to carry out the fieldwork. Two senior research assistants worked with me on the preparation and analysis of the findings, i.e. Dr Nessa Winston and Ms Caroline O'Kelly, MA. Financial support for the project came from the Irish Jesuit Provincial, Rev. Professor Andrew Greeley of Chicago and St Patrick's College, Maynooth.

Valuable help was also received from 'the Ireland Fund'. Regretfully, I was not able to procure any State research funding for the work. The bias in favour of research in the precise sciences – biology, chemistry, physics, econometrics, medical research, etc. seemed to be getting the lion's share of research funding. I do not have to point out the sad results of this unbalanced distribution of research funding when one looks at the dysfunctional state of our modern society to see the effects of real lack of State support for objective (non-sponsored) social research. (I was very pleased when the Government gave the 2007-08 survey a generous grant, which marked a welcome change in policies.)

Moving from Greater Dublin to the Republic of Ireland was made possible by being able to commission the ESRI to carry out the fieldwork, i.e. a ninety-minute interview-questionnaire of a national sample of 1,347, 73% of whom (1,005) were interviewed. This sample was arrived at from the 1988 Register of Electors using the tried-and-tested ESRI 'Ransam Programme'. The interviews were carried out during the period of November 1988 to April 1989.

Another new and valuable dimension of the 1988-89 survey was the cooperation of the Department of Sociology of the *Catholic University of Nijmegen*, in the Netherlands. That Department had been monitoring inter-group attitudes in the population of Holland for a number of years. We were able to measure attitudes on similar scales and, as a result, compare and contrast the findings in our respective national populations. I also exchanged the data with Nijmegen, where some scholars were able to carry out analyses of the findings and share them with me for inclusion in my publications. Such international cooperation was most useful because of the growth of international migration into Europe from outside and between countries within the Continent. I was to find this connection/relationship very helpful academically and I was enabled to avail of the Nijmegen data-analysis, which was highly sophisticated at the time. (My previous familiarity with the Dutch language was also a great help.)

The main problem for me was time, since I would not seek sabbatical leave for reasons I have explained earlier. The lecturing, correcting and advisory role in Maynooth, of up to eight hundred undergraduate students taking sociology in Arts, not to mention the growing number pursuing post-graduate studies in sociology was my priority. During 1986-87, I worked on the new questionnaire. Father (Professor) Andrew Greeley asked me to include a module on attitudes towards religion and the family, as part of a European values and attitudes study. It was his payment for the module that enabled me to employ the ESRI. Also, I would have access to relevant data from his module, as he was free to tap-in to some of my data elsewhere in the questionnaire. Before the ESRI was satisfied with the structure and content of the questionnaire, I had to modify it somewhat, without interfering with the principal questions and scales. A number of pilot interviews were also necessary to sharpen up the questions.

By the summer of 1988 an agreed questionnaire was arrived at and the ESRI set about printing the 'schedule' (i.e. the questionnaire) in a format conducive to interviewing and to entering into the computer on completion. During the early autumn, I had a conference with a large team of ESRI-appointed interviewers to ensure they were familiar with the various questions and scales. In September they were ready to go. It felt like the beginning of a match – 'the ball was in, the match was on'. I now had to await the reaching of 73% of the sample, which would be a satisfactory response rate. According as the completed questionnaires returned from the interviewers in the field, they were entered in the computer in the ESRI.

The anticipated findings included a significant reduction in the case of racialism, ethnocentrism, anti-Semitism, sexism, homophobia, political prejudice, religious prejudice, anti-British attitudes, etc. This was based on an examination of the potential trends found in the 1972-73 survey. As the overall level of participation in education had increased since 1972-73, when the O'Malley free second-level education scheme had not been of benefit to the sample (which was at that time beyond the second-level age). Other changes in attitudes were expected to happen because of the introduction of equality legislation introduced to Ireland since joining the EEC in 1973. In a real sense, the 1988-89 survey would measure the impact on social attitudes of the very substantial increase in participation in education, although I had my reservations about the quality of education being promoted, i.e. greater emphasis on science and technology and a withdrawal of emphasis on the 'liberal arts, philosophy, theology, etc.' (which would result in greater tolerance towards minorities). Pragmatic education, which would be more accurately defined as technical training, would be more or less neutral in relation to attitude change. (This failure of more education to result in the 18 to 25 year-olds being more tolerant in the 2007-08 survey confirmed the above hunch!)

The second factor to be measured would be the impact of our membership of the EEC during the sixteen years between the surveys. Here again, I would have been cautious. Ireland's very strong support for joining the EEC was probably more pragmatic than idealistic, i.e. we joined because of perceived economic advantages, rather than a desire to be closer to the other European nationalities. The rhetoric used in the pro-EEC campaign would not reflect the reasons why the people voted so strongly for Ireland's entry. Later referenda have shown a gradual disillusion with the integration of the European Union. The findings of the 1988-89 survey could well test the level of perceived solidarity with European nationalities among the respondents.

The introduction of the Anomie Scale, meaning the degree of normlessness in the Irish population, into the 1988-89 survey, which was an omission in the 1972-73 survey, was most useful and was interesting. During the six months from September 1988 until April 1989, I once again felt like 'an expectant parent', waiting to see what would come out of the 'womb of the computer'. It is better to defer commentary on the findings until the next chapter of this book.

The late 1980s marked the beginning of the end of the communist political superstructure of Eastern European States. A 'bloodless revolution' was underway in Poland, in Eastern Europe and in other

Eastern States. The 'to-ing and fro-ing' between Poland and the Vatican and the role of the Protestant Churches in the Democratic Republic of Germany (Eastern Germany) contributed to the momentum of this non-violent revolution. There were more people crossing the 'iron curtain'. The more open regime in Moscow under the astute leadership of President Mikhail Gorbachev was beginning to 'ripple down' to the Eastern European satellite States. The role of 'people power' seemed to gain momentum in changing the State superstructure, and in the more open disposition to the popular demands. A similar exercise of 'people power' took place in the United States during the 1960s and the 1970s and brought about an end to racial segregation and the withdrawal of US forces from the pre-emptive war in Vietnam.

The fall of the Berlin wall in November 1989 was inevitable and won ecstatic reaction throughout Europe and the whole Western World. The 'Fall of the Wall' symbolised the liberation of a people who had felt the strain of a very restrictive system of government. Western political commentary had 'demonised the Communist system' and portrayed the alternative liberal capitalist system as an 'idyllic political structure' that was conducive to freedom and socio-economic progress. But reality was not going to be so black and white. A total collapse of the old regime without any replacement was in danger of leading to a degree of anarchy and social chaos. It did not turn out to be too chaotic as the transition was carefully controlled by wise leaders on both sides of the socio-political divide. This did not mean that the 'end of socialism' and the victory of 'liberal capitalism' were all rosy or just. More about the advantages and disadvantages of this relatively left-right change for so many people later. (Nineteen years later, in 2008, the world was to witness a much greater crisis in liberal capitalism with negative global consequences.)

The one event that tarnished the non-violent revolution was the summary execution of President Ceausescu and his wife in Romania at the fall of the Communist regime during the Christmas season of 1989. It cast 'a cloud of indignity' over the change of power. This tragic execution was a violation of the 'rule of law' and seemed to be more an act of revenge than an act of justice. Thankfully, the new government pledged to honour the European norm of the abolition of capital punishment.

13. *MÁMÉAN* PILGRIMAGE REVIVES

After the establishment of the Stations of the Cross and the consecration of the new *Carraig an Aifrinn* (Mass Rock) in August 1980, an annual programme of pilgrimages was planned. In August 1981, the Auxiliary Bishop of Armagh, Most Rev Dr James Lennon, led the annual *Turas*. This acknowledged the traditional links between patrician shrines and Armagh in medieval times. During the 1980s, a number of significant improvements and additions were carried out at the shrine to meet the devotional and liturgical needs of pilgrims. These included the upgrading of the Stations of the Cross, the building of a Sacristy Chapel, the erection of a life-size statue of St Patrick and the digging of a new Holy Well.

The artistic and devotional contribution to the upgrading of the Stations of the Cross is acknowledged in the creative genius of Sister M Pius (Margaret Dyer) of the Convent of Mercy, Westport, who designed the images on each of the fourteen stations. They are carved on black marble plaques by sculptor John Coffey from Westport. The same sculptor created the special *Máméan* Cross for each of the stations. These mini Celtic crosses have elicited much praise from pilgrims as have the images on the plaques. A special feature of *Turas na Croise* in *Máméan* is the singing of *Caoineadh na dTrí* Mhuire in the *sean-nós* tradition by Joe John Mac an Iomaire (Cill Chiaráin).

The building of the Chapel was necessary because of the level of wind and rain, which frequently blew and fell during pilgrimages. The chapel was built by Tommie Coyne (Tír na Cille) assisted by voluntary labour. Later in 2006, Hughie Golden (Carrowholly, Westport) re-roofed the chapel with original Bangor slates (in memory of his late father, Patrick, RIP). The chapel was named *Cillín Phádraig* and consecrated by Archbishop Joseph Cunnane DD (Tuam) on the 8th of September 1985 to mark the 1600th anniversary of the birth of St Patrick in 385AD. Special stain-glass windows of Our Lady, St Joseph, St Brigid and St Patrick were also created by Sr M Pius (Dyer) to adorn the little chapel appropriately.

A life-size limestone statue of the young Saint Patrick was carved by one of Ireland's best sculptors, Ms Cliodhna Cussen in 1986 and unveiled and blessed by the Bishop of Clonfert, Most Rev Dr John Kirby, at the following pilgrimage. The statue, which was entitled *Pádraig Mór na hÉireann, Aoire Mhámean* (Big Patrick of Ireland, Shepherd of *Mámean*). The young Patrick is dressed as a shepherd with a blanket folded over his shoulder and a crios around his waist with Celtic and Christian symbols. The sculptor created a disposition of 'peace and welcome' on the face of the young Patrick. A sheep nestles at his feet. The statue stands at the centre of the shrine.

Later in 1993, a new Holy Well was dug and blessed. The original well (which is a sump-well) was proving inadequate for the demands of the increased numbers of pilgrims. This new well, which was named *Buntobar Phádraig*, was dug at the spring from which the water flowed into the original Holy Well (*Tobar Phádraig*). The Auxiliary Bishop of Tuam, Most Rev Dr Michael Neary (later to become Archbishop of Tuam) solemnly blessed the new well during the national pilgrimage in August 1993. It has a constant supply of clean holy water.

The above-listed additions fit snugly and aesthetically into the physical environment of the *Mámean* shrine. It is to be hoped that in the future the simplicity of this shrine will be preserved and every effort be made to maintain its Gaelic and spiritual traditions. The Irish language is the medium of *Mámean* religious ceremonies. The three miles of path from Gleann Fhada to Doire Bhéal an Mháma have been improved and maintained by local employment schemes under the guidance of the late Micheál Ó Mainín (Oorid, Maam Cross) and Terry Ó Cianáin (former Garda an Maam). Sadie bean Uí Chadhain is the current (2014) chairperson of *Coiste Tacaíochta Mhámean*. The late Michael Keogh (of Peacocke's Maam Cross) and his son Basil were among the biggest benefactors of the *Mámean* shrine during the 1980s. Michael's late daughter, Lorna Keogh, was our first honorary treasurer. The late Michael Conroy, Curr, was a key original supporter of the revival of the *Mámean* Pilgrimage.

Chapter Seven

THE 1990S
A DECADE OF PROGRESS AND REGRESS

1. A DECADE OF CHANGE

Every generation seems to believe that their current experience must mark the greatest era of change ever. And yet, time seems to deflate 'heady' decades of perceived change into less exciting memories. Will the nineteen-nineties be any different in time? In my opinion, the decade under review in this chapter has heralded more than a normal dose of cultural, economic and social change in Irish society and elsewhere. Irish urban and rural environments have gone through the beginnings of change, which have begun seriously to alter the visual perspective of our town and country scapes. The root causes of the changes of the nineties were by and large sociocultural and institutional. Leadership also played a significant role as instruments of the socio-culturally determined developments.

The collapse of the Eastern European collectivist-communist system in 1989 precipitated the unchallenged rise of *laissez-faire* capitalism as a dogmatic political ideology. This was to reinforce individualism with a corresponding demise of collectivism, which had given support to the basic social needs of people. The 'backlash' to this most recent political distortion has later begun to show emerging signs – in response to the symptoms of social dysfunction even in Irish society. *Examples of such malaise are – the acute rise in homicide and suicide rates; the alarming growth until recently in the percentage of our adult population in prison; increases in rates of marital and domestic breakdown and flagging support for indissoluble monogamy; and the widening of the gap between the rich and the poor resulting in a greater sense of relative deprivation.* In my opinion, the collapse of economic progress due to the spread of deregulated liberal-capitalism and consequent effects in 2008 in Ireland and elsewhere is, among other causes, a product of the rise of materialistic individualism!

Side by side with the negative symptoms it must be said that there were many positive changes during the nineties. There was a definite improvement in the material standard of living for the vast majority of the people. Telephonic communication improved to the state of 'universal telephonisation', which was achieved without much fuss or bother. Other forms of telecommunications, i.e. television, websites, e-mails, etc. began to transform offices and homes.

The untimely death of my only sister, Mary (Sr M Gregory, SSL) RIP, took place as a result of a brain haemorrhage, in the St Louis Convent, Monaghan, at the age of fifty-seven years, in June 1993. Mary was one of the most intelligent of our family. She was artistic with a genuine love of the poor and young children. She was a primary teacher in Carrickmacross, Dundalk and elsewhere. She had poor health for over twenty years. She never lost the common touch and was gifted with a keen sense of humour. *Ar dheis Dé go raibh a h-anam uasal.*

My career as a senior lecturer continued in St Patrick's College, Maynooth (NUI Section) until the age of statutory retirement on the 30th September 1996. I worked until the very end. During the early years of the nineties, most of my spare time was engaged in analysing the findings of the 1988-89 national survey of intergroup attitudes in Ireland. As I have said already, the reading of the printouts with new findings and correlations was always one of the most exhilarating experiences of my academic life. It often confirmed something totally new (although anticipated). When a hypothesis is confirmed, one feels great and grateful. Of course, some of my findings confirmed attitudes in Irish society that were truly negative and detrimental to weaker minorities such as Travellers, gays, and certain ethnic and religious categories. The only consolation one gets from unearthing these prejudices is the conviction that '*a prejudice exposed is a prejudice undermined*'. Here is not the place to go through the mass of findings taken from the 1988-89 national survey. They are all presented in the text *Prejudice in Ireland Revisited* (Maynooth, 1996, 97).

I acknowledge the help received from many friends and colleagues, especially my two senior research assistants, Nessa Winston and Caroline O'Kelly. John O'Connell and his staff in the Computer Centre in St Patrick's College, Maynooth, could not have been more helpful. The support of the Department of Social Studies in Maynooth was highly to be praised under the benign stewardship of that most brilliant of real scholars, Professor Liam Ryan. Cooperation with the *University of Nijmegen* in The Netherlands added very much to the value of the findings and confirmed the validity and reliability of some of the key tables. It was a hectic five years of processing and analysing of the data, which had been collected by the Survey Research Unit of the Economic and Social Research Institute (ESRI) under contract. The Head of the Unit, Professor Brendan Whelan, was also very supportive as was Professor Damian Hannan.

While it is better to leave an examination of the findings to a study of *Prejudice in Ireland Revisited* (1996-97), some results did point to noteworthy changes in Irish society. As noted already, the first change to strike me forcefully when I read the initial printout was the decline of the 'blue-collar' worker in the Irish workforce, when compared with 1972-73. By 1989 there was evidence of a trend towards 'class homogenisation', i.e. the swelling of a 'big belly of the middle class' with the decline of the 'working class'. This was serious for the social justice capacity of 'majority democracy', which would result in major political parties seeking to satisfy a range of nuances of middle-class wants and priorities. The day when the poor or the 'lower-class' had the voting power to determine Government policy was well passed and passing further. The best chance for the poor to exercise influence would be in a 'hung *Dáil*' where the minority of representatives genuinely representing the poor could exercise some influence and ensure the weaker people's needs were not ignored. In that context it is probably a good thing that the two major parties were separate, middle-class parties. If the *Dáil* were divided on social class lines the representatives of the poor would rarely be heard in the future or taken seriously.

The rise into dominance of the middle class, which was becoming more urbanised, would have a very significant influence on Irish values and norms. The 'rural and urban peasant' was becoming a dwindling minority. In rural Ireland there was a large influx of non-farming, rural residents. They could be classified as 'ex-urbans'. The new middle class were quite socially and geographically mobile. Bourgeois communities were taking over, especially in regard to fashion and recreational patterns. 'The Golf-Club/Tennis Club/Bridge-Club syndrome' would increase. The owning of a yacht and ponies were important items of conspicuous consumption! Leisure was becoming more commercialised. Even in farming areas, family horticulture declined. Holidays outside one's community were more popular. By the 1990s nearly as many Irish went on holidays abroad as foreign tourists came to Ireland. The Irish had now become so middle class that many of the menial blue-collar jobs were being done by first generation immigrants. This was to become very clear as the standards of living improved materially.

The 'de-ruralisation' of the Irish people in the 1980s and in the 1990s confirmed that the growing (socially and geographically mobile) urbanised middle class was inevitably changing the cultural ethos of the Irish people, with its priority vested in the family and the local community. A student of mine, around this time, did a small research project in which he measured the degree of attachment of a sample of middle-class, white-collar workers (in positions of senior management) to religion, community, extended family, and Irish culture. To his surprise he found a very low level of attachment to all four areas and came to the conclusion that the self and career were the number one and two. There was some attachment to this nuclear family of procreation. This small study confirmed what was to become more evident later, namely, our upwardly mobile middle class were more strongly individualist and quite detached from country, community, religion, extended family and Irish culture. Such people would thrive in the multinational areas, such as the European Union! But how functional is such an ethos in the overall and in the long run? A meaningful life requires serious attachments that are deep and rewarding. One cannot love a 'position'! One can love only persons (in families and communities). Modern Ireland was becoming a more lonely place for many, even successful, people. Such institutions as family, neighbourhood, community, religion and informal recreation are just as necessary as success in highly competitive jobs. Irish society has become a more competitive place to live in. Professor Liam Ryan once remarked at a conference on education today and its 'points race': '*only rats win rat races*'! 'Cooperation' is an integrating social process while 'competition' is basically dissociative.

The 1988-89 survey of Irish intergroup attitudes was particularly valuable in that it was possible to measure the degree of change which had taken place over a period of sixteen years. This coincided with Ireland's first sixteen years in the European Economic Community, during which time the country experienced mixed fortunes. Nevertheless, for better or worse, our membership of the EEC affected Ireland and put our society into an almost irreversible trend of change. *I feel that it marked major economic success at the macro level, and quality-of-life failure in many cases at the micro level.* Hopefully, it will be possible to recover control of our destiny before it is too late and the State has not surrendered all its 'home-rule' authority and power to Brussels! The influence of *television* on the agenda of thinking and on the lifestyle of the people was threatening the uniquely Irish culture and character. Membership of the European Union has obviously accelerated the above-mentioned changes, despite the fact that it contributed very little to the provision of alternative employment for those of the working class whose livelihood was taken away by the socio-economic order that was emerging.

The period of EEC membership (1974-89) was of mixed benefit to Ireland. Unemployment and inflation were severe for most of the time (see table on page 221 above). Granted, Ireland benefited from a range of grants in agriculture and some infrastructural developments. These infusions of cash were not distributed in an equal manner. The strong seemed to grow stronger while the weak grew relatively weaker. The emigration of both 'brawn' and 'brains' was the safety valve, which I always thought was a double fault. Those most qualified to bring about an indigenous revival of Irish communities in the weaker parts were leaving the country while, very often, those least educated had to stay behind to keep things 'ticking over' until the new dawn would come.

As already noted, in my last lecture to those graduating every year in the late 1980s and early 1990s, I would tell them that *it would be better for their local communities if they stayed at home on the dole (rather than emigrate) and generate a dynamic for change through local enterprise and local politics.* Of course, going away for a short period could serve as an apprenticeship or experience for home development. The real beneficiary of emigration was always the host society. (We see this in reverse later with talented people working in Ireland from lesser developed societies, where their services are more urgently needed. This is especially true in the case of engineers, doctors, nurses and those technically qualified employees.) It does not appear socially just for us in Ireland to benefit from the services of those highly skilled migrant workers from weaker countries where their services are much more urgently needed. Is it not ironic that we were now exploiting the talent from weaker societies to enhance further our overdeveloped society while enjoying a very high material standard of living? The same dynamic that kept Ireland down for so long is, unwittingly, keeping other developing societies in relative poverty! Will we ever learn? (It will become clear that after the 2008 economic 'crash', Irish well educated [at the expense of the State] young people were leaving this country where their talent was most needed!)

Other symptoms that emerged from the 1988-89 survey were the growth of secularisation and the beginning of a decline in religious practice. The most likely explanation for this change was a definite increase in the ideology of materialism and consumerism. This, in turn, led to an acceptance of individualism and a weakening in the long collectivist tradition of Irish Catholicism. Institutions such as 'the family' and the 'local community' were losing out to the unrestricted advance of individualism. There was a rise in domestic breakdown. The withdrawal of pivotal support (in terms of norms of behaviour and material help) for the family was soon to reap a sad reward for many people. The major media commentators seemed to lack a critical understanding of this (structurally caused) lowering of the quality of life in Ireland.

The ideology of 'individualism' seemed to be functional for the rise of 'capitalism' in Ireland during the latter half of the 1990s, greatly boosted by the competitive ethos of multinational companies originating, for the most part, in the United States of America. Even the moderate presence of the 'collectivism' of trade unions was to become ideologically repulsive for those 'giants of progress'! Their opposition to trade unions was, for me, indicative of a regressive change in Irish industrial relations.

This process leading to 'individualism' was to find an ally in the parallel process of 'privatisation', which was quite foreign to the newly emancipated Irish State. 'Privatisation' was on the agenda of Irish governments, especially in the case of those senior civil servants and advisers who 'worked their way' into the corridors of power. Service in response to the needs of the people was to be replaced by the profit motive.

As regards the Catholic Church, the level of conviction in the post-Vatican Two generation, which put new emphasis on social justice and the re-integration of the Sacred Scripture as pointing basic Christian communities towards their collective liberation, was to lose its progressive momentum. 'Liberation theology', which brought so much hope, was to be silenced by degrees. A more individualistic theology was to focus more on personal sanctification than on the structural change of society necessary to bring about greater social justice for all. This is not to deny that, in many of his encyclicals, Pope John Paul II did counter the blatant social injustice of unrestrained individualism and *laissez faire* competitive capitalism. But the world media barely recognised the Pope's social teaching and concentrated on his teaching on sexual matters, almost to the exclusion of his teaching on matters of social justice. This suited the bourgeois society and compartmentalised religion and morality away from the level of structural (social) injustice. *Preoccupation with private morality issues (including sexual sins) seems to cloud the issues of structurally-based social injustice and curb the prophetic role of the Churches!* Of course, private morality is very important, and he or she who ignores it is not following Christian teaching.

The rate of increase in participation in second- and third-level education between 1972-73 and 1988-89 was significant and very substantial. This policy of 'investment in education' of the late 1960s was to pay dividends later in the 1990s when highly qualified graduates and technicians would be required for the influx of new jobs in medical, pharmaceutical, information and electronic professions. This suited the move to 'white-collar' and highly paid work.

The findings of the 1988-89 survey were to point to the effects of the shift away from liberal humanities to more scientific and technological subjects on more tolerant attitudes towards different ethnic, racial, religious and other social categories. The results were somewhat disappointing in that the level of increases in tolerance was not commensurate with the level of improvement in educational participation. A tolerant society requires a well-educated population in the area of the humanities, i.e. arts, creative literature, philosophy, theology, psychology, sociology, anthropology, history, geography, and so forth.

By 1988 the (formal) educational achievement of women in Ireland had begun to outperform that of men. When compared with men, the proportion of women completing second level was 18% higher. This could have been practically explained by the percentage of men ending their formal education at Junior Certificate in order to pursue a skilled or semi-skilled trade. Nevertheless, it gave concrete evidence of the ascent of women into the white-collar professions. By the end of the 1990s, men of the working class were becoming the deprived gender in Irish society and it appeared that feminism was moving away from gender equality to gender privilege (in the case of the middle class). This created a certain disillusion among those of us who had hoped that the gender equality movement would be sex blind. Obviously, it was not so!

The findings of the 1988-89 study in relation to prejudice and tolerance were also very interesting. For some categories, prejudice scores were reduced when compared with 1972-73. Socialists, black and coloured people, Protestants (since over 93% of the adult population were Catholics), and a number of other groupings recorded a significant drop in prejudice. It was very strange that Irish people's acceptance of socialists had increased just as the Soviet Union was about to lose its Communist grip. The gap between our attitudes towards socialists and capitalists was barely significant in the 1988-89 results. This was not to prevent the country from embracing the free-market capitalist system less than a decade later. *The emerging problem of global capitalism could well become a source of serious conflict of interest in the decades ahead. It will create a situation where a sense of powerlessness at national level could well lead to socio-political unrest.* It is a most serious threat to local democracy and makes one suspicious of the real motivation behind Global Free Trade. It will inevitably lead to the dominance of the strong. International Trade Unions seem to have been remiss in relation to the manipulation of the world labour market to exploit cheap wages and low-cost raw materials. Ireland is also a player in the multinational club. The inevitable result of Irish manufacturing industry being closed down and work going to countries with cheap labour has long since been heralded.

Between 1966 and 1999, I gave lectures on different aspects of industrial relations in the *College of Industrial Relations* (later renamed as the *National College of Ireland*). During the 1980s and 1990s, it became apparent that the critical (academic) subjects taught were being replaced by applied subjects teaching more the techniques of managerial skills. A good example of this was the replacing of Industrial Sociology by a subject named Human Resource Management. The latter lacked the critical dimension required of a Human Science. I am afraid that similar watering down of academically critical standards in favour of 'applied' technical skills has crept into the whole university system. Technical Institutes have clamoured to become Universities, e.g. Dublin City University and Limerick University. Universities themselves were becoming more like Technical Institutes. This move has serious implications for the future of both University Education and Technical Training. In my opinion, both essential dimensions have suffered because of the watering-down of the intellectual independence of universities and the status of technological training.

2. Signs of Hope in Ireland

The socio-economic development of Ireland was to become a more central factor of the 1990s. Once the first steps towards a lasting peace in Northern Ireland began to become more real, thanks to the work of John Hume, Gerry Adams, Martin McGuinness and representatives of the Irish Government, i.e. Albert Reynolds, Bertie Ahern and advisers such as Martin Mansergh. The influence of President Bill Clinton, British Prime Minister Tony Blair, Secretary of State Dr Mo Mowlam, Senator George Mitchell (US) and others at home and abroad, supported the momentum for a change within the Provisional IRA to move towards an exclusively pacifist and political methodology and engage in the democratic process. *The role of para-military prisoners in persuading the leadership to declare a ceasefire was critical.* This has had a positive impact on economic developments. Without peace in Northern Ireland, economic progress on the island of Ireland would be constrained. The recognition of the State and the ending of abstention from *Dáil Éireann* and from Stormont enabled *Sinn Féin* to enter mainstream politics. For many, hostility towards *Sinn Féin* and the Provisional IRA would take some time to abate and enable them to accept these leaders 'in from the political cold'. The role of Gerry Adams has been pivotal in the peace process.

Economic Development in the Republic of Ireland has been very imbalanced (regionally) leading to the rapid growth of Dublin, Cork and Limerick and the decline of wide areas of the West, Border Counties and parts of the Midlands. Communities had almost died owing to lack of population, i.e. schools closed, and two-thirds of the young people migrated out of some of these areas. The improvement in educational participation did not arrest this haemorrhage of young talent throughout 1970s, 1980s and the early years of the 1990s. In my opinion, the bureaucratic leadership in Dublin and Brussels seemed to be more in favour of the 'gentrification' of the West and North West rather than its development!

A change of policy (at least in principle) seemed to emerge during the latter half of the 1990s. This may have been due to the growing unpleasantness of urban congestion and suburban traffic problems *et cetera* and the new attractions of working and living in 'the provinces'. One clear example of the lack of attraction of Dublin has been the exodus of third level students and unattached young workers every Friday back to their home parishes. In the fifties and sixties, the young people would go to Dublin during the weekends (if they had the resources). Was the new direction of this traffic going to be followed a generation or so later by a serious attempt to build up our provincial towns and cities as moderately sized centres of population? It is, as yet, too early to say. Perhaps future generations will decentralise development from within by the talented young people themselves. Ireland had become very lopsided. Government in Dublin became the Dublin Government! The first stage in correcting the situation is to acknowledge the problem of imbalance. (The sad fact about the new Government elected in 2011 was the fact that only one Cabinet Minister [*An Taoiseach*] represented a constituency west of a line from Dublin to Limerick!) It is more just to bring jobs to the people than to force them to go to where the jobs are!

The situation would improve somewhat in the year 2000 and following. Government programmes, such as *Clár,* would direct extra resources to communities throughout the country, which had experienced a massive decline in population since 1926, i.e. between 1926 and 1996. Another significant policy which was to be agreed by the Government was the National Spatial Strategy, which identified a number of centres 'earmarked' for major urban growth, i.e. so-called Gateways, such as Sligo, Galway, Athlone, *et cetera*. In between the 'Gateways', there would be urban areas knows as 'Hubs', which would experience medium levels of growth. The main purpose of the National Spatial Strategy was to generate 'balanced regional development' to counter the trends of over-expansion on the eastern and southern areas, mainly around Dublin. The creation of the Western Development Commission and the Border/

Midland/Western Council (BMW) were intended to provide structures for the channelling of extra infrastructural funding into the lesser-developed parts of Ireland. Unfortunately, to date the delivery of 'balanced regional development' has not been impressive. This, in my opinion, is due to the over-powerfully centralised State bureaucracy. (The 2012 Budget has 'slashed' the programme of de-centralisation!!)

The campaign for the restoration of the cross-radial rail link from Sligo to Limerick (later to be known popularly as the Western Rail Corridor or WRC) was viewed by us on the Western Inter-County Railway Committee as a pivotal inter-regional infrastructure. It would provide *'front-loading' infrastructural investment* in the West of Ireland, which would contribute much to 'balanced, regional development'. In the early 1990s we made a real breakthrough when the then Minister for Transport, Mr Séamus Brennan TD, agreed that the disused rail track would not be abandoned until the Government had had the opportunity to evaluate its case for restoration. Up to that point, CIE had been sending me (as Secretary of the Western Inter-County Railway Committee) an annual bill for the cost of keeping the track *in situ*, which came to £86,000. On the day of the meeting with Minister Brennan I gave him the unpaid bill and heard nothing about it afterwards. In effect, the Minister had on that day, preserved the thoroughfare from Collooney to Limerick for the people of Ireland. If one were to have to buy it back in 2005, it would cost around 500 million euro. We had achieved Box-Car Willie's advice to us in 1981 when he said at a country-and-western concert in Castlebar that, 'if they took up the track we would never get it back'. (Box-Car Willie was a Country & Western singer.) I will return to the railway project again.

3. RENEWAL OF PIONEER TOTAL ABSTINENCE ASSOCIATION

In December 1991, I was asked by the Jesuit Provincial, Fr Philip Harnett SJ, to chair an interim Board of Management of the Pioneer Total Abstinence Association of the Sacred Heart, which was founded in December 1898, under the guidance of the late Father James Cullen SJ. In addition to administering the Pioneer Association, the Board was asked to *'carry out a Review of the PTAA, which has been commissioned by the Jesuit Provincial in consultation with Central Council and the*

Episcopal Conference and produce a Report'.

The Interim Board was asked to produce a Progress Report by November 1992 and a Final Report by 31ˢᵗ March, 1993. Both Reports were to be submitted to the Jesuit Provincial. The Board's appointees were in office for a two-year period. In addition to chairing the Board of Management, I was asked by the Provincial to chair Central Council for the period of the Board.

Despite a very busy schedule, it was possible to get down to business on the PTAA straight away. I must admit that the extra work was interesting and stimulating. Some, of course, would once again see me as an activist and workaholic, which did not bother me as long as the worthwhile work was being done. When asked one time about my busy workload, I replied that 'when you don't drink you must do something'! Really, I always allowed myself ample time for quiet reflection. Otherwise, it would be impossible to analyse findings in a critical manner.

On the 30ᵗʰ November 1992, the Pioneer Board's progress report, *What the Pin Stands for Today*, was finished and submitted to the Provincial. It was printed in February 1993 and circulated to all the Pioneer Centres and other Units of the Association. Comments and suggestions were invited for the next stage of the Board's review of the PTAA. There was a very fruitful response over the following month (March). In order to do justice to the 200 serious written comments and suggestions and to prepare the final report within the time constraints laid down by the Provincial, the Board assigned certain areas, i.e. Spiritual basis of the Association, Membership, Structures and Procedures, to different members. The meetings were given progress reports on each area. It worked out very well indeed. In my experience of taking part on various Working Parties, I must admit that the Interim Pioneer Board was among the most competent and committed group of people I had worked with. By 2ⁿᵈ June 1993, we had *the final report* ready for submission to the Jesuit Provincial. It was accepted by him and approved by Central Council and the Bishops' Conference. The title of the final report was *Towards A Second Century*, which was, in effect, a new blue print or constitution for the Pioneer Total Abstinence Association. *Moladh go deo le Dia*.

The new structures and procedures proposed were quite radical. Transparency and active and representative participation in guiding, administering and monitoring the Pioneer Association were achieved. The structure proposed was analogous of that of the Houses of the *Oireachtas*, i.e. A President, a *Dáil* (Central Council) and a Government (Board of Management). The President, whose role would be non-executive, would be elected every three years by the members of Central Council (from among the Council's members). The Central Council members were to act as an 'electoral college'. Since the PTAA was 'an apostolate of the Society of Jesus under the patronage of the Irish Episcopal Conference', both the Chairperson of the Board and the Central Spiritual Director would be appointed by the Jesuit Provincial. The appointment of the Chairperson would be after consultation with Central Council and the Irish Bishops' Conference. The membership of the Board of Management would be 'functional', i.e. the Officers of the Association and Chairpersons of Central Committees – Finance, Leisure, Education and Training and Spirituality (Youth would be added later). Three members would be co-opted. In 2003, on the establishment of the Provincial Activities Committees, their Chairpersons would be added to the Board's membership. The shift from a one-person Central Director to the collective directorate of the Board took some time to sink in. It must have been quite difficult for the outgoing Central Director, Father Bernard McGuckian SJ, to adjust to the new role of Central Spiritual Director.

The Association operated under *Towards a Second Century* as its constitution and rules for nine years until 2003, when an amended revision was agreed and issued under the title, *Constitution and Rules of the PTAA*. A lay CEO, Mr Pádraic Naughton, would replace the Jesuit Central Director in September 2002. Fr McGuckian SJ, would become the Central Spiritual Director of the Association. Time would prove that the structural changes proposed in *Towards a Second Century* would be more or less effective and elicited genuine interest from the membership to participate. Of course, from time to time, there would be murmurs in favour of the old structures, when the Reverend Central Director exercised 'supreme command' of the PTAA. Such structural nostalgia was hardly surprising in an organisation served by a single and benevolent authority for almost one hundred years. I will return to the Pioneer Association later.

4. CHALLENGES TO THE CATHOLIC CHURCH (INCLUDING CHILD-ABUSE SCANDALS)

Ever since 1967 there had been a growing change in the Irish people's attitude towards religion and the church. Since over 90% of the people in the Republic were Roman Catholic, it was inevitable that the form of this change would be seen in the practices of Catholics. The first area to feel the pinch was in the field of vocations to the priesthood and to religious orders – male and female. Mass-going and participation in the Sacrament of Penance gradually declined. There seems to have been a one-generational lag between the drop in vocations and the rate of decline in going to Mass and to the Sacraments. *In my opinion, the decline of domestic prayer, e.g. the family rosary, has led to the decrease in Mass attendance.*

By the mid-nineties, all signs indicated that a very substantial proportion of Roman Catholics had discontinued going to Mass every Sunday. With regard to 'Foreign Missions' the mission changed from evangelisation to development–plus–evangelisation. The decolonisation of the British protectorates in Africa and elsewhere was complete by the end of the nineteen-seventies. The impact of the failure of the Biafran campaign for IBO independence in Nigeria, with the forced return of many of the Irish missionaries, seemed to have had a serious and negative impact on vocations to the Foreign Missions.

The emergence of the joint committee on the Conference of Religious Orders and Congregations under the title of the Conference of Major Religious Superiors in Ireland was a move towards centralisation, which did not succeed in stemming the decline in vocations. In fact, it created a kind of a 'super order or congregation' and could have weakened the unique character and impact of individual orders and congregations. The Conference's title was modified to read 'Conference of Religious in Ireland' (CORI) later for politically-correct reasons. It would be unjust to conclude that CORI did not make a significant impact because of its collective strength. Its role in raising public awareness of social injustice in Ireland was significant and contributed to the church's prophetic role. CORI also enabled the religious orders to respond more effectively to the child-abuse crisis and to provide appropriate norms for the protection of minors from possible abuse by religious in future and deal more adequately with any allegations. Nevertheless, it lacked the charisma, which individual orders and congregations possessed.

The advance of materialism and consumerism was probably the most serious cause of decline in vocations and religious practice. The reduction in the size of the average family to between two and three children was to have a serious impact on the numbers of young men and women available for celibate vocations to the priesthood and religious life. Only sons or only daughters would be less likely to consider a vocation in to celibate state.

To add to the problem of the rise in materialism and the decline in vocations and religious practice, the early 1990s were to witness the exposure in the national media of sex-abuse scandals associated with a small minority of priests and religious. It was also alleged that the bishops and those in authority failed to act promptly in support of the victims of paedophile priests and religious. I must admit that the revelations totally shocked me. My experience of priests and religious was in the role of child defenders rather than child abusers. The revelations were most depressing and painful. As bad as they were for us priests, they were a million times worse for the unfortunate children who were abused. *Nostra culpa*! It must be admitted that the bringing in of procedures in 1996 was a most important move, to the credit of the Bishops and those in charge of Religious Orders and Congregations. It would take time, however, to identify and process cases yet to be revealed. The whole question of compensation had to be worked out and on whose shoulders it should fall. In the case of those abused in institutions run by the Church (for the State) it was necessary to share the costs, because of joint responsibility.

The sexual scandals exposed in the early 1990s were to undermine the credibility of the Church in the eyes of some, especially those who were feeling marginalized within the Catholic Church. *'An rud is annamh is íontach'* ('That which is rare is more noteworthy') as the Irish proverb says. *The total incongruity of the idea of some priests and religious abusing children and, by so doing, shattering the trust which the people had placed in this privileged body of moral guides and spiritual leaders was to result in a very serious situation for the Church in Ireland for some time.* For that reason it was no wonder that the media writers and presenters would try to bring the Church leaders to task and overemphasise their alleged negligence. In time, some people in the media would overkill, which would not help the cause of the innocent victims. In all, the Church was going to endure a 'decade of unparalleled humiliation' because of the sins of some of its ordained and professed members. If such 'humiliation' leads to a sense of guilt and intro-punitive response, it will enable the chastened institutional Church to revive as a humble servant of the people of God in the future. This, in my opinion, is the only way forward. The self-cleansing power of the Holy Spirit will enable us to climb this mountain towards recovery. Also, paedophilia itself must be examined as a form of compulsive behaviour. Demonisation and criminalisation are not adequate to deal with it and prevent it throughout society.

'A bad priest does not make a bad Mass' was a saying often quoted during my time of training in theology (1966-70). I do not remember its author. Certainly a minority (+2%) of abuse allegations referring to priests does not invalidate the priesthood or its Ministry. That may be objectively true but we live in the subjective world of attitudes and values. All priests have suffered in their public standing because of the scandals. One day a friend of mine intimated that I cease wearing the Roman collar and wear 'mufti' instead, i.e. collar and tie. I refused and insisted that now was the time to profess my priesthood (without parading it, of course). So I have continued to wear the collar in solidarity with my brother priests in the order and outside it. As a result, at times one can get a whiff of the cold wind of 'avoidance' by strangers, which was not so in the past. It does bother me sometimes. Anyhow, because of my public involvement in multiple causes, I am privileged to have more than my due share of public support. Naturally, I am extremely upset that a priest should abuse a child, which injures the victim and undermines the trust required of his vocation.

The outcome for the Priesthood and Religious Life is the generation of a negative stereotype by articulate and sometimes hostile media. The real danger is to define priests and religious (as social categories) in accordance with the negative behaviour of a minority and to limit or even avoid publishing the positive traits or activities of the majority of clergy and religious. *This is social prejudice by definition.* Voltaire and others poisoned the mind of the elite of Bourbon Europe with reference to the 'evil' character of the Jesuits in the 18th century. This led to the tragic suppression of the Society of Jesus by Pope Clement XIV, at the behest of the Bourbon monarchs in 1773. Some more extremist journalists and political commentators seem to me to be applying this propaganda strategy (unwittingly, I hope). Luckily, we have a free press and a free democracy where courageous journalists and politicians have challenged the narrow view before it becomes a 'self-righteous bandwagon' leading to discrimination and persecution. *'Go réidh, a bhean na dtrí mbó'!* ('Hold it, oh woman of the three cows'!)

A final reflection on the child-abuse scandals in the Church is to look back at times of corruption and scandals in the history of the Church. After the 4th century scandals came reformers St Martin of Tours, St Patrick and many other great priests and bishops. After the corruptions of the Renaissance papacies came Martin Luther, St Ignatius, St John of the Cross, St Teresa of Avila, St Francis Borgia, St Francis Xavier and many others. We may expect a similar response to the passing current crisis, *le cúnamh Dé.* Our hope must always be in the power of the Lord we serve.

In justice, it must be stated that the leaders of the Church, in my experience, did respond courageously *after* the revelations were exposed. Most Bishops and Superiors committed themselves totally towards the prevention of further abuse and to the making of amends to those abused. Access was given to Gardaí and other State Officials to the relevant records. This led to trials and imprisonment of offending clergy and religious. (The tragic situation in the Diocese of Cloyne was the failure of the Church authorities, in that Diocese, to implement the Church's procedures to the full.)

With regard to the issue of child abuse in general, as I already stated, there is a serious need to study what causes such an unacceptable activity. It seems to me that the causes are psycho-socio-cultural. Any weakening of the incest taboo would also be relevant. Current acceptance of pornography, even of the 'soft' class in print or film, is also a possible contributory factor. Greater censorship may be required to prevent the people from harming innocent children. The liberal acceptance of promiscuity inevitably leads to decadence. We must protect the innocent and respect each other at all times. Of course, allegations of child abuse against adults (including clergy and religious) are open to abuse. This is especially true where there is monetary remuneration for victims. Very strict sanctions should be applied against those who make false allegations. The good name of the falsely accused can be irreparably damaged in the current atmosphere.

Leaving the sad issues of child abuse I would like to comment on changes in moral norms in general. During the early 1990s I was giving a Novena of Grace (nine days' public retreat) in Dublin. It involved offering a public Mass at 12 noon each day, during which I would preach a sermon following the Spiritual Exercises of St Ignatius. During the morning and afternoon I would hear confessions. The church was full most days. The congregation of one thousand plus were from the parish plus those who had come from neighbouring parishes. A large proportion of those attending would be parents and retired people. It was a real treat for me to minister to this large believing congregation who manifested a solid faith and a most charitable disposition.

In the course of meeting the retreatants, especially talking to them in the confessional (after their confession), I discovered many felt a great sense of failure in relation to their children, their late teenagers and young adults. They would ask themselves the question: '*Where did we go wrong? We tried our best to rear them well and hand on the faith and teach them what was right and wrong. We sent them to Catholic schools and now they have given up going to Mass and do not abide by the Church's teaching in other areas (e.g. in regard to relationships).*' This would be the gist of their conversation. I felt very sad for these very good and conscientious parents. They were suffering because of the failure of their children to have the wisdom to follow their advice, instead of opting for that of their peers and the 'false prophets', who counselled norms of behaviour that distanced them from the teaching of Christ. Hopefully, these young people would come to their senses later and be influenced by their parents rather than misguided by the 'unredeemed world's' prophets.

Near the end of the Novena, I raised the issue in a sermon. I put it like this: '*What would you like to be written on your tombstone, i.e. what would your epitaph be?*' Before putting the question I told the congregation of my concern for good parents' feelings of failure because their grown children did not always follow their sound counsel and example. I thought they were unjustly judging themselves as failures. They had done 'the best they could'. At that stage in the Novena, I must have been hearing confessions for at least nine hours over a number of days. There was a perplexed reaction to the question. After a few minutes

I offered them what I would like to be written (in Irish, of course) on my mythical tombstone. '*Here lies the mortal remains of Micheál Mac Gréil. The world is bad enough, but it might have been worse without him. May he rest in peace.*' I told them to rejoice in the good they had done for their children and not persecute themselves for the decisions some of their children had made.

We sometimes neglect to appreciate how much inner pain grown-up children cause their parents when they, often in a cavalier and sometimes insolent manner, dismiss the sincere advice and good example of their parents. In our popular culture we have so many agony aunts and uncles who do not have the understanding or moral courage to advise young people of the wisdom of governing their lives in a sober, moral and dignified manner. In fact, some popular writers and broadcasters may have led young people astray and encouraged self-indulgence instead of sensible asceticism in their lifestyle, i.e. excessive drinking, vulgar language, etc.

At the same time, pastors, teachers and parents must also take some responsibility in failing to convince young people of the importance of the freedom to grow and develop themselves, by adhering to the basic moral norms tested over centuries. Pragmatism and materialism often come into conflict with the moral teaching of Christ. The ethic of cooperation and service comes into direct conflict with that of competition and profit.

The commercialisation of leisure puts pleasure for sale. The 'good life' is no longer one characterised by love and service. It is, rather, characterised by hedonistic pleasure. Of course, it is difficult for young people to resist the 'snares and arrows' of the hedonist model. Hopefully, the young will return to 'the straight and narrow', when they discover the shallowness of the secular alternative! During the 1960s and 1970s in the United States, many overindulged young people became bored with the 'good life' and drifted into a more austere 'hippie culture', which really failed to satisfy their thirst for meaning. For me personally, the Christian/Catholic way of life can best provide 'meaning' and 'interest' for the young, middle-aged and old. To this end, our pastoral guidance of young people should be directed, i.e. to enable them to live a full life and, as St Ignatius of Loyola says at the end of his Spiritual Exercises, 'seek to find God in all things'. That is possible, if we try to live an ordered life.

5. NORTHERN PEACE PROCESS GAINS MOMENTUM

The politics of the early 1990s in Ireland were dominated by the ongoing 'Troubles' in Northern Ireland and the endless loss of life and property as a result of the paramilitary war. It became known that behind the scenes talks were taking place between John Hume MP, MEP, and Gerry Adams MP, the President of *Sinn Féin*. John Major MP, succeeded Margaret Thatcher MP, as Prime Minister of the UK in 1990. Mr Peter Brooke MP, was appointed Secretary of State for Northern Ireland and he brought about a new climate for dialogue and negotiation. In August, 1990, shortly before my Uncle John (McGreal) died, he told me that he thought Mr Brooke MP, was a good man, and he (John) felt that there was a real hope of peace. In his earlier years, my uncle had been in the Old IRA and was quite Republican in his outlook all of his life. He died in hope of a peaceful solution. The Major–Brooke change was most important and the Irish Government, under Charles J Haughey TD, Albert Reynolds TD, and John Bruton TD, were able to talk to Prime Minister John Major MP, in a way that the previous British regime did not facilitate – so it would appear from a distance. The net result of the changes was to bring about a negotiated solution to the awful problem of conflict in Northern Ireland. It was only to be expected that some would question the sincerity of the negotiations. *The secret was that no side was seen to lose or be humiliated.* Those seeking 'unconditional' surrender had to be overruled!

Much credit has to be given deservedly, to *An Taoiseach*, Albert Reynolds TD, (from Longford), for his courageous initiative in welcoming Gerry Adams MP, and Martin McGuinness MP, to Government Buildings in 1993 and giving public support to the Hume–Adams talks. *I would consider John Hume, Gerry Adams and Martin McGuinness to have been the main internal political vanguard of the Northern Peace Process on the Nationalist side.* At the ground level on the constitutional and paramilitary sides, there were other key and courageous people. Notably, among the latter was Father Alex Reid from the Clonard Monastery of the Falls Road, Belfast. Martin Mansergh (later to become a Senator TD, and Minister of State) from County Tipperary was a key adviser to the Irish Governments on the Northern Peace Process. (Incidentally, Martin Mansergh was a helpful supporter of the campaign for the restoration of the Western Rail Corridor as far back as 1980.)

As I have already noted, the mid and early 1990s were tough years in Ireland for young people seeking jobs. Many of our traditional industries had collapsed and a new category of jobs was emerging in the technological and services industries. The number of graduates was increasing every year. The northern docks in Dublin were developing as a massive financial services centre. The Haughey dream was becoming a reality. It was the dark before the dawn!

6. FUTURE OF HIGHER EDUCATION IN IRELAND AND OTHER ISSUES

In the field of education, the Government, under Minister Niamh Bhreathnach TD, was addressing the third-level system. The National Youth Council of Ireland nominated me as the Council's representative on the *Special Committee on the Future of Higher Education in Ireland* set up by the Minister to examine the third-level needs and structures excluding universities. At the same time, the Department of Education was preparing the new *Universities Act*, which would become law in 1996. One of the main tasks of our Committee was to prepare a report on the future of regional third-level colleges to be renamed Institutes of Technology. There were serious divisions among members of the Committee over the non-location of Regional Technical Colleges in North Dublin City and in County Mayo. The compromise in relation to the latter was to make Galway RTC a 'double-barrel' institute, i.e. the Galway-Mayo Institute of Technology, with a campus in Castlebar, County Mayo.

Regretfully, North Dublin City lost out to Blanchardstown as a desired location for a new RTC. This was despite the fact that the North City in the Kilbarrack-Coolock area merited such an institution on relative-deprivation grounds. In my opinion, North Dublin City should have been prioritised.

Two new third-level institutes, i.e. the Art College in Dun Laoghaire and the Special College in Tipperary were not even on the agenda. The members of the 'high-powered' committee which prepared the published report were not invited to its launch or presentation. Was it felt that some of us would raise embarrassing questions on the occasion? Despite my dissatisfaction with the *modus operandi* of the Committee, I trust the Special Committee did some good for the fairer participation of young people in third-level education. The situation was bad enough but it might have been worse without us! The country had failed to devise a system whereby equal participation and achievement across the classes had or has been won. Even the abolition of university fees (under Minister Niamh Bhreathnach TD) has failed to change the privileged elites getting the most advantage!

The mid-nineties in Ireland were very interesting. With movement in the political scene in Northern Ireland, a new air of optimism had begun to dawn. This enabled the 'normalisation' of socio-economic development on each side of the border. War-torn Belfast was beginning to get a much-needed facelift. The commitment of President Bill Clinton of the USA and his wife, Hillary, in favour of the 'peace process' also had the latent function of encouraging US investment in Northern Ireland and in the Republic of Ireland. Cross-border movement increased and the public image abroad of Northern Ireland, which had been that of a violent community, was changing to that of a people trying to come together for the sake of reconciliation and integration. We were beginning to convince ourselves that there would be 'peace at last'.

In 1993, the government of *Fianna Fáil* and Labour under *An Taoiseach*, Mr Albert Reynolds TD, and *An Tánaiste*, Mr Dick Spring TD, (Kerry), collapsed. The cause was ostensibly because of the proposed appointment of the Attorney General, Mr Harry Whelehan SC, to a high judicial appointment by *An Taoiseach*. It had been discovered that the reaction of the Attorney General's Office to the prosecution of Father Brendan Smith in relation to child abuse had not been satisfactory. It was never made clear in the reports published to what extent, if any, the Attorney General was directly involved in any obstruction of proceedings. Once the issue had been politicised it gained a frenzied momentum in the media with the net result of a good government being brought down. To add to this tragedy was the putting in danger of the success of the Government in progressing the Northern Peace Process. Reading the whole story in the papers, I was never fully convinced that the 'Whelehan Case' was the only cause of Labour's exit from Government. The results of a Cork by-election at the time may also have been relevant! I would like to see a serious analysis of what was really going on within the Labour Party at the time.

In my opinion, the Reynolds-Spring Government was one of the best coalition Governments in Ireland during my politically conscious experience. It was a centre-left Government, which suited the development of our country. In a broad sense, it was closer to the ideal of Christian caring of all the people, be they strong or weak, rich or poor. In both of my own surveys I discovered that the people who voted for *Fianna Fáil* and for Labour were more or less from a similar social-class-position background. It (the *Fianna Fáil*/Labour Government) represented the small farmer and the city working-class. These categories of citizens have rarely had a strong voice in Government since the rise of the urban middle-class.

When the Reynolds-Spring Government fell, the President, Mrs Mary Robinson SC, did not dissolve the *Dáil* and call for a General Election. Instead, she requested the *Dáil* to explore the possibility of forming an alternative Government, which would get the support of the House. After some negotiations a new Government was formed under *An Taoiseach*, Mr John Bruton TD, (Leader of the *Fine Gael Party*) and *An Tánaiste* Mr Dick Spring TD (Leader of the *Labour Party*). A third party joined this new Coalition, i.e. the *Democratic Left,* which was formerly part of *The Workers' Party,* which, in turn, was previously known as *Official Sinn Féin.* The new Government was often referred to as the 'rainbow coalition' (blue, pink and red?). Mr Proinsias de Rossa TD, of the Democratic Left became a Cabinet Minister, while two other members of the party got positions as Ministers of State, i.e. Mr Pat Rabbitte TD, and Mr Eamonn Gilmore TD. The 'rainbow coalition' was a study in itself of representatives with previously held radical views on the 'right' and on the 'left' of Irish politics able to compromise beyond recognition. Nevertheless, it seemed to work reasonably well for a few years until it was defeated in the General Election of 1997.

My own regret, or should I say criticism, of this rainbow government was its lack of reasonable support for the Nationalists in Northern Ireland, largely because of the strongly-held anti-Republican views of spokespersons of the Democratic Left and the traditional 'Republican neutrality of *Fine Gael*'. Both parties had developed 'compulsive alienation' against their *Sinn Féin*/Nationalist roots. Of course, one must admit that the Bruton/Spring/De Rossa Government played an important role in winning Unionist confidence and enabled open dialogue in relation to the Peace Process. In the evolution of affairs, such a period of confidence-building was necessary. To the credit of Mr Dick Spring TD, the Minister for External Affairs, he seemed to remain open to dialogue with the representatives of the Nationalist/Republicans side. His personal position was greatly appreciated by many keen on proceeding with the Peace Process. The complexity of Irish politics is not always appreciated.

As I have already noted, the Minister for Education in the Rainbow Coalition Government, Ms Niamh Bhreathnach TD, of the Labour Party, addressed the vital question of the future development of third-level education. It was under her direction that the special working party or committee was set up (chaired by Mr Lindsay). She brought in the *Universities Act*, which granted a high degree of autonomy to the four colleges of the National University of Ireland (NUI), i.e. UCD, UCG, UCC and NUI Maynooth. There were three university colleges outside the NUI, namely Trinity College, Dublin (TCD), Dublin City University (DCU) and University of Limerick (UL). The latter two were Institutes of Technology that were renamed as universities. I could never see the logic of such re-naming. The change of status was, in my opinion, neither good for the legitimate status of technological education and training, nor for the universal status of university education. A similar process of third-level homogenisation had also taken place in Great Britain.

The granting of full university status to the Recognised College in Maynooth (*Ollscoil na hÉireann, Ma Nuad*), on a par with UCD, UCC, and UCG, was something that IFUT in Maynooth had campaigned for since 1982. It was my first policy initiative of the ASA when becoming Chairperson of the local branch of IFUT, occasioned, as stated earlier, by the visit of Professor Dooge when he was canvassing for a seat in the Senate representing the graduates of the National University of Ireland. The recognition given to St Patrick's College, Maynooth, in the *Bhreathnach Universities Act* was a real 'feather in the cap' of the Recognised College. Credit is also due to the mature foresight of the Trustees and Senior Executives of St Patrick's College, i.e. President Michael Ledwith and Vice-Presidents, Matthew O'Donnell and Séamus Smyth. Dr O'Donnell succeeded Dr Ledwith as President and Dr Smyth became Master of the Recognised College in 1993.

There were two aspects of the new legislation that I was disappointed with, i.e. the omission of representative(s) of Kildare County Council on the NUI Maynooth Governing Body and the retention of the feudal academic structure. IFUT policy would favour the rank of professor for all senior academics and the rotation of the position of departmental heads. This would be in line with the more progressive Continental European practice. I was also disappointed that the 'Pugin Image' of St Patrick's College was not included in the crest of the new NUIM. This seemed a little petty to me, and like an attempt to dissociate NUIM from its worthy ancestor! Of course, I welcome the new status.

7. Retire as Lecturer
and Publish *Prejudice in Ireland Revisited*

The year 1996 was very significant for my academic and research career. The findings and interpretation of the 1988-89 survey of national intergroup attitudes were published under the title, *Prejudice in Ireland Revisited.* Mr Mervyn Taylor TD, former Minister of Equality and Law Reform, launched the book in the Academic Staff Room (New Arts Block). The book was well received and the first printing sold out in a short time. A second printing was issued in 1997 and it also sold out. It was very difficult for me personally to manage the distribution of the books to bookshops and libraries. The book was published by the Survey and Research Unit of the Department of Social Studies, Maynooth.

The second event in 1996 was my retirement from lecturing in September and going out on pension. While it was a major event and marked the end of a quarter of a century lecturing undergraduates and advising graduates in Maynooth in Sociology it was not that traumatic. I suppose I had anticipated the event. It was sad to retire from the informal company of colleagues in the Department. I missed the mass of undergraduate students and the chores of preparing lectures and correcting papers and theses. One thing was very clear, namely, organisations such as Colleges do not have memories. The employee is essentially a functionary, i.e. a worker, a lecturer or an administrator, etc. Just as when the King dies we say, 'the king is dead, long live the king'. It is not as in the case of a family or a religious community, although some religious communities may be in danger of seeing their active members as functionaries and just 'carrying' the retired members.

Modern society has become quite formal and we are always being advised (subtly) not to be too personal. Maynooth College is probably better than most institutionalised organisations. Retired academic staff are welcome to maintain contact with the College as 'Academic Associates'. I had the added advantage of continuing my social/survey research activity and continued to be a member of the 'Survey and Research Unit' of the Department of Social Studies, thanks to the understanding of Professor Liam Ryan. He reminded me in 1996 that I was retiring only from the position of Senior Lecturer. Professor Liam Ryan welcomed me to continue research in the Department of Social Studies, as did his successor, Professor Seán Ó Riain (2007 to 2011).

Working under Professor Liam Ryan for over twenty-five years was a privilege and a very rich experience. He gave me confidence and full academic freedom. He tried to run the Department on the principle of consensus. By his unobtrusive manner he drew the best out of all of us. He was genuinely student-centred. I admired his moral courage when he supported the basic rights of Professor Patrick McGrath and Lecturer Malachy O'Rourke in the 1970s, when they were dismissed from their academic positions because of their move toward laicisation. The local branch of IFUT (Maynooth Academic Staff Association – ASA) stood firmly behind both members' rights. Of course, there was a small minority of members who disagreed with our position.

Professor Ryan was 'laid back' in his approach to administration and he seemed to expect that our department would automatically get its fair share of resources. Some of us in the Department of Social Studies, at the time, felt that sociology, despite its popularity with undergraduates and, later, with graduates, did not receive a fair distribution of administrative, teaching and research resources. Other departments, with fewer students seemed to be receiving proportionally more than their fair share. Professor Ryan had not got the peasant's limited vision as noted by Mairtín Ó Cadhain, i.e. 'their world ended at their 'mairn' (or boundary fence)'. And, yet, when one looks back from the present day out of his Dept. of Social Studies have emerged five autonomous departments, i.e. *Sociology, Anthropology, Applied Social Studies, Adult and Community Education and Psychology*. This is not a bad legacy to the 'quiet man' at the head of our Department. Liam has had credibility in the Church and in society.

During the 1990s in Maynooth, the signs of change were being consolidated in the University. The Humanities, i.e. arts, theology, philosophy and the human sciences, which were the hallmark of this distinguished College right up to the 1980s, were being overtaken by more vocational subjects or departments, i.e. biology, physics, chemistry, computer studies, economics and financial studies, information technology and pragmatic linguistics. Mathematics (which was both an arts and a science subject) was designated as the Department of Mathematical Science. On the positive side, this trend, which was happening in other universities, resulted in a significant number of our graduates qualifying for the highly technical jobs, which were coming on stream in Ireland in the late nineteen- nineties. The fact that INTEL and other similar factories were being located in County Kildare was another incentive towards the boosting of the technological training side of the NUI Recognised College (later to become NUI Maynooth). In terms of cash investment, new buildings housing the 'sciences' were soon to outshadow the one-storey and cheaply built new Arts Block. These campus constructions clearly confirmed the new character of Maynooth. It would only be a matter of time until an 'industrial or technological campus' would be erected nearby. This change is also very problematic for the nurturing of future intellectuals.

8. SURVEY OF TUAM DIOCESE – *QUO VADIMUS*

As I retired from my position as NUI Senior Lecturer in Sociology in St Patrick's College, Maynooth, my work as social researcher continued. Former colleague in Maynooth and our Archbishop of Tuam, Dr Michael Neary (my home Diocese), asked me if I would be willing to help out in carrying out research into *the pastoral needs and resources of the Archdiocese.* It was agreed that I would help out, with the necessary permission of my Jesuit Superiors. After a number of meetings with the Tuam Diocesan *Pastoral Planning Committee,* (under the chairmanship of Fr Séamus Cunnane) which was set up in 1994, a methodology was agreed. A *Parish Enquiry Questionnaire* would be sent to each of the fifty-six parishes of the archdiocese. A full-time research officer would be employed to assist in the research and an office was provided in *Cnoc*

Mhuire. The research officer appointed was Mr Neil Sheridan (from Balla) a graduate (MA) of the Department of Social Studies, Maynooth and a member of a well-known football family from Balla, County Mayo. Later on, assistant research officer, Ms Karen Downes (also a graduate of Maynooth) from Westport, was employed to help with the fieldwork and carry out a survey among the laity. Unfortunately, owing to limited resources, the latter was never completed as originally planned.

During the period 1996-98 the research was finished and an initial report, *Quo Vadimus,* was presented to the Archbishop, priests and lay leaders of the parishes. The report documented, in some detail, the pastoral needs, resources and level of participation of the faithful throughout the Archdiocese, which covered large stretches of Counties Mayo, Galway and a small part of County Roscommon. The level of lay participation in the liturgical, spiritual, pedagogical and administrative life of the parishes varied. The decline in vocations to the priesthood and religious life was reported. Although I suggested it to the Pastoral Committee, the state of the domestic Church, i.e. family prayer and devotion, was not included in the Parish Enquiry Form. The decline of family prayer and devotion has been very serious in Ireland over the past twenty-five years.

The *demographic profile of the parishes*, i.e. the vital statistics of annual births versus annual deaths, revealed a wide disparity. While some parishes showed dynamic growth, especially those influenced by urban growth areas, other parishes were static or in decline. The inland parishes of East Mayo and East Galway and some of the parishes in the more remote western areas, i.e. Achill, North West Connemara, were in a very serious state of community population decline. One of the positive outcomes of this finding was its influence on Minister Éamon Ó Cuív TD, (who launched the Report). (He later launched the *Clár* National Programme, which singled out communities that suffered a fifty per cent or more decline between 1926 and 1996, for special favourable status in relation to State-aided development grants. Such criteria make sense to anyone committed to the maintenance of local viable communities.)

When I called for special support for the weaker (demographically) parishes at the launch of *Quo Vadimus* (in 1998), a journalist disagreed with me and said that we should be directing resources where the population was and leave the dying communities to fend for themselves. In other words, we should follow the population trends into Dublin,

Galway, London, Manchester, *et cetera*. It would appear that some people would be indifferent to the moorlands and highlands of the West of Ireland being stripped of their population, as were the Highlands of Scotland in the past. Thank God, such a regressive attitude has not as yet taken over fully in our rural West.

It is very difficult to assess the impact of *Quo Vadimus* on the Archdiocese. At least it raised the level of awareness for pastoral leaders as to the current state of the parishes. It was not easy for some clergy to accept the obvious decline of their administrative and pastoral supremacy within their respective parishes. There was a time in Ireland when the parish priest was a central authority figure (without necessarily being authoritarian) and most exercised their leadership roles to the benefit of a downtrodden people. The post-Vatican Two move towards greater participation of committed laity, i.e. 'core Catholics', encouraged the priests to share their pastoral and administrative responsibilities with the laity. *Quo Vadimus* reported the level of serious lay participation in the pastoral, administrative, liturgical, spiritual and pedagogical ministry.

The most satisfactory findings were in relation to lay participation in the parish liturgy, i.e. Ministers of the Eucharist, Readers, Choirs, Altar Society and Ushers/collectors. Participation in the parish structure, i.e. Parish Pastoral Councils and Finance and Buildings Committees left much to be desired. In all probability this would change significantly over the following ten years or so because of the traumatic decline of vocations to the priesthood and religious life. The question of merging smaller parishes would not be acceptable. The clustering of such units would be a better solution, when a Priest could serve two parishes and the local Parish Pastoral Council would be responsible to the Archbishop for administering the parish.

Arising out of the greater involvement of laity, the urgent need for the *theological, spiritual and pastoral formation of the 'core Catholics'* becomes a priority. Otherwise, there was a real danger of 'fundamentalism' or a lack of self-confidence among the committed laity. One of the most attractive characteristics of the priests in the Roman Catholic and Anglican Churches has been their careful academic formation in the 'Sacred Sciences'. This explains the relatively low level of religious fundamentalism in these Churches in modern times. Any serious reduction in this training would greatly undermine the Church's standing, especially, among a growingly sophisticated congregation. Even those of us (priests) who have spent many years studying philosophy, theology and related sciences, needed ongoing courses in order that we may keep abreast of the challenges and questions being raised by a better-educated faithful. I must admit that I was a little disappointed by the lack of a sense of urgency in relation to the question of lay formation for future Ministry. It was a pity that the former major seminaries such as Clonliffe, Kilkenny, Carlow and others were not geared for the training of 'core Catholics' in preparation for serious Ministry. The introduction of a permanent deaconate should be brought about without undue delay throughout the dioceses.

After the publication of *Quo Vadimus*, comments were invited from a range of involved persons. I interviewed most of the parish priests and some of the curates of the fifty-six parishes and wrote a follow-up report entitled *Ar Aghaidh Linn* (Let Us Go Forward) in June 2000. In this report a set of definite recommendations was also appended. Each priest in the Archdiocese received a copy of the report. It is difficult for me to assess what effect this document has had. Surprisingly, I received no reaction after delivering the texts (copies) of the Report to Father Brendan Kilcoyne, secretary to Archbishop Neary, at the end of June 2000 (or in early July). I assume the priests read the document and discussed it among themselves. I was happy to observe later that a campaign to establish Parish Pastoral Councils in every parish was carried out. It seems to be difficult at times to get some clergy to share power with the laity or of the laity to accept responsibility for parish ministry at a deeper level. Do we priests suffer from 'induced dominance' or do our lay friends have a sense of 'induced submissiveness' when it comes to matters spiritual or pastoral? This may be understandable in light of the past history of benevolent priestly dominance! Despite all the challenges and limitations, I found a very high standard of pastoral care in the Tuam parishes during my research and discussions with the clergy.

9. CENTENARY OF PTAA

The Pioneer Total Abstinence Association (PTAA) was founded in Dublin on the 28th December 1898 by four noble 'middle-class' middle-aged, pious women, i.e. Mary Bury, Frances Sullivan, Lizzie Power and Ann Egan, under the spiritual direction of Father James Cullen SJ The Board of Management decided to celebrate the *Centenary of the PTAA* during the year from 28th December 1998 until 27th December 1999. Throughout the five years 1994-99 plans and programmes were agreed and different sub-committees and individuals were assigned responsibility for the execution of an interesting programme of events. While my role as Chairperson was involved (*ex officio*) in all committees, I was assigned special responsibility for the Centenary Rally to be held in *Páirc an Chróchaigh* (Croke Park) on Sunday, 30th May 1999. As Chief Organiser of the 1999 Croke Park Rally, I had the very competent assistance of Mrs Mary Brady, from Corballis, Garlow Cross, Navan, County Meath. We organised the event on a very systematic basis. All around the Association we contacted key promoters who urged members to register and book seats in Croke Park. By the end of December 1998 we had a substantial number of bookings. The GAA gave us the use of Croke Park free of charge, as was the case in 1949 and 1959.

There were quite a number of arrangements to be worked out, i.e. security, stewarding, liturgy, music, the building of the altar, public address, all within Croke Park. On the streets of Dublin, we had to prearrange parking for coaches and cars. The majority came to Dublin on coaches (482 coaches) arrived on the morning of the rally. Each Diocese had its own band and each Centre had its banner. The Mass was televised live on TG4 and that night a summary one-hour highlight of the rally was transmitted on RTÉ1 at 10.30pm and attracted a very big viewing public. The outside TV had to be arranged and paid for by the Association.

The day of the rally came. It was cloudy and dry, but bitterly cold. *The Irish Times* reported that there were 45,000 present, including *Uachtarán na hÉireann*, Her Excellency, Mrs Mary McAleese and *An Taoiseach*, Mr Bertie Ahern TD. Some twenty-four bishops, two cardinals and the papal nuncio and over two hundred priests took part. His Eminence Francis Cardinal Arinze (Nigeria and Rome), preached the sermon. His Grace, Dr Desmond Connell, (Archbishop of Dublin), presided at the Mass. Fr Bernard McGuckian SJ, Central Director, welcomed the participants.

During the musical interlude, Mr Aonghus McAnally was MC and Ms Niamh Murray and Dr Ronan Tynan led in singing appropriate songs and hymns. Over twenty bands from all over the country came to play in Croke Park according as they arrived from the parade, which lined up on O'Connell Street and marched around Parnell Square, through Great Denmark Street and marched around Mountjoy Square, down Fitzgibbon Street and on to Jones' Road and in to Croke Park. The 482 coaches (from every county in Ireland) brought Pioneers to Dublin for the Centenary Rally. The parade was led by the band of the *Garda Síochána*. In all, the rally went off very well. It was a 'people's rally'. Despite the very cold day, the spirits of the people were high. There were delegates from abroad, i.e. England Scotland and Wales, the United States and Canada, Australia and New Zealand, Sub-Saharan Africa, South Africa, Bolivia, India and elsewhere overseas. The largest foreign delegation (outside Britain) came from Kenya. It was a day to remember, *Deo gratias.*

As part of the Centenary Celebrations, it was decided to hold the first International Conference of the PTAA in St Patrick's College, Maynooth, on the first weekend after the Croke Park Rally. There was a good attendance of delegates from abroad and from Central Council. At that Conference it was decided to establish a pan-African Committee to help to coordinate affairs of the PTAA in Africa. At the time, it was estimated that there were a quarter of a million pioneers in Africa, throughout eight countries, i.e. Kenya, Uganda, Zambia (and Malawi), Tanzania, Zimbabwe, Namibia, South Africa and Nigeria. It was hoped to establish National Pioneer Councils in these countries with an active presence of Pioneers in three or more dioceses. The problem with Pioneers in the foreign countries of the so-called 'Developed World' was their being mainly among emigrants from Ireland or members of their families. I had urged the Pioneers in England, for instance, to try to attract members from other ethnic groups (in addition to those of Irish background). Similarly, in the United States, we had failed to extend membership beyond the Irish-Americans to any great extent so far.

The growth of the Association in Sub-Saharan Africa was almost totally within the indigenous population. It was also a different type of movement. Father James Cullen's idea was for Pioneers to live positive lives as parents, as workers, as members of various professions, as sports people, as members of Church and non-Church voluntary organisations, as members of political parties and as leaders in their local community. The PTAA as an organisation in itself was more or less a seedbed for 'core Catholics' (in the mind of Father Cullen). Local centres would spread the membership. As in Ireland, women Pioneers constituted 70%

of those serving as 'core Catholics' in Africa. The Legion of Mary played a major role in promoting the Pioneer Association in Africa.

In some countries in Africa, however, regular attendance at meetings and a high level of spiritual prayer and renewal were expected of the membership. I was later to discover that in some of the more active dioceses in places like Kenya and Zambia, up to ninety per cent of Pioneers were actively involved in local centre activity. In Ireland, one would be grateful if between five and ten per cent of Pioneers would attend local meetings on a regular basis. In Ireland, our public influence is more 'indirect', while in parts of Africa, membership seeks to influence people 'directly'. In South Africa, where original membership was established early in the twentieth century, the structure was more akin to the Irish model, particularly in the cities such as Cape Town and Port Elizabeth.

Some Pioneers do not seem to grasp fully the vision of Father James Cullen SJ, who wished to influence society through a kind of infiltration method. As a spiritual body he hoped we (Pioneers) would influence society through our prayer, personal sacrifice and good example. He was very keen, for instance, that clergy and religious would become Pioneers, as examples of Christian asceticism. From time to time, attempts by the leadership of the PTAA to lobby and to engage in the public media as part of an 'instrumental' social movement have met with only very limited success. My efforts, as Chairperson, to urge centres to adopt a special ministry in aid of those with drink and drugs' problems were not very successful to date. Social action was rare in the history of the Pioneers in Ireland. And yet, the PTAA has been one of the most influential agents of positive change in Ireland over the past hundred years.

Collective involvement of Pioneers in Ireland has been mainly in relation to outings, rallies, religious pilgrimages, leisure and sports activities, largely for the members themselves. It was an attempt to provide an alternative lifestyle, or should I say, recreational style, which would be free from drink (strangely enough, I found the same to be true in Africa). Such functions as regional and diocesan dinner-dances were also very important and are still receiving very good support throughout the whole country. Masses and special liturgies provide spiritual occasions for meetings. Around Confirmation time, we try to have an occasion for public enrolment of 'Young Pioneers'. We also try to set up clubs in second-level schools.

A special publication on the history of the PTAA, *A Nation of Extremes*, by the eminent Irish historian Prof Diarmaid Ferriter was launched as part of the centenary events. Seminars and conferences are very worthwhile events for the Association to raise membership awareness of the Pioneer mission to different age groups.

10. ADDRESSING THE DRINK PROBLEM TODAY

By the end of the twentieth century we still had around 180,000 Pioneers in Ireland in over 1,000 centres. The total world membership was around a half-a-million members. Our prayer has always been: 'for the sober use of alcohol and the conversion of excessive drinkers'. The Pioneer Association has never been against drink in moderation. So far, we have not been able to organise 'moderate drinkers' into our mission, apart from enlisting their support for some of our events. The structuring of 'moderate drinkers' in a supportive way has met with strong opposition within the Association, because of the danger of 'watering down' the total abstinence commitment of members. I have always felt that there was a place for some kind of a tenuous formal link with moderate drinkers who are interested in supporting the PTAA.

One of the most optimistic aspects of the PTAA has been the revival of interest by the youth in joining. We adopted the slogan: *'abstain from drink until you are eighteen and from illicit drugs for life'* and invite them 'not to give up drink but, rather, to take up life without drink'. Young people like a challenge but they need to be addressed in a positive manner. Condemnation and demonisation of youth are having the opposite effect on them from what those who condemn and demonise them may intend. I have always believed in the power of the self-fulfilling prophecy theory, i.e. if we define situations as real they become real as a consequence of our definition'. Priests, teachers, parents, Gardaí and others who are anxious to control young people's behaviour should always think of this approach. In other words, if we define young people in a positive light, they will respond to us in a responsible manner. Recognition for the good they do and encouragement are far more powerful than criticism of their faults and 'writing them off'. As the Irish proverb says: *'Mol an óige agus tiocfaidh sé'* ('Praise the young and they will respond').

When attracting young people to abstain from drink, we should be aware of the heroism required for the young person to go 'against the tide' of peer pressure and the example of some adults. Second-level schools are very important 'structured peer environments' where Pioneers can do much good. Thankfully, since 1997 the revival of school centres gained momentum. The setting up of the National Youth Committee in 1997 as a central committee of the Board of Management was a very significant development. Some of us seniors had to be prepared to take 'some stick' from time to time from the new youth leaders. They are quite demanding but that is as one would expect. Of course, there is always a danger of mini 'power games' being played and the possibility of 'power cliques'. I would be more concerned about 'power cliques' than 'power games'. The major change that has taken place within the PTAA has been its democratisation and an enabling of many members to share in decision making. The National Youth Committee is intended to give representatives from each of the four provinces a say in the running of services to young pioneers. (Unfortunately, one of the regrettable consequences of the child-abuse scandals has been the restriction of voluntary youth work within the PTAA as a precautionary measure.)

In the early years of the Pioneers in Ireland, the leaders adopted the slogan: *'Ireland sober, Ireland free'*. In other words, freedom was the gift of sobriety. Addiction is the enemy of freedom. Great liberating leaders like James Connolly and Big Jim Larkin were important moral supporters of the Pioneer Association. Many social commentators saw the importance of the success of the *Irish Independence Movement* to enable the people to avoid addiction to alcohol. Mr Ulick O'Connor stated on a recent interview on RTÉ that the Pioneer Association was one of the most significant movements in the process of the emancipation of our people from their colonial dependence and sense of inferiority. Many of the most effective leaders in the Irish Freedom Movement were Pioneers. The working-class people in Dublin and in other Irish towns and cities were being prevented from liberating themselves because of their dependence on alcoholic drink, i.e. drinking to excess provided them with an escape from the misery of their condition. An obvious example of a noble people 'hooked' on alcoholic drink was the Native Americans (the Indians). Some Travellers have at times used alcohol as an escape from their total deprivation and the biased attitudes of members of the settled community.

What is true for society is doubly so for individuals. Once an individual becomes addicted or psychologically dependent on alcohol, personal freedom is at risk. This is very important for young people and for adults with families, and other responsibilities. Unlike in the early twentieth century in Ireland, when excessive drinking was most visible among the poor adult males and those on low income, today's excessive drinkers tend to include middle-class youth of both genders, male and female. Many of our very heavy 'binge drinkers' do not lack income or education. Some tend to wreak havoc on themselves and on those around them. Most serious of all, they become addicted very young in life and develop a dependence on alcohol, which impinges seriously on their personal freedom and on their social and personal lives.

The Pioneer Association's policy of advising young people to abstain from alcohol at least until they are eighteen years of age is based on our understanding of the absence of moderation in the *'Irish drink subculture', i.e. which sees drinking to excess an aim of the 'good night out'*. This is a most infantile and uncreative aspiration being pursued almost equally by some young men and women. The proliferation of 'Irish Pubs' throughout Continental Europe and elsewhere abroad is spreading this 'drink sub-culture' to the dissatisfaction of many parents and responsible citizens in these countries, where the culture of drinking alcohol was/is more moderate. Again, this is being promoted by the multinational drinks industry. Governments may have to intervene for the sake of their young people.

In my experience, the impact of advertising and sport-sponsorship by the drinks industry was crucial in promoting the acceptability of alcohol among young people. Modern advertising has become very powerful and can have a seductive effect on late teenagers and young adults. It seems that such an intrusion in the lives of people (especially through radio and television in their homes) should be strictly restricted in the interests of the health and welfare of our young people. All sponsorship of sport by the drinks industry should be 'anonymous' or not at all. The association of drinking and group sport in Ireland is notorious. The major sports organisations have really failed in their responsibility to the physical, social and personal welfare of young people, whose games are intended to promote physical fitness and character formation. The growing commercialisation of group sport in Ireland has been part of the problem. Voluntary amateurism has been greatly eroded. The media have also become the masters in many ways. The media in Ireland have too much influence and, at times, seem to act irresponsibly in matters of glamorising intemperate lifestyles.

Another unwelcome development in Ireland throughout the last quarter of the 20th century has been the proliferation of 'off-licence' outlets. This has been instrumental in providing relatively easy access to under-age drinkers and to those with addiction problems. According as our people became more affluent, the home has become better stocked with drinks. In some homes one can find 'cocktail bars'. This has added to the unhealthy increase in the consumption of alcoholic liquor. Again, I feel that the State has been remiss in its liberal attitude towards 'off-licences'. The Pioneer Association made representations to the *Oireachtas* Committee involved in the preparation of legislation on the extension of opening hours for pubs, clubs and hotels and the availability of intoxicating liquor in off-licences and food and vegetable stores. Our submission called for much stricter control of 'off-licences' as well as the printing of 'health warnings' on all bottles and cans. A strong plea was made to outlaw drinking in public places other than licensed premises. Regretfully, our appeals were mostly in vain. Commercial interests seemed to outweigh the welfare of the young people.

At least, we raised the public awareness of the issues raised. Until the drinks industry is compelled to take its proportionate responsibility for the negative consequences of alcoholic drink on drinkers, their families and others injured or damaged because of the influence of drinking irresponsibly, it is hard to see a serious change. *I believe that the most effective way to control the negative effects of the abuse of alcohol is to take the drinks industry to court, as has happened in the case of the tobacco industry.* This suggestion of bringing the alcohol industry to account for its 'proportionate responsibility' for all cases of negative (serious) outcomes of alcoholic drink in society has not been successful as yet. The costs to the medical services in caring for those suffering from the physical effects of alcohol on the body should be part of the bill to the drinks industry. Also, the loss of working hours, study time, social support, and so forth, results in serious deprivation resulting from the abuse of alcohol.

By the end of the nineties the ugly spectre of 'binge drinking' by

291

young Irish men and women was to become a regular feature in the Irish public media. Our negative stereotype of 'drunken Irish' was being borne out by concrete evidence. And yet, the State refused to intervene, except in a minimal way. Driven by the pressures of commercialisation, a *laissez-faire* position was being adopted. One has to question the priorities of the Irish establishment, including the State, Trade Unions, IBEC (Management), farming associations, sports and hospitality industry, *et cetera*, in promoting commercial and economic development before the welfare of our young people! It is very sad and extremely difficult to understand such a decline in patriotism and idealism. Repeated disappointments with the State's inertia and also its deafness and blindness to our appeals, disappointed the Pioneer Board of Management. We would also have wished a stronger line from the Conference of Bishops and from the Conference of Religious in Ireland (CORI). By the end of the decade, however, we sensed a change in the public attitude towards the PTAA by journalists in RTÉ, TG4, national newspapers and, most of all, local radio stations. Some weeks I would be interviewed three or four times, i.e. as Chairperson of the Pioneer Association. It really proves the point that in this world all we can hope to be is 'seeders' rather than 'harvesters'!

Before leaving the Pioneers, it is necessary to explain our commitment to total abstinence for life. We do this as the self-denial of something good 'in reparation to God for the sins of intemperance'. I would love to drink in moderation but, for purely spiritual reasons, I will deny myself that good for the greater good of the love of God and of my neighbour! Through our self-denial, we take on some of the pain of Christ, which He suffered for us in His passion. Again, unfortunately, the Catholic Church seemed to underplay the importance of 'reparation' and 'atonement' after Vatican Two. The ascetic way of life has not been promoted sufficiently in recent times, in my opinion. This may have been as a response to an over-pessimistic view of the 'world' of some religious leaders in the past. Did we 'throw out the baby with the bathwater'?

Fr Cullen, our founder, did not see the Pioneer Association as a Pledge Movement. As noted above, it was a spiritual association of believers who did not drink and were willing to deny themselves of their right to enjoy moderate drinking in reparation for the sins of intemperance and to pray for those with drink problems. By wearing the pin, they would give good example. Many well-disposed, even Church leaders and pastorally-oriented persons, fail to grasp this essentially spiritual nature of the PTAA. It was never intended to be 'anti-drink'. It is promoted by getting adults to join it. The promotion of the temporary pledge among young people is to prepare them for moderation in adult life.

11. PRESIDENT MARY ROBINSON (1990 – 1997)

During the decade 1990-2000 the Republic of Ireland elected two distinguished women as Presidents of the State. In 1990, Her Excellency, Mrs Mary Robinson, from Crossmolina, County Mayo, was elected by popular vote. In 1997, her Excellency, Mrs Mary McAleese from Rostrevor, County Down (originally from Belfast, County Antrim), was elected to succeed President Robinson. The six Presidents of Ireland up to 1990 were all men, i.e. *An Dr Dubhghlas de h-Íde* (1938-45), *Mr Seán T Ó Ceallaigh* (1945-59), *Mr Éamon deValera* (1959-73), *Mr Erskine Childers* (1973-74), *Mr Cearbhaill Ó Dálaigh* (1974-76) and *Dr Pádraig Hillery* (1976-90). After such eminent male predecessors, the 'two Marys' were most successful in adding grace, gravitas and meaning to the Office in their own unique manner. Traditionally, the Office of President was characterised by reserve and political neutrality. This was to change somewhat in the 1990s, at least in its image.

The relatively brief periods of office of Presidents Erskine Childers and Cearbhaill Ó Dálaigh were due to the sudden death of the former and a resignation on a point of principle of the latter. In 1976, President Ó Dálaigh had referred a piece of legislation to the Supreme Court for the purpose of checking if it was in harmony with the Irish Constitution. The Bill in question dealt with security matters. The then Minister for Defence made a derogatory (vulgar) remark about the President at a subsequent after-dinner speech in Mullingar. This was reported in the local and national media. It was seen by President Ó Dálaigh as serious and improper behaviour by a Minister and tantamount to an insult to the Presidency. The Government failed to take the necessary action to restore equilibrium and President Cearbhaill Ó Dálaigh resigned on principle, thus avoiding a constitutional crisis. It was to the credit of President Patrick Hillery, who succeeded President Ó Dálaigh, that the status of the Office of President was restored after it had been damaged by the Minister's unfortunate remarks. He carried out his duties with firmness and quiet dignity.

I had the personal privilege of knowing and working with Presidents Mary Robinson and Mary McAleese in their careers prior to their election to their high office. As reported already, Mary Robinson SC had invited me to give evidence from my research in the David Norris Constitutional Case against the criminalisation of homosexual behaviour of consenting male adults (which he eventually won at the European Court in Strasbourg). In the case of Mary McAleese we worked together on the MacBride Commission investigating the Irish Prison System during 1980 and 1981. She was a Professor of Law in Trinity College, Dublin, at the time. Both relatively brief experiences enabled me to appreciate the excellent character and outstanding ability of the two future Presidents of Ireland.

President Mary Robinson both led and symbolised the campaign for gender equality and the whole area of civil rights. She would have been identified with the so-called liberal agenda, which was promoted by the former *Taoiseach*, Dr Garret Fitzgerald. Politically, she would be classified in the 'liberal left' camp. She was part of a vital and articulate collectivity of academics, clergy, religious, lawyers, politicians and trade unionists, who raised issues concerning civil rights. They were more than adequately reported in *The Irish Times*. This broad coalition of liberal thinkers had been around Dublin since the late 1960s, i.e. after Vatican Two. Some Jesuit colleagues of mine and I would often attend meetings of '*Flannery's Harriers*', as they were called, in the Clarence Hotel on the Quays, where the 'brave new world' of justice and equality would be discussed usually without dissent. Professor Enda McDonagh, St Patrick's College, Maynooth, Fr Jack Kelly SJ and Father Austin Flannery, OP, Editor of *Doctrine and Life* (after whom the Harriers were named) were among the numerous members of the clergy who participated regularly.

Concern for issues of civil rights outside Ireland was also central to the agenda of '*Flannery's Harriers*' and other liberal groups, which continued to meet and communicate through journals and the letter columns of *The Irish Times*. *The Irish Press*, prior to its unfortunate demise was, if anything, more radical than *The Irish Times* in its addressing of issues. Its readership would not include many of the upper-middle-class elite. People like Reverend Professor Terence McAughey (a Northern

Presbyterian Minister) and Dr Kadar Asmal (later Minister for Education in South Africa) led the *Irish Anti-Apartheid Movement (IAAM)*. Mrs Louise Asmal was a Trojan worker for the cause. I became a member of the IAAM.

I always saw President Mary Robinson as a worthy member or sympathiser of such a range of groupings who were committed to improve our world. She had always been a champion of the Women's Liberation Movement. During the 1980s and 1990s, there was a growing reaction to the 'Liberal Agenda' in the United States and there were echoes of such opposition beginning to be heard in Ireland also. By the mid-1980s, however, the feminist movement had penetrated the *Social Science Departments of the Irish Universities* as it had done earlier in Britain and the United States of America. Most of the graduates of the Social Science Studies' Departments were articulate women from middle and upper-middle class backgrounds. It is very interesting to observe that pre-1970s the majority of departments of Social Science/Studies were under the direction of clerical academics, e.g. University Colleges in Dublin, Cork, Galway and Maynooth. Would many of the 'liberal set' today be happy or willing to acknowledge their academic roots that sprouted from the rostrum of Priest, Sister and Brother Professors and Lecturers? But history confirms the Church's primary role in a social awareness of informal discrimination.

In my experience of Kent State University (1965-66) and Ann Arbor in 1974, I found communities of liberal academics. In Belfield in the 1970s and early 1980s, I noticed the rise of a very strong feminist ethos among the academic staff. At times, one would almost have to apologise for being a man, much less for being a male cleric! The liberal–feminist movement extended to outside the departmental staffrooms. New courses were devised in feminist sociology, psychology, history, literature, *et cetera*. The effects of this new awareness of women's rights would be communicated throughout Irish communities by enthusiastic feminist graduates from the social and human science departments.

Mrs Mary Robinson's presidential election campaign was effectively organised and supported by committed feminists and local community leaders around the country. Civil rights' groups were also very supportive of her at the local level. Local community adult-education groups affiliated to AONTAS (the national adult-education umbrella organisation) were strongly committed to women's rights and contributed to the Robinson manifesto. I was very much involved in AONTAS at the time and was president during 1994-95. The county Vocational Education Committees (VECs) were losing their dominant position on the national executive of AONTAS during the 1990s.

Looking back now, it was clear that President Mary Robinson was very necessary for the cause of 'women's liberation'. The fact that some more militant feminists may have gone 'over the top' at times and seemed to be anti-male in their rhetoric and action, should not take from the value of the movement, just as cases of extreme nationalists during the Irish independence campaign did not undermine the legitimacy of the cause of national freedom. The de-radicalisation of the more extreme aspects of the feminist movement will follow its relative success.

The progress made by the feminist movement in Ireland in the 1990s was substantial. All institutions, i.e. family, religion, law, economy, polity, education and recreation were forced to adjust their norms to facilitate the change. This was a very painful process for many. Those who stood to lose in the new power-sharing were the males who had most power at the top of the social ladder and those at the bottom of the power-spectrum. Males in the poorer and weaker groups were to suffer because they would lose not only their imagined power superiority (which they had not got) but also their basic 'social status' in many cases. By the end of the nineties, in my opinion, the most deprived and discriminated-against gender category was the males at the bottom of the social ladder. Their women colleagues had begun to lift themselves up both psychologically and socially, while the men were left behind. This showed a serious lacuna in the feminist movement's ideology because it was basically more bourgeois than socialist in my opinion. Had it been more socialist (with a small 's') it would have been better able to bring the men along with the women.

Now that the feminist movement has asserted itself it may be time to establish *a more socially inclusive movement* made up of men and women, i.e. an inclusive gender liberation movement. The cause of women's rights in areas where they are still being denied should remain on the agenda. Such a change would mark the success of the exclusively feminist movement by its incorporation into an inclusive one. It would be a classic case of '*floreat ut pereat*', i.e. 'blossom to cease to be necessary'.

(Father Michael Hurley SJ took this as the motto of the *Irish School of Ecumenics.*) I would also like to see a movement for social equality between men and women, which would focus more on the social class issues in a non-condescending manner. Also, some women who assume positions of power are open to the temptation of becoming as authoritarian as the men whom they replace. It is an established fact that authoritarianism is not correlated with intelligence or, for that matter, with gender!

Another area where feminism had an impact was on the family itself. Male and female roles were redefined. Both men and women were being encouraged to pursue full-time occupations outside the home. The time and space in the lives of mothers for child rearing was to be restricted. It may be too early to assess the overall impact of this reduction of the mother's nurturing role on the development and socialisation of the young. This is an area that cannot be resolved by feminism alone. *Husbands and fathers have complementary roles* to those of *wives and mothers.* There was an extraordinary growth in the number of single mothers during the nineties, some of whom did not have the support of a committed male partner. It is disappointing that the feminist movement failed to correct this trend. It is owed to every child born in our society that he or she has a reasonable chance of maturation and socialisation. These children's welfare needs much more attention and resources than have been afforded to date.

In the ideal order, every child is entitled to good home life with a father and a mother to care for her or him during childhood and early adolescence. I would have expected the feminist movement to give great priority to child rearing in the family by both mother and father. This is another important reason for moving the gender question into the post-feminist inclusive stage. This should not be taken to mean that I was opposed to the necessary work done by the feminist movement during the 1980s and 1990s. The assertion of women's rights was necessary and timely and President Mary Robinson was a very significant leader of that movement. Also single mothers are to be admired and praised.

President Robinson tried to open up the Office of the Presidency and invited various groups of Irish emigrants abroad to visit her in Áras an Uachtaráin. She also addressed the assembled members of the *Dáil* and the *Seanad*. Because of the constitutional delineation of the role of the President, it was only possible for her to become publicly involved in a way that could not be seen as political or partisan. Because of President Robinson's background and profession, she possessed a high degree of leadership self-confidence in the positive sense of the word. Most people with an upper-middle-class background accepted her as one of their own. At the grassroots she won the respect of the people. The President won admiration abroad when representing Ireland. She always carried herself with gravitas.

It came as a surprise and, I would say, disappointment, when President Robinson announced that she would resign from Office before the end of her seven-year term to take up a senior position in the United Nations. While her being appointed to this high office was a great honour for Ireland, it was felt, nevertheless, that she should have deferred taking up the position until she had finished her term in the Presidency. Yet, she had been elected to office for a full term and was expected to complete it. As was her personal right, she opted to resign and take up the position in charge of Human Rights in September 1997, i.e. three months before the end of her term. So ended the reign of Ireland's first woman President and prepared the way for a presidential election. Apart from being the first woman President, Mrs Mary Robinson was also our first President not nominated by the *Fianna Fáil* political party or by party consensus. The Irish Labour Party had nominated her and Mayo was proud of her.

12. PRESIDENT MARY MCALEESE (1997 – 2011)

The presidential election of November 1997 was won by Mrs Mary McAleese from Rostrevor, County Down. She was the nominee of the *Fianna Fáil* party. Being a woman from Northern Ireland or 'the Six Counties' (as some more republican-minded people call it) caused a certain, if muted, hostility against the former Trinity Professor and the Vice-Chancellor of the Queen's University, Belfast.

She was also known as a very committed Roman Catholic, who had worked for and represented the Irish Conference of Catholic Bishops on the All-Ireland Forum in the 1980s. Further, she was perceived as a strong Irish nationalist. The more dominant 'liberal' media did not support her candidacy with any great enthusiasm. And yet, she 'walked into office'. The vast majority of Irish people felt they could identify with President Mary McAleese.

As already noted, when President McAleese was a Professor in Trinity College, Dublin in 1979 and 1980, I worked with her on the MacBride Commission into the Irish Prison System. Mr Sean MacBride SC (former Minister for Foreign Affairs and son of Major John MacBride, hero of 1916) was Chairperson of the Commission. This Commission of Enquiry into the state of the Irish Prison system was called together by the Prisoners' Rights Organisation, under the influence of its spokesman, Mr Joe Costello (a *Labour Party* TD and Minister of State). It was the first real enquiry into the Irish Prison System since 1881. Professor McAleese was one of the active members of the Commission and wrote the chapter on the history of prisons in Ireland. She also made very valuable contributions in every aspect of the report, i.e. alternatives to prison, rehabilitation of offenders, the problem of recidivism, sentencing policy, and so forth.

During the nine months in which we were preparing our Report, which was published in 1980, I got to know Mary McAleese as a scholar and as a multifaceted personality. She was very warm, motherly and personable. Her concern about justice and peace in Northern Ireland was contagious. Although her family was violently threatened and their family home in Belfast was shot at by Loyalist paramilitaries, resulting in their being forced to leave their 'mixed' neighbourhood, she continued to keep contacts across the religious and political divide. The family's public house was later destroyed by Loyalist paramilitaries. Because of all this unjust persecution, Mary's family, the Leneghans, moved to Rostrevor in County Down, where they lived in peace.

President McAleese's love for all things Irish (including Gaelic football) was borne out by her becoming fluent in the Irish language, after a number of refresher courses in the Donegal Gaeltacht. She is a principled ecumenist and a very committed Roman Catholic at the same time. I would place her slightly left of centre on the political/ideological spectrum. She possessed a range of qualities that made her an ideal candidate for the position of *Uachtarán na hÉireann* (President of Ireland). Her subsequent performance as President has borne out her ideal suitability for the position at this time in our history.

On assuming Office as President, Mrs Mary McAleese set out to serve the nation in her own inimitable style. She and her husband, Dr Martin McAleese, kept very close relations with both sides in Northern Ireland

and were well received by those on the Protestant and Unionist side. Her reception of Holy Communion at a Church of Ireland celebration raised eyebrows among some Roman Catholic clergy. She did so in a spirit of ecumenical recognition as Head of State and thus established President McAleese's credentials as President of all the people. This did not in anyway diminish her loyalty to the Catholic Church, although it may have weakened her public image (used against her by certain commentators) as an 'exclusively Roman Catholic' President. It raised for me the urgent need for progress towards intercommunion and mutual recognition of Holy Orders between the Roman Catholic and Anglican/ Lutheran Churches. Had Pope Paul VI survived for another ten years as Pope, I believe that such an important goal in the path towards Church Unity would have been reached. Many serious Catholics and Protestants desire intercommunion and so do I.

President Mary McAleese attended the Pioneer Centenary Rally in Croke Park on the 30th May 1999. She was our 'Guest of Honour'. Her concern about the growing problem of binge drinking and loutish behaviour by young Irish men and women was commented on by her at a special Summer School on Irish Culture in the United States some years later. It was her lot during the first decade of her being *Uachtarán* to preside over an Ireland with an unprecedented rise in our economic prosperity. Her public addresses were both complimentary in praising and recognising our new affluence on the one hand, and alerting us to the obligations of social justice within Irish society and between nations abroad on the other hand. She also reminded us of the importance of spiritual values necessary to make our materially rich lives more meaningful. *Vis-à-vis* the *Dáil* and *Seanad*, the President observed a most discreet distance.

From the start she strove to build up a good relationship with the British Head of State, Her Majesty, Queen Elizabeth II. Their joint visit to the War Graves of the First World War in Belgium in 2003 was seen as a gesture of long-term significance. This would help to heal the resentment felt by many families whose ancestors had fought and died for a cause they thought noble, i.e. the freedom of small nations in World War One, at a time when their fellow Irish men and women were engaged in military conflict with the British occupation forces in the Irish War of Independence, 1916-21. The majority in Northern Ireland had contributed so much to the 1914-18 War and viewed the 1916 Insurrection in Ireland as a treasonable action at the time. It has required a degree of mutual understanding and patriotic forgiveness on both sides to reach the stage when we could honour one side without dishonouring the other. Herein, I see the invaluable gesture in Flanders. (It was to be President Mary McAleese's privilege to welcome Queen Elizabeth II to Ireland on a State Visit in May 2011.)

13. The Pro-Life Challenge

During the mid-1990s, the pro-abortion rights' lobby became very active in Ireland. They used a tragic case (the X Case) to advance their cause, with some success. An amendment to the Constitution (which had outlawed abortion except in the case of it happening as a result of a medical intervention to save the life of the mother) was passed that permitted information on termination abroad. The indirect termination of pregnancy in defence of the mother's life is fully in line with the teaching of the Churches. In some of the rhetoric used to promote the right to abort the unborn child the emphasis was on the mother's right to choose such a termination. It was, therefore, seen by some people as part of women's rights and they would state so without apology.

For me abortion, i.e. the 'deliberate termination' of a pregnancy can never be justified, except when the mother's life is in imminent danger and the death of the unborn child is not the primary purpose of the medical intervention. The Roman Catholic Church has always allowed such intervention. I cannot accept that anyone has the right to end the life of another human being, either outside the womb or inside it. I know that some people do not recognise the pre-born to have the same rights as the born. When society fails to defend the life of the unborn it is in the process of dehumanising itself. Just as when society ceases to support the life of the disabled it dehumanises itself. We have now reached a certain level of hypocrisy when the early detection of handicap in the child in the womb can be used as justification for abortion in some countries. Abortion is one of the scourges of modern civilisation. It is a crime against the innocent! Those who seek to protect the unborn must rank among the true heroes of our time. *I consider the unborn the weakest and most vulnerable of all minorities!* The deliberate killing of the unborn is an anti-life tragedy.

The importance and sacredness of the life of the unborn have been brought home to me on numerous occasions when I visited expectant mothers in hospital. The trauma and real sense of loss and mourning of a mother and father when they suffer a miscarriage is something to experience. The recent clarification by the Church on the status of the unborn in the sight of God, i.e. the scrapping of 'Limbo', tells me that God will bring the unborn to heaven, *consummatus in brevi* (brought to the fullness of life in a brief moment), as a full person in the prime of life. Our faith tells us that. Therefore, it is consoling to know that *all the aborted innocent unborn children are now in the prime of life with the Lord, as are all unborn children whose untimely death was caused by unavoidable miscarriage.* With God nobody is lost.

Unmarried mothers, no matter what their age, are to be praised and thanked for their heroic love for the child they give birth to in circumstances, which, at times, are far from ideal. *Unmarried mothers are loving mothers* for going ahead with their pregnancy. They deserve the fullest social respect and support. Today's inhuman and sometimes callous attitude towards the unborn often masquerades as 'liberal' in this regard. Abortion, in my opinion is one of the most illiberal activities practised in modern society. Thank God, up until 2013, Ireland refused to legalise abortion. But how long will this 'oasis of civilisation for the unborn' be able to survive in a world that seems to be losing its value for life?

I am sure that some of my 'liberal friends' may be surprised at my very strong defence of the 'unborn'. The way I see the world I could do no other. However, we live in a world where my views on the rights of the unborn are not held by all good people. In some strange way, many have been persuaded in good faith that abortion is permissible. I accept their good faith but I feel they are unwittingly in serious error on the issue. The challenge facing civilisation is to find a way of persuading good people of the inviolable right of the unborn to live. Confrontation and name-calling will not work. The issue is highly emotional and sometimes a number of active pro-life campaigners have been associated with 'right-wing politics'. I would hope that I would be seen as a tolerant, left-wing pro-lifer!

14. THE COLLEGE OF INDUSTRIAL RELATIONS CHANGES

In September 1998 I was transferred from Sandford Lodge (the Jesuit Community attached to the College of Industrial Relations) to Upper Gardiner Street, Dublin 1. I became a member of the Jesuit Community attached to St Francis Xavier's Church. It was quite an upsetting change in that we were, in effect, being put out of the CIR residence to facilitate the sale of Sandford Lodge. The dynamic Director of the College of Industrial Relations (now re-named National College of Ireland [NCI]), Professor Joyce O'Connor, had procured new premises in the newly developed North City Docklands. It was located on trendy Mayor Street. Dr Joyce O'Connor and I (as already noted) had the distinction of being the first two graduates of the National University of Ireland to qualify for a PhD in Sociology in 1976. Her drive to change the CIR was most impressive. It was a classic case of change following the dominant social forces of 'Celtic Tiger' Republic of Ireland. She was successful in changing the College radically. The direction in which trends were going made me and others very worried. The CIR was to lose much of its unique character and ethos as an educational organisation that was established by the Jesuits in 1951 to serve the needs of workers, supervisors and lower/middle management.

The College under the Jesuits was imbued with the radical spirit of the Gospel, which strove for justice and fair play. It instilled into trade union leaders a sense of moral courage to defend the workers' rights against all kinds of manipulation by wealthy industrialists whose 'bottom line' was profit. Lecturers communicated a 'patriotic spirit', which kept community and country to the fore. Philosophy and social ethics, as well as Catholic social teaching, were taught without apology. I was given the more empirical subjects to teach, i.e. industrial sociology, social institutions and industrial anthropology. As noted earlier I taught part-time in the CIR (later the NCI), for thirty-three years – from 1966 until 1999.

Some of Ireland's most successful leaders of industry were graduates of the College. I had the good fortune of living in the residence attached to the CIR for twenty-eight years and three months (June 1970 – September 1998). I commuted from there to St Patrick's College, Maynooth and to other places when I was lecturing. It was also possible to keep an ongoing connection with Milltown Institute of Theology and Philosophy.

The College of Industrial Relations was a most inspiring community of Jesuits with whom to live. Stimulating conversation on matters of interest in the affairs of industry and of society was to provide a most challenging atmosphere to 'the Junior Academic-cum-Researcher' who was keen and, maybe overzealous, to enquire into and solve all of the social problems of the day! For me, it was the ideal environment to take on what appeared to others to be demanding tasks of research and lecturing. I could do it because of the support and encouragement and, most of all, patient tolerance and help, which I received from my Jesuit colleagues in the College of Industrial Relations, i.e. Fathers Tim Hamilton, Bill McKenna, Kevin Quinn, John Brady, Tony Baggott, Michael Connolly and others, in the early years. Miss May Fox, the 'housekeeper', kept us all 'true priests' and Jesuits. Brother Jim Barry SJ, was a caring provider and Brother Herbert Monaghan SJ, was Plant Manager.

So much was I impressed by this place that I suggested that it become a residential research and teaching institute for Jesuits of the Irish Province who were committed to the broad field of 'faith and justice'. I was worried that the 'direct-contact with deprived communities', which was most admirable in itself, would not be so powerful a challenge to structural injustice, as would an enhanced research (residential) unit in the CIR. It also had the advantage of being close to the Milltown Institute of Theology and Philosophy. But, alas, these views and this vision were not shared by the 'powers that be' during the 1970s and 1980s. Living with the poor and deprived or engaged in 'coal-face' remedial activity was to win the day and get the resources, i.e. of that slim section of the Province's ministry funds explicitly assigned to the justice apostolate.

Critical analysis of social injustice is a necessary and complementary aspect to serious work for the improvement of society in relation to justice and equality. I thought for years that the College of Industrial Relations should have gone into the research-plus-teaching role. But the *praxis* rather than the *analysis* seemed to dominate the post-Vatican Two Society of Jesus! Admittedly our *praxis* was never totally void of analysis. I feel we 'missed the boat'. It was from the College of Industrial Relations that I prepared my first major book, *Prejudice and Tolerance in Ireland* in 1976-77.

There was another very significant change or source of change entering the affairs of the CIR namely, the decline of volunteerism. Jesuits worked just for their keep and did not claim overtime for the long hours labouring for their students. There were also voluntary lay participants on the staff. Financial backing to pay staff the going professional wages would, of necessity, have meant our having to qualify for State funding or else get very generous contributions from very wealthy people. A third option was to raise the students' fees. The annual budget shot up in the late 1980s and right through the 1990s. This meant up-grading degrees and courses in the public market. Materially the graph was to be 'up-up-up'. Jesuit Province subsidy could not suffice, nor would it be justified, once the ethos of the College went mainstream.

Now, those 'who paid the piper would call the tune'. Value-laden and intellectually stimulating courses would be phased down while applied and pragmatic programmes would dominate. Even my own course in industrial anthropology was dropped from the syllabus in 1999 (without even a letter of explanation). Not only was the College leaving its old physical base in Ranelagh to move into the supra-modern premises in Dublin's 'City of Oz', the North Wall Financial Centre *situ*. It had changed its name to National College of Ireland (NCI) with 'Certificate, Diplomas, Degree and Postgraduate courses' on offer. Of course, I wish it well, and all credit to Dr Joyce O'Connor who steered the change through with determination.

Some would see the setting up of the new NCI as a positively progressive development. It certainly was tailored to follow changes in society. But, would it challenge the capitalist model of the 'New Ireland'? It was too dependent on the State and on big business to rock the boat structurally, in my opinion. Also, its curriculum was, of necessity, pragmatic as well as being academic. It may be too soon to pass judgement. Perhaps, I would not be the most objective judge, having suffered with many other veterans of the old CIR. We knew the real price paid for the current success. The real tragedy is that Ireland (in Celtic Tiger days) needed the critical analysis from the CIR even more than when we were struggling with emigration, unemployment and widespread poverty. Humanising our suddenly affluent Ireland and filling the 'culture-lag', which has followed the 'roars of the Celtic Tiger', called for a group of committed teachers and researchers, who were not impressed by the pretensions of

305

wealth and economic power. This was the case of the Jesuit team and their voluntary lay colleagues in the fifties, sixties, seventies, eighties and part of the nineties. I hope I do not sound like *Oisín* after the *Fianna*. (Since the collapse of the Celtic Tiger, there is need for a change to the ethos of the pre-boom Ireland College! Hopefully, the NCI will be able to respond to this need.)

The true strength of such a more radical group would be its material weakness! Otherwise, it would not have the freedom of poverty of spirit to challenge the economic and political establishments. Education, to a large extent, had become a major industry in itself, as well as being the silent servant of the socio-economic establishments. I do not wish to imply that the old CIR was anything but a very modest, relatively unknown (outside its associates) centre of learning and critical analysis. In my experience, however, it 'punched above its weight' and achieved its mission's aim. There is the material for a worthwhile study or book on the role of the College of Industrial Relations, earlier known as The Workers' College and originally called The Catholic Workers' College. In my judgement, its demise was premature and ill-advised.

Perhaps, there is room in our society for both the College of Industrial Relations and the National College of Ireland? Maybe younger teachers and academics might someday come together and re-constitute the CIR or a college like it. Irish society needs such a critical and independent college. All they require to start is a room downstairs in an underused house and invitations to concerned workers, supervisors and managers, to come together to discuss the current state of industrial relations, relative poverty, alienation, and such like topics. Things could take off from there! That was how the Catholic Workers' College started in the early nineteen-fifties in the basement of Sandford Lodge in 1951.

15. THE WORLD POLITICAL SCENE IN THE 1990S

After the fall of the Berlin Wall in 1989, there was an end to the Cold War and the assumption of world dominance by the United States of America as the single major superpower. It was armed to the teeth with weapons of mass destruction (conventional and nuclear) and soon began to flex its muscles. The Soviet Union disintegrated and Russia, under a wobbly administration, experimented with Western capitalist democracy, especially under the reign of President Yeltsin. The former-communist states of Eastern Europe embraced free-market capitalism, with mixed results. Western speculators, as well as the indigenous wealthy class, soon bought up much of the assets of land and industrial property, which had been the collective possession of the people. Early in the 1990s, I visited Eastern Germany to meet a couple who had stayed a few nights in the family cottage in Loughloon. They had been living on a collective farm, which was now 'up for grabs'. It would have been an ideal opportunity to make it a co-operatively owned farm, as Michael Davitt would have preferred to have happened after the 'buy out' of the Irish Landlords after 1903. My friends were worried and disappointed.

The whole break-up of Yugoslavia was a tragic blunder and handled with inept leadership both within and outside the federal state. The noble stance of the Serbs against the Nazi invasion during the Second World War seemed to have been forgotten. The religious animosity between Roman Catholics (Croatia), Greek Orthodox Christians (Serbia) and Muslims (Kosovo) was a volcano ready to erupt. For the German Foreign Minister to initiate the secession of one of the Federal States of Yugoslavia, i.e. Slovenia, alarmed me in the context of the sacrifices made by the Serbs against Hitler's Army. I could not believe the level of European political misunderstanding of the residue of resentment between the different ethnico-politico-religious peoples. The difficulties could have been avoided if the Confederation of the States had been negotiated and the socio-economic support had been forthcoming from the rich to the poor. The secession of Slovenia (the richest state in Yugoslavia) was the precipitating factor that unleashed a level of military and paramilitary violence of a most brutal nature. Combat fatigue and the rather indiscriminate military intervention of NATO (mostly US) led to an unsatisfactory solution. The ordinary people of all groups paid an unnecessarily heavy price for Western and Eastern deficiency in political leadership. The Yugoslavian conflict brought out the need of real ecumenism between the Greek Orthodox, Roman Catholic Churches and the Muslim Religion. Had Pope John XXIII lived he would have been very active in this regard, i.e. promoting real pluralist ecumenism between the three religious groups.

The Middle East was a most unstable area during the latter decades of the twentieth century. The establishment of the State of Israel after the end of the Second World War (1948) on the land of Palestine was never integrated properly. The indigenous population was treated as deprived refugees and were expelled from their own lands and denied their rights as full citizens. America (the US) and Great Britain supported the 'Israel solution' as a response to the unjust dispersion of the Jewish people by European and other anti-Semitic regimes. But one wrong does not justify another. The tragedy of the Israel solution was its injustice to the Palestinians, who had little to do with the persecution of the Jews in Europe.

The West's support for Jews who were persecuted so much and for so long by European Governments and the Western power elite was understandable. The Christian West felt a sense of collective guilt for the survivors of 'the holocaust'. Biblical literalism naturally attracted the Jews to the lands of their religious ancestors. The failure of their host States in Europe to defend their personal and property rights ensured that they would build a 'fortress State in Israel' and defend it with vigilant military efficiency. The combination of these factors created an Israel living under permanent martial law. From the perspective of the poor Palestinians this meant perpetual second-class and underclass citizenship within the 'claimed' territory of Israel as little more than refugees in their own land. I fear that the current image and behaviour of Israel could lead to greater anti-Semitism, which has been one of the most serious forms of social prejudice and discrimination ever researched. The Jews themselves have most to lose from Israel's image.

The military build-up of Israel made it look like a massive 'Western aircraft-carrier on dry land', i.e. an outpost of the major world superpower! This elicited a paramilitary, guerrilla response from the Palestinian defenders of their lands. As Jean-Paul Sartre is reputed to have said, 'terrorism' (which is the term used today to describe this informal violent response to superpower military force) was the reaction of relatively speaking (in military terms) weak opposition. A similar response was used by the Irish freedom fighters against the British superpower between 1916 and 1921, and between *the Jewish guerrilla fighters themselves* and the *British army in Palestine* in the nineteen-forties. Most informal paramilitary action against political and military regimes, which has 'established legitimacy', is defined as 'terrorism' in today's world. Those who wish to wage 'war on terrorists' may unwittingly be reinforcing even greater 'terrorism' in response. In other words, in many cases 'terrorism' is a symptom of the existence of perceived and irreconcilable injustice. It is very difficult to convince the 'superpower' that it may be acting unjustly. Instead, the powerful push the level of injustice even further in an attempt 'to destroy' the 'terrorist groups'.

I believe the Israeli-Palestinian conflict is a series of pyrrhic victories. Even the total dispossession of the Palestinians from Jerusalem and from their land would be pyrrhic, because the more the Palestinians are persecuted the wider their support in the Arab world of the Middle East and abroad and the deeper the festering of hatred towards Israel and the West. The Jews themselves, as I have said, have most to lose by the total destruction of the Palestinian people. So far, the United States has tolerated the violation of various United Nations' resolutions in relation to illegal occupation of non-Israeli lands and the facilitation of the possible breach of nuclear proliferation, i.e. by permitting Israel to possess suspected nuclear weapons and the obstruction of an UN inspection of Israel for weapons of mass (nuclear) destruction. Other nations would have been sanctioned by the UN for ignoring such resolutions!

Another unacceptable practice that has been permitted or allowed to happen, for which most other countries except the United States and Israel would be brought before the International Criminal Court[4] in the Hague, is the killing of suspects without trial or arrest within the territory of another sovereign state. Such supreme exemptions from the norms of international justice are very unwise. It is akin to situations of 'absolute power'. At the same time, the acts of suicide bombers are never justified even in the face of intolerable provocation. Such acts are the 'last straw' in paramilitary counter-attack.

The exercise of absolute power has worried many genuine friends of the United States over the past decade. I would consider myself as a friend of the people of the United States and of the Jewish people. I have relatives on all sides of the family living in the US. Most of my friends were very worried about the prevailing disposition of the US

---

4 The United Nations Treaty Database entry regarding the International Criminal Court, retrieved on 10th March 2010, states that: '...Israel, Sudan and the United States have informed the UN Secretary General that they no longer intend to become States Parties and, as such, have no legal obligation arising from their former representative's signature of the Statute of Rome (in 2000)'. *Wikipedia*. (See: www.icc-cpi.int/en_menus/icc-Pages-default-aspx)

power elite. One thing on the side of the US, however, has been the capacity of its own people on occasion to change its ruling elite and bring in more civilised policies. This happened twice in my memory, i.e. the liberation of the Black People or Afro-Americans from segregation and discrimination and the forcing of the US Government to withdraw from Vietnam. A similarly radical change is now necessary in relation to US involvement in the Middle East.

The United Nations Peacekeeping Troops should, in my opinion, be stationed in Palestine and the original boundaries should be restored and protected, from intrusion by either side. Nothing less will ensure peace between Israel and Palestine. In return for such an agreement, Muslims, Christians and Jews would coexist as normal neighbours and the rest of the Middle East would become normalised and use its human and natural resources to develop its citizens to the cultural and religious excellence of which they are capable. Such a transformation can be achieved only by a fundamental change of policy on the side of the United States of America. But is it in the perceived interests of the Western power-elites to prevent pluralist integration in the Middle East in order to maintain control?

A country with supreme power carries an awful responsibility, which can lead to peace (based on just harmony) or to war (establishing the supremacy of the strong). It will be shown in the chapter dealing with the first decade of the 21st century that supreme power and terrorism have continued, so far, on their futile violent interaction to the cost of thousands of innocent lives and the deterioration of Israeli-Arab relations. If only the money, expertise and human energy wasted on propaganda of hate and on war were devoted to spreading justice and peace, what a wonderful world we would be building! However, we must not lose hope that one day sanity will prevail! *In my opinion, the coming together of Christians, Jews and Muslims in real ecumenical dialogue is a prerequisite for peace and harmony in the Middle East. Exclusively secular efforts seem to be counterproductive and unlikely to succeed.*

After the election of President Putin in Russia, in March 2000, a restoration of discipline and economic control was likely to be on the agenda. Terrible violence had been taking place in one of Russia's southern states, which was the meeting place of Muslims and formerly Orthodox Russians, e.g. Chechnya. Again, we are seeing here a clash for independence, on the one hand, and for the maintenance of the status quo, on the other. Militarily, Russia is still a major power – and about to grow by the end of the 1990s. It would take some time for it to reach the status of 'superpower', which the Soviet Union had during the post-Second World War years until the 1980s. It would also take time for it to renew its military weapons. Russia is very advanced in the field of space exploration. Russia's possession of enormous resources of oil and gas has made her a force to be reckoned with, especially, once she reorganised her economy and established discipline, which the new President seemed determined to do. State control would increase under President Putin. While Russia was not a totally open society, it was more accessible than in the past. There was a degree of tension (at the end of the century) on its southern border with the Ukraine, which was going to come to a head in 2004-05 and in 2014.

By the end of the 1990s China was to re-emerge as a major world power while still under a Communist One Party system of Government. It succeeded in getting its economic system into high production and opened its doors a little to the West. Its military power was formidable. The return of Hong Kong as a province of China in 1997, from being a colony of Great Britain, went through quite smoothly. The Irish Jesuits, who had served under the colonial regime in Hong Kong, continued to do so under the Chinese supreme control. It has worked out fairly satisfactorily since 1997.

Throughout China, however, there was and is a very restrictive control of religion, e.g. Tibet. China refused to allow the spirit of reform to occur, as happened in Russia. Its economic growth was unique and substantial, which proved to me that capitalists are prepared to work under any type of regime so long as they are allowed to gain profit out of their efforts. Such capitalists are basically apolitical! At times they seem to be able to turn a blind eye to such matters as human rights and equal distribution of income and wealth! Of course, they would argue that the Chinese people are naturally better off by working with Capitalists to build their economy (and make profit at the same time). The main players in the field of Chinese industrial growth have been the Chinese themselves. If they can maintain their pace of growth, which emerged in the late 1990s and early 2000s, China could well end up as a challenge to the United States' status as a 'superpower'! The unfortunate continuity of capital punishment rates the society to be less civilised.

The population of India reached the one billion mark at the end of the 1990s. This great country's economy was also showing signs of 'coming together'. India, like China, had been a country of great and ancient cultural tradition. Between the two they are about to challenge the supremacy of Western Culture. I often felt embarrassed when I read or listened to Western Europeans looking down on and joking about the culture and traditions of China and of India and the rest of the Far East. In Ireland we have a welcome minority of citizens and in-migrated workers of Indian and of Chinese origin, who are a real addition to our cultural wealth today. We Irish have so much to learn from peoples from the East. The time has come for courses at the second-level in our schools, which would introduce our young people to the language and culture of India and China. Indians and Chinese form an integral part of modern, multicultural pluralist Ireland! (In the 2006 Census in the Republic of Ireland, 1.3% of the population was born in Asia.)

Central and Southern America continued to 'keep their heads above water' during the 1990s and suffered badly from repressive regimes, internal conflict and violent strife in a number of countries. The positive and negative influence of the United States and the developed world over the whole continent of America was manifest. In addition, the exploitation of raw materials, such as oil and gas, was evident. Also, the production of food was changed to provide cash crops suitable for export to the Western Market. Commodities such as coffee, tea and fruit would also become part of the multinational agri-business crops. On the other side of the coin, Western exports' subsidies would force South America to sell its beef, for instance, at very low prices. European dumping of surplus beef would further undermine exports from natural beef-producing countries. In their pursuit for cash-crops for the Western Market, some countries neglected the cultivation of native nutritious crops, such as potatoes and others, for their own people. Brazil was beginning to assert itself as one of the major national economies in the world, despite its internal social difficulties.

The internal land-ownership structure created a landlord hierarchy in some countries of South America reminiscent of medieval Europe, but much more extreme. The initial progress of liberation theology to bring about structural change in the 1970s had been fairly well suppressed in the 1980s and 1990s. Regimes like that of General Pinochet in Chile and the dictators in other countries had appalling human rights' records. The export of drugs to the United States from Columbia and elsewhere was to arouse great concern in Washington. One commentator said to me one time that '*the United States exported guns to the South American dictators which were used to kill the poor and underprivileged, while the poor of South America exported drugs to the United States which, in turn, contributed to the destruction and death of US youth.*' It was an exchange in instruments of mutual death and destruction! The dominance of Mexican drug barons constitutes a very serious threat to social stability in the region. A United Nations intervention may be necessary to establish an acceptable level of security and peace in the region.

The real tragedy of Central and Southern America in the twentieth century has been the failure of the socio-economic and political system to bring about equality and the full integration of all of the people. As happens very often in history, the tough circumstances produced heroic people, many of whom were martyrs and, sooner or later, the fruits of their labours were made visible. By the end of the 1990s, against all of the odds, some notable changes were beginning to take place and more representative, as distinct from populist, persons were being elected to high office. Also, corruption and repression were being reduced. The twentieth century ended with some rays of hope for the downtrodden people in parts of Latin America. The survival of the Republic of Cuba, despite the very restrictive sanctions of the United States, manifests the commitment of the Cuban people. This is not to mean that a greater level of popular participation of the people in Government in Cuba is not desirable.

The state of affairs on the continent of Africa during the nineteen nineties was not good. The optimism resulting from the release of Nelson Mandela and the earlier expectations from the removal of the yoke of colonisation was countered by the neglect and exploitation of the 'developed world'. The rising scourge of AIDS was also demoralising many of the young people. The condition of HIV positive was (largely) being transmitted through heterosexual promiscuity in seriously congested poor communities. Some of the affected communities had up to one third of their young people with this deadly disease. Serious civil wars leading to mass killing took place, e.g. in the Congo, Rwanda, Sudan and elsewhere. The great powers and the United Nations failed the African people again and again. Just contrast the interventions in Yugoslavia and what was the case in Rwanda. It was as if white Western citizens were more valuable than non-white Africans, i.e. a legacy of the Eurocentrism and racism of the Enlightenment!

Attempts to control the spread of AIDS have not been that successful to date, especially in Africa. The radical solution lies in a change of lifestyle and the practice of sexual continence, i.e. total abstinence outside marriage or a permanent partnership. Contraception and so-called 'safe permissive sex' does not seem to be that successful. The Pioneer Association discovered that young people who abstained from alcohol, as Pioneers, rarely got AIDS. Their moral strength to avoid casual or promiscuous sexual activity saved them from the deadly scourge. The proliferation of sexual pornography and promiscuity in Western culture via movies, internet and television is part of the problem of the spread of AIDS. Liberal ideology appears to be incapable of seeing the awful consequences of this lifestyle. Asceticism as a source of human strength and freedom is often rejected as reactionary. Coupled with the power of the alcoholic drinks industry, sexual promiscuity has become a killer of many of our youth through the spread of AIDS. The practice of 'safe sex' may save some from contamination among the 'sexually active', but the risk is too great to the protection of all of our youth from the premature 'death sentence' which is AIDS. We evade facing the issue of AIDS at our peril. It is devastating the populations of large sections of Africa (and elsewhere). Radical action is urgently needed. Also, the most advanced medical care must be made available to those already contaminated.

Africa is, so far, the neglected Continent. It has such resources of human talent and natural advantages that would make it a tremendous place to live in and bring up children. The family and children are still valued for what they are, unlike our partially materialist Western society. Indigenous cultures are humanly and environmentally very rich. We in the Western World have had a poor record in Africa. The scandal of slavery and the racism accompanying it have been among the most shameful happenings in the history of civilisation. The great scandal of the 18th century Enlightenment was its implicit support for racism! In addition to our failure to respect the human dignity of African peoples, we added insult to injury by not recognising the rich cultural ethos of the people of Africa.

Thank God, the 'black baby' mentality (which portrayed our evaluation of the people's indigenous culture and religious understanding of God as primitive and superstitious) has changed. In fact, many anthropologists would argue that the upper Nile region of Africa may have been the cradle of our civilisation. During my visit to Uganda in 2004, I got the idea that the 'Garden of Eden' could have been located there. Also, there is evidence that the ancient peoples of the Mount Kenya area of Kenya had reached the concept of monotheism around the time of Abraham. This would go to show that God was speaking to his people through their own African religions long before the completion of these revelations came to them through the revelation of Christ in the Gospel. It is indeed tragic that 'Euro-centrism' may have distorted the Christian message of the Universal God.

One of the great advantages of Irish missionary work has been the fact that Irish missionaries themselves came from a colonised rather than a colonial country. This should have given us a more sympathetic understanding of local people's culture. This would have been especially true of Irish Missionaries who supported the Irish language and culture at home. They had already felt the indignity of cultural imperialism in Ireland, which almost destroyed our own indigenous culture and language. Regretfully, some of our Irish teachers and leaders had succumbed to the false propaganda of the anglicisation of Ireland. Even more tragically still, some of our Church leaders (diocesan and religious) were converted to the sense of inferiority of the native Irish culture. This was to weaken our advantage as a colonised missionary country. During the era of European expansionism into Africa, America and Asia, the Christian evangelists followed the colonising armies, with very negative results for the native cultures and religious heritage of local peoples. I fear that our new awareness of this sad history of cultural and religious colonisation may have come too late for many people (including the Irish people themselves).

One of the most interesting discoveries I found in my research into Irish attitudes towards the British was the level of *post-colonial attitudinal schizophrenia*, i.e. 'looking up' to the British while at the same time feeling hostility towards them. My analysis of what I found out to be a 'looking up to the British' was, in effect, 'looking down on ourselves'. This means that colonised or suppressed people eventually accept the lesser definition of themselves that their 'masters' had of them. In other words, we develop a sense of collective inferiority. This is true of most minority- statused groups. My reading about and experience of visiting and meeting people from former colonies and from people suffering minority status at present is their tendency to accept the indignity of inferiority self-perception. This can lead to great frustration and tension, which result in violence and aggression at times.

Much of the violence and failure of the African people to avail of their human and natural resources to date has, in my opinion, been due to this 'post-colonial' impaired sense of subconscious inferiority, which is totally unmerited. What Africa needs most now is self-confidence and a re-appraisal of its own culture and traditions, not as something weird and exotic, but as a heritage of invaluable human richness. A certain scepticism of the so-called superiority of Western materialist cultural values and norms would also help them. Less dependence on loans and hand-outs from Western Banks, including the World Bank, and more reliance on their own resources would be a far wiser approach. They need to emancipate themselves from the tyranny of the superiority of Western culture! The recent reports of external multinational companies buying up land in the poorer parts of Africa are outrageous. All land should be nationalised.

Local corruption is an obvious result of the current state of external dependence and local poverty. Multinational commercial and industrial exploitation of cheap labour and low prices for basic raw materials are in themselves a real form of corruption which, in turn, breeds bribery and servitude. The transition from extended family personal (informal) social control to urbanised, formal, bureaucratic and impersonal rules, is very painful and often inhuman!

The Western World's superiority in terms of technology and wealth is very evident in Africa. Commercial television, i.e. Sky, CNN, etc., push consumerism, while the African viewers cannot afford the luxurious lifestyle portrayed. This results in an unnecessary level of discontent among the poor and misdirection in relation to self-improvement. In Nigeria, for instance, I was surprised at the number of second-hand cars and trucks imported from Europe. While the old Mercedes and the old BMW and Renault cars were still working, thanks to the skills of local mechanics, it was sad to see one of the biggest oil-producing countries in the world unable to give its people newer vehicles. It is so often the case that the rich make of the poor a mobile dump for their second-hand cast-offs. One sees that in Ireland too in the case of Travellers being given second-hand cast-offs. The late Bishop Peter Birch of Ossory, for instance, would never insult the Travellers in that manner. When a Traveller needed a pair of boots he would invite him or her into a shoe-shop and pay for a new pair of good, hard-wearing boots or shoes. Only the best is good enough for the poor!

A major problem facing Africa, as in the Middle-East and Eastern Europe, during the last quarter of the twentieth century, has been the animosity between the Muslim peoples and the Christians and those of other faiths. The Muslim belief is very strong in the Northern section of Africa. In sub-Saharan countries Christianity is more prevalent. At present, Christians face Muslim expansionism, and their insistence on establishing an 'Islamic State' where they achieve a majority. The tensions in Nigeria, Uganda, Sudan and elsewhere, have to be addressed at the global level and a peaceful and pluralist *modus vivendi* will have to be worked out between the religious supreme leaders to enable such coexistence in modern society. *Religiously monolithic societies are no longer feasible in our 'global village' today.* At the same time, we need to preserve and respect the religious richness of the Muslim, Christian, Jewish, Hindu and the local religious traditions. The view that the solution is in a secularist world, void of religion, was retrograde and inhuman. The possible tyranny of the secularist state, e.g. The Third Reich in Germany or Stalin's Communist Totalitarian State, is just as unbearable as that of an extreme religious regime. Of course, the world requires a tolerant society where there is place for variety in belief or in unbelief. In my view, genuine religion is an essential ingredient of a civilised society. What is ideal is an integrated pluralism which respects and supports cultural and religious differences and, at the same time, integrates the various groups on a basis of total equality. Secularism fails to satisfy the quest for meaning! The quality of life is lessened in the absence of meaning.

In the Australasian region of the world there were areas of conflict and persecution during the 1990s. I was, in a small way, involved in the East Timor Liberation Campaign. This was a case of where a relatively small country of Christian citizens had been occupied by a large (100 million

Muslims) country, i.e. Indonesia. Eventually, the United Nations, with the support of former-coloniser, Portugal and neighbouring Australia, succeeded in liberating the small state. It was a very important victory for the United Nations and for World opinion. *Irish Pax Christi* campaigned for East Timor's freedom. (The closure of our Embassy in East Timor in 2011 is to be regretted and shows a short memory in our Department of Foreign Affairs. It appears to me to be short-sighted!)

Australia is a country to which many young Irish were deported (prior to 1850) and to which numerous Irish men and women have emigrated ever since. It has not had a good world reputation for its attitude to non-whites. The plight of the native Australians, often referred to as 'Aborigines', is evidence of racial and ethnic prejudice and discrimination over centuries since the European colonisers arrived there in the 16th and 17th centuries. During the late 1990s, Australian policy towards regional immigrants and refugees has been unwelcoming. How long this position can endure is a matter of speculation. Sooner or later the wealthy countries will have to admit those who have not got sufficient to live on in our gross imbalance of wealth. May I repeat the words attributed to St Ambrose *'the superfluities of the rich are the rights of the poor'*. I believe strongly in the primacy of equality for all at the global level over superfluity for some. In more recent years, the 'pluralist integration' of the Native Australians has been on the agenda.

16. THE GOOD FRIDAY AGREEMENT (1998) AND OTHER DEVELOPMENTS

In 1997, Mr Bertie Ahern TD, (*Fianna Fáil*) became *Taoiseach* of the Irish Government and headed a *Fianna Fáil/Progressive Democrat* Coalition. Ms Mary Harney TD, (Progressive Democrat) became *Tánaiste*. The Government was a centre-right one and ruled over an economically booming upturn in relation to gainful employment and wealth. The new *Taoiseach*, Mr Ahern TD, was able to employ his considerable negotiating skills to facilitate progress towards the bringing about of *Sinn Féin's* commitment to a purely political role and the ultimate signing and electoral support North and South for the *Good Friday Agreement* in 1998. As already stated, that removed the political institution from its temporary 'pivotal position' in Irish society and enabled the economic institution to replace it at the centre.

This provided the structural framework for industrial and commercial development as a priority over family, polity, religion, recreation, law or education. In fact, we were soon to realise the full realignment of the institutions, with the possible exception of the religious institution, to 'dance to the tune' of the maestro economic institution. Some would go so far as to say that our country was to become 'an economy' with the consensus of all major political parties. Nevertheless, it had to be admitted that we needed some of the benefits accruing from the new improvement in our economic activity. The overall reduction in unemployment and the ending of forced emigration were welcome. The renewal of housing stock to a level of material comfort more conducive to pleasant living and the removal of domestic hardship from those doing the normal housework were to be welcomed unbegrudgingly. The possibility of improving our basic infrastructure, i.e. roads, railways, seaports and airports, telecommunications, water supply, sewerage, waste control, *et cetera,* was something the people deserved. Education and health services were to be upgraded from the point of view of plant and payroll. Security forces and the legal and court services expanded in response to new demands.

In all, the Republic of Ireland was experiencing the beginning of a period of unprecedented expansion and improvement in the material standard of living fuelled by the new wealth caused by our economic growth (which was to end 'with a bang' in the summer of 2008). There was very wide support for the manner in which the Government was able to control and facilitate this growth. I say this while I would be very critical of aspects of its policy in relation to the distribution of our new wealth and its failure to protect the family from the demands of the economic machine. Reference has already been made to some aspects of such failure. In my view our families, with their high fertility, provided a young workforce. It was owing to these 'Celtic Cubs' that growth was possible in the Republic of Ireland.

The blame for our failure to apply the new wealth more fairly is not due to the Government alone. Religious and community leaders must also share responsibility for the negative effects of our new wealth. Up until 1998, most people worked for their needs while thereafter many were working for their surpluses. *The day has long passed when we require a strict maximum incomes policy, i.e. there should be a figure above which nobody should be allowed to earn or keep.* This could only be achieved by high tax on income above the level, say twice the average wage. This would stem the rise of greed and reduce the gap between the rich and the poor. In hindsight, it would curb speculation. Opulence, i.e. excessive wealth, is very bad for society and it is a scandal to the young. It also stimulates crimes of theft, robbery and other forms of corruption. It makes the awareness of relative deprivation greater and increases white-collar crime and corruption.

What is true of disparity between individuals is also true of imbalance in wealth between communities and between countries. It is very difficult to restrain the wealth of rich communities and countries in order that the weaker ones may improve. One area where measures could be taken to generate greater equity is in the area of unearned income, which should be minimalised. This would control financial speculation, which leads to serious imbalances in areas of wealth. Society is healthier when all income is earned or received due to personal social need, i.e. welfare payments (which should be at the level of average income). *The divorce between work and wealth is most dangerous and leads eventually to economic failure.*

One particular example of unearned income which has had serious implications for many people in Ireland today has been sites for houses in particular districts. In my opinion, the ground area of a town or city should be 'municipalised' or be in the ownership of the urban authority for the citizens and made available at a standard price. Urban site speculation would be, thereby, removed from the equation and it would be easier to institute house price-control by the public authority as a result. The price of development land should be strictly controlled. Of course, the prevailing socio-political policy between 1996 and 2008 was 'self-regulation' in financial matters.

A phenomenon that has grown substantially in the latter decades of the twentieth century in Ireland (and elsewhere) has been the superstructure. This includes all the services and agencies involved in responding to the needs of the people, i.e. banking, insurance, revenue, security, mortgage agencies, financial services, stock markets, environment agencies, agricultural control agencies, *et cetera*. A cadre of professional and highly paid personnel are employed to run this very elaborate superstructure. Ordinary citizens have to spend more and more time filling-in repetitive bureaucratic forms. The European Union has added much to this bureaucratic burden on the backs of the people. In my opinion at least half of the superstructure is redundant and a high-powered commission of enquiry should tackle this problem before the people collapse under its weight. Public money should be invested in infrastructure rather than for the services of excessive superstructure! It would be very interesting to carry out serious research into the link between the European 'highly codified legal system' and the overgrowth of bureaucracy. The common-law tradition seems less conducive to excessive bureaucracy!

Local Government should and could take back many of the services it had lost to those agencies which have taken over its function, e.g. mortgage services, environment control and so forth. All this expansion of our superstructure has added to our cost of living and landed many of our people in lifelong debt situations, which, to people of my generation, appears absolutely crazy. Is it not time 'to call stop', in the words of the late John Healy, a most observant journalist of the 1960s and 1970s? Functions have been taken from State departments also and handed over to semi-State and privatised companies under licence. All this adds to the super-structure! The inevitable result of this is the massive increase in the numbers employed in the services, as distinct from manufacturing industry and agriculture. The 'financial centre' in the docklands of Dublin feeds this 'superstructure dinosaur'. Our Irish bureaucratic professionals are so good as to serve in the European Superstructure and even in the emerging Global Superstructure. The rise of the aptly designated Information Technology is an essential component of the 'super superstructure' expanding on all sides. What is going to happen when we discover that half of it is probably redundant to the real needs of our people?

During the 1990s an uncle-in-law of mine, the late PJ McMenamin[5], who at 86 years was a perceptive critic of society, remarked to me a few weeks before he died in 1996 that modern society was beginning 'to lose the run of itself'. May I repeat his comment to me was '*This country will never be right until the ration book is back*'! Our capacity

---

5 PJ was married to my mother's late sister, Maggie Coyne, who was one of my favourite aunts. She was a kind and witty woman.

to survive with the minimum of superstructure and of wasteful surplus would be truly tested. The 'throw-away society' of the West would have to spare and mind durables like footwear, clothing, cars and other such items. The virtue of thrift would be called for; at least, the return of the ration book would test our mettle. Most of all, it would make it possible for the developing world to enable its people to reach a more adequate material standard of living and a reasonable average life-expectancy as a result.

I missed PJ very much when he died. We spent many a long night analysing and 'passing judgement' on the 'goings on' in Irish and world society. He would cast a cold eye on leaders and on systems. He was a positive sceptic of the 'superstructure'! At times he would urge me to write a letter to the *Mayo News* or *The Irish Times* about issues that needed public airing. He would say to me, with a glint in his eye, '*I think Micheál it might be time for you "to ski a drop of ink" at that*'! *Ar dheis Dé go raibh an anam uasal.* (I will be returning in a later chapter to the Celtic Tiger and its impact on the life of people.)

As we leave the nineteen-nineties it is good to remember that the decade witnessed three major developments, which were sure to leave a lasting imprint on Irish society for many years to come, i.e.

    (i)   the Peace Agreement in Northern Ireland;

    (ii) the fall in Religious practice; and

    (iii) the upturn in the Irish economy.

Each of these areas of change could form a topic for a doctoral thesis or a post-doctoral *magnum opus*!

Developments in the peace process in Northern Ireland, in changes in religious attitudes and practices and in Irish economic development constitute major themes for a commentary for the first decade of the 21st century. Developments in Great Britain, in the United States and in the European Union affected the situation in Ireland during the nineties.

After eighteen years of Tory Party Rule in the United Kingdom, the Labour Party (New Labour) got into power in Westminster in 1997. Mr Tony Blair MP (1997-2007) became Prime Minister and there were great expectations in Britain that a more collectivist approach would be pursued in relation to social and community issues. The preparatory work in Northern Ireland under John Major MP, (Tory Prime Minister) and, most of all, the contribution of Secretary of State, Mr Peter Brooke

MP, in the early 1990s, were significant. John Major had been able to relate well with Mr Albert Reynolds TD, and with Mr John Bruton TD, who were *Taoisigh* at a vital stage in the process.

Prime Minister Tony Blair MP, and *Taoiseach* Bertie Ahern TD, seemed to have been very successful in patiently ironing out the problems in relation to the Northern Irish Peace process. In Britain itself, Prime Minister Blair introduced a number of structural changes, i.e. *devolution of representative authority* to Scotland, to Wales and to Greater London. He also set out to reform the House of Lords and reduce the proportionate membership for inherited peers. His attitude to the Trade Unions was completely different from that of Prime Minister Margaret Thatcher, when she reigned as Prime Minister. Still, he did not restore their strong position, which had been the case under previous Labour administrations. In fact, New Labour, under Tony Blair was closer to the 'Centre' than to the 'Left' on the ideological spectrum. This enabled the party to get significant support from the middle classes, who constituted the majority of the adult (voting) population in Great Britain. A minority of committed 'left-wing' MPs were dissatisfied with the inevitable compromises to the middle ground.

The personal commitment of Prime Minister Blair and *An Taoiseach* Bertie Ahern to the Northern Peace Process was most admirable. Prior to the signing of the *Good Friday Agreement* in 1998, both men spent much time in Belfast to facilitate minor amendments to the draft texts. After its eventual signing, the political skills of both leaders were also proven when the agreement was ratified by both parliaments and subsequently approved by a large majority of the Irish people in referenda carried out on the same day in the Republic and in Northern Ireland. The election of the Northern Ireland Assembly and the appointment of a devolved administration with Mr David Trimble (Official Unionist) and Mr Séamus Mallon (SDLP) as *First Minister* and *Deputy First Minister* respectively went through without a hitch. *Sinn Féin* and the DUP were given Ministries although the latter did not participate in the Cabinet. Things looked fairly optimistic, despite the refusal of the DUP 'to play ball' in the spirit of the Agreement which they opposed all the way. Their representatives on the Administration refused to attend 'cabinet meetings' with *Sinn Féin* colleagues. It all looked petty and a case of 'sour grapes'. In fact, it was a refusal to accept the democratic vote of the people of Northern Ireland. Nevertheless, the new arrangements seemed to be working despite the extreme elements in the DUP whose heart was not in the new arrangement.

The Provisional IRA ceasefire of 1996 held and this was an essential condition of the Agreement. A breakaway element of the Provisionals (called the 'Continuity IRA') continued to operate outside the terms of the Agreement. One of the most awful and tragic actions perpetrated by these breakaway paramilitaries happened in Omagh on the 15th August 1998 when mayhem and murder were indiscriminately inflicted on innocent people. The bombers did not give adequate warning and unsuspected citizens were blown to eternity while many others suffered serious injury, including burns. It was a very traumatic final act of destructive violence, which happened after the ceasefire of the Provisional IRA. It proved to me the dangerous futility of violence, while the *Good Friday Agreement* proved the power of positive action.

Northern Ireland had many inherited problems to solve before a completely acceptable way of coexistence between Roman Catholics and Protestants, or Nationalists and Unionists, or Republicans and Loyalists could be worked out. The tradition of the Orange Parades, which were public rituals of Protestant supremacy and Loyalist fidelity were most intimidating for Roman Catholics and nationalists, especially when they marched through predominantly Catholic/nationalist neighbourhoods. It was difficult and dangerous for a Catholic to be in the vicinity of those Loyalists returning from the rousing parades with their inflammatory speeches and emotionally arousing music. Add to that a few drinks and one can imagine the need to avoid confrontation or even contact. Some of the leaders, religious and political of the Orange Parades, could be quite demagogic in their appeal. Most notorious of the controversial parades took place in Portadown in a district called Drumcree, where a Catholic housing estate was on the traditional 'return route' of the parade. Eventually, it was diverted from the Catholic estate – to the great annoyance of the more militant Orangemen. This annual stand-off was to become a major irritant in the Peace Process right through the 1990s, even after the *Good Friday Agreement. Symbolism is very important in Northern Ireland.* I look forward to the day when both sides can enjoy each other's parades as pageants representing pre-pluralist days!

From 1992 until 2000, Mr Bill Clinton, was President of the United States of America. It was said of him that *he was the best President of the United States that Ireland ever had.* From very early on in his Presidency, he took a pro-active and very positive interest in the Peace Process and assigned Senator George Mitchell to preside over the negotiations as an honest broker. He became very popular in Ireland as was made manifest during his visits. In the United States, President Clinton had his problems with the ultra-right Republican opposition. They tried to have him impeached from office because of an alleged affair with a young woman. It appeared to me that the whole relationship with the young (adult) woman was exploited by those who wished to get President Clinton out of office. My attitude to such areas of personal deviance is to let them rest so long as a crime has not been committed. *'Let he or she who is free cast the first stone,'* says the Lord in the Gospel! Anyhow, we should not make known the hidden faults of others, unless a party has been injured! If only the media abided by this rule, which follows on the 'eighth commandment', our society would not be so demoralised as it is today, as a result of sensational low-standard journalism feeding on the hidden personal faults of others.

One aspect of President Clinton that I could not condone, was his apparent acceptance of capital punishment when he was Governor of Arkansas. What is wrong with the United States? It is so primitive in relation to the death penalty. Even US Roman Catholics seem to go against the advice of the Pope on this question. In my opinion, capital punishment is un-Christian and demeans the society that practises it. The United States also permits people to carry personal firearms, and efforts made by President Clinton to curtail the sale of guns were not successful. There is still an element of the 'wild west' about the US.

President Clinton had a good rapport with Prime Minister Blair and *An Taoiseach*, Bertie Ahern, and this helped in the work towards the *Good Friday Agreement* in Northern Ireland. He also presided over a very successful period of economic growth in the United States, which, no doubt, helped the growth in US investment in industry in Ireland. What I liked about Bill Clinton was the fact that he did not take himself too seriously. The attempts of Mrs Hillary Clinton (later US Secretary of State) to draft a progressive healthcare bill in 1993 was shot 'out of the water' by a reactionary Congress. While by our standards the

Hillary Clinton idea would be very modest, it was nevertheless, too radical for the Congress of the United States at the time.

United States relations with Iraq during the 1990s had been very problematic, beginning with the attack on that country under the presidency of Clinton's predecessor, George Bush (Senior), because of Iraq's incursion into part of Kuwait (which was originally part of Iraq). After the forces of Iraq were pushed back from Kuwait the US forces withdrew and a period of serious sanctions imposed on President Saddam Hussein's regime as well as ongoing air surveillance of the country. Arising out of the sanctions, human misery prevailed in Iraq right through the nineties. It was ironic that the United States, under previous presidents, was an ally of Iraq in the Iraq versus Iran war (1980) and helped to strengthen the army of President Saddam Hussein. 'Yesterday's friends were today's enemies'! It should be noted that Britain and a number of other countries were allies of the United States in the war on Iraq at the beginning of the nineties.

What was really frightening about the War against Iraq was the display of grossly superior air power and the mass destruction of Iraq's infrastructure and the killing of thousands of its citizens. The use of modern technology has turned the US armed forces into a frightful killing force. The strategy of 'overkill' and destruction of civilian homes and means of living has been a military tactic ever since General Tecumseh Sherman's (1820-91) *March through the Carolinas* during the American Civil War in the 1860s. Those who kill and destroy most in modern warfare are immune to counter-attack because of the remoteness of the major fire-control. It is only when the major powers' troops and administrations have to occupy the territory attacked that they are confronted by the survivors in a guerrilla war situation. Because of the need to preserve the deposit of oil, there was a limit to the extent of the US-led attack. The real tragedy about the West's military invasion of the Muslim states, i.e. Iraq and Afghanistan, is the long-term damage done to future international relations. The sanctions against Iraq led to human misery on a major scale, including mass malnutrition. In my opinion, victories are always pyrrhic in the long run, when there is widespread destruction and the death of innocent people. President Clinton's Government implemented the sanctions regime against Iraq.

17. Farewell Greeting from Bishop Jeremiah Newman

Before ending the commentary on the nineteen-nineties, I must record a meeting I had with the late Bishop Jeremiah Newman, Bishop of Limerick (1974-95). He had been President of St Patrick's College, Maynooth, when I was refused a year's leave of absence without pay, to analyse and write-up my research into prejudice. The interviews for this research were carried out in 1972-73 and the findings were to be my PhD thesis and the material for *Prejudice and Tolerance in Ireland*, published in 1977. As a result of the college's refusal, I was compelled to resign my position as a junior lecturer for one year. At that time, I got the impression that President Jeremiah Newman was trying to get rid of me. It is in this context that his calling me aside at a bishops' meeting in Maynooth shortly before he died (3ʳᵈ April 1995) had significance. The conversation went somewhat as follows:

> Bishop Newman: (in St Joseph's Square): '*Mick Mac Gréil, come here*'
>
> Mac Gréil: '*How are you, Bishop Newman?*'
>
> Bishop Newman: '*All right. I want to tell you something. Your appointment to the college staff of this college was a good decision. Your research work is serious stuff and not like some of the half-baked (or words to that effect) reports we read today.*'
>
> Mac Gréil: (a little stunned): '*Thank you, Bishop. I do my best.*'
>
> Bishop Newman: '*I wanted to let you know what I thought. God bless.*'

(The above is my recollection of our brief conversation more or less.)

I was a little overpowered by his unsolicited recognition of my work as lecturer and researcher. He himself had been the Professor of Sociology in Maynooth before Professor Liam Ryan. He had a brilliant mind. His critique of Ludwig JJ Wittgenstein (1889-1951) the Austrian philosopher of language was highly praised. Also, he was the real force behind the opening-up of St Patrick's College, Maynooth, to the admission of lay students and the increase of the Arts and Science faculties. As I already said, Jeremiah Newman was the second founder of Maynooth University. While I was not happy with the manner in which I was treated in 1974 by him as President of the College, I always acknowledged his contribution to our development. In the end he proved he was a man of moral principle by his encounter with me on St Joseph's Square shortly before he died. I went to his sad funeral in the Cathedral in Limerick shortly afterwards. *Ar dheis Dé go raibh a anam uasal.* All is forgiven and we both were reconciled in a typically Jeremiah manner. *Laus Deo Semper.* This is a good note on which to end the commentary on the 1990s.

Chapter Eight

THE TWENTIETH CENTURY
IN RETROSPECT[6]

1. A WAY OF UNDERSTANDING MACRO SOCIAL CHANGE

Before proceeding with a report and commentary on the 21st century, it is useful to cast a summary look at some of the developments of the twentieth century just ended. It is possible to look on society as a network of related 'social institutions'. By 'social institution' is meant *a set of norms centred around an area of need.* The recognised major social institutions include *family, polity, religion, economy, education, law and recreation.* It should be noted that social institutions are abstractions from the social reality, i.e. 'family' does not exist while the O'Connors, Hunts and Murphys in the local village do exist. People's lives are made up, day-in day-out, in behaving in accordance with the norms of these seven major institutions. Sociologists, who analyse society along institutional norms, are identified as 'structural functionalists'.

Among the more eminent leaders of this school were: Herbert Spencer (1820-1903), Emile Durkheim (1828-1917), Talcott Parsons (1902-79), Robert K Merton (1910-2003) and Leslie White (1900-75). In the course of my lecturing in Sociology, I did try to teach the writings of these eminent scholars. That was not to say that I viewed them as I would Sacred Scripture! It should be added that during the 1970s and 1980s, 'structural functionalism' was out of favour because of its alleged 'conservatism'. *The structural functionalist sees the explanation of all behaviour patterns in their functions,* i.e. *objective consequences for society.* In this way the structures of society strive to maintain social equilibrium.

The more popular theory in vogue since the 1960s has been a 'conflict theory of society'. Karl Marx (1818-83) was identified as the theoretical

---

6 Some readers may wish to skip this chapter as it is a sociological reflection on macro social change in the twentieth century in Ireland. In Chapter IX there is a return to the 'ongoing present'.

father of this school. I tried to introduce students to 'conflict theory' also but I felt it tended to be open to a political stance and, thereby, cease to be non-normative and value-free, which was the aim of the more objectively scientific approach. Of course, it could be argued that all approaches are to some degree normative and value-laden. In all honesty, I found it easier to be objective when adopting the 'structural functional' approach. Being in or out of fashion should not worry a lecturer that much!

Using the social institutions (sets of norms centred on areas of human need) to explain the change taking place in Ireland during my lifetime, I adopt the *'pivotal institution approach'*. (I hope I am not getting too technical for the reader.) This approach goes as follows: *Major social change takes place when the hierarchy of social institutions changes.* At different times in various societies particular institutions occupy 'pivotal positions', when the functions of the other institutions tend to serve the needs of the pivotal ones. For instance, where the family is pivotal, society is domestic-oriented, i.e. religion, law, the economy, education, the polity and recreation are all centred on supporting the family. Also, in times of crisis and unrest the political institution becomes pivotal and all other institutions are expected to support the emergency needs of the State or of the 'Revolution'. Some societies have the religious institution in the pivotal position and likewise family, education, economy, law, polity and recreation are characterised by their support for the religious needs of that society.

2. Shifts of Pivotal Institutions

Looking back at Ireland since 1900 one can detect significant shifts in the pivotal institutions. Up until the mid-1920s one could identify the political institution occupying a pivotal position, i.e. World War I and the struggle for Irish political independence followed by an unfortunate civil war at the beginning of the Irish Free State. The family, religion, education, law, the economy, and recreation were all dominated by the political issues of the day. The country was living in an almost continuous state of emergency.

Over the following four decades (1926-66), except during the 1939-45 Emergency period, there was a certain return of religion and the family into the centre. Education was very family-and-religion-centred and the values emanating were family-based and religion-influenced. The political will of the vast majority of the people was in support of both family and religion (but not as a 'State Church'). The unfortunate result of the Partition of Ireland in the early twenties was to result in Protestant dominance in Northern Ireland and Roman Catholic predominance in the Free State/ Republic of Ireland. While the political institution was to enter the 'pivotal ring' for the period of the 1939-45 Emergency (during the Second World War), Ireland's neutrality worked to preserve the prominence of the family and religion.

By the early 1960s we witnessed signs of the replacement of family and religion as pivotal institutions by the economic institution and the focussing of the political institution on such themes as planned economic development, a marked decline in the agricultural workforce (with its strong family ties) and a growing and more autonomous secular order. This was in part made easy by Vatican Two's acceptance of the autonomy of the secular. Even on the Foreign Missions the emphasis was to move from evangelisation to economic development! A brave new economy-centred Ireland was emerging before our eyes. A delayed 'industrial revolution' was underway. Urban populations were on the increase. The extended family was to make way for the nuclear family to facilitate industrial society. Community at the local level was under strain as was neighbourhood. Mixed farming was to make way for specialised farming, i.e. agri-business. And we all cheered as we hailed the 'progress' ahead! Joining the EEC in 1972 was to consolidate further the growing pivotal role of the economy. After all, it was the European Economic Community.

Education was to bear witness to this change most clearly. There would be a new emphasis on *'Investment in Education'* as the title of Professor Patrick Lynch's Report (1966) indicated. The World Bank's role in this change in making the educational institution serve the needs of economic development rather than that of the person, the family, and religion, has never, to my knowledge, been explained clearly. The 'O'Malley Free Secondary Education Scheme', introduced in the late sixties, was part of this change and was to de-radicalise young people, i.e. 'emancipate' them from their parents' cultural, religious and social values! And again, at the time, we all went along uncritically with this 'new age' economy-centred revolution. (By revolution, I mean *a radical and rapid change of society's value system.*) Such culturally enriching subjects as Latin,

Greek and even Irish were to be dropped or downgraded (in the case of Irish). The big in-words were 'relevance' and 'usefulness' for jobs. The loss of the people's 'cultural memory' was not considered to be serious. Such 'memory' would impede the de-radicalisation of our young people. Pragmatism and expedience were to replace idealism and morality!

But something happened in 1969 that slowed down the path to economic dominance, namely, 'the Troubles' in Northern Ireland. This restored the pivotal position of the political institution and challenged the rise of the economic institution. I remember the reaction of some of the 'high priests' of the economy at the time. Such words as 'irrational', 'stupid', *et cetera* were used in conversation about the Northern Troubles. Some saw them as a throwback to unenlightened times. There was a famous remark of a comedian, when he was mimicking an air hostess, announcing to the passengers arriving at Aldergrove Airport in Belfast, i.e. '*Turn back your watches four hundred years. You are now landing in Belfast*'. The Troubles made no sense to the leaders of the economic institution. But, they must have made sense to many committed people in Northern Ireland. Culture and tradition were still very important to committed Roman Catholics and Protestants and to Republicans and Unionists. *The success of one side was interpreted as the demise of the other.* The late Bishop Peter Birch of Ossory anticipated the bloody struggle which was to characterise Northern Ireland right through to the mid-nineties largely because of mutual intransigence. John Hume MP, MEP, never underestimated the danger of victory for one side. The solution had to be a compromise, which respected both cultures and religions.

By the mid-nineties there were signs of an agreed settlement, which ruled out humiliation or defeat for Republicans or for Loyalists. Of course, some people's negative reaction to the apparently generous concessions to paramilitaries was understandable from the 'on-the-fence' perspective or from the vested interest in maintaining the violent and 'criminal' *status quo*, but it was not politically wise. I would have gone further and offered pensions to all genuinely political paramilitaries on both sides 'for their service to their struggle'. I say this as one who was totally opposed to the armed struggle. Failure to do so created a regular-income problem for ex-paramilitaries who have found it difficult to get gainful employment after so many years 'on-the-run'. There were many problems to be worked out after the ceasefires. These will be considered later when commenting on the *Belfast Agreement* (which is popularly referred to as the *Good Friday Agreement*).

3. RISE OF THE ECONOMIC INSTITUTION

By 1996 the coast was clear for a renewed economic institution to occupy, for the first time in Ireland, the exclusively pivotal position. The resultant rise of materialism would further undermine religion and the Christian emphasis on cooperation and service. The new emphasis was on competition and profit. The European Union had, from the start, placed pivotal emphasis on the economic institution. So we were now in tune with the leadership of the EU. Our progress in economic development would gain much prestige for Ireland.

The new role of the family was to provide *workers* and *consumers* for the new economic order. Women, who heretofore saw rearing children as a primary role, were now urged to become 'productive members' of the growing workforce. More than that, they would be penalised for staying at home as a result of the 'individualisation' of the income tax system. The day of the 'family wage' would become history. In fact, the basic unit of Irish society, under the dominance of the economic institution, would be the individual and not the family of parents and children. From now on the economic advantage of getting married would be greatly reduced. Hence the proliferation of unmarried and single parents. The *laissez faire* and unrealistic rise in house property had become most dysfunctional. A family home, i.e. house, had become more a unit in the speculative property market, in many cases, than an essential right to a family in Ireland (and elsewhere in Europe). Its monetary value was to be determined by the market. State price-control of basic housing has been quite inept. If one were to define exploitation as the *'capitalisation of a basic human need'*, then the growing artificial inflation of house prices in Ireland could be defined as 'exploitation'!

For those parents, who are forced to work outside the home, the rearing of children has become a major burden. Crèches, pre-schools and 'post-school caring' have become a most elaborate and commercially expensive alternative to home-rearing. The transmission of the family's religious and cultural values and norms to the young is now left to agencies outside the family. In an Orwellian situation where the crèche and preschool will be located within the employment environment, it will be possible to socialise the young within the economic and work culture in a more complete manner. *It is the new 'family farm' without the family!* Thank God, the Irish have not, as yet, fully sold their attachment to the family as the best way to hand on their culture to the young, but, we are in danger of surrendering to the dictates of our economic masters. My hope is the growth of political pressure to call a halt to the dangerous trends, which emerged when the economy assumed dominance in Ireland in recent years. A weakening of the role of parents in the education of their children could well become enshrined in our renewal of *Bunreacht na hÉireann*, to bring it into line with the economy's need and a major blow to the family.

The function of the religious institution in society is seen to be in the provision of meaning to our lives and especially in addressing the problem of death, evil and human weakness. It authenticates the fundamental moral order required to enable social integration. Religious belief *is a commitment to God's existence and to living one's life according to the will of God.* For Christians, the will of God is revealed by Christ as recorded in the Sacred Scripture. It is from such revelations that we Christians believe that the true and real meaning of our lives finds its completion. In addition, reading the reflections of truly holy and wise believers on the teachings of Christ in Sacred Scripture gives us further insight into the meaning of life. This in no way takes from the discoveries of science and technology, which enable us to understand more clearly the wonderful secrets of nature, which is part of divine ongoing creation.

For Christians, the Church is (as noted earlier) the *corporate presence of Christ on Earth through the indwelling of the Holy Spirit.* Vatican Two saw the Church as the 'People of God'. For most media commentators, however, the Church is seen as an organisation made up of ordained, professed and lay members. The Roman Catholic Church has a visible concrete structure with a hierarchical chain of command made up of the laity, the pope, cardinals, bishops, priests, religious and other functionaries. It has a territorial structure of dioceses and parishes. Most faithful believers expect the clerical hierarchy to speak with authority on issues of faith and morals. Responsibility for the preservation of the 'deposit of faith', i.e. the essential doctrine or teaching of Christ, from one generation to the next, rests with the *magisterium* (the teaching authority of the Church). From time to time certain issues or questions arise within the Church which may be only indirectly related to the 'deposit of faith' and permit a plurality of opinion. On some of these issues in recent times, Popes and Bishops have given their considered opinion and counsel, which are worthy of serious consideration by all believers, e.g. on social issues, ethical questions relating to war and capital punishment, *et cetera*. On questions relating to the 'deposit of faith' the Catholic Church's judgement, issued at an Ecumenical Council or by the Pope in virtue of his office, commands universal acceptance.

I trust that this summary statement of my understanding of the Roman Catholic Church is clear and reasonable. The sister Christian Churches are part of the broader family of baptised followers of Christ and loyal adherents to his teaching in Sacred Scripture. Their structures are different from that of the Roman Catholic Church. The divisions within the Christian Church are the sad product of history and their reconciliation must be of ongoing priority to all Christian Churches, if we are to be true to the will of Christ: 'that they may be one'. I long for the day when Roman Catholics, Orthodox and Protestants can come together as an inclusive ecumenical council of the Christian Churches.

In relation to the economic institution, the Church is not necessarily committed to its pivotal position or to the prevailing ideology at any time – be it 'free-market Capitalism' or 'bureaucratic Communism'. It is to the credit of the Churches in Ireland that, despite their continuous criticism by media commentators, they have maintained a constant critique of the social injustices in times of prosperity. They have also challenged the unrestricted rights of private property and defended the social priority of the 'common good'. Regretfully, most of the mass media have not given due prominence to the Church's social teaching. I hope this is not due to auto-censorship among journalists because of the commercial interests of their owners and advertisers. Media who depend on private owners and advertisers are not totally free irrespective of their claim to be a 'free press'. They are also servants of economic and commercial interests.

Individual priests and religious of the Irish Catholic Church have played a critical public role in drawing attention to areas of neglect, marginalisation and maldistribution of wealth. Journalist and commentator, Mr Vincent Browne, once said (during the nineties) that: *Whatever we say about the Catholic Church in Ireland, it must be admitted that behind nearly every voluntary service group or lobby group for the deprived, one will always find a priest or religious or an ex-priest or an ex-religious* (or words to that effect). That being said, I must admit that during the final quarter of the 20th century, there was a slowing down of the zeal for the mission to the underprivileged. The message being perceived seemed to tone down the more radical drive to identify with the cause of the poor. The move away from seeking structural change to seeking remedial help for the individual victims of social injustice would enable the Church to live with the imbalances of capitalist society. The net result was obvious on the ground in the world and in Ireland at the end of the 1990s.

The demise of the 'Liberation Theology' approach in the Third World was to be replaced by a growth of person-oriented evangelist movements throughout South America and Africa. There was a sister movement in the Roman Catholic Church often referred to as the 'charismatic movement'. The seeds of the latter began in the United States (Ann Arbor) in the early 1970s. The focus of such movements is the sanctification of their members, which is, in itself, a very good thing. They do not see themselves directly involved in the creation of a socially just society. In the words of Max Weber, they are more 'other worldly', whereas liberation Christian Movements are 'this worldly'. 'Other-worldly' movements can coexist with class-structured inequitable economic structures. *In fact, 'other-worldly' movements provide an outlet for religious expression, which also may provide relief and tension-release to the suffering poor, without in any way threatening the privileged classes.* Such movements are sometimes in receipt of generous support from the wealthy and the politically strong patrons in society. A critical analysis of these movements in relation to the achievement of social justice and universal human equality, which seems to me to be at the core of the Christian message, is urgently needed within the Church and within society. What is really needed in society is both 'other worldly' and 'this worldly' movements in the Church.

4. THE ECONOMIC INSTITUTION AND EDUCATION

According as the economic institution[7] resumed its ascent to the pivotal position in Ireland during the second half of the twentieth century (i.e. after Ireland's entry to the EEC), its strongest supportive institution was to be education. The Irish educational programme and syllabus was (as noted above) being oriented to serve the needs of the economy. Through the schools and colleges young Irish talent was being prepared for service in industry, services and agriculture. No longer was the production of *'Saints and Scholars'*, poets, theologians, philosophers, priests, religious, dramatists, historians, writers and critical intellectuals to be the top ambition of our universities and other third-level institutes of learning. Such a programme would find little priority among the bureaucratic pragmatists and financial backers of our 'research and development'. Eminent academics heralded the advance of the pragmatic approach and even invited industrial research complexes into or close by the university campuses. Industry needed the universities and institutes of technology to provide super-skilled experts to oversee the semi-skilled technicians operating the computerised factory programmes. Some factories would be engaged in producing the computer software and hardware for military, medical, communications (including transportation), bio-manipulated seeds, automated-manufacturing, *et cetera*.

On the commercial services side, specialised personnel would be required in the accountancy and financial control areas of work. Policing and crime detection were also in need of sophisticated computerisation. 'Big Brother' will soon be able to monitor the day-to-day routine of every member of the human race and put an end to the privacy which each of us is entitled to. Technological advance will soon be able to provide universal surveillance. If it is in the interests of the economy, who can prevent it? Hence, the need for intellectuals who will persuade the political powers to check what is happening to the quality of life of all of the people. Was it not a pity that some intellectuals or moral leaders did not counsel the scientific creators of the nuclear bomb and not make the knowledge available to the US military or to any other

---

7 In the following paragraphs the emergence of the economic institution into the pivotal position in Irish society in the mid-1990s will be examined in order to demonstrate the theory of social change based on the change of 'the pivotal institution'.

such groups willing to misuse the product of scientific genius? Such awesome power in the hands of an amoral or misguided leadership courts disaster for all life on earth. *Because we can do something is no reason why we should do it!*

The answer to the problem of the educational system supporting the scientific and other skills required by the economic institution or, in the case of the nuclear bomb, the political institution is very challenging. However, it would be unreasonable to expect universities and other colleges not to respond to the technical and scientific needs of industry, the services and agriculture. Perhaps, the most reasonable approach would be an obligatory foundation in arts and humanities for all third-level students of science and technology. This would be good for the graduates themselves and for society. An 'intellectual' scientist or economist (as distinct from a merely 'academic' scientist or economist) would be a check on the excesses of the monopoly of economic interests. Some universities around the world require a basic arts degree for all of their graduates in science, law, medicine, accountancy, *et cetera*. It is time for us to insist on such a 'well-rounded' education for all of our graduates. You may ask who would pay for the extra three years at third level. My answer would be let those who benefit from the expertise (including employers abroad) pay for the training of their workers, i.e. pay the costs of a fuller education. The State should cover the costs of the basic arts degree for all.

By the time I retired from lecturing in the university (30th September 1996), I was becoming disillusioned somewhat by the direction university education was taking in Ireland. In the past, it appeared to me that our universities had not made as great a contribution as they could have to the social needs of the people because of their elitism and refusal to provide intellectual leadership commensurate to their potential. Of course, there were notable exceptions. In the 19th century and earlier, Irish universities did not reach out to the vast majority of our people. Where were they during the Penal Laws? Where were Trinity and the Queen's Universities during the Famine and in its wake? The same could have been said about our elitist secondary schools. They seemed to fulfil the function of 'pattern maintenance' i.e. reproduce the professional leadership required by the prevailing establishment. Where were they when the Irish language was being neglected and suppressed in the 19th century?

The universities have frequently served the wants of the elite and not always addressed the needs of the people, which goes to prove again what the sociologist, Talcott Parsons wrote, i.e. that *the function of the (established) educational system was 'pattern-maintenance'*. Some idealists were led to believe that we in education were to lead social change and respond to the needs of all the people. Pattern-maintenance became very clear to me in the 1990s, when I was a member of Minister Bhreathnach's *Working Party on the Future of Higher Education in Ireland* and on the *Governing Body of St Patrick's College, Maynooth (The CEC)*. The move away from arts and humanities towards more pragmatic disciplines was an adjustment to the 'maintenance' of the requirements of the economy, with even less likelihood of producing more intellectuals as distinct from high quality academics. It was undiluted pattern-maintenance for the growing Irish economic order and its accompanying 'bureaucratic superstructure'.

We were gradually becoming cultivators of a very materialistic culture in Ireland, which I felt was doomed to collapse because of its own weight and emptiness (the collapse of 2008 would seem to some degree to confirm my fears!). Education, far from being creative (even for those in the lecture halls) as a source of change, was becoming the obedient instruments of change (already taking place) and of cultural de-radicalisation, i.e. removing the young from their family culture. If left unchecked, it would leave them highly skilled and very knowledgeable (academically), but could also make some of them anomic, i.e. members lacking in meaning and being personally normless. The dominance of the economic institution was in danger of 'demeaning' education. This rather pessimistic view of our higher education's direction at the end of the twentieth century has been commented on by a number of very experienced teachers and lecturers over a number of years. It does not give me any pleasure to be so critical. I feel, however, that one of the reasons why we won Independence for Ireland was to be in a position to ensure that our education system would respond to all the needs of our people and not to the narrow requirements of a most powerful elite with money and resources to dictate educational policy. Of course, it would be wrong to fail to appreciate the value to society of advances in science and technology in all areas of life including health care, communications, *et cetera*. The problem is the devaluing of the humanities and of the obligation to transmit the people's culture to the young.

Commenting on the role of education in countering social prejudice and promoting tolerance, the late Professor Chuck Hildebrandt (of Kent State University) said back in the 1960s that 'Ireland needed more education, while the US needed better education'. I believe that his commentary on our education in Ireland today would be that *'we now needed better education'*, with a greater input from the arts and humanities. The sooner we grasp this fact the better for the quality of life of future generations. Otherwise, the old adage *'we eat to live'* could well be turned on its head to read *'we live to eat'*, which is the description of a society exclusively dominated by the economic institution. All this being said, it should be stated that necessary economic progress required the support of the education institution, in the interests of 'the common good'. What worried me was its tendency to dominate the priorities of the Irish education system, to the detriment of the formation of intellectuals.

5. Support of the Legal and Political Institutions

When the economic institution becomes pivotal, the legal institution will reflect and reinforce it. The preoccupation with *property protection, banking, exchange, litigation, tax evasion and avoidance, industrial law, et cetera*, dominates law enforcement (Gardaí and civil servants), the application of the law (courts and tribunals) and the legislators (Houses of the *Oireachtais*). It was not a mere coincidence that a plethora of Tribunals and Enquiries into tax and property problems emerged in the later decades of the twentieth century. This was a sign that the regulation of the economic institution and its minor commercial institutions was crucial for the success of the economy. The banks and organisations dealing with 'money' also had to be regulated in a more appropriate manner. The rise of white collar crime was indicative of the new situation. The French sociologist, Emile Durkheim, once wrote that *the function of deviance 'was to clarify the norm'*. Much of the legislators' time has been in relation to laws pertaining to the economy, as have most of the numerous regulations coming from the European Union. The real irony was the rise of personal ethical deviance in a time of neo-liberal, self-regulated, free-market capitalism.

In a period of dominance of the economy in modern society, the whole area of regulation of industrial relations becomes central. During the 1970s when Mr Michael O'Leary TD, was Minister for Labour, a broad range of laws governing employment was introduced, principally because of Ireland's membership of the EEC. Regulatory agencies were enhanced, i.e. the Labour Court, the Conciliation Services and the Rights' Commissioners. Industrial strikes were reduced or shortened. Also, under *An Taoiseach*, Charles J Haughey TD, a 'social partnership' was called into being between trade unions, management, farmers and the State. Later, bodies representing the poor, youth, the marginalised, the old and others were added to the original four parties. This fifth partner was to be known as the 'Social Pillar'. It is interesting to record the 'genius' of Charles J Haughey to involve the trade unions at the highest level, when his counterpart in Britain at the time, Prime Minister, Mrs Margaret Thatcher MP, gave the trade unions the 'cold shoulder'. (It is very interesting to note that the 'social partners' have escaped major criticism for the rise and fall of the Celtic Tiger in our critical media!)

An Taoiseach, Charles J Haughey TD, believed that economic development could not maximise its progress without the cooperation of the 'social partners'. It is also interesting to note that the Minister for Labour at the time was a young TD named Mr Bertie Ahern TD. All governments from the 1980s until 2011 continued the 'social partnership model'. The setting up of the Labour Relations Commission, under the former General Secretary of IFUT, Mr Kieran Mulvey, would complement the Labour Court and other agencies in dealing with serious issues affecting workers and management. The Commission would cover unionised and non-unionised workers. Unfortunately, quite a number of US employers in Ireland did not recognise trade unions. This was something I have always considered a serious aberration. It broke the solidarity of the workers *vis-à-vis* the owners and managers. When I was chairperson of the County Kildare Council of Trade Unions, I tried to put pressure on these foreign-based multinationals (such as Intel) to recognise trade unions. It would be the mature thing to do!

The support of the Irish political institution for the economy in the 1990s has been direct and indirect. Legislation was enacted to facilitate competition, foreign investment, industrial relations, taxation (favourable to industry) and other measures as required. State Agencies, such as the IDA (Industrial Development Authority), *FÁS* (Training Authority) and

Udarás na Gaeltachta, were resourced to promote industrial development and training. Elections were fought and won on economic issues. Former US President, Bill Clinton's famous saying: 'It's the economy, stupid!' when canvassing for election as President, could be aptly applied to Ireland in the 1990s (once the Northern Problem was coming under political and non-violent control).

At the time it seemed that the State really 'got its act together' in relation to the economic development of our country in the late 1990s and was to win the admiration of commentators around the globe. Our joining the euro currency in 2000, while Britain refused to do so, was seen as revealing our economic muscle and independence from Britain. Political ideology moved towards the centre-right in the left-right scale. However, the euro curtailed our political independence and our ability to prevent our economy overheating in the next decade! (This was later confirmed, unfortunately!)

The new growth resulted in the incredible increase in the workforce and the temporary end to the scourge of emigration, which had bled our country of its 'brains and brawn' for one hundred and fifty years. It was great to see Irish emigrants returning to work in their own country. Also, we had an influx of migrant workers from Eastern Europe and elsewhere abroad. A massive investment in infrastructure, i.e. roads, rail, air and sea ports, telecommunications, was approved by our Government. This was long overdue, but we did not have the resources until then to undertake the work.

It had become clear to supporters of the restoration of the Western Rail Corridor that it was dependent on a 'political' decision. The Western Inter-County Railway Committee, which had been campaigning for the reinstating of the railway from Collooney to Limerick since 1979, invited Minister of State, Mr Éamon Ó Cuív TD, who was later to be responsible for 'Rural Development' in the new *Fianna Fáil*/Progressive Democrats Government (1997-2002), to address a meeting at Horan International Airport (renamed Knock Airport in 1998) in 1997. At that meeting our sights were raised. The Minister advised us to apply for a modern, up-to-date, welded track on reinforced concrete sleepers. The restored line had to be a 'first-class line'. At the time our Committee was even prepared to accept second-hand track, which was lifted from the mainlines which were being re-laid with welded rails. This was to me a most significant meeting and gave me an insight into the new dynamic approach to our project and to the expectation of serious socio-economic development. A new era was awakening. The introduction by the Government of such policies as the *National Spatial Strategy, Clár, and 'Decentralisation'*, was also an attempt to spread the development throughout the country. This exemplified the political dimension of a socio-economic transport infrastructure and, in a subtle way, redirecting the 'economy' towards social needs! The question to be asked later was the extent of support for the railway project among the elite economists! (The renewal of the track from Limerick to Athenry was achieved recently. Approval to proceed further to Claremorris is expected!)

The Government's neo-liberal taxation policy was also development-oriented. It was very much geared to the workforce. The lowering of income tax to 20% and 42% (top rate) and the individualisation for working couples' tax allowances manifested the Government's priority in favour of the economic institution over the family and the rearing of children at home. This was, in my opinion, a disastrous decision and would have very serious consequences 'down the road'. But, the people supported it, with a limited amount of protest from a minority in the media. There were other signs of withdrawal of support for local communities in the reduction in community employment schemes (which was to cost the Government a loss of votes in the 2004 Local Government elections). It was a very strange phenomenon that, according as the country was getting richer, community support was becoming less. *Redistribution of the new wealth to the needy* was already being reduced through the substantially lower tax rates on the rich! The weaker urban communities were to feel the pinch as relative deprivation increased. *I would attribute some of the rise in urban crime to this neglect.* Also, there was little or no control of the price of houses. In fact, housing development was very much 'developer- and speculator-led' rather than 'community controlled'! While one could welcome the improvement in employment and the reduction in emigration, there was concern about the less egalitarian face of the 'brave new Ireland', where development lacked class and regional balance. It proved that *'when the "economic tide" came in, not all boats floated'*!

In terms of electoral power in the new Ireland, it was very clear by the end of the 1990s that the majority of the Irish-born were becoming 'middle class' and urbanised (in world view, if not in area of residence). The results of such a change would mean that the deprived and the poor would become an almost insignificant minority, that is, unless they were strategically placed with the balance of power in a 'hung parliament'. It was clear also that *Sinn Féin,* having recently been gaining political status, was trying to organise the voice of those left behind by the rapid economic growth. This would be very interesting down the road, when *Sinn Féin* would be acceptable as a partner in a centre-left coalition. The history of the Troubles in Northern Ireland had anchored that party in 'the community of the outsiders'. Of course, the routinisation of *Sinn Féin*, as a result of their representatives entering conventional politics and administration, will in time de-radicalise them and place them in the middle-class camps.

Routinisation always de-radicalises revolutionaries and converts them into safe reformers! It happened to *Cumann na nGael* and to *Fianna Fáil* in the 1920s and 1930s and to the Democratic Left in more recent years. The revolutionary roots of the Irish Labour Party are also a fact of history. The *Good Friday Agreement* was a most astute 'process' towards routinisation in the cause of peace. Of course, there will also be those prophetic leaders who will revitalise the revolutionary spirit, when the situation becomes over-routinised. That is why it is wise for every major political party to have a broad spectrum, which can embrace the more radical members, especially those on the Left. It keeps their policies sensitive to minority needs and concerns and challenges the very rich and powerful in our unequal society.

Needless to say, it is the ideology of the ruling parties that, in reality, counts at the end of the day. The commitment to free-market capitalism among the Government parties after 1997 was a key factor in attracting multinational companies to Ireland. Such companies follow cheap labour and low capital-gains' taxes. As Ireland became richer, its labour became more expensive and the attraction of our country to investors in labour-intensive employment reduced. When that adjustment comes, it will no doubt cause disappointment. In the meantime, incomes were going up and so were prices for food and other items. *Housing was the most notorious example of cost-of-living rises.* And yet, we were told that inflation was very low! *Bank interest was very low and this, in turn, kept down mortgage interest costs. Had we not been in the eurozone, our Government could have put up interest rates to cool demand.* The eurozone must bear some of the blame for Ireland's housing/building 'boom to bust'.

A strange change took place among the Irish people with the arrival of the Celtic Tiger. We became a nation of borrowers, i.e. for houses, cars, holidays, *et cetera.* Saving had to be (artificially) made profitable by the State. The old Keynesian rule of *Production = Consumption + Savings = Consumption + Investment* seemed to be ignored. When I was studying economics, the professor advised that Savings/ Investments should be over 20% of production to ensure ongoing economic prosperity. It was quite confusing for me to understand the theoretical base of our new prosperity, having been trained in the Keynesian School. I sometimes wondered were we living in a false pre-crash paradise. Hopefully not! When it happened, I hoped it would have a soft landing. (Unfortunately, when the crisis came in 2008, it was fairly catastrophic!)

6. COMMERCIALISATION OF RECREATION AND LEISURE

In my analysis of social change I have added recreation as a seventh major social institution. Recreation and leisure are not that easy to define. The most obvious definition of *recreation/leisure time is that spent free from work or obligatory service to family, religion, politics, et cetera.* The function of recreation/leisure is 'tension-management', which is essential for healthy and fruitful survival. It is also seen as the main function of the family. In the past (pre-industrial society) most of the people's recreation was informal and based in the family, the neighbourhood and the local community. When religion was more pivotal, all holidays were holy days, and periods of communal celebration and relaxation were centred around religious feasts, i.e. Christmas, Easter, 15th August, All Saints and others. Ireland's national holiday was St Patrick's Day. Periods of non-celebration were also observed, i.e. Advent and Lent. Ever since the rise of the Enlightenment at the end of the 18th century there has been a gradual playing down of religious feasts and their replacement by secular holidays. The arrival of the 'Bank Holiday' was evidence of the growing ascendancy of the economic institution. Other obligatory periods of non-working were also to be decreed. The Bank Holiday replacing the Holy Day manifested the rise of the economic (secular) institution!

The commercialisation of leisure had advanced in Ireland with the decline of informal recreation in the home. The old idea that the family home was to be the place where '*one let one's hair down without losing status*' had declined. Annual and regular holidays in hotels and apartments away from home were originally bourgeois conventions and rarely availed of by the mass of the Irish people in the past. They, rather, went to visit family friends away from home for a short period and such friends reciprocated by coming to them. This was the routine in my family right up to the 1980s. Maybe, we could not afford anything else? Conventional commercialised holidays have little attraction for me to this very day. They seem counterfeit! We would go to the bog on Easter Monday!

Ireland itself became a holiday location on a highly organised basis from the 1960s forward. Tourism, which is a recreation/leisure industry, was discovered to be a lucrative service. Our hospitality became a valuable commodity! Many of our visitors were third or fourth generation emigrants from the United States and elsewhere abroad. Looking back at it now, we must have presented an attractive image of a people who were relatively poor, very religious and family-centred. Most of all, we were friendly and happy to talk to the enquiring visitor. At the time, our town and countryside were relatively unspoiled by high density traffic on the roads or ostentatious rural and ex-urban housing. Our rivers were clean and providing life for many fish. Some saw Ireland as a quiet haven for the bourgeoisie from highly industrialised and polluted societies of the 'developed world'.

Our cost of living was low and prices were relatively cheap. Reading some of the literature of the time, one gets the impression that Ireland would become another semi-third-world holiday centre and it was more important to gentrify rather than develop it. Such a fate would result in a gradual depopulation of the numerous local communities of the rural West, North-West and South-West of Ireland. *This idyllic, underdeveloped Ireland was not viable.* I was to discover this in a survey of parishes of the Archdiocese of Tuam carried out in 1996. Our approach to tourism had to change if and when our indigenous economy began to develop. There was a possibility of retaining friendliness and an aesthetically beautiful physical and human-made environment, which would make Ireland a quality destination for visitors. This, however, would require community control of development and the maintenance of high-quality accommodation and entertainment at reasonable prices. To achieve this in a 'free-market' society would not be easy.

By the end of the 1990s the Irish themselves were changing their recreational patterns of behaviour. Many were 'going abroad' on an annual basis. In the past, such trips were limited to honeymoon trips, funerals and family celebrations, and the occasional visit to Lourdes, Fatima or Rome, on pilgrimage.

At home, 'dining-out' by families was on the increase. Baptism, confirmation, weddings and funerals were mostly celebrated (after the religious ceremonies) in hotels, clubs, and pubs. It was ironic that according as homes/houses became bigger with more function rooms, they became less used for family celebrations. This resulted in a staggering increase in commercialised leisure outside the home. Even wakes at home began to decline (although there has been a welcome return of this age-old tradition in the more recent past). The undertaker's funeral parlour became the commercialised form of waking the dead! Lurking behind all the change has been the pivotal economic institution. The gradual destruction of the Sabbath as a 'day of rest' by the retail trade and others has been a retrograde development. Is shopping in supermarkets replacing worshipping or is it a new form of 'worshipping the economic God' on the Sabbath day?

The latest effects of the commercialisation of leisure have not yet been fully analysed. One area of life, which has suffered most, has been the place of voluntary personal and social leisure. Sport is a classic example of this, where 'amateurism' is under serious threat. The fictitious application of the title 'professional' only to those who play for money is an insult to the professional amateur. The family/neighbourhood/ community structure has also been undermined by the commercialisation of leisure. This also can affect the stability of marriage in that it empties the home so often. The rise of marital breakdown and divorce has tended to commercialise marriage itself!

One industry to benefit enormously from the commercialisation of leisure is the alcoholic drinks industry and its retail outlets, the pubs, clubs and hotels, not to mention the off-licences and supermarkets. The experience of the Pioneer Total Abstinence Association has enabled me to appreciate the far-reaching impact of the consumption of alcohol on the lives of the people and the proportion of our fellow-citizens for whom drinking alcoholic liquor has impeded their personal freedom and development and, in numerous cases, wreaked havoc in their families. The growing power of the multinational drinks industry and compliant Governments has greatly strengthened its addictive grip on Irish society. The commercialisation of leisure has facilitated its deeper penetration into the lives of the people through advertising in the media. No wonder, then, young people have been seduced by its appeal!

7. SUMMARY OF INSTITUTIONAL MODEL OF CHANGE

Just to conclude this rather lengthy and winding *commentary on social change* in Ireland between 1900 and 2000, using the *'pivotal institution model'*, I trust I have not lost many of my readers. Seven major institutions were identified, i.e. family, religion, education, law, polity, recreation and economy. By institution, as I said, is meant *a set of norms centred around a central area of human need and activity.* Norms are human ways of doing things. *For example, the economic institution includes all the norms relating to the production, distribution and consumption of goods and services and the adaptation of the physical environment (to enable such activity) to meet the needs and comforts of the people.* The people's day-to-day lives fluctuate from activities in one or other of the institutions. It is part of the human social condition that we are compelled to conform to the acceptable current norms of the time we live in. Otherwise, social living would be impossible. *Also, it should be noted that change in one institution affects change in each of the other six, e.g. spread of change in the role and status of women.*

Despite the relatively large amount of text devoted to the understanding of social change in modern Ireland, what is written is totally inadequate to explain the elaborate process that lies behind what most people take for granted as normal. The norm is perceived as the only way, in their mind, of doing things. Of course, our current social system is but one way that seems to be viable for the present time. Even those who occupy positions of authority in the system are themselves products of the system and are committed to operate it effectively.

As already noted, the concepts of the various institutions are abstract. In the concrete reality there is no such thing as 'the family', or 'religion', or 'polity', or 'law', or 'education', or 'economy' or 'recreation'. These are all abstract universal concepts. What we find on the ground, are 'the Kelly family', the believer praying, '*Dáil Éireann*', 'the *Finance Act 2012*', 'Brackloon National School', 'Jacob's factory' and the 'All-Ireland Final'. For rational discussion we must, of necessity, use universal concepts, with a foundation in reality. A further qualification must be made that when sociologists or others analyse social change, they do so in generalisations and use a method known in the literature as 'ideal typology', i.e. models which are rarely found complete in any society at a particular time because social change does not happen in uniform patterns. In many cases even the conditions of change do not exist to the same extent. Also, the various social institutions may not be pulling together in the one direction, that is, unless one lives in a totalitarian state. But, even under such systems coercion does not produce the desired result because the full commitment of the people may be lacking. Allowing for such shortcomings, I would hold that the *'pivotal institutional model'* is a very useful framework by which to diagnose and explain social change (at the sociocultural level) in society.

The biggest threat to the pivotal position of the economic institution is the failure of an exclusively materialistic system to provide meaning, despite its potential capacity to satisfy all the people's material needs and comforts. Such issues as social equality, environmental protection, cultural pursuits, religious beliefs and practices, literary pursuits, personal relationships, family loyalties, political ideals, *et cetera,* can impede the advance of the economy. The level of personal satisfaction with superfluity is problematic. For instance, the hippie revolt in the United States in the 1960s was an expression of the failure of materialism/consumerism to satisfy many of the younger affluent generation. What they turned to in its place left much to be desired.

Pitirim Sorokin, the Russian-reared student of macro social change, saw it differently. *He held that 'change was cyclical' at the level of civilisation.* He discovered that the ethos alternated between 'ideational', i.e. spiritual, and sensate, i.e. material and empirical. European Culture changed from being 'ideational' in the Medieval era to becoming 'sensate' in the post-Enlightenment era (19th and 20th centuries). The Renaissance era was a transitional phase in the ongoing process of cyclical cultural change. Sorokin felt that there were signs of the post-Enlightenment sensate era reaching saturation point. During 'sensate eras' we find rapid material change, while in the 'ideational era' there is a high level of spiritual growth and aesthetic genius. Small societies like Ireland may have only become absorbed into the 'sensate culture' over a hundred years after it had been established in the rest of the Western World. Have we just arrived when the pendulum is going to swing back to a more spiritually characterised ethos? There are signs of sensate fatigue, i.e. the difficulty of the economic and scientific/technological establishment to recruit some of the most intelligent students away from arts and humanities, despite its financial appeal. The 21st century is going to be a most interesting one! A slowing down of the sensate, for instance, may give the environment a chance to breathe! It may also herald a return to the spiritual and religious pursuit of meaning! *The post-2008 collapse of the voracious rate of material 'progress' may well be a sign of sensate fatigue!*

At this stage the reader may ask me if I had an ideal (utopian) model for society. I have one such model. My ideal society is domestic-centred, namely, the family would be the 'pivotal institution' with all the other social institutions supportive of it and a move towards the ideational ethos. Human beings are the 'longest nesting animals', who are slow to mature physically and slower still to develop their personality, internalise their culture (including their religion) and learn the necessary social and occupational skills to play an adult role in society. *From all the studies I have been able to do and read about and from experience of life in Ireland and elsewhere, it appears to me that we will always need a well-supported family. This will be a great challenge for our leaders in the 21st century. The family needs the support of both the neighbourhood and the community.*

8. Vatican Two: A Major Event in the 20th Century

So much for the institutional model of Irish society! It is now intended 'to change gear' and highlight a number of historical events which characterised the twentieth century for me. The most revolutionary changes in the Roman Catholic Church during the 20th century happened in the early 1960s. In 1959 in Rome, the old Pope, Angelo Giuseppe Roncalli, from Bergamo in Italy (1881-1963), who took the name John XXIII, was contemplating the scene at the time and realised that something radical was needed to rediscover the Church's relevance in a world that was becoming more and more disillusioned. His own experience of Eastern Europe and elsewhere told him that the poor relations between the Orthodox and the Catholic Church were a tragic scandal. A group of bright theologians, i.e. Karl Rahner, Edward Schillebeeckx, Carlo Martini, Joseph Ratzinger and others were producing new insights into the Church's teachings. Fr Teilhard de Chardin SJ had helped to show the possibility of *evolution or development* in the Church's teaching. The idea of *semper idem* (always the same) was being challenged. Other Jesuits, like Henri de Lubac, were articulate in presenting an understanding of the Church that was pastorally relevant in an ever-changing world. In South America we had bishops such as Archbishop Helder Camara who were desperately trying to give pastoral leadership and encouragement to those lay people working for the poor and trying to bring about structural change.

And then it came. Pope John XXIII called the Second Vatican Council and asked the universal church to look at itself in the early 1960s. For the next six years or so, our Church became alive with great expectations. (I have already commented on the Council's deliberations). In the overall context of the twentieth century, Vatican Two and the letters to the world by Pope John XXIII changed, at least for a time in the public eye, the relationship between the Catholic Church and the world. It also opened the door to greater lay participation in the liturgical, spiritual, pedagogical, pastoral and administrative life of the local church. Bishops were also given a wider role, especially through the local 'Conferences of Bishops'. The terms 'dialogue' and 'collegiality' were seen as very important for the life of the Roman Catholic Church. It was a new Pentecost with formal recognition of the place and sanctity of other Christian Churches. A more respectful attitude towards the Jewish faith was adopted and a new dialogue was encouraged with other world religions. By the end of Vatican Two we all looked forward to a better Church and a spiritually healthier relationship with what was good in the world around us. The fear of 'Modernism' seemed to fade away somewhat. Vatican Two ranks for me as the major (positive) event of the 20th Century.

9. POWERFUL SOCIAL MOVEMENTS OF THE 20ᵀᴴ CENTURY

In the news media a number of interesting essays were written on the century and millennium just ending. The 20th century was one of radical change in Ireland, started with the buy-out of the landlords and the rise of a number of powerful movements, i.e. the Gaelic League, the Gaelic Athletic Association, the Labour Movement, the Pioneer Total Abstinence Association, the Cooperative Movement, the Suffragist Movement, the Literary Movement (including the Abbey Theatre), and *Sinn Féin.* We were still part of the British Empire, with a growing demand for Home Rule in the late 19th century under Charles S Parnell. The success of the Land Movement, under the leadership of Michael Davitt (assisted by Parnell), had given the people the necessary confidence to pursue the higher goal of national independence. History tells us how successful those diverse movements have been over the century now ending. The previous chapters of this book have monitored the social, economic, political, religious and cultural developments after the achievement of independence for twenty-six of the thirty-two counties of the Island of Ireland. *The Insurrection of 1916 and the War of Independence (1919-21) contributed to the establishment of the Irish Free State in 1922 and the partition of Ireland with six counties of Ulster constituting Northern Ireland.*

The rise of fascism in Europe was facilitated by the outcome of World War One (1914-18), the Wall Street Crash (1929) and the ill-advised *Treaty of Versailles.* The Spanish Civil War in the 1930s was a tragic event with acts of extreme violence on both sides. The victory of General Franco was aided by support from the German Third Reich government. It should be noted that Franco did not get involved in the Second World War on the side of Hitler.

The rise of Nazi fascism under Adolf Hitler was facilitated by the humiliating misery imposed on the German people following their defeat in 1918 and the effects of the Wall Street Crash in 1929 and the failure of Liberal Capitalism. Germany's military expansionism throughout continental Europe shocked the people of the world, while the obscene cruelty of totalitarian genocide against Jews, gypsies, homosexuals, certain ethnic groups and others reached an unprecedented high in State brutality. The Third Reich was defeated in 1945. The war against

Japan was won mainly by the Americans (US) in 1946. Unfortunately, the US used the 'atomic bomb' as a weapon against Japanese cities, which was a gross act of 'overkill'. Nevertheless, the US was essential in the Allied victory.

To the east of Germany, the ruthless purge and persecution of whole categories of people by the totalitarian Communist regime (which had replaced the Tsarist monarchy in 1917) under Joseph Stalin numbed the civilised imagination. This same Soviet regime was to expand its area of influence after the Second World War. This was not to deny the enormous cost in human life the USSR was to pay for the defeat of Hitler in 1944-45. Without the sacrifice of the people of the Soviet Union and the bravery of its army, the outcome of the Second World War would have been very different. The first half of the twentieth century, then, was one of gross violence in Europe and elsewhere in the two World Wars and the rise of totalitarian regimes between the wars. After the Second World War we had a tense 'Cold War' between the West and the East. This led to the establishment of the so-called 'Iron Curtain'.

Trouble in the Middle East grew during the second half of the century. The process of decolonisation was formally and painfully conceded throughout Africa and Asia. (Ireland's decolonisation had been partially achieved in 1922.) Paramilitary trouble broke out in Northern Ireland in the 1950s and again in 1969 and continued until 1994. Violence between tribes and countries in Africa was very tragic. Many of the former colonial territories when liberated were arbitrary and not in harmony with traditional tribal and cultural boundaries. Also, there was the ongoing clash between Christianity and Islam. Many of these problems continued into the twenty-first century. It was a painful century for Africa before and after decolonisation. Conflict in Indo-China (renamed Vietnam) was post-colonial and ideological.

10. THE POST-WAR EEC

The rise and expansion of the European Economic Community (the Common Market), later re-designated the European Union, was the most significant political development in post-Second World War Western Europe. For Germany, France and Italy it was perceived as the best guarantor of non-aggression between European powers, which caused such pain, and destruction in both World Wars (1914-18 and 1939-45). This ideal is to be commended. But, in my opinion, this tendency towards a centralised integrated 'United States of Europe' (a dream of Caesar, Napoleon and others) seems to be taking over, resulting in the alienation of the people because of the remoteness of the centre of authority. I, personally, voted in favour of Ireland joining the EEC in 1972 but I voted 'no' in subsequent *referenda* seeking to integrate the member states further than that of a common market. I was happy that the European Court of Human Rights, which was outside the EEC/EU, kept a watchful eye over our civil rights legislation, *et cetera*.

Ireland was to be a beneficiary of European structural funds but I am not so sure that the Irish Government distributed such funds equitably throughout the country. The Common Agricultural Policy (CAP) was a double-edged sword, which has led to the decline of small farmers and the disruption of our agricultural production. Country-wide horticulture, i.e. the growing of fruit and vegetables, has slumped practically out of existence (by the end of the century). *Agribusiness seems to have replaced family mixed farming*! This has disenfranchised many small farmers and their rural communities. Commercial interests have disrupted locally integrated rural communities in Ireland and throughout most of Europe. It has become clear to me that the European Union had fast become very much a free-market, capitalist-dominated union of 'states' (some would be so cynical as to say 'statelets') or rapidly heading in that direction by the end of the 20th century. I am sorry if this 'European sceptic' view will annoy some readers!

What was most positive about the ideal EU would be its ability to elicit cooperation between independent states, i.e. independent in relation to cultural and diplomatic affairs and, most important of all, in relation to military alliances. We in Ireland must be able to remain neutral and non-aligned. As a formerly colonised country, we have learned the hard way the dangers of dependence. It almost cost us our native language and culture.

11. DECOLONISATION

It was a painful century for the people of Africa both before and after decolonisation. Colonisation was a product of European expansionism in the 17th, 18th and 19th centuries. *Racial prejudice*, i.e. prejudice against people because of their different colour and genetically inherited traits was practically non-existent prior to the renaissance period of European expansionism. This was one of the greatest failures of the so-called European Enlightenment. Prejudice against 'black people' was to prove the most degrading of all. Some white Christian Europeans defined the black peoples of Africa as *'less than human'*! So much was this perception of inferiority believed by slave-owners that they even tried to deny the black slaves the right to religion, which was reserved for humans! The emancipation of 'black' and 'coloured' people took a very long time and the residue of racism is still with us. The tragedy of it all was its utterly false basis. *The colour of one's skin is as humanly significant as the size of one's boots!*

There were two areas in particular that highlighted 'the dangerous myths of race' for me, i.e. the 'Deep South in the United States' and the 'Apartheid Segregation in South Africa'. Both 'reigns of terror' were formally defeated to a point during the twentieth century. The leaders who bravely guided the civil rights campaigns against the evil systems would, in my opinion, rank among the greatest heroes of the century, i.e. the Reverend Martin Luther King (1929-68) and Mr Nelson Mandela (1918-2013). Martin Luther King paid the ultimate price for the cause when he was martyred in a most cruel and vicious way in 1968. Nelson Mandela spent twenty-seven years in penal servitude for the cause of the black and coloured People of South Africa. Another heroic person who deserved to rank among the greatest liberators and pacifist leaders of the twentieth century was Mr Mahatma Gandhi (1868-1948) of India and South Africa. *Knowing about people like King, Mandela and Gandhi helped me to commit myself in my own small way to the cause of civil rights.* My method of campaign was through research and publication of the findings of the people's racial and ethnic attitudes. I also lent support from time to time to public protest against situations of prejudice in Ireland (e.g. towards Travellers) and abroad (e.g. through the Anti-Apartheid Movement).

Another outstanding person who came to the attention of the world as a champion of the deprived during the latter part of the twentieth century was Mother Teresa of Calcutta (1910-97), who identified with the destitute people and, thereby, recognised their equality of human dignity. In fact, women have been very much to the fore in the campaign for racial, ethnic and social equality.

Archbishops Hurley of Durban and Tutu of Cape Town of the Catholic and Anglican Churches respectively were noteworthy opponents of apartheid in South Africa. It was very good to see leaders of the churches united in their public campaign for justice. Many local people told me on my visit to Africa in 2004 that most Churches were agencies for justice and equality.

Such recognition from the victims of racial and ethnic prejudice and discrimination was most necessary and encouraging for me at a time when the media in Ireland were reluctant to publicise any positive news about the Church. As I said earlier in this text, some of our most vocal critics of the Catholic Church in the media seemed to have developed a degree of compulsive alienation from the Church of their earlier life. This is quite a regular phenomenon in times of rapid social and religious change. This disposition may be called the 'apostate complex'. People with such a psychological handicap tend to emphasise the negative and play down the positive about the body or group to which they once belonged and from which they are subconsciously alienated. They also tend to over-identify and praise their current group or ideological position. It is very difficult to be objective in our assessment of bodies to which we have had an attachment. Such is the weakness of the finite human condition. This condition can and does develop also in relation to political views and parties.

The arrival of AIDS in the 1980s was to become a massive scourge. Its proliferation was enhanced by heterosexual and homosexual promiscuity as well as by the use of contaminated needles for the injection of drugs into the bloodstream. The world's reaction to AIDS was one of shock and alarm. Patients were treated strangely in the beginning. In Western society, sexually active gay men were the group most severely hit by this new killer disease. The medical profession tried hard to find a cure or a vaccine, which would prevent its spread without taking the necessary behavioural precautions, i.e. against promiscuous sexual activity and using needles already contaminated with the blood of others. So far, the only sure way to avoid contamination with the HIV virus is avoidance of casual sexual activity and drug-injection by means of used needles. This is ideologically repugnant to those who believe in 'free sex'. Liberal society believes in the hedonist approach to sexual relations and, in my opinion, is leading youth astray and, unfortunately, in the case of many to sexually transmitted diseases.

In Africa, the spread of AIDS among the poor was most devastating. I have already commented on this fact when discussing developments of the nineteen-nineties. It is very difficult to measure the impact of AIDS on the newly emancipated countries. It was tragic that the scourge of AIDS struck just as the Republic of South Africa was emerging from the indignity and pain of apartheid. Other countries in sub-Saharan Africa were being seriously decimated by this killer of the young and the vibrant. The negative consequences for poor families have been inestimable. And yet the wealthy world powers did relatively little to ease the burden. Tribal sexual norms would have to change, if the people themselves were to take control. Leaders like Fr Michael Kelly SJ, of Lusaka University and his colleagues working for the prevention of the spread of AIDS and the human treatment of those affected deserve great praise, support and recognition.

In addition to the pain inflicted on the people of Africa by racial discrimination and by AIDS, internal conflicts have bedevilled many African nations during the twentieth century. These were in addition to the struggles for independence by the indigenous peoples, e.g. the long war of independence in Kenya under Great Britain. This was a result of the colonial territories having arbitrary divisions *vis-à-vis* national tribal boundaries. The Biafran War in the 1960s was a classic case of such inappropriate divisions. This was compounded further by the conflict between Islam and Christianity south of the Sahara and near the 'Horn of Africa'. The growth of big cities and the migration of young people from rural and remote districts had led to the sudden emergence of 'shanty towns and gross congestion'. Tribal and family social-control norms were undermined and the rise of juvenile delinquency followed. I remember a mature student from Nigeria telling me in the mid-1970s that the Western influence on African society made the people poorer and more deviant by this rapid urbanisation and the undermining of tribal order which was more cultured and more humane. The West brought much misery to Africa.

The twentieth century in the Far East was marked by wars and revolutions of a very bloody nature, i.e. in China, Japan and South East Asia. The partitioning of India after Independence and the subsequent violence were tragic happenings after the great work of Mahatma Gandhi. Burma, Indonesia and Indo-China were also among the countries to suffer the privations of internal conflict. Japanese expansionism into China and other neighbouring states led to terrible persecution. The war between Japan and the United States was won by the latter in 1946. As already stated, the most horrific act of war, in my opinion, was the dropping of two atomic bombs on two Japanese cities by the United States, which brought that conflict to an end. Five years later, we had the Korean War, which was won by neither side after unnecessary bloodshed. The US led allies stopped at the border of North Korea in 1952, leaving the country divided.

Further to the South the French occupying forces were engaged in an ongoing war with 'rebels' in French Indo-China, now known as Vietnam. Eventually the French were forced to withdraw leaving the country divided between North Vietnam under Ho-Chi-Min, and Southern Vietnam under President Diem. The Northern part was under a Communist regime, while the South was more akin to a Western (Christian) State. In the early 1960s, the US got engaged in defending South Vietnam from a Communist take-over. Some would see the US involvement as quasi-messianic. The result of this engagement was to bring death, misery and destruction to hundreds of thousands of *Vietnamese, Cambodians* and *Americans*. It went on for over a decade, leading to the withdrawal of the US forces. The Vietnam War showed clearly the devastatingly destructive nature of 'conventional weapons of mass destruction' (CWMD).

In Central and Southern America, the century was marked with a whole series of Civil Wars and suppression of oppositions by dictators. The Mexican Civil War in the 1920s was particularly vicious. The Castro-led socialist revolution in Cuba was successful (in defeating the Batista dictatorship) and the regime succeeded in surviving even after the 'fall of the Berlin Wall'. Internal movements for civil rights met with bloody suppression in a number of countries. The battle for social justice, aided by '*the liberation theology*' movement, began to decline after the death of Pope Paul VI, Argentina, under the dictator General Galtieri, failed in its military attempt to take back the Malvinas Islands, (known to the British as the Falklands), thanks in part to the support of the US under President Ronald Reagan, in the early 1980s. The British Prime Minister, Mrs Margaret Thatcher MP, ordered the military recapture of the islands, which was successful. It was like the good old colonial days! The *coup d'état* by General Pinochet (1915-2006) in Chile in 1974 was an example of the ruthless dominance of might over democracy. It was alleged that the (US) CIA supported the General. In 1974, when attending a course in the University of Michigan, Ann Arbor, I got to know a Chilean student who was the son of a Chilean Ambassador to an Eastern country during the brief reign of President Allende. He gave me an insight into methods of South American dictatorships. Persecution in El Salvador and elsewhere in Central America resulted in much pain and occasional martyrdom.

12. OTHER DEVELOPMENTS AND CHANGES

While there were many more atrocities happening throughout the world during the twentieth century, there were also some very positive developments. There was serious progress in relation to the reduction of *sexism, ethnocentrism, racism, homophobia, anti-Semitism, class prejudice* and *Christian sectarianism* in large parts of the world. This was helped by the public outcry against *Nazi xenophobia*, as revealed during the decades after the war. The Second World War had a traumatic effect on the people of Europe. The social sciences were beginning to 'come of age' in the 1950s and 1960s and were able to examine the psychological and social causes of intergroup hatred and persecution. Intellectuals like the late Gordon Allport of Harvard University (USA) made an enormous contribution to our better understanding of social prejudice. The study of authoritarianism by Adorno and colleagues (in Berkeley, California) after the Second World War was an attempt to explain the mindset that produced the Nazi leaders and seduced so many people to follow them. Other studies tried to identify social structures conducive to the suppression of the people.

The advance of cultural and social anthropology in the universities of the 'Western World' provided an analysis of modern cultures and also helped us to understand the socio-cultural influences of contemporary society. A revival of interest in the work of Max Weber (1864-1920), the eminent German sociologist, was to lead to a better understanding of bureaucracy, which was essential for the growth of the industrial and commercial corporation. It seemed to me that Weber's ingenious description of how bureaucracy worked became '*an ideology of bureaucracy*'! I could refer to many more examples of the 'descriptive' and 'prescriptive' role of the human sciences in the 20th century, especially, psychology, sociology and anthropology. Sigmund Freud (1856-1939) helped to make us aware of our psychological make-up and enabled us to live with our personality limitations (even if we disagreed with some of his philosophical conclusions).

One would have expected that the improvement in our capacity to diagnose and to explain (scientifically) the structures and behaviour patterns of people would have obviated or prevented our drifting into social crises. But, such an expectation is naïve because people behave irrationally and selfishly, unless they are imbued with a morality of altruism and social justice. This is something beyond the capacity of the human sciences, since they are 'non-normative', that is, if they are scientific. This is where I see the role of religion, based on an altruistic ethic of truth, love and social justice. The cumulative contribution of Christian missionary work has been a welcome antidote to the exploitation (by colonisers and conquerors) of indigenous Africans and others over the nineteenth and twentieth centuries.

In the decade after the Second World War, the Christian Churches began to question their failure to be effective in preventing the awful inhumanity in the world, especially in the Second World War and the Nazi Concentration Camps. The appalling injustice throughout the developing worlds of Africa, Asia and Central and Southern America and the social imbalances within the strong developed world did not respond to Christian standards. The concept Fourth World was applied to the hideous poverty in the deprived areas of large cities of the rich world where equitable distribution of wealth did not prevail. When I joined the Jesuits in 1959, we had very little awareness of this post-War self-questioning in the Roman Catholic institutional Church. The new interest in Sacred Scripture (promoted by Fr Carlo Martini SJ, in Rome) and in Liturgy was breaking through to those studying theology in the nineteen-fifties. *Some well-intentioned critics seem to herald the defeat of 'institutionalised religion' as the remedy. This is also naïve since all human behaviour is institutional. What is needed is certain changes in institutional religious practice!*

The notable advances of medicine and disease-prevention increase the life expectancy of many. Bodies such as the World Health Organisation (WHO) achieved much success in the control of diseases such as leprosy and polio but were not given the resources required. The inequality between the levels of health care in the countries of greatest need is still grossly inadequate. The coming to grips with the scourge of tuberculosis (TB) in Ireland by Minister Noel Browne TD, and his Department in 1950 was a notable example of positive change. The developed world seemed to have attracted medical personnel even from the Third World to add to the relatively strong services in the rich community. This tended to aggravate an already under-resourced care system in the developing countries. *The free movement of talent from poor countries to the relatively strong ones needs to be controlled in the interests of justice.*

The growth of ecumenism after Vatican Two raised the hopes of many that the post-Reformation Christian Church would move towards Christian unity. So far we have not made sufficient progress. Hopefully, the momentum towards unity will revive in the decades ahead. This would be very good for Ireland. The survival of a viable Christian Church in Western Europe could well be dependent on advances in Christian ecumenism. The positive work of the Irish School of Ecumenics, inspired by Fr Michael Hurley SJ, in the late 1960s, was an ongoing beacon of true enlightenment. Pope Paul VI seemed to have grasped the urgency of pluralist Christian Church Unity. Tentative moves towards dialogue between Jews and Christians and between Catholics and Muslims are to be welcomed.

During the twentieth century, science and technology made very significant and substantial advances resulting in improvements in the material standards of living of more people. There were great improvements in medicine, communications (including transportation), engineering, *et cetera*. To cope with such advances, education and training became an 'industry' in itself. Needless to say, the benefits of such advances are not equitably distributed. The 'culture lag' between technological advance and its incorporation into cultural and social norms is a real problem.

One of the latent effects of scientific specialisation has been the massive growth of pollution (as noted earlier by philosopher, Bernard Lonergan SJ). The world's physical environment has come under threat because of the effects of our new method of living. The significant increase in human population coupled with excessive use of pollutants has inevitably begun to threaten our God-given physical environment. Numerous species of animals and plants are being destroyed. Even the atmosphere, air and water, are under threat, unless we correct our collective ways. The greatest danger is coming from the most developed societies, whose material standard of living has become unsustainable. The scarcity of unpolluted water is a global problem facing the human race!

By the end of the 20th century, the Green Question had become more important and more urgent. The protection of the environment will, of necessity, become a top priority in the 21st century, that is, if our planet is to sustain us. But can we depend on collective human motivation to correct our behaviour in relation to the environment before it is too late, since motivation is basically negative? We do not tend to behave (collectively) until we feel threatened if we do not! Then it may be too late! The material standard of living of advanced ('developed') societies seems to me to be unsustainable, that is, if we are to give a fair chance to the developing peoples. Perhaps the current (post-2008) economic crash is 'a blessing in disguise'!

13. CONCLUSION

In this chapter an attempt has been made to comment on the social changes that took place, especially in Ireland, during the twentieth century (as experienced and observed by the author). Use has been made of changes in the pivotal institution to explain the macro force influencing change at the structural level. I am aware that many current sociologists and commentators on macro social change interpret social change from other theoretical perspectives. It appears to me that most of our behaviour and structures are socio-culturally determined, i.e. in conformity with the prevailing institutional norms. Hence, human freedom is limited by these basic norms.

In addition to macro social change, particular historical events and international circumstances, which helped to influence the development of Irish society during the twentieth century, were reflected on and noted. Changes in the Christian Churches were given special mention. Voluntary (social, cultural and political) movements during the first quarter of the twentieth century were pivotal in helping to create the new Ireland. The impact of the Second Vatican Council has been critical.

The events that took place in Europe, i.e. the First World War, the Second World War and the setting up of the Common Market (now the European Union), were seen as significant factors in the development of modern Ireland. Of course, Irish society has also made its contribution in the affairs of Europe and the world over the past century.

It is now proposed to comment and reflect on the events of the early years of the twenty-first century in the following pages.

Chapter Nine

THE DAWN OF A NEW CENTURY
2000-2012

1. A NEW CENTURY AND A NEW MILLENNIUM

As expected the new century began with great ceremonial spectacle at midnight on the 31st of December 1999, as we said farewell to the *20th century* and to the *second millennium*. I celebrated the occasion at an ecumenical service in the car park in Murrisk, County Mayo, at the foot of Croagh Patrick (near the Famine Monument). It was organised by the local committee under the leadership of Johnnie Groden. Our prayer service began at the moment of the sunset, which marked the end of the last day of 1999. The next sunrise would be on the morning of New Year's Day 2000 AD. The car park was fairly packed as Catholic and Protestant priests joined in prayer under the Holy Mountain. I felt privileged to be part of the religious celebration at this historic moment in time. I thought of my late father who attended Midnight Mass in St Mary's Parish Church, Westport, to mark the beginning of the twentieth century. On both occasions the people took part in a religious service – to indicate it was the '*Year of the Lord*'.

Other celebrations were more superficial, but impressive in their own way. Of course, television channels competed with one another to capture the imagination of viewers. I always preferred the live performance where we could interact with each other. Television, unfortunately, has had a negative effect on those who become addicted to it, in that it turns people into passive viewers and tends to dictate their agenda for thought. It 'massages' people and limits their capacity for self-recreation. (For that reason, I have refused to have a television set in the family cottage in Loughloon where I spend much of my time when in the West of Ireland. In that same cottage, I have written reports, essays and books without the intrusion of television or website.)

I must admit I went to a friend's house in Drummindoo (Jimmy and

Mary Reynolds) to view the Church celebrations at home in Ireland and in the Vatican on New Year's Night. The Holy Father, Pope John Paul II, gave an exhortation to us all to work for peace and justice in the new millennium. The Catholic and Protestant leaders in Ireland prayed for peace in our land. President Mary McAleese greeted the new millennium with optimism. She noted that it was also a Christian celebration marking two thousand years since the birth of Christ. There were programmes of self-analysis taking place in all Christian Churches. And yet, we were living in the silence of the dark before the dawn.

The demise of the twentieth century with all its varied memories and the arrival of the twenty-first century were in reality an anticlimax. This goes to prove that time, as such, does not exist! As already stated, it is but *'a measure of activity with reference to before and after'* (to paraphrase Aristotle). It is the activity that makes the historic moment significant and not the time. Of course, the ongoing momentum of activity leads to fatigue on the part of the actors in the various institutions and requires constant renewal of personnel and adjustment of norms.

Nevertheless, the occasion of the beginning of the new century was duly celebrated by the public media and by political and religious bodies. Because the end of the twentieth century also marked the end of the second millennium since the birth of Christ, it was to be expected that we would have a spate of prophecies of doom coming from more fundamentalist sources, which tended to reify time and number. Amazingly, we were spared such frantic outbursts. Were we coming of age?

2. THE PRESENT WORLD SCENE

Perhaps the most interesting happenings of the occasion were the various commentaries on the past hundred/thousand years and attempts at looking forward to significant changes in the coming decades. Since most affairs of people are largely socioculturally determined, there was relatively little that could be done to alter the worrying path towards the consolidation of power and influence by the dominant politico-economic (and military) elite societies. By the year 2000 it was possible to identify a number of *dominant world groupings*, i.e. the Western Bloc made up of the United States, the European Union, Canada and the countries of Australia and New Zealand, the Eastern Powers of China and emerging

India. Russia, under President Putin, would show signs of its recovery as a significant power, especially with its wealth in oil and gas. Should the day come when Russia, China and India form an Eastern Alliance, the balance of power would move in their direction. The role of Japan, with its strong United States' orientation could, at that stage, become very strategic. The Middle East, from the Mediterranean to India, appeared to be the most volatile area in the world at the beginning of the 21st century. The demeanour of Israel *vis-à-vis* the Palestinians coupled with the importance of oil reserves in the area constituted a very (politically) explosive situation. The failure of the US and the Western Alliance to bring about stability and social justice in the Middle East forces the question: *Does the West want ongoing unrest and division in the area?* This prevents the emergence of a strong united Middle East power. The North-African states with 'supreme monarch' rulers would feel the pressure to their systems of government.

Other areas of the world in Africa, Latin America and a large part of South Asia were by no means trouble-free. Their potential was yet to be realised. The negative residue of colonialism and globalisation was still stifling the progress of liberation and emancipation. The clash between Islam and Christianity was finding expression in the Northern half of Africa. AIDS, as already noted, was becoming a cause of enormous misery throughout sub-Saharan Africa and elsewhere.

At the same time the Western World was suffering under the weight of its hypochondria, which resulted in grossly expensive health services – privatised to a large extent. All this was happening despite the fact that the greater health-needs were not in the Western World. Life expectancy in sub-Saharan Africa was under fifty years of age, while it was creeping into the mid-to-high seventies in countries like Ireland. It was sad to see so many doctors and nurses from the developing world working in Ireland and elsewhere in the Western World, while the needs in their own countries were much greater.

Multinational companies continued to exploit conditions in the weaker societies. While it could be argued that the drive for 'globalisation' had the potential to be of benefit to all peoples, it seemed to me to be geared to the further strengthening of the strong. Political unrest and famine (due in part to climate change) were causing huge refugee problems and premature death. Rich countries like the European States had adopted a *fortress policy* towards refugees and asylum-seekers from the developing world. *The economic 'success' of neo-liberal, free-market, capitalism was showing no sign of its onward march towards a massive crash within less than a decade. We were living in the false security of perpetual progress, (i.e. until we were to be shocked in 2008).*

One of the issues, which seemed to get much publicity at the end of 1999, was how to get our computer networks to adapt to the new date 2000. Millions were spent to equip our blind machines to serve us in the new millennium. Metrification and decimalisation had come to dominate our lives in weights, volume and spatial measures, and any other area where the 'robotic machines' could intrude. It must be very frustrating for 'Big Brother' that we still honoured non-metric numbers, i.e. seven days in the week, a variety of month lengths, three hundred and sixty-five days (plus one quarter) in the year. One would be forgiven for suspecting that the aim of our 'metric masters' was to dehumanise and depersonalise all weights and measures. God be with the days when we measured horses in 'hands', distances in 'yards' and 'feet' and oats in 'maums'! Bureaucracy and technology are forces for measured uniform conformity, which by degrees strip aspects of the human, the personal and the unique character from normal living. George Orwell had a good grasp of this form of the massification (measurable) of human society. It is practically impossible to resist this insidious and incremental process towards the facilitation of bureaucratic control of people's lives. Eventually, those who control the technology and the computer systems will control the world, if we are not careful. At that stage society will become more 'virtual' and 'less meaningful'!

Some readers may think that these views are 'anti-progressive' and 'anti-scientific'. Such an interpretation would not be true. What I wish to see is all change to be controlled by its benefit to the quality of human life, i.e. its contribution to material comfort and to the culturally meaningful enrichment of the lives of all the people. The latter would also include the whole environmental challenge. Current trends seem to reverse the source of control from the person to abstract measuring norms.

The Republic of Ireland was in a unique position between two major blocs of economic and political power, i.e. the Brussels-centred European Union and the Washington-centred United States of America. Neither bloc seems to me to be that good for our social and cultural health. Our

Tánaiste (at the time), Mary Harney TD, when Minister for Enterprise, Trade and Employment, was reputed to have said that Ireland was 'closer to Boston than to Berlin'. Foreign investment by United States' corporations in the Republic of Ireland has been substantial. The positive influence of the American President, Bill Clinton, in supporting the peace process in Northern Ireland, was evidence of the mutual respect the Irish had for the United States of America and *vice versa*. The ambivalence towards the *American Military Forces' use of Shannon Airport* in relation to the invasion and occupation of Iraq in 2003 should not have surprised the keen observer of diplomatic intrigue and compromise. This does not justify such a breach of Irish neutrality but it helps to explain it. The initial defeat of the *Nice Treaty* (2003) and the later decisive defeat of the *Lisbon Treaty* (2008) were evidence of our growing detachment from, and opposition to, the moves to integrate us into 'the United States of Europe' (USE) by stealth. Nevertheless, the people were pressurised to accept both treaties on second *referenda*. Ideally, we might be wise to welcome an involved-yet-marginal position between the two blocs, i.e. the USE and the USA. This would allow the Irish people to maintain their independence from both blocs, at least to some degree!

One of the welcome features of the increase in economic strength in Ireland during the early years of the 21st century has been the arrival of workers from Eastern Europe and elsewhere in the world. This has changed Ireland radically, i.e. from being an emigrant society to becoming an immigrant one. In time this will (should this trend continue) affect every aspect of our cultural, religious, social and political priorities. The old ethnico-religious divisions between nationalists and unionists, Catholics and Protestants, Republicans and Loyalists are fast becoming less central. It is only a matter of time before the coin will drop for those with old allegiances. The new Irish society will have to be inclusive and culturally pluralist, that is, if we are going to benefit from the cultural richness of our new immigrant citizens. It is very important that we give our ethnically different citizens an opportunity to become familiar with the Irish language and culture and also try to get us indigenous Irish to know migrants' languages and cultures. This has serious implications for the teaching of languages in our schools' systems. Another positive effect will be the presence of well-educated blue-collar workers to correct their demise among the indigenous population.

One of the features about the migrants to Ireland over the past decade and a half is their healthy value system (for the most part). It seems that they are mostly family-centred and children are seen as a priority to them. They also seem to be less secularised than many of our modern Irish of the younger generation. Of course, there are exceptions. The Roman Catholic in-migrants value worship with the community. Also, Muslim immigrants seem to have sober lifestyles, worship regularly and are family-centred. Hopefully, these religious and family values will do something to counter the trends away from religious and family values and practices among many of our upwardly mobile young Irish adults. In a real sense, the foreign workers and their families coming to Ireland in recent years are a welcome 'leaven' to our new pluralist Ireland. The challenge facing the host society is to strengthen our Irish cultural identity and share those aspects, which will help to integrate our new neighbours in a truly pluralist manner. It was timely, therefore, that it had been possible for me to carry out a third national survey of the prejudices of the adult population of the Irish Republic during 2007-08. This research was sponsored by the Irish Government. (The results were published in 2011 under the title, *Pluralism and Diversity in Ireland.*)

3. WESTPORT, A QUALITY DESTINATION FOR VISITORS

To return to the local scene in my home parish of Aughaval (Westport), in the year 2000, I was asked to direct a survey of the town of Westport[8] in County Mayo as 'a quality destination' for visitors (tourists). This was the third such study of Westport that I had done, i.e. one in 1987 and another in 1992. It was decided to survey three populations, namely, the providers of accommodation, the visitors/tourists and a random sample of the adult population of Westport. The commercialisation of holidays had been a fact ever since the industrial revolution and had become a very important industry in Ireland in the post-Second World War period. Four features contributed to our attraction during the years 1960 to 1995, i.e.:

    1. Our prices for accommodation, etc. were relatively cheap;

---

8 The Report on Westport was published in 2002 by WTO, i.e. Mac Gréil, Micheál, *Westport, a Quality Destination.*

2. Our country was particularly of interest to second- and third-generation Irish from the United States, Canada, Australia, New Zealand and from Britain;
3. We were gifted with exotic scenery, moderate climate and a popular Irish culture; and
4. We were a very friendly and welcoming people.

After joining the EEC in 1973 Ireland became part of the *tourist destination* for people from Continental Europe, many of whom had come here to improve their English language skills. During the 1980s and 1990s there was a substantial upgrading and expansion of facilities to cater for the needs of the visitors, e.g. bed-and-breakfast and guest-house accommodation, hotel expansion, the building of self-catering apartments, etc. Semi-state bodies were set up to coordinate the tourist trade. The national airline, *Aer Lingus* and *Irish Shipping* ferry services played an important role in improving access to Ireland for potential visitors/tourists. During a period when the Irish economy was not performing that well for various reasons and emigration was demoralising our people, tourism played a very important role in correcting the socio-economic decline. This was particularly true in the poorer parts of Ireland, whose remoteness made them attractive to the cosmopolitan visitor.

By the end of the 1990s the role of tourism had begun to change in Ireland. The general economic position of Ireland started to improve relatively rapidly and this meant that the cost of living became more expensive. Also, our relative dependence on tourism for income would be greatly reduced. There was a substantial increase in the numbers of Irish people going on holidays abroad. Young Irish men and women were in pursuit of white-collar jobs and fewer numbers were satisfied with work in the catering and accommodation services. In other words, there was a clearly defined move up the social-class-position scale for the majority of the young 'Celtic cubs'. It was an interesting reversal of roles for the Irish to become consumers rather than producers of the touristic services. Some would see this as progress.

The State used various tax incentives to improve the quantity and quality of visitors' accommodation and services. The new areas of growth were apartments and hotels. The rise in bed and breakfast and guest-house accommodation was to peak in the year 2000 and, apparently, began to decline a few years later. The increase in manual jobs created by the upward social mobility of the young Irish worker was to be filled by the arrival of willing and very able 'foreign' workers from Eastern Europe and elsewhere abroad. In a matter of one or two generations many heretofore Irish working-class families and the sons and daughters of small farmers would become middle and upper-middle class professional people. This would follow the pattern of upwardly-mobile sons and daughters of Irish emigrants to Great Britain, the United States and elsewhere. The full significance of this 'mass social change' has not as yet been fully appreciated. Immigrants to Ireland from Eastern Europe, Africa and Asia have been filling many of the 'blue-collar jobs' vacated by the upwardly mobile 'native Irish' young 'Celtic cubs'! *These are the new 'lace-curtain Irish' in Ireland.* Westport was an interesting and representative 'case study' of the effects of socio-economic change on the Irish tourist industry, despite its unique features. (Of course, the post-2008 economic recession would slow down this change somewhat.)

The effects of this most recent social change on visitors to Westport in the 2000-01 survey were becoming evident. There was a trend towards more upmarket visitors. The extraordinary rise in hotel and other categories of accommodation by the year 2000 within the Westport urban catchment area resulted in the following:

Hotel Bed-Nights	1,519	(34.59%)
Apartment Bed-Nights	1,534	(34.93%)
B & B places	1,071	(24.39%)
Hostel Accommodation	268	(6.10%)
Total Bed-Nights	4,392	(100%)

In addition to the above accommodation, quite a number of visitors to Westport stayed with family and friends i.e. returned emigrants. The above figures meant that there was roughly (in 2000) the same number of bed-nights for visitors/tourists as there was for the four thousand or so residents. And yet, Westport was not just an exclusively tourist resort. It had a viable community with employment for practically everyone available for work in factories, administration and other services. The leaders of the *Westport Tourism Organisation* (who had commissioned my research) were very conscious of the importance of maintaining the viability of the local community, while welcoming such a wide range of visitors. In addition to the provision of accommodation, etc. for holidaymakers and tourists, Westport had become a popular location for multi-day conferences, and other such meetings. The latter took place outside the normal holiday season. Musical and other cultural festivals found Westport to be a most congenial location. Off-season holiday breaks for retired Irish citizens were enjoyed in Westport hotels throughout the year. As a member of a tourist delegation from Limavaddy in Northern Ireland pointed out to me, Westport had succeeded in building up an attractive visitor/tourist infrastructure.

The real challenge facing a location like Westport with its outstanding and attractive natural environment was, and is, not to 'overdo' the exploitation of the physical environment. It was very noteworthy that the majority of Westport residents voted for limited urban expansion, i.e. a cap on development, and agreed that *all developments should be community- rather than developer-led*. I fear that the power of money can undermine the protection of the physical environment from the voracious drive for profit in our 'free-market' society. *I tried to warn the citizens in this regard and pointed to the possibility of the stretch of seashore from Rosbeg to Old Head becoming like 'Atlantic City', New Jersey, United States of America, with miles of artificial beaches and areas of concrete roads and summer houses.* The latter would, of course, be reserved for the upwardly mobile rich people. This would reduce almost totally the rugged beauty of the southern border of Clew Bay. I must admit that there are a number of environmentally sensitive bodies, who would resist such a vulgar intrusion, hopefully.

Westport is almost a unique urban community in the West of Ireland. Ever since the 1930s it has provided employment to most of its own community and for quite a number of men and women who commuted to the factories, the port, the mills, the large shops, *et cetera*. Much credit is due to the policy of local investment by the local industrialists and commercial families in attracting manufacturing industries to the town. Of course, rationalisation and profit-seeking outside Westport was to become stronger than the original '*Sinn Féin*' industrial policy of placing priority on the local manufacturing jobs. Some would argue, however, that wages could have been better in the 1930s, 1940s, 1950s and 1960s. I was disappointed at the speed with which our indigenous industries were transferred to countries of the Third World to avail of relatively cheaper wages and raw materials in the latter quarter of the 20th century. Entrepreneurs switched their manufacturing jobs to countries of extremely low wages. This is a widespread capitalist, free-market policy, which, at the end of the day, is counter-progressive in the human sense. Our entry into the Common Market facilitated the double-edged exploitation, i.e. of the cheap wages abroad and the loss of blue-collar jobs at home in Westport and elsewhere in Ireland.

Of course, Westport benefits from a fairly strong multinational industry, i.e. Allergan, which has provided good pay and conditions for up to a thousand local workers over a number of years. But, what would happen if the foreign owners and directors were to decide that it would be commercially more viable to transfer the plant to a country with cheaper labour, even within the European Union? It would be more secure if a number of indigenous employers, including local and central government, were to provide socially useful and personally satisfying jobs (in addition to Allergan).

Since the collapse of the Iron Curtain in 1989, the erroneous belief has become popular that *the State's ownership of some of the means of production is wrong and unproductive*. We saw in Ireland how false and deceptive this pro-capitalist belief was, i.e. the privatisation of our telephone communications systems. The European Union has, in an almost deceptive manner, denied the State the right to invest in such companies as *Aer Lingus,* thereby forcing their ultimate privatisation. The European Union has, in my opinion, become a capitalist club in everything but name! And this makes many very influential and articulate protagonists of the free-market quite pleased to herald the demise of State-owned industry. In my opinion, services such as banks, vital communication industries, electricity suppliers, water and sewerage services, forestry and other such key industries should be under public control, whose management would be responsible to the people. (The collapse of the economic boom in 2008 was partly due to its artificial rise because of inadequate regulation in the Republic of Ireland and at the EU level. The recent imposition of the selling of State assets by the *Troika* is degrading our society.)

It has always been problematic for me to integrate international capitalism and democracy because of the anonymity of money and the undemocratic power of business – both in manufacturing industry, commercial and agri-business. On the other hand, one has the contradiction between rigid bureaucratic control and democratic power. It is very difficult to establish and maintain democracy, which gives power to the people. Perhaps Alexis de Tocqueville got it right when he saw democracy working best in a situation where *central authority, local authority and voluntary organisations* were equally balanced in a countervailing exchange of dialogue. In Ireland, the weakest leg in the three-legged stool of democracy has been real 'local government'. In social partnership, which was so important for the planning of economic and social 'progress', we had a two-legged stool again, without the voice of local government. In Ireland, because of the powers given to county and city managers, who are civil servants in the pay of central government, the role of the elected local councillors is very limited. Hence, the grossly imbalanced (regionally) development of Ireland. (In 2012, it had been decided by central government to diminish 'local authority' further by centralising water services.)

Returning to the study of Westport as a 'quality destination', which was defined as *'a place and a community which provide the visitor or tourist with a holiday experience that is attractive, enjoyable, relaxing, culturally and socially enriching and of high quality as regards material comforts and needs which are reasonably priced. It is also a community where local people are friendly, courteous and welcoming.'* Some time was spent on this comprehensive definition and various elements or notes of it were used as the criteria by which to assess Westport as a quality destination. (In June 2012, Westport was judged to be the best place in Ireland to live – see *The Irish Times*, 25th June 2012.)

Westport Tourism Organisation and other bodies who had adopted a more critical view of how Westport had and was developing as a tourist destination deserved great credit for keeping the area a quality destination and adapted successfully to the changing needs without lowering the quality of the experience for visitors. It was clear that it would be very necessary to continue monitoring social change and the rise of affluence, which could 'vulgarise' the district and do irreparable damage to the social, cultural and physical environment. It was clear that the bed-and-breakfast and guest houses, which were an essential dimension of the mixed Westport experience, could easily be swamped by an over-dominant and efficiently organised local hotel confederation. Hostels and camping accommodation had declined since 1992 and this was to be regretted because most young foreigners were introduced to an area like Westport via camping and staying in hostels. Traffic problems were becoming acute but some plans were being worked out. The need to protect the physical environment from the intrusion of development was pointed out. Activities (indoor and outdoor) would be very important in the future. The results of the survey were published in a special report in 2002.

It was around midday on the 11th September 2001 my research assistant, Eoghan Murphy, called and informed me of the 'bombing' (by the deliberate crashing of three passenger jet aircraft into the buildings in New York and Washington by suicide pilots) and said to me in his Waterford accent – '*This is something big, very big!!*' or words to that effect. I then went to a television set and actually witnessed the second plane crashing into the second tower and creating the collapse in flames of both buildings. We were witnessing an outrageous act of cruel brutality and murder of innocent people. *Ar dheis Dé go raibh a n-anamacha uaisle*.

The instant TV reporting was similar to the CNN reports on the horrific bombings of Baghdad in the first Iraq War. Of course, the two were part of a pattern in which innocent people died. The 'September eleventh incident' was different in that it was on American soil, the home ground of the superpower. The failure of the United States to intervene and prevent the attack was evidence of the fallibility of its intelligence to anticipate this form of attack. This must have increased the paranoia of the people and made them disposed to accept the most stringent of new counter measures. Because of the terrible events in the US we ended the interviewing of visitors, having gathered information from over nineteen hundred respondents. Two days earlier, Westport won the National Tidy Towns' Award. (I will be returning to the '9/11' incident itself later.)

The challenges facing communities like Westport in 2001, (which has been one of the most successful host communities for visitors in Ireland) came from the rise of economic wealth in the local community and the decline of Westport people willing to engage in the personal services of catering and accommodating visitors. Most of our young people, as noted earlier, were not willing to be 'blue-collar' workers in the personal services and were opting for 'white-collar' careers, which they judged to be more prestigious. The exit from small farming of young people was but a prelude to this change, which was now becoming evident in the so-called 'tourist industry' at this time.

The commercial impact of increased numbers of visitors had been a bit too much for many locals. Our major shopping street, Bridge Street, which had quite a range of grocery, clothing, victualler shops, etc. was gradually turned into a street of exotic pubs, boutiques, cafés, fancy-goods and souvenir shops, etc., geared for the visitor trade. *One could not now buy a loaf of bread on Bridge Street.* Also, at Westport Quay the former warehouses were turned into apartments to attract self-catering visitors. Cafés, restaurants and tourist-servicing shops and stores replaced the fairly active centre of exports and imports by 'tramp-streamers'. The harbour that was once a commercial and industrial haven was now to be wholly transformed into a leisure/pleasure location. A case was made to build 'a marina' for the yachts of the rich (new and old). Pleasure-cum-leisure activity was gradually becoming a feature of the commercialisation of western beauty spots.

Gentrification of the West of Ireland could soon replace the necessary drive to develop the local communities and towns where men and women would be able to earn a livelihood in all-year-round jobs. A 'gentrified' West of Ireland without jobs for its people, except in tourism and the environmental-protection services, would not be socially viable. Of course, the jobs provided should be environmentally friendly. The West needed balanced and sustainable industrial and commercial development. At the present time (2014 AD) it is difficult to predict how things will turn out. The current economic downturn will put the people to the test. The material standard of living seemed to me to be too high in terms of housing, holidays, motor cars, etc. prior to 2008. *There needs to be some 'curtailment of the consumer's choice of the privileged'* (to quote from Karl Mannheim) *to enable an advance in the public welfare of all the people and of all peoples!* Otherwise, the gap between the rich and the poor grows too wide and, in such a grossly unjust world, strife and revolt will continue to fester. The latest survey of Westport as a 'quality destination', which was carried out in 2011-12 measures the impact of the 2008 crisis. The report, *Westport Eleven-Twelve*, was published in the spring of 2013. The impact of the economic depression is reflected on in this document.

4. THE 9/11 NIGHTMARISH TRAGEDY AND ITS CONSEQUENCES

The nightmarishly tragic event of the eleventh of September 2001 was carried out by followers of Osama Bin Laden, who commandeered passenger airplanes with passengers on board and deliberately crashed them into the World Trade Centre and the Pentagon. A fourth plane believed to have been set for the White House in Washington was forcibly crash-landed *en route* by the brave revolt of doomed passengers on board. The event stunned the whole world and exposed the vulnerability of even the world's superpower to the unpredictable attack by highly sophisticated 'terrorists'. This was the first time in more than one hundred years (apart from Pearl Harbour) that the United States was attacked at home in an organised conflict. The first reaction was shock, horror and even disbelief in the United States. The whole Western World expressed solidarity with the people killed and injured by the attack. In a short time feelings turned into a sense of paranoia and collective insecurity in the USA. This developed into anger and rage in the United States, and a strong demand to have the attack avenged was soon on the agenda. The immediate target was the Taliban regime in Afghanistan, where Bin Laden and his chiefs were supposed to have been protected.

The attack on Afghanistan (following the 9/11 attack) took place under the leadership of the United States' very powerful security forces. The tacit support of the Pakistan Government was achieved and this facilitated an all-out attack on Kabul and other centres of Taliban strength. The war itself opened with the usual Star-Wars bombardment of urban targets, communications networks, etc. by a most powerful array of conventional weapons of mass destruction unleashed on a relatively undeveloped society. It was hoped to capture or kill Bin Laden and his lieutenants. The regime was defeated but the overall victory has not as yet been won (although Osama Bin Laden was later assassinated in Pakistan in 2011). The Taliban regime was so fundamentalist that they had very few friends even among Muslim nations. The obscenity of the visual reporting on round-the-clock television of systematic bombing and killing of people of Afghanistan and the destruction of their homes and local infrastructure showed *how really barbaric we still were – 2000 years after the coming of Christ – and was feeding the viewers' primitive voyeurism.* Viewers were not unlike crowds watching public executions in earlier times. Will we ever learn? It would drive one to total despair or to total commitment to Christian pacifism. The outcome of the response-slaughter was the partial defeat of the Taliban regime and the setting up of a conforming local parliament and government, which appeared to be an improvement on the extreme Taliban. Unfortunately, the ongoing violent activity has continued and shows little sign of ending.

But the agenda for military aggression by the United States in the region was far from over. A second attack on Iraq was launched on Good Friday 2003 by the United States Military Regime aided and abetted by the United Kingdom. Ostensibly, the reason was the supposed possession of nuclear and biological weapons of mass destruction by the Government of Saddam Hussein (which, incidentally, was not true). The invasion went ahead without the sanction or approval of the United Nations. The United States Government, under the presidency of George W Bush, seemed to have long since decided to invade Iraq and remove President Saddam Hussein by force. The real reasons have never been stated. They were probably related to a number of issues, i.e. protection of the State of Israel; the guarantee of the supply of oil; and the growing fear of the rise of militant Islam. It could also be the early signs of United States' colonial ambitions in the Middle East and the US leaders felt *the need for establishing regimes, which would be accommodating to its interests*. Every superpower in history has had such ambitions. Islam seems to have replaced communism as the 'ideology' to be curtailed. The real tragedy is the *counter-productivity* of the United States' strategy and tactics.

The more aggressive and penal the approach, the more determined and zealous the militant defenders of Islam and their national territories of the Middle East become. It is not possible today to defeat totally with military weapons or with inhumane sanctions the will of a people to be free and independent. At the end of the day it is the vast numbers of innocent people and civilian populations who are forced to pay the supreme price for high-tech weapons. We have seen this in Ireland, where the military power of the United Kingdom was unable to defeat the paramilitary actions of a few hundred militant republicans and loyalists. Much of Britain's military and police activity was counterproductive. But the strong are the most impervious to the need to negotiate and remedy the causes of the insurgency. Someday, there will have to be a negotiated peace in the Middle East, which will be based on social justice and mutual recognition of religious and cultural differences. The sooner the better for all of us! But, would a united Middle East be seen as a greater threat to western ambitions? As already stated, it seems to me that a divided Middle East would be more acceptable to the US and its closest allies.

The repercussions of the attacks on the New York Financial Centre and on the Pentagon Offices in Washington on the 11th September 2001, plus the successive invasions of Afghanistan and Iraq on the whole world were for the most part negative. Draconian legislation and restrictive movement of people followed, not to mention the occasional acts of terror, e.g. the railway bombings in Spain and London, which have led to an all-round rise in collective paranoia. The lowering of civil liberties' standards and acceptance of literally anything in the name of 'defence against terrorism' have resulted in the disregard for the rights of prisoners and the justification of summary execution of suspected 'terrorists' by the United States and Israel even in territories or countries outside their own jurisdiction. Also, the United States opted out of recognition of the International Criminal Court, having been, at the same time, anxious to see to it that other leaders who were suspected of violating human rights were sent to The Hague (see page 309 above). In the United Kingdom a raft of emergency legislation was enacted to counter terrorism. By degrees there would be a slide towards highly policed society with the electronic storage of information on most citizens, all in the name of security. Thank God, we in the Republic of Ireland have remained a relatively free society so far.

5. THE SECOND WAR IN IRAQ

The threatened War in Iraq brought widespread protest around the World during late 2002 and early 2003. I had the privilege of being invited to speak at the launch of 'Westport against the War' (in Heneghan's Pub, Westport on 6th February 2003) and to march in the mass demonstration (100,000 people) in Dublin. I also addressed meetings in County Kildare. My reason for becoming active was inspired by justice and the folly of the military option. As a member of *Pax Christi* and *Amnesty International*, it was imperative for me to act in support of the strongest possible pacifist stand being adopted by *'neutral and non-aligned' Ireland*! The abuse of Shannon Airport to ferry troops and prisoners to and from the battle zone was very embarrassing for Irish peace-loving people. *Our protest against the war was not anti-American.* In fact, it was in solidarity with those citizens of the US, who were adamantly opposed to what was going on in their name. In the end, the only way to change US policy would have to be from within the US itself, that is, unless things escalated to a point of no return. When I was in Kent State University in the mid 1960s and in Ann Arbor University in 1974, I witnessed the courage and strength of the American people in forcing their Government (and the military-industrial elite) to withdraw from the crazy adventure in Vietnam.

In early 2006 there was a fear and growing unease that George W Bush would dig his country in deeper in the 'killing fields' (or should I say, desert plains) of Iran. He would then have united the Shia and the Sunni Muslims as well as the Arabs and the Persians, against him. How would Palestine, North Africa and Indonesia react? Russia, China and India would also have much reason to worry in the event of all-out hostilities between the Arab-Muslim alliance and the West (including Israel). Lesser events had been the precipitating factor in world conflict. The countries of Western Europe and Scandinavia would need to ponder their reaction. One shudders even to think of the level of potential destruction, which could be inflicted on the world should we not be able to establish some modicum of justice and mutual cultural and religious respect between peoples. The technology of war and the lethal capacity of weapons of mass destruction (conventional and nuclear) are so frightening that peaceful coexistence is the only viable option. The orgy of violence following 9/11 was ill-advised and leaves the world a less secure place.

If only the same amount of human energy, economic investment, research efforts (in both the human and natural sciences) and political and religious commitment were devoted to the creation of a pluralist global society, which would ensure a totally fair distribution of goods and services as was being wasted on the protection of privilege, we would be a much safer and culturally richer human race. *At present there is too much injustice and hatred in the world for a lasting peace.* The United Nations has been stymied by the superpower(s) for far too long. It appears to me that the only world structure likely to guarantee international justice would be *an effective and reformed* United Nations. Nothing less has any chance of procuring peace with justice. The current United Nations is too dependent on the 'super' five, i.e. United States, Russia, China, France and the United Kingdom, which is a distortion of history. I would love to think that the weakness of the current system would force a change in the UN. It would be better, in my opinion, if the headquarters of the United Nations were located in a secure neutral non-aligned country rather than in the territory of a superpower.

6. RESTORATION OF WESTERN RAIL CORRIDOR POSSIBLE

So much for global politics for the moment! Let me return to the West of Ireland. One of the most satisfying developments of the early years of the new century in Ireland for me was the announcement by the Minister for Transport, Mr Martin Cullen TD, on the 1st November 2005 of the Government's decision to reopen the Western Rail Corridor from Ennis to Collooney in two phases, i.e. phase one Ennis, County Clare, to Claremorris in County Mayo and phase two from Claremorris in County Mayo to Collooney in County Sligo. As I have commented earlier, a special Western Joint RDO Railway Committee (representing Counties, Sligo, Mayo, Roscommon, Galway, Leitrim, Clare, Limerick and Tipperary North Riding) was set up in 1979 to campaign for the restoration of this cross-radial rail link. On the demise of the RDOs in 1987, a special Western Inter-County Railway Committee carried on the fight. Two Reports were carried out in 1981 and 1992 for the committee in support of the project, but their findings fell on deaf ears!

It appeared very clear to me that neither the Department of Transport nor *Córas Iompair Éireann* were that interested in reviving the line at the time. In fact, there was gross neglect by all governments in Ireland up until the 1990s of any serious investment in railways (with the exception of the electrification of the Dart Line in Dublin). The only victory our committee achieved during the 'dark years' was the commitment by the late Mr Séamus Brennan TD, when Minister for Transport in the early 1990s, to preserve the track and thoroughfare in public ownership until the Government had made a considered decision in relation to the rail link between Limerick and Collooney in County Sligo. Our committee was made up of county councillors and county development officers and three non-elected persons. I was one of the latter because of my call for restoration of the Collooney to Claremorris line in 1979 and the fact that I had surveyed potential use of the rail link and presented the first report in 1981. Since 1987 I have been the Honorary Joint-Secretary of the Western Inter-County Railway Committee.

By 1997 there were optimistic signs from government of support for railways and it was becoming clear that Transport Minister, Mary O'Rourke TD, had committed a large capital budget to railways in Dublin, i.e. *An LUAS*, and throughout the country. The relaying of new welded tracks on the mainlines, and the acquisition of new passenger rolling stock were agreed. The 'sun was rising' again for rail! But, alas, our track (from Collooney to Ennis[9]) was not included in *Iarnród Éireann's* (Irish Rail) part of the National Development Plan of 1997. The idea of a cross-radial (now Dublin-centred) major rail infrastructure seemed to be summarily dismissed by Dublin bureaucracy and their so-called experts. The decline of the Western regions always appeared to me to be a case of strategic neglect. Would it interfere with the 'gentrification' concept? In fact, in the 1997 plan, the Dublin to Westport line was downgraded from the status of main line! Nevertheless, the line has operated as an inter-city mainline since 1997 with four trains each way every day.

As already noted, at a significant meeting of the Western Inter-County Railway Committee at Knock Airport, on the 4th November 1997 the newly appointed Junior Minister for the *Gaeltacht* and Rural Affairs, Mr Éamon Ó Cuív TD, (grandson of the late Éamon de Valera) put new life into the Committee and encouraged us to pursue our campaign for a restoration of the Western Rail strategic corridor as a high-quality line, i.e. welded track on reinforced concrete sleepers. There should be no 'cap-in-hand' mentality.

Minister Ó Cuív TD, met our Committee again in the Knock House Hotel on the occasion of the launch of his *Clár* development support programme (10th November 2001). *Clár* identified communities which had lost more than half of their population between 1926 and 1996 and singled them out for special advantage with regard to development

---

9 The section of the line from Limerick to Ennis had been restored for regular service in 1988. We had to wait a further 22 years until the Ennis to Athenry section was opened in 2010!

support including infrastructural development. It so happened that the Western Rail strategic corridor went through *Clár* areas from Collooney to within one mile of Tuam. By July 2002 a new momentum of support was gathering force, i.e. from the County and City Development Boards, Border / Midlands / Western Assembly (BMW), regional authorities, the political parties and the local authorities.

The Government had commissioned consultants Booz, Allen and Hamilton to prepare a National Rail Strategy for inclusion in a broader national development plan. We were invited, among many other groups, to address these experts in a hotel in Sligo on the 19th July 2002. It was quite superficial and could not pass for serious consultation of a group with our 'track record'. We were never taken that seriously by the department. The civil servants did not seem to respond to the views of the people. Was it a case of the 'tyranny of superior knowledge'? Still, our committee did expect to be consulted seriously. It was remarkable that all the economic, social and cultural strategies published by City and County Development Boards from Donegal to Cork in 2002 supported the revival of the Western Rail Corridor from Ennis to Sligo.

In November 2002, *Iarnród Éireann* cut the crossover link (at Athenry) to the Northern line to Tuam/Claremorris/Collooney. This, in effect, meant that the corridor was broken. *The reaction was swift, vocal and public.* I doubted the legality of such an action by CIE without consultation. It stirred up more public support for the restoration of the Collooney to Limerick rail link. It became a *felix culpa* (a happy fault). On the 16th December 2002, our Committee met the Minister for Transport, Mr Séamus Brennan TD, (on the occasion of opening the N17 road bypass at *Cnoc Mhuire*). He expressed support for the Corridor and promised that his department would work in greater cooperation with our Committee on the case for the project. This was later (June 2004) to be translated into our participation in the McCann Committee. Minister Séamus Brennan TD, was later transferred to another department and replaced by Minister Martin Cullen TD. When the history of the restored Western Rail Corridor is written, the contribution of Minister Séamus Brennan TD, to its revival will merit a most positive mention.

The publication of the Booz, Allen and Hamilton Report, *Strategic Rail Review* early in 2003, while mentioning our project, did not commend the Western Rail Corridor. It seemed to exaggerate the costs and, by implication, make it financially prohibitive. Still, it was in the overall a positive report for the future development of the Irish Rail Network and the improvement of railways in Dublin, but it lacked an understanding of the need for 'front-loading' investment in railways in the West of Ireland. A special conference was called in Claremorris by the Western Development Commission to respond to the *Strategic Rail Review* (Report). Minister Séamus Brennan had already intimated that he did not necessarily agree with all of the recommendations of the Report. Naturally, we interpreted that to mean that the Western Rail Strategic Corridor was still a possibility. The conference was extremely critical of the treatment of the corridor by the consultants. Incidentally, I have always believed that the decision to reopen the railway from Limerick to Collooney would have to be a political (Government) decision and would not come from the bureaucracy or from consultants engaged by the department. On the 17th October 2003, I was invited to address an Inter-Regional Transportation Conference in Tralee on the case for the Western Rail Corridor. It was the annual conference of the Associations of Irish Regions.

In April 2003 a new group, West-on-Track, was set up involving voluntary community organisations along the track from Sligo to Limerick. It was led by two very dynamic leaders, Colman Ó Raghallaigh and Martin Cunniffe of Claremorris. I was invited to become its patron, which I accepted. Frank Dawson, Deputy County Manager of Galway (and chair of the National Network of Directors of County Development Boards) and one of the most knowledgeable members of the Inter-County Railway Committee, supported the 'West-on-Track'. It succeeded in a relatively short time in raising the community consciousness of this valuable people's rail infrastructure. West-on-Track complemented the largely behind-the-scenes work of the Western Inter-County Railway Committee. We now had the ideal recipe for the final push for the railway and, very soon, politicians of all parties would feel the lobbying pressure of representatives of every community along the track – all eighteen of them. The West-on-Track leaders were experts in raising public support. They were invited to send representatives to our general meetings on the Western Inter-County Railway Committee. In September 2003 Colmán Ó Raghallaigh and I were given the Taisce Award for the 'best transportation initiative of the year'. (We were given the awards because of the work of our respective committees.)

After the local government election of 2004, Cllr Michael McGreal (Roscommon County Council) was elected Chairperson of the Western Inter-County Railway Committee, on the resignation of Martin Joe O'Toole (former Senator TD, and County Councillor) from Kilsallagh, Westport, County Mayo. On the 13th of April 2004, Minister Séamus Brennan TD, visited the railway stations on the corridor at Tubbercurry, Charlestown, Kiltimagh, Claremorris and Tuam. It was further evidence of his support for the 'Western Rail Corridor'. He also invited Mr Pat McCann (CEO of Jury-Doyle Hotels) to chair a working party, which would investigate the case for restoring the corridor. Both the Western Inter-County Railway Committee and West-on-Track were given three places each on the Committee. The Committee was set up in June 2004. Minister Brennan's successor, Mr Martin Cullen TD, (Waterford) continued the Brennan policy with regard to the corridor.

In May 2005, Mr Pat McCann sent a Report (known as the *McCann Report*) in his capacity as chairman to Minister Cullen recommending restoration on a phased basis: (1) Ennis to Athenry; (2) Athenry to Tuam; (3) Tuam to Claremorris; (4) Claremorris to Collooney. Three and four would be conditional on the securing of sustainable freight traffic and on further evaluation in 2008 respectively. A special seminar was called in Breaffy House Hotel, Castlebar, to evaluate the *McCann Report* on the 13th May 2005, at which I was asked to reply to Minister Cullen's Response which was positively cautious, as if he was still trying to persuade CIE, *Iarnród Éireann* and the Civil Service to come on side. Others were more critical of McCann. On reflection, McCann was very clever and went as far as the establishment could take at that stage. The Minister was preparing a 'Transport Envelope', which would cover rail infrastructural capital investment for the following ten years. This would later be known as 'Transport 21'. Our task now was quite clear to me, namely, how to get our project into the 'Transport Envelope', against the opposition of some powerful voices in the Civil Service and in CIE. I had a number of meetings (with Minister Éamon Ó Cuív, Cllr. Michael McGreal, Mr Terry Byrne, Frank Dawson, Martin Cunniffe, Colman O'Raghallaigh and others), so that we could prepare a strategy. In the meantime, *An Taoiseach*, Mr Bertie Ahern TD, announced in the *Dáil* (in reply to a Parliamentary question) *that the money would be available to restore the Western Rail Corridor once the Minister for Transport had analysed the McCann Report.*

The Western Inter-County Railway Committee met in Tuam on Friday, 29th July 2005 and discussed the *McCann Report*. There was great concern that McCann would be used to limit the restoration from Ennis via Athenry to Tuam. We agreed to the following motion:

> *The following was agreed unanimously by the members present:*
>
> (1) *The McCann Report was welcomed as a significant and supportive document for the reopening of the Western Rail Corridor from Collooney to Ennis which would be a most valuable transport infrastructure and would provide concrete proof of the State's commitment to balanced regional development.*
>
> (2) *It was further agreed the line should be reopened in two phases, namely,*
>
> > *Phase One – from Claremorris to Ennis;*
> > *Phase Two – from Collooney to Claremorris.*
>
> (3) *It was also agreed that during the construction of Phase One (i.e. from Claremorris to Ennis) CIE would carry out the work of renewing the fencing, clearing the overgrowth from the track and reopening the drains in the section of the line from Collooney to Claremorris.*

The above motion summarises the current strategy agreed in regard to the restoration of the Western Rail Corridor.

It was decided that the above response would be communicated to the government and made known to the public. Minister Éamon Ó Cuív TD, who called in on the Tuam meeting, agreed that the response was reasonable and agreed to give a copy to *An Taoiseach*. West-on-Track and the Western Inter-County Railway Committee kept up the pressure on politicians from all parties. On the 5th October 2005, at 7.00pm a briefing session was called in The Earl of Kildare Hotel, Kildare Street, Dublin 2, to explain the case for the Western Rail Corridor, to which all TDs, senators and ministers from the Western counties were invited. The session was addressed by Frank Dawson (Galway County Council) and Gerry Finn, (Director of the Border, Midland and Western Regional Assembly). There was a reasonably good attendance. Practically all present expressed support and optimism. Still, nothing was delivered.

We were forced to await the announcement on the 1st November 2005.

The scene for the grand launch of Transport 21, a 3.4 billion euro capital investment over ten years took place in Dublin Castle with great pomp and ceremony. Everyone who was anybody in transportation was invited. Of course, nobody from either the Western Inter-County Railway Committee or from West-on-Track was invited to 'join the suits'. On the Sunday before the Tuesday (1st November 2005) I received a phone call from Minister Éamon Ó Cuív TD, to suggest that we have our own launch (of whatever would be offered to us) at the railway station in Claremorris. Since I had to be in Dublin on Pioneer business, we decided that I would take the midday train from Dublin to Claremorris and the Minister would greet me as I arrived. I would come out the second door of the first carriage. I immediately rang around to assemble the thirty plus county councillors of our committee. West-on-Track was also notified. The Minister's office arranged for a full array of television and radio reporters (in Irish and English).

The Government had agreed to restore the Western Rail Corridor in two phases over nine years (at a maximum). I was literally thrilled. What was dead as an infrastructure would come alive. The Government at last had listened to the people and to their local representatives. Of course, there was dissatisfaction with the unnecessary length of time it would take. When Jim Fahy, RTÉ, asked me if I was unhappy about the length of time, I said to him *that it was not a question for today. It was something we would have to negotiate tomorrow. Today we rejoiced in a most positive decision made by the Government in the interests of the West of Ireland.* He seemed not to like my answer. But, I reminded him that when he had interviewed me in Castlebar in 1981 for RTÉ at the launch of our first Report, he had alleged that *I was quixotic* if I thought the cross-radial link would be restored. *'You should now eat your words,'* I suggested! (This I said to him in jest.) He took it well but edited it out of the news report. It was, indeed, a great occasion. Later in the year, Brian Cowen TD, the Minister for Finance named the project in his Budget for 2006.

The reason why I have recorded so much detail about the restoration of the railway is to put on record the difficulty people in the West of Ireland have had in getting their rights from native Irish Governments. (At times one would be forgiven for thinking that the *'Irish Government in Dublin'* was *de facto* the *'Dublin Government in Ireland'*.) What we have succeeded in achieving is a step towards the emancipation of the regions from the centralised, radial and Dublin-centred focus of all Irish life. Via the Western Rail Corridor people from the Western Regions can travel by train to other regions without having to go through Dublin. This symbolises a new decentralisation of movement. Also, our project proved that the people could and had to win their infrastructure by working together (voluntary and statutory) for their rights and for the common good of all. Needless to say, the campaign must continue until we have the maximum use of the line to the benefit of all the people. Great credit is due to many people for their support and stamina. The professionalism of West-on-Track in making the case had impressed even our critics. The support of the local media (radio and print) proved most valuable. Of course, there would be much to do before the Rail Corridor was restored. Those who opposed the project would try to delay and obstruct its delivery. (While the decision of 1st November 2005 is still in place in 2014, only the phase Ennis to Athenry has been delivered. The remainder was deferred in the 2013 Budget.)

7. PIONEERS AND THE ABUSE OF ALCOHOL

The growth of the commercialisation of leisure was one of the most characteristic changes in recent times in Ireland, as was the new monopoly of the lounge bar for indoor recreation in many of our towns and villages in the case of certain age groups and social classes. The drinks industry has been 'on the ball' to capitalise on this new extra-home (and at-home) recreation and leisure. According as people spent less time recreating themselves at home, they joined various clubs and recreational groupings. Many of these clubs and groupings are social-class-position determined, e.g. Golf Clubs, Tennis Clubs, Bridge Clubs and Yacht Clubs (for those near the ocean, sea or lakes) and constitute structured peer environments for the middle and upper-middle class. Working and lower-middle class tend to follow football, fishing and just enjoy passive leisure in pub relaxation. The supporters of Gaelic Football and Hurling seem to be both middle and working class. Soccer attracts a similar backing while rugby is more upper- middle class (except in Munster). The arrival of television facilitated more passive recreation at home, mainly for parents and younger people.

The rise of support for group-sport was indicative of social change, i.e. towards a more urbanised (at least in mentality) industrial and post-industrial society in more densely populated living quarters. Some social psychologists would see competitive group games as providing 'legitimised outlets' for pent-up aggression arising from the stresses of modern living in industrial and post-industrial largely urbanised societies. Hill 16 in Croke Park, when Dublin was playing, provided a good proof of the psychologists' theory. It was a safe outlet for displaced aggression.

One dimension of modern lifestyles which has been of special interest to me, because of my role as Chairperson of the Board of Management of the *Pioneer Abstinence Association of the Sacred Heart (PTAA)*, has been the alarming growth in the abuse of alcoholic drink, especially by teenagers and young adults (male and female). With the rise of affluence and the decline in self-discipline and self-control, '*drinking to get drunk*' seemed to be the aim of a number of our very foolish young people – male and female. Contributing to this alarming situation among young people are the availability of so much disposable income (prior to 2009), the rise in consumerism and the lack of control or influence of parents or wiser people on the behaviour of young people. Soap operas on television seem to present a problematic domestic scene at times and a hectic pub life. The popular culture into which young people are attracted or 'seduced' is quite *anomic*, i.e. normless. The more popular print media exploit this culture. Clever advertisements for alcoholic drinks also exploit the association between young people drinking and sexual intimacy. Also the association of alcohol and sport continues, despite its possible destructive influences.

The State, far from curtailing the situation, seemed at times to be adding to it in relation to the liberalisation of liquor licensing laws, especially in relation to off-licences, supermarkets, nightclubs and late-night drinking in pubs, hotels and various clubs around the country. When Micheál Martin TD, was Minister for Health and Children, we had hoped that, at last, the State would do something concrete to curtail access to alcoholic drink by young people, i.e. the Task Force Reports on Alcohol. But, alas, later policy seemed to have taken a different line in relation to the abuse of drink and had left almost everything mainly to the control of 'self-regulation' by the drinks industry! Unfortunately, self-regulation has not been that effective.

As said elsewhere, *we (in the PTAA) had been hoping for a test case in Court which would hold the drinks industry responsible for its proportionate share in the damage the excessive use of alcoholic drink had caused to people's personal, domestic and social life.* Because of the damage caused by drink there is, in my opinion, a *prima facie* case against advertising of drinks in the media or on public signboards. The success of cases against tobacco companies is a good precedent.

The PTAA, in March 2000, adopted a policy (motion) to give priority to the promotion of the juvenile (8-11 years) and the young pioneer (12-18 years) in response to the rise in young people drinking irresponsibly. We encouraged them to take up life without drink until they were (at least) eighteen years old. The National Youth Committee and all units were advised to make this their priority. Some progress had been made during the first six years. At times, the National Youth Committee seemed to be more interested in 'youth affairs' than in 'youth work'. The latter was to be its main mission. As happened in many youth organisations, some leaders seemed attracted to the political power game of 'youth affairs'. This was understandable.

The support of schools and colleges is central. There are, however, growing difficulties in getting into schools to organise or spread the news. The bishops have relaxed their efforts to persuade young people to take the Confirmation pledge. Child protection policy, which is understandable and necessary, has led to a serious withdrawal of voluntary adult support for the under-eighteens. Parents are not that much available to help out either – so many young people are being left to their own devices. The lack of non-alcoholic youth-work and youth-leisure outlets in many, if not most, local communities, has been very disappointing. In my visitation (2006-08) to 994 centres of the PTAA, I have recommended that each parish should support a Pioneer Club in the second-level school that its students attend in order to counter peer pressure to drink. This promotion from the grass roots is more likely to succeed than that from higher Committees of the PTAA. The work of No Name Clubs is highly to be commended.

The pub, until recently, has had almost the monopoly of extra-home indoor leisure facilities in the vast majority of small towns and villages in Ireland! Still, it would not be right to blame the publicans for all the abuse of alcohol, many of whom try to prevent it. The main problem is the lack of alternative recreational facilities, which would be attractive to young people. We all must accept a share of blame for this neglect of our young people. The Pioneer Association acts as an organisation, which tries to encourage young people to take up life without any dependence on drink. The PTAA urges all adults to be moderate in their use of alcoholic drink. We also ask young people to abstain from drugs for life. The danger of easy access to alcoholic drink in 'off-licences' is, in my opinion, much more conducive to the abuse of alcohol than are public houses. The latter provides control of over-indulgence as well as being suitable for moderate social drinking.

The growth of the PTAA in Africa has been most encouraging. It was calculated in 2004 that there are about 250,000 Pioneers in Africa at present. In Kenya, Zambia, Zimbabwe, Uganda, Tanzania, Namibia, South Africa and Nigeria, which I visited that year, there seems to be great fervour among the local Pioneer leaders. In South Africa, where the association was established in the early twentieth century, centres there operated more on the lines of their counterparts in Ireland. In Nigeria there was an obvious disruption caused by the Biafran war. The Ibo people were defeated and the missionary church suffered setbacks. Nevertheless, there is still a good core spirit in the Ibo dioceses. Lagos and other non-Ibo dioceses have strong enclaves of Pioneers.

I visited the Pioneers in each of the eight countries mentioned above in 2004. The visitation took seventy-eight days with over one hundred meetings. I spent most of the time in the rural parishes and stayed in the various seminaries and religious houses. The Legion of Mary and Irish Missionary Congregations and Orders were the initial stimuli for the spread of the PTAA in Africa. It is now sufficiently established to generate its own propagation in a growing number of African dioceses. From the point of view of organisational structures, the PTAA is to a large extent self-sufficient on the ground. The centre at the parish and sub-parish level is the basic unit.

In Africa, in contrast with Ireland, there is a constant influx of new young adult members. Our emphasis at home on recruiting the young Pioneers may have led to the neglect of the constant need to recruit adults into the association. We should also encourage reformed alcoholics to become Pioneers. Of course, there is a very strong 'faith dimension' for the Pioneer, who dedicates his or her total abstinence from alcoholic drink to the glory of the Sacred Heart of Jesus, i.e. the symbol of the humanity of Christ, in reparation or atonement for the sins of intemperance, and for the love of the neighbour. The Heroic Offering, which is the special prayer of the Pioneer, spells out the motivation of the Pioneer's abstinence for life from intoxicating drink:

(a) 'For the greater glory of the Sacred Heart';
(b) 'To give good example';
(c) 'To practise self-denial';
(d) 'To make reparation for the sins of intemperance'; and
(e) 'For the conversion of excessive drinkers'.
(f) The Pioneer is not anti-drink but, rather, is willing to deny himself or herself something good for a better cause or motive as indicated in the Heroic Offering. Fr James Cullen SJ, who founded the PTAA in St Francis Xavier's Church, Upper Gardiner Street, Dublin 1 on the 28th of December 1898, had already launched the Heroic Offering in St Peter's Cathedral, Belfast in 1889 and encouraged people to recite it twice daily and live accordingly. The theology of reparation or atonement, which is central to our understanding of the suffering and passion of Christ, is at the heart of the Pioneer devotion. *Unfortunately, after Vatican Two there seemed to have been a significant change in relation to the whole idea of asceticism for the love of God and of the neighbour.* This, in my opinion, may have militated somewhat against the perceived spiritual value of being a Pioneer. The decline of the ascetic way of life associated with religious virtue has facilitated consumerism and self-indulgence, which, in turn, may have weakened the moral fibre of the faithful. As noted earlier Irish National Labour leaders like James Connolly and Jim Larkin appreciated the positive significance of the PTAA in their time and their asceticism.

I would suggest that there is ample evidence in the lives of many in Irish society and elsewhere today to manifest the harmful effects of the absence of self-denial on their personal, domestic and social lives. It is not accidental that committed young Pioneers in communities riddled with AIDS in parts of Africa are relatively free from this killer-disease. Self-denial in relation to alcohol enabled young believers to practise it in relation to promiscuous and casual sex and indulgence in drug-taking. The grace or moral strength which the young Pioneer received gives him or her the freedom to say no. In Ireland and in Western Society, in general, our young people need to acquire the necessary self-discipline to protect their personal freedom from addiction and destructive and dissipating self-indulgence. This is something that membership of the PTAA can give them. At its essence the Pioneer Association is a 'freedom movement' for the individual and for society. It was interesting to hear the remarks of the social commentator, Ulick O'Connor, attributing to the Pioneer Association the credit of being a major positive influence on the liberation and emancipation of the Irish nation during the early decades of the 20th century. The old adage, *'Ireland sober Ireland free'*, which was often used by the early promoters of the PTAA, did, in reality, bear fruit. I was very pleased to see the slogan *'Africa sober, Africa free'* displayed at the *Pan-African Pioneer Conferences* in Nairobi in 2001 and in Cape Town in 2004.

At the March meeting of Central Council in 2003 the document – *Towards a Second Century,* was updated in a number of areas and the amended document was published as the *Constitution and Rules of the PTAA.* It was a most satisfactory outcome of the thorough process of structural change at the level of administration and organisation. The three most significant changes brought about in 2003 were:

(i)   The official recognition of Provincial Activities Committees;

(ii) The clarification of the role and functions of the President of the Association, as a non-executive position; and

(iii) The organisation of the PTAA in Africa and elsewhere outside Ireland within the Association was regularised.

The President would be elected every three years, i.e. by the members of the outgoing Central Council, who would constitute the 'electoral college'. This was to avoid the politicisation of the position. The indirect and relatively discreet electoral procedures were also chosen (by those who drafted the Constitution) to facilitate a say by delegates from countries outside Ireland. A more direct electoral procedure could be justified if the President represented only Ireland. (Unfortunately, some local leaders were anxious to make the position one of direct election, rather than the 'electoral-college method'.)

In March 2006, my reappointment by the Irish Jesuit Provincial as chairperson of the Board of Management of the PTAA (which is the 'government of the Association') was approved by Central Council and by the Conference of Irish Bishops. This was in accordance with the Constitution and Rules of the PTAA. Fr Provincial, John Dardis SJ, appointed Fr Joe Dargan SJ, to replace me as chairperson of the Board on the 1st June 2008. In all, I was chairperson for sixteen and a half years.

One of the first tasks I agreed to on reappointment in 2006 was to complete my visitation of every centre of the PTAA in Ireland (1,077 centres) over a period of eighteen months. I began this onerous task in the Meath diocese on the 7th February 2006. It had been my intention to visit every active and lapsed centre and make contact with local Pioneer leaders and the parish priest. When this 'field exercise' was completed, I would have visited practically every Catholic parish in Ireland, which is an extraordinary privilege. Each evening during the visitation, I would write up the facts about the centres, the views of the officers and clergy I met and my own observation. The visitation has shown that there was still a great interest in the Pioneers and our task would be to find ways and means of reviving the spiritual and pastoral zeal of committed Pioneers (young and old) at the parish level. It was also clear that there was a very high level of awareness of the challenge facing young people in relation to alcohol and drugs. Parents, teachers and clergy were seen to play key roles in relation to the protection of young people from drinking. The association of sport and alcohol provided a lethal cocktail for many young people in the view of most people consulted. The parish visitation was expected to continue until the end of 2008. Because of my replacement in the chair on June 1st 2008, it meant that I had not completed my plan to visit all 1,077 of the parishes/centres (I had visited only 994 parishes/centres). An individual confidential report was sent to each centre visited. I regret I was not able to visit every local centre before retiring as Chairperson in 2008.

8. Illness and Bereavement in the Family

In early August 2002, I had an operation for a hip-replacement in Mount Carmel Hospital, Dublin under a very competent Dr McGoldrick. For the previous six years I had experienced serious pain and discomfort in my right hip with echo pains in my right knee. A fall earlier near the *Mámean* shrine may have contributed to my damaged hip. It was time to do something about it. During the Croke Park Rally in 1999 and at the first Pan-African Pioneer Congress in Nairobi in 2001, the bad hip was causing quite an amount of pain. The operation was a great success, thank God. After two weeks in hospital and a further fortnight convalescing, I was back in action. On St Patrick's Day, 2003, I succeeded in climbing *Mámean*. Thank God I did not look back for twelve years. This was my first real experience of hospital and being forced to be a patient. The sense of being tied-down was new to me and helped to make me more aware of what it must be like for those with chronic illness. I was advised to use a walking stick for the rest of my life! *Deo gratias.* (In the spring of 2014 the top of the new hip shifted needing further surgery.)

Shortly after my recovery, my sister-in-law, Eileen (née Kelly), wife of my brother Seán (retired Lt Colonel), got seriously ill. She passed away on the 14th April 2003. It was very traumatic for my brother and very sad for her children, Austin and Kathleen. Eileen was a member of a well-known Westport family (PJ Kelly & Son). On 21st November 2003, my brother Seán got a very severe stroke. As a result of the stroke, he suffered brain damage leading to a loss of memory and loss of his eyesight. He was totally blind in a short time and did not know where he was. He was treated in Merlin Park Hospital for six weeks and took up residence in the Monastery Nursing Home, Corrandulla, County Galway, where he received excellent care and attention for over six years. I tried to visit Seán every Sunday and offer Mass for the patients and staff of the Home. The Home Manager, Mr Michael Hayden, his wife Noelle, and his staff were kind, caring and efficient with my brother and the other patients suffering from vascular dementia. Seán passed away on the 10th February 2010, RIP

My brother Seán (known affectionately in the Army as Jack) was highly thought of in the Defence Forces. He became the *Ceannasaí an Chéad Cathláin* (Commanding Officer of the First Battalion in Galway).

He also served as Training Officer with the FCA in the West Mayo area. His funeral Mass in Galway Cathedral attracted a large congregation of mourners. It was good to see such a large turn-out of retired NCOs and privates from both the regular Army and the FCA. *An Taoiseach*, Mr Brian Cowen TD, was represented at the funeral by his ADC.

The experience of my brother's long illness and death have been sad but fruitful for our family and brought out the true quality of mutual care. In my experience, we are better people in times of great illness and sadness than we often are in times of success. The former brings out the best in us and lets us experience the grace of God in our lives. Another fact that I have experienced so often in my life is that the grace of God rarely comes in advance of when it is necessary.

I did not realise how close I was to Seán until his terrible illness knocked him out. He was only eleven months older than me. We both started school on the same day. We received our First Communion and Confirmation together. We were both Cadets together in the *Fórsaí Cosanta* (he was ahead of me) and we both served as Second and First Lieutenants in the Curragh Camp together (in different Units, of course). I left the Army to join the Jesuits on the 30th August 1959. We kept continuous contact down the years. But both of us went our different ways. After his stroke I became much closer to him and to his family. This has, in itself, been an extraordinary grace. *Ar dheis Dé go raibh anamacha Eibhlín agus Sheáin.*

9. Suicide, a Sociocultural Problem in Modern Irish Society

In recent years in Ireland, suicide has become far too common. In all, I have known thirty-six people who had taken their own lives. They were mostly young adults and teenagers, the vast majority of whom were males. While each case has an individual and unique causal dimension, there must be something dysfunctional in modern Irish society and culture, which causes the vulnerability of young males especially to attempt the termination of their precious lives. In my view, *social anomie*, i.e. a sense of normlessness, due to rapid social change that is not culturally consolidated and the loss of the support of religious beliefs and morality, are likely causal factors. Emile Durkheim, the very eminent French sociologist, was the first to discuss anomic suicide. In my study of Irish intergroup attitudes of 1988-89 and in 2007-08, I included a modified version of Srole's Anomie Scale. The findings show a substantial level of social anomie, which indicated a degree of growing normlessness and uncertainty about life in the population. When religious belief and communal practice weaken, the danger of social anomie is likely to increase.

Another factor that is likely to contribute to the rise in suicide and attempted suicide is the decline of group identity and support, which causes people to *feel isolated and on their own*. In a time when family (nuclear and extended), neighbourhood and community provided support and personally secure identity to a person, the levels of suicide were less frequent. Stress and competitiveness were minimal. People were less ambitious or anxious for greater wealth and achievement. In modern Ireland there has been a marked increase in the level of individualism and a weakening in the family, neighbourhood and community bonds. Upward social mobility and competition have replaced security of identity (social class wise) and the ethic of cooperation. It is almost like a return to 'the survival of the fittest mentality'. The possibility of achieving success is negatively balanced by the reality or fear of failure. In such a socio-cultural environment, it is not that surprising that the suicide rate would be high, not to mention the level of heart failure due to stress and worry. The phenomenon of post-binge depression due to excessive drinking of alcohol could also be a factor in some cases of suicide.

Striving for material success can become a trap for many people. Hence the importance of a revival of community-oriented religion, domestic-centred political policies and a playing down of ambitious individualism. The profit motive should be modified substantially by the service motive. What we need, in a nutshell, is a multidimensional move to re-humanise our society. The substitution of the professional (waged) help for the personal, informal support does not seem to work in many cases. Of course, there is need for professional assistance in acute problem areas, even in cases of good domestic and community support. As it seems at present, not only in Ireland but across the European Union as well, the economy is taking precedence over family, neighbourhood and community. Quantity of life (i.e. materialism) is seen to be more important than quality of life (i.e. creative spiritual life) because of the dominance of commercial and economic interests.

One of the most disappointing results of the welcome advance in social equality between men and women has been the largely individualist option made by many emancipated women. I had hoped liberated women would opt for improvements in domestic, neighbourhood and community life. Instead many of the more successful women in various fields seem to have reinforced our existing system. Careerism, which had enhanced male ambition in the past, is equally strong in the new male-female order of things. (I had better leave it at that before I get myself into conflict with some feminist critics!) My support for the feminist movement has been constant, save when I discovered that some leaders were more individualist than collectivist. The quality of life of all is greater than the advantage of either men or women. We should all strive to replace competition with cooperation and reduce stress, normlessness and individual isolation. In such a society (utopia) *service would replace profit as the prime motivation*! Such a change would be likely to reduce the suicide rate and improve the quality of life for most people.

10. PLURALIST INTEGRATION IN IRELAND

Among the aspects of Irish society with which I am most concerned is the need for pluralist integration of our new brothers and sisters from many nationalities, religions and political systems. As observed previously, Ireland's minorities in the past were historical and indigenous because of the fact that we had been an emigrant society throughout the 19th and 20th centuries. Since the late 1990s this began to change and this under-populated island began to experience a long-overdue economic boom. Increased employment attracted, in the first instance, the return of Irish emigrants back home to fill the new vacancies. This was followed by migrant workers from less prosperous countries in the European Union, especially from Eastern Europe, where there was a good work ethic and range of skills. Workers, with special skills, e.g. nurses, were recruited from outside the European Union. Naturally, it was only a matter of time until workers and people from the poorer countries of Africa and Asia would gravitate to Ireland as 'economic' and 'social' refugees. In a short period our streets and public transport were filled with a rich spread of nationalities and languages. Within the sixteen years 1996-2012, Ireland was to become an immigrant society. My only regret has been that I was not twenty years younger so that I could carry out more ongoing surveys of people's attitudes to the various groups and groupings. It is hoped that the recent slowdown in the economy will have been corrected in a number of years.

The findings of my previous surveys in relation to racial, religious, political and ethnic prejudices towards categories of people outside Ireland were, for the most part, measuring dormant prejudices, since there were very few people from these groupings living in Ireland. Of those with whom our people had actual contact most were, in the main, students, foreign doctors, tourists and some working in Indian and Chinese cafés and restaurants. Irish migrants who had returned from Britain and the United States would have had a certain amount of contact with people from other racial groups and ethnic minorities.

Our returned Irish foreign missionaries had a more personal experience of other ethnic peoples in Africa and Asia. In fact, the experience of Irish missionaries was a significant factor in reducing Irish racial prejudice and, where it did exist, making it more benevolent or patronising. Our missionaries' role in opening the Irish people to a healthier attitude to foreigners from the 'Third World' has not been fully acknowledged by the 'chattering classes' in the media and in politics in Ireland. In fact, it should be pointed out that academics in the human sciences have also failed to research the positive influence of the Irish Foreign Mission's effort over almost one hundred years. This was probably due, in part, to the hypercritical attitudes of what was perceived to be Church or religion-related. Is this a further manifestation of the 'apostate complex', i.e. a compulsive alienation from what we were and an over-identification with what we perceive ourselves to be in this brave new secular world?

The arrival of migrant workers, asylum seekers and refugees to Ireland is a most exciting challenge to us all. In time, it will change Irish society. On the positive side, it could implant new family and community values and help us to regain some of what we may have lost in our pursuit of wealth and comfort. It will, in my view, also enrich our cultural life and broaden our experience and outlook beyond the very narrow confines of 'adolescent' cultural values. Because most of the immigrants value family and children, this will bring a new vitality to our schools and Church congregations. In time, because of the possibility of favourable contact between Irish and other ethnic groups, we can become more tolerant of cultural diversity and move towards a society *that will be both integrated and pluralist*. The skills, industry, intellectual ability and commitment to work hard of so many migrant workers will add to the wealth of our communities. In the areas of sport, music, drama, writing, *et cetera*, there is an enormous potential in our new brothers and sisters sharing this piece of earth with us. We must also be realistic in relation to those among immigrants who may misbehave.

Of course, there are negative consequences if we fail to approach our new guests in an open and mature way. Unfavourable contact, avoidance and fear could lead to the difficulties experienced between poorly integrated minority groupings. There is a very serious responsibility on the host society to prepare for the fair integration of our new guests, while recognising and respecting their cultural and religious differences. *The law of the land must be clear on the minority rights of our new immigrants*. The Civil Service and the Gardaí should ensure that prejudiced and xenophobic groups are prevented from in any way interfering with the rights of our guests. Total equality with regard to wages, work opportunities, health services, housing, welfare, education and freedom of religion between the dominant and minority groupings should be guaranteed and enforced. The mass media of communication must avoid all forms of 'anti-locution', i.e. ridicule, reporting the group identity of those who break the criminal laws. It will be very important that hostile ethnic jokes and other forms of vulgar anti-locution are kept in check. We in Ireland have been at the wrong end of 'anti-locution' in England in the past as an under-esteemed minority. Now that 'the boot is on the other foot' we should be careful not to repeat the hate-jokes and name-calling that our ancestors received. This is our opportunity to show the dignity of our culture and the universal solidarity of our religion. True pluralist integration requires structural duplication to ensure the continuity of cultural diversity, i.e. denominational schools, separate language schools, different places of worship, *et cetera*. Separation in such cases is not segregation!

The whole question of intergroup relations should form a significant module of the Irish Educational Curricula at the second and third levels. *To study prejudice and tolerance is self-therapeutic*. (I certainly found it to be so!) *We should also remember that a prejudice exposed is a prejudice undermined.* It is very important that tolerance of different ethnic and religious groupings should be a major aim of our religious teaching. In the case of Christianity, this tolerance of others was central to the preaching and teaching of Christ, i.e. his attitudes towards women (in a sexist time); his attitude towards Samaritans; his respect for sinners; his love of enemies and, most of all, his universal definition of who was my neighbour! It has been a terrible distortion and political manipulation of that clear teaching which turned 'Christianity' into a justification of hatred and bigotry in the unenlightened past. We in post-Reformation Ireland (on both sides) have suffered from this turning of the teaching of Christ on its head, causing so much misery, deprivation and even death, at times. Such an obscene abuse of Christianity must be resisted to the maximum in the new multicultural Ireland.

11. RECENT TRENDS IN IRISH EDUCATION

As noted already, recent trends in Irish education away from arts and the humanities (including human sciences) are very worrying because of the danger of our failing to produce 'intellectuals', i.e. persons able to be in support of their culture while at the same time being critical of it. It was very significant that among the first people to be rounded-up in Paris after Hitler's army's overcoming of the city, were the 'intellectuals'. When the Gestapo, for instance, came to arrest the philosopher, Jacques Maritain on the day of the fall of Paris, he was luckily away in the United States. Under the reign of Senator McCarthy in the United States in the 1950s, there was a purge of the intellectuals. The aim of any worthwhile educational system should always be the enabling of the students to become intellectuals with a tolerant interest in the welfare of all people. When studying social psychology, I found it to be a sobering fact that there was an absence of a correlation between intelligence and authoritarianism (which is highly correlated to social prejudice). This meant that the most intelligent or the least intelligent person in a group could be most authoritarian. We have seen this down through history with authoritarian leaders displaying great intelligence and academic ability and attracting authoritarian supporters who were equally intelligent. This would imply that open- and closed- mindedness, (the latter is highly correlated with authoritarianism) are learned phenomena, hence the vital importance of an educational curriculum which enables the student to be open-minded.

In old Irish culture the status of the scholar was held in high esteem – *'aoibhinn beatha an scoláire'* ('wonderful the life of the scholar'). *In my desire for a broad, open and liberating education, I do not intend to underrate the precise sciences or professional education and training. Society needs an ongoing supply of skilled and professional people to maintain the economy and the services.* What is required is the availability of a very good foundation in the arts and humanities for all students, that is, if we want to have an integrated pluralist society with a high level of tolerance in the population. Ideally, an integral part of the arts and humanities' curriculum should be the study of philosophy and of the theology of the people's religions. Theology itself should be open to intellectual debate, while accepting that faith is always a *commitment to God's existence and a willingness to live according to His will.* The study of social prejudice and discrimination is very self-therapeutic, as already pointed out. (One of the most disappointing findings of the 2007-08 survey of Irish prejudices has been the poor performance of the 18 to 25 year-olds sub-sample despite their high level of participation in higher education. I will refer to this finding later in the text.[10])

12. The 'Celtic Tiger' – Positive and Negative Aspects

The twelve years under review in this chapter (2000-12) have been quite dramatic and hectic in terms of social, economic and political change. They were *'the best of times and the worst of times'* to quote Charles Dickens[11]. The period began after the arrival of the 'Celtic Tiger' following the successful achievement of the *Good Friday Agreement,* which put an end to the nightmare experience of the recent Northern Ireland 'Troubles'. This enabled the economic institution to occupy the pivotal position in Irish society, i.e. replacing the political institution as the area of central concern which had concentrated national socio-political energy for almost thirty years. The self-regulated 'free market' under the dominant Neo-Liberal ideology and the joining of the Euro Club provided a stimulating incentive 'to plough ahead without restraint'!

---

10 Mac Gréil, Micheál, *Pluralism and Diversity in Ireland,* Dublin, Columba, 2011.
11 The opening lines of *A Tale of Two Cities* by Charles Dickens.

Following on the rise of the 'Celtic Tiger', the economy began to expand, unemployment decreased, involuntary emigration was replaced by immigration of workers from abroad. The in-migration included returning Irish emigrants, the descendants of Irish emigrants, and migrant workers from Eastern Europe, Africa, Asia and elsewhere abroad. The improvement, (or should I say, renewal) of infrastructure, i.e. housing, hospitals, roads, railways, offices, harbours, airports, communications, hotels, schools, colleges, *et cetera*, were to become the lasting products of this extraordinary decade of economic growth. The Dublin Docklands alone are monuments to this dynamic period of 'Ireland at work'. The golden age of material progress and success had arrived in 'poor old Ireland'. *Ar feadh aga bhig dúnadh an bhéal bhocht!* (For a brief time the poor mouth was shut!)

So pleased were the people of the Republic of Ireland that they returned the *Fianna Fáil* Government to power for 'three terms in a row', i.e. 1997-2002, 2002-07 and 2007-11. Mr Bertie Ahern TD, (from an inner-Dublin working-class background) was returned as *An Taoiseach* for 'three in a row'! (He stepped down from being *Taoiseach* in May 2008 to be replaced by Mr Brian Cowen TD, (a publican's son from Clara, County Offaly). In politics, nothing succeeds like success!

The unexpected collapse of the 'Celtic Tiger' in the summer of 2008, following weakness in the banking system in the US, (i.e. the crisis of Lehman's Bank), the UK, Ireland and elsewhere in Europe experienced a slump in the overpriced building trade. It soon became clear that there was a failure in financial regulation at national and international levels. 'Reagonomics' in the US supported by Thatcherite deregulation in the UK over two decades earlier was to sow the seed of a future unregulated financial crisis! This new progress had been accompanied by an increase in the powerful financial *superstructure*, i.e. in banking, mortgage, insurance, *et cetera*, became socially and politically contagious. It spread under the title of Neo-Liberalism, which became the ideology of Europe, the United States and other like-minded political elites. The fall of the Berlin Wall in 1989 deflated the collectivist challenge. The Soviet system, it could be argued, had been over-regulated. The common euro currency had removed the capacity of the Irish Government to check financial over-heating. Cheap money suited Germany at a time when dearer money would have put the necessary brakes on over-borrowing in the Republic of Ireland.

The Irish Government and fellow-European Governments were also taken by surprise by the extent of the collapse of the financial system in 2008. Economists, accountants and the majority of so-called financial experts (with rare exceptions) seemed to be unaware of the shaky structural foundation of the 'free-market' economy across the 'western' world. The 'Celtic Tiger' had cross-party consensus in the Republic of Ireland and even competed in favour of ongoing economic growth and expansion, i.e. see election manifestos, etc. Of course, they are all aware now of 'what should have been done' after the event. But are they? A serious in-depth study should be carried out on the inability of the experts to warn and guide the elected leaders in relation to the dysfunctional basis of neo-liberal, free-market (*laissez-faire*) ideology, which informed Irish financial rules and regulations. They seemed to lack the intellectual ability to stand outside this same ideology. Neo-liberal, free-market ideology had almost become a secular faith!

To quote an American sociologist, Milton Yinger (when talking about change in the religious institution), it is important 'to keep the trains running while changing the station'. That was what the late Minister for Finance, Mr Brian Lenihan TD, was forced to do when the news of the collapse became clear. The tragedy was that he was not given the true extent of the problem from the banks and elsewhere. *An Taoiseach*, Mr Brian Cowen TD, to his credit, supported Brian Lenihan and received Cabinet and *Dáil* backing for the remedial rescue of the State. The harsh 'emergency budgets' to follow took courage. The forcing of the Republic to seek support from the European Central Bank and the IMF in the autumn of 2010 added 'insult to injury'. This, plus the austerity programme of recovery, inevitably cost the Government parties an unprecedented loss of popularity in the polls. *At least the Government's brave response to the crisis has 'kept the trains running'!* This collapse was another classic case of 'the morning after optimism'. Of course, harsh emergency budgets are not enough to generate wealth to ensure economic sustainability for Ireland.

Perhaps, it would be opportune at this stage to reflect on what happened during the 'boom' or Celtic Tiger years. The most outstanding achievement of the 1997-2002 government of *Fianna Fáil*/Progressive Democrats was its contribution to the Peace Process in Northern Ireland.

The consensus-based all-party devolved-government in Belfast was followed by the voluntary disarmament of the major paramilitaries, the withdrawal of the visible presence of the British Army and the move towards a mutually acceptable local police force. These were real advances of substance which people like me had hoped for but did not expect to be realised in our lifetime. More than that, the manner in which the developments took place was guided by the wisdom and negotiating ability and patience of the political leaders. These leaders and their advisers merit the Irish people's lasting indebtedness. Political leaders such as John Hume, Gerry Adams, Martin McGuinness, Séamus Mallon, the Rev. Ian Paisley, Peter Robinson, David Trimble, David Ervine, Bertie Ahern, Albert Reynolds, John Bruton, Dick Spring and others within Ireland and Tony Blair and Bill Clinton outside the territory do, in my opinion, deserve to be acknowledged. The unique role played by Senator George Mitchell (USA) merits the gratitude of the Irish people. *An Taoiseach*, Mr Bertie Ahern TD, went to Belfast on the evening of his late mother's funeral to spend long hours completing the negotiations for the *Good Friday Agreement* in 1998. This was a manifestation of genuine commitment. The role played by Dr Mo Mowlam MP, Northern Ireland Secretary, and the prisoners in the Maze Prison in the lead-up to the historic agreement should not be underestimated.

From 1998 onwards, economic development was to replace political action in relation to Northern Ireland as the main concern of the Government in Dublin. In other words, the economic institution was assuming a *pivotal role* in Irish society and all other institutions were being geared to serve its needs. Education would place greater emphasis on the needs of the economy, i.e. economics, commerce, science and technology would be given a higher priority than arts and the humanities. The family would also have to adapt 'to dance to the economy's tune', i.e. both parents would be pressurised to seek gainful employment and full-time child-rearing would be implicitly discouraged. Income tax would be individualised. Recreation would become more commercialised. Politics would focus on economic development. Law would be dealing more with industrial and property issues. The rise of materialism and consumerism would present a real challenge to religion. Looking back at the changes between 1998 and 2008, it is possible to discern such institutional changes in Irish society. The rise of white-collar deviance, i.e. tribunals, *et cetera*, were further signs of the change.

The General Elections of 2002, and again in 2007, returned *Fianna Fáil*-led Governments with Mr Bertie Ahern TD, as *Taoiseach*, i.e. 2002-07 (*Fianna Fáil* and the Progressive Democrats) and 2007-11 (*Fianna Fáil*, the Green Party and Progressive Democrats). The neo-liberal policies pursued by these Governments were in line with most Western Governments. The structural weaknesses of such policies were concealed and an enormous degree of development took place before our eyes. The *renewal of housing* was badly needed and was the greatest (relatively-speaking) since Minister Sean T Ó Ceallaigh TD, 'removed the thatch' in the late 1930s. Tens of thousands of immigrants were housed in new homes and apartments. The whole area of communications infrastructure was upgraded to the highest standards, i.e. roads, railways, air and sea ports, telecommunications, *et cetera*. For example, some billions of euros were invested in motorways! Water schemes, new sewerage plants, colleges/ schools, hospitals and clinics, theatres, Garda barracks and other necessary infrastructures were renewed and built during the period 1998-2008. *They are all there now 'over the ground and the recession cannot take them back'! When the economy recovers, all the above infrastructural achievements will be there to be added to and new priorities will be identified when that time comes.*

The Celtic Tiger changed the material face of Ireland, especially its capital city, Dublin. That change is akin to the *Georgian expansion* in the late eighteenth century. Will future historians call the 'Celtic Tiger' expansion the '*Albertonian Expansion*'? Will those who see a previous *Taoiseach*, the late Charles J Haughey TD, as the initial driving force behind the new Dublin renewal and expansion call it the '*Carolinian Expansion*'? Both Haughey and Ahern seemed to have been happy with *the Dublin skyline like a forest of builders' cranes*! (So much for fantasy!) It should also be remembered that services such as education, training, medical care, security, etc. also expanded during the 'Celtic Tiger' decade.

The downside of the above era of growth and optimism was its un-sustainability due in large part to the unprecedented borrowing and lending policies – not only in Ireland but throughout *the self-regulating neo-liberal international banking systems*. For most of the era of the 'Celtic Tiger', there was a contagious epidemic of excessive borrowing and mortgaging. This led also to an overvaluation of property, an acute rise in the cost of wages and services and an unhealthy drop in personal savings. *The free- market engine seemed to go into overdrive!* Where were the watchdogs in the large accountancy companies, the expert economists, the political (Government and Opposition) leaders, the public servants, the national Central Banks, the EU and, most of all, the financial regulators? I believe most of us were seduced and we got too greedy for our own good! The 'God of materialism' seemed to have blinded us to sober reality! The secular alternative failed our people! It is a sobering fact that the four criteria of social dysfunction, i.e. suicide, homicide, percentage of adult population in prison and domestic break-up, all increased during the materially prosperous years of the 'Celtic Tiger'.

In my opinion, the real problem was structural. Hopefully, it will be corrected in time to prevent a future 'boom'. The pain of the 'burst' is too great for the majority of the people. Also, in the interests of equity, a tough maximum incomes policy at national and international level is imperative. The austerity reaction seems to me to be more centred on the rehabilitation of the 'liberal capitalist system' than on the future sustainability of societies like Ireland.

Between 2002 and 2006 the main banks seemed to be changing their focus from serving the needs of depositors and moderate lending to viable projects at sustainable terms. They seemed to enter the speculative market and were lending beyond their capacity. They also moved into dealing in 'hedge funds' at the international level. For all practical purposes, they seemed to be 'self-regulated'. By 2004, vast numbers of people began borrowing literally 'beyond their means', i.e. for houses/apartments, motor vehicles, holidays abroad, education, *et cetera*. Interest rates were low and *a shift from thrift towards reckless borrowing seemed to take over*. We were to become a nation living on credit. House prices, services and wages soared. Were we beginning to live as if there was never going to be a real tomorrow? Income tax was being lowered and the highest earners' income tax was down to 42%. Redistribution was minimal thereby not reducing the gap between the 'rich' and the 'poor' within Ireland. Relative to previous decades, social-welfare benefit was more generous. There seemed to be a divorce between 'work' and 'wealth'.

When Mr Brian Cowen TD, took over as Minister for Finance, there was a modest shift towards social solidarity. Another welcome development was the *Spatial Strategy Policy,* which put new emphasis on regional development. Those of us involved in infrastructural development in the West of Ireland, e.g. the Western Rail Corridor, became more optimistic at the arrival of the new spatial policy. We still await the completion of the Limerick – Sligo rail restoration project. By 2014, we are only as far as Limerick to Athenry.

The General Election of 2007 once again returned a *Fianna Fáil*-led Coalition Government (with the Green Party and two Progressive Democrat TDs in support). By this time, prices had become very high and the economy seemed to be overheating. The Government (as a member State of the Euro) had lost its power to raise interest rates. Alarm bells were being rung and questions were being asked about when the upward spiral would stop or slow down. We were being assured that it would be a soft-landing when, and if, it happened. *The economic system seemed to be predicated on continuous progress and ever-growing expansion.* We were now 'part of the global economy'! It seemed to me we were beginning to 'walk on water', without a regulated structural foundation. Were we living on confidence alone? *An Taoiseach,* Bertie Ahern TD, resigned in May 2008 and the Minister for Finance, Mr Brian Cowen TD, succeeded him. Mr Brian Lenihan TD, succeeded Mr Cowen as Minister for Finance. By this time, the European Union had expanded to twenty-seven states and after a second Referendum on the *Lisbon Treaty,* it was taking to itself (in Brussels) more sovereign power from the member states. Despite its growing bureaucratic power, *the EU failed to anticipate the 2008 financial crisis.* The dominance of the neo-liberal ideology resulted in a high level of free-market self-regulation. In reality the capitalist system had failed the people once again!

13. THE FAILURE OF NEO-LIBERAL FREE-MARKET CAPITALISM

The financial crisis of the summer of 2008 began in the United States with the collapse of Lehman's Bank and spread to Europe. The Republic of Ireland was hit a double blow, i.e. the banks' crisis and the collapse of the construction industry. The latter resulted in unemployment and an immediate increase in social-welfare expenditure. The State's revenue from taxation decreased rapidly while its expenditure increased.

The globalised and self-regulated free market, which was the foundation of the dominant political ideology, i.e. neo-liberalism, had, once again, failed the Western World, including Ireland, the United States and the European Union. This was the second time in recent history when liberal capitalism proved dysfunctional, namely, the first being the Wall Street Crash in 1929 and its consequences for the Western World.

What was happening in Ireland since the autumn of 2008 was also spread throughout the European Union and the United States of America. The reckless borrowing and lending by people and the banks proved unsustainable. The Irish Government was suddenly faced with the problem of borrowing money to keep services going and to bail out the banks, one of whom (the Anglo Irish Bank) had built up an enormous debt. *This crisis exposed the structural weaknesses of the neo-liberal, free-market capitalist system.* The popular reaction in the media was to scapegoat leaders rather than highlight the basic structural weaknesses. Had the government not bailed out the banks, it would appear that local credit unions and private pension funds would have been in very serious trouble.

Frantic efforts were made to remedy the crisis and save the free-market capitalist system. Austerity regimes were called for 'to restore' the State's finances. These resulted in higher unemployment; cutbacks in health services, education, capital investment, social welfare and other services; and a serious rise in involuntary emigration. The State's revenue receipts from taxes were further reduced. In the autumn of 2010, the international moneylenders raised the lending rate to the Republic of Ireland to plus 7%, which forced Ireland (despite its highly praised austerity efforts and without serious social unrest) to seek help from the ECB and IMF. It was ironic that those partially responsible for the original crisis, i.e. the international money lenders, were forcing the Republic of Ireland into submission to the IMF/ECB! *This brought home to Ireland who was really running the world, namely, the international moneylenders.* This source had already forced Greece and would later put pressure on Portugal into the same destiny. Also, it would create a crisis in the eurozone, bring about a change of government in Italy and threaten other countries in Europe, i.e. Spain, France and Belgium.

Who are these international moneylenders? Should they have such unrepresentative power? This may be a question for the United Nations to address. Speculative lending to banks (and States) leads to financial crisis and can ultimately lead to the exploitation of a country's vital wealth, i.e. the fruit of people's labour. The current globalised financial structure will inevitably lead to the survival of the fittest and the destruction of the weakest societies. Such a world is certainly and basically unethical in the Christian context! A just world is based on cooperation and social equality.

Much criticism has been made of the manner in which the Irish Government responded to the situation before and after the crash. Its behaviour was, as far as I can see, in conformity with the free-market, neo-liberal ideology, which dominated the whole of the EU, the USA, Canada and all Western countries. In fact, the Republic of Ireland was complimented during the 'Celtic Tiger' years and later in our initial reaction to the crisis in the 2008 and 2009 budgets. But 'eaten bread is soon forgotten' when the pinch of corrective measures was being called for. Inevitably, Government leaders were to be scapegoated and 'sacrificially slaughtered' in the 2011 General Election. *One of the accessory functions of a leader is to become a scapegoat in times of difficulty.* Nearly every government forced to implement austerity programmes in Western Europe has been defeated and put out of office since 2008. What is going to be the destiny of those governments who have replaced the defeated ones and are being compelled to continue the austerity programmes necessary to satisfy the international moneylenders? Only time will tell.

As far back as the 1930s, the late Professor and author, Karl Mannheim, noted that *there cannot be progress in social justice and equality without a curtailment in the consumer's choice of the privileged*[12]. Part of the solution to the current crisis must be the operation of a maximum income's policy at the individual, community, national and international levels. This would help to change the primary motivation (at all levels) from profit to service. If the result of the current crisis moves in this direction then, it may be said, it was a 'happy fault' (*felix culpa*). The lowering of the wasteful material standard of living in the 'developed world' is also to be welcomed in order to give the 'developing world' a chance!

The problem of emigration has, once again, returned to the Republic of Ireland and is beginning to drain the 'brains and brawn' out of the country to the stronger economies in Australia, England, Germany,

---

12 See Mannheim, Karl, *Man and Society in an Age of Reconstruction*, New York, Routledge and Kegan-Paul, 1942.

Canada and elsewhere. This raises the structural question of the *laissez-faire*, free-market of labour, which is, in my opinion, one of the greatest impediments to social justice and equality between societies and within countries. Talent, in our system of profit motivation, is inevitably drawn to regions and countries where there is socio-economic strength and wealth and away from the relatively depressed areas and societies, where talent is most needed. This makes the already strong communities and countries stronger and richer while it causes the weaker societies and communities to become even more deprived.

We in Ireland have clear evidence of the effects of free movement of labour during almost two centuries of emigration and the recent decade of immigration during the 'Celtic Tiger' period. Intra- and international social justice is well nigh impossible unless there is serious regulation of migration of workers. *The host societies or communities should be obliged to compensate fully the societies and communities of origin for immigrants entering their workforce.* The more qualified the immigrant, the greater the compensation should be! Such control should be regulated by a reformed United Nations.

14. A THIRD MAJOR SURVEY OF PREJUDICE IN IRELAND 2007-08

The welcome arrival in the Republic of Ireland of so many in-migrants between 1996 and 2007, largely to undertake the blue-collar work (which Irish workers had been deserting in favour of white-collar work), raised the question of carrying out a new national survey of intergroup attitudes. Having directed two major surveys on this topic in 1972-73 in Greater Urban and Suburban Dublin and at a national level in 1988-89, it seemed to me that a new survey would measure the changes in social prejudice and tolerance in response to various happenings, which had taken and were taking place in Irish society since 1988-89. I discussed the project with Professor Brendan Whelan of the ESRI and a number of other advisers. It was generally agreed that such a research project would be of much benefit to the understanding of intergroup relations in a more pluralist and diverse Ireland.

The problem was to get funding for such a major social survey exercise. I intended to commission the ESRI to carry out the fieldwork as was done in 1988-89 (under Professor Brendan Whelan). During 2005 I began searching for funding and updating the questionnaire. When I approached the Government, the response was positive from the departments dealing with Equality and Community Affairs. A formal application was submitted to the Ministers, Michael McDowell TD, (Equality) and Éamon Ó Cuív TD, (Community Affairs). They approved a grant for the research project, which included payment for the fieldwork (ESRI), the employment of a senior research officer (for eighteen months) and research secretaries (part-time)[13]. As director and author of the Report, I would not claim a salary (apart from travel and related expenses). Professor Sean Ó Riain of the Department of Sociology, NUI Maynooth, provided an office from which the work proceeded and any grants received were processed.

The fieldwork was carried out by means of an interview questionnaire of a national random sample of 1,015 respondents between November 2007 and March 2008. The average length of the interviews was forty minutes. The processing and preparation of the data for analysis and presentation took place between June 2008 and March 2011[14]. The report was published under the title, *Pluralism and Diversity in Ireland* in Dublin by Columba Press in May 2011. To complete the funding, Atlantic Philanthropies (Mr Chuck Feeney) gave me a generous grant which covered the preparation of the final text and subsidised part of the printing costs so that the book could retail at €25, which would be within the range of students and people of modest means. The printer, Crotare (Mr Liam Killion), produced a very handsome book at a reasonable cost. Mrs Teresa Hunt was the 'originator' of the text. Mr Éamon Ó Cuív TD, (former Minister), wrote the Foreword to the book and launched it in the Royal Irish Academy, Dublin on Wednesday, 18th May 2011.

The findings of the 2007-08 survey were for the most part positive and recorded an overall increase in social tolerance in the population when compared with the 1988-89 findings (published in *Prejudice in Ireland Revisited,* Maynooth, 1996) and those of the 1972-73 survey (published in *Prejudice and Tolerance in Ireland,* Dublin, 1977). In all, prejudices

---

13 *Senior Research Officer*: Mr Fergal Rhatigan, M Soc Sc; *Research Secretaries*: Mrs Maria Woulfe and Mrs Teresa Hunt.

14 The actual interviewing took place between November 2007 and March 2008. The Survey Division of the ESRI was commissioned to carry out the fieldwork.

towards some fifty-one stimulus categories were measured (see page 407). These included: cultural, ethnic, political, racial, religious, social and a number of special categories. Among the fifty-one categories, forty-six were replicated from the 1988-89 national survey. Despite people's reduction in social prejudice in the overall findings, there still remained an unacceptable level of intolerance towards a number of minorities such as 'Travellers', 'Muslims' and persons with compulsive behaviour problems. A number of surprises were found in relation to the attitudes of the youngest age group (18 to 25 years) who were not as tolerant as their educational standard reached and socio-economic security would have predicted.

It was anticipated that there would be a reduction in social prejudice (with a corresponding increase in social tolerance) in the 2007-08 survey for the following reasons:

(a) *The social and economic security generated by a decade of economic growth, increased gainful employment and reduced emigration;*

(b) *The relatively successful resolution of the Northern Ireland problem and an end to military and paramilitary violence;*

(c) *The favourable contact with migrant workers into the Republic of Ireland from Eastern Europe and elsewhere abroad;*

(d) *The continuous increase in participation in education among young people and mature students returning to college;*

(e) *Tourism into Ireland and the increase in the number of Irish people going abroad for business and for leisure.*

A factor that had a positive influence on ethnic and racial attitudes prior to the arrival of the Celtic Tiger was the tolerant influence of Irish foreign missionaries and those lay people on foreign voluntary service. The economic recession, which took place after the fieldwork was completed, is likely to lead to a reduction in social tolerance if we are not careful because of the insecurity and frustration ensuing. Frustration creates tension which, in turn, seeks expression or release in aggression. Social prejudice is *an easily available form of displaced psychological aggression*. Hence, the danger of an increase in prejudice (and discrimination) in times of economic downturn.

The '*morning-after-optimism phenomenon*' is another factor to take into account. It appears from history that people are most insecure and volatile after a relatively sudden collapse of optimism. It is a time when political leaders are most susceptible to being blamed by the popular media, and punished in the ballot box. As will be seen, the Government of the Republic of Ireland became a main scapegoat on which the voters gave vent to their negativity in the election of 2011. The problem with such scapegoating is that it fails to correct the problem, since it prevents the addressing of the real source of the crisis, which in my opinion has been structular.

The challenge facing Ireland is, as stated already, to maintain the momentum towards greater tolerance despite a less favourable socio-economic environment. Based on the understanding that '*a prejudice exposed is a prejudice undermined*', it would be reasonable that the subject of intergroup relations should be part of the curriculum of the senior-cycle of second-level education and also a required subject in undergraduate courses at third level in a country which is becoming more culturally diverse. The Republic of Ireland has become such a country, i.e. over 14% of the national population was born abroad according to the 2006 Census.

15. PUBLISH *PLURALISM AND DIVERSITY IN IRELAND*

Changes in attitudes towards Great Britain and Northern Ireland in the 2007-08 study confirmed the very positive effect of the *Good Friday Agreement* of 1998 and the *St Andrew's Agreement* of 2006 in the Republic. One of the most striking changes happened in relation to attitudes towards Northern Unionists. In 1988-89 national survey, only 33.4% would welcome 'Unionists' into their family through marriage, while in 2007-08 some 66.2% would admit them to kinship, i.e. a nominal increase of +32.8%. Willingness to 'deny citizenship' to 'Unionists' dropped from 18.6% to 8.0% over the same period of time, i.e. a nominal drop of -10.6%. These are very optimistic figures indeed and are indicative of a significant and substantial peace dividend from the above agreements. Similar results were recorded in other questions relating to Northern Ireland in the survey.

The relative position of 'Northern Irish' (with 75.1% 'admitting to kinship') as an ethnic category was disappointing. In terms of social distance, they ranked seventeenth in a scale of fifty-one categories behind the following:

Would Admit to Kinship

1st 'Roman Catholics'	(91.1%)	9th 'Euro-Americans'	(81.3%)
2nd 'Working Class'	(85.6%)	10th 'English'	(81.0%)
3rd 'Irish Speakers'	(84.4%)	11th 'Unemployed'	(80.9%)
4th 'People Physical Disab.'	(83.0%)	12th 'Canadians'	(80.1%)
5th 'Unmarried Mothers'	(82.4%)	13th 'Protestants'	(78.4%)
6th 'Welsh'	(82.4%)	14th 'French'	(78.4%)
7th 'Scottish'	(81.7%)	15th 'Trade Unionists'	(77.8%)
8th 'Gardaí'	(81.4%)	16th 'British'	(77.2%)

See: Table of Rank-Order of Stimulus Categories by Mean-Social-Distance[15].

In the normal course of events 'Northern Irish' should be next to 'Irish Speakers', i.e. according to the *principle of propinquity*. The most realistic way to improve this relative situation is to increase the experience of favourable contact between people from the Republic and those in Northern Ireland. Sport and cross-border tourism, i.e. people from the Republic going North, are two possible areas with the potential for favourable contact. An All-Ireland soccer team would also be a most positive source of favourable contact among Irish working class. Improving cross-border meeting of people might well become a priority policy in the years ahead!

Irish attitudes towards the British also improved significantly between 1988-89 and 2007-08. A special *Anti-British Scale* measured socio-political dispositions[16]. Even attitudes towards the 'British Establishment' were more tolerant. The important supportive role of the British Prime Minister, Mr Tony Blair MP, and his Northern Irish Secretary, Dr Mo Mowlam MP, in the peace and reconciliation process is acknowledged. (The reception for Queen Elizabeth II on her visit to Ireland in May 2011 confirmed such improved attitudes.) If the brief decade of the 'Celtic Tiger' were to do no more than create an environment of economic security to enable the Irish people to rid themselves of their post-colonial 'hang-ups', which apparently happened by 2007-08, it may have been worth it!

Irish attitudes towards the Irish language continued to be positive,

---

15 See Table on page 407 below.
16 See: Mac Gréil, Micheál, *Pluralism and Diversity in Ireland*, Dublin, Columba, 2011, pages 255-261.

especially among those with higher social class position in society. Reasonable competence in the native language increased to 47%, which is probably the highest it has ever been since before *An Gorta Mór* (The Great Famine) of 1845-48. Unfortunately regular use of the language was still too low at 23%. It was clear that structural impediments restricting the greater use of Irish exist in current Irish social norms. Also the support from the current Irish education system for the language leaves much to be desired!

Attitudes towards and practice of religion in the adult population were measured in the 2007-08 national survey. Over the previous thirty-five years, religious collective worship had declined substantially. Regular monthly worship for Roman Catholics was still as high as 55% with 9% stating they had given up going to Mass. This was still a considerable level of collective Christian worship in a society that had become more materialist and individualist. Only 4.4% of the Irish population declared they had 'no religion' in the *2006 Census of Population* report. Some 72% of respondents in the 2007-08 national survey admitted they prayed 'once a week or more often'. As many as 47% said they prayed 'daily or more often'. Ten per cent stated they never prayed. In reply to the question of 'perceived closeness to God', 71% replied that they felt a degree of closeness, i.e. 'extremely close' (22%) or 'somewhat close' (49%), while 4% said they 'did not believe in God'. The latter confirms the 4.4% of 'No Religion' in the *2006 Census Report*. These statistics about religious practice and disposition should help to give the reader an idea of the situation in the Republic of Ireland at the beginning of the twenty-first century and correct the distorted image often portrayed in some of the Irish media which could well become a negative self-fulfilling prophesy of decline in religious practice.

The greater part of *Pluralism and Diversity in Ireland* is devoted to the levels of social prejudice against diverse social minorities and how they have changed over the period from 1972-73 to 2007-08. The following summary Table (407 below) gives an overview of the level of closeness to which the national sample of over-eighteen-year olds were prepared to admit members of fifty-one different 'stimulus categories'.

Respondents were asked to indicate the closest to which they would welcome/admit a member of each of the fifty-one categories listed. Those

416

receiving a mean-social-distance (MSD) of 1.500 or less were ranked as 'in-groups' in Irish society, while categories with over 2.500 merit attention. This scale was devised in the mid-1920s in the United States by Emory Bogardus[17]. The rank-order of preferences is an important measure in that it groups together (generally speaking) those we perceive to be closest to us in terms of religion, ethnic group and nationality, racial grouping, social class, political ideology, *et cetera*. This is referred to as the *principle of propinquity*. When this principle is not confirmed in the order of preference, e.g. in the case of 'Northern Irish', there may be a conflict of perception or experience or cultural influence at work. Reflection on the following Table tells citizens of the Republic of Ireland much about themselves. People who are interested in advancing towards a wholly tolerant society are advised to read the text itself, i.e. *Pluralism and Diversity in Ireland*. Also, it would be advisable to carry out a similar research project in every country with cultural and religious diversity. From what I have studied and read about intergroup relations in other countries, the Republic of Ireland is probably one of the more tolerant (intergroup) societies when the whole picture is taken into account, i.e. when historic intergroup conflict has been allowed for. The findings of *Pluralism and Diversity in Ireland* (2011) confirm this opinion. Of course, from time to time one reads very negative commentaries on Irish society by writers, which are not borne out in the evidence, or they may be in relation to specific incidents, which merit such negative views. It is very important to test negative generalisations against the evidence.

While welcoming the overall improvement in intergroup tolerance between 1988-89 and 2007-08, there are a number of categories towards which the level of prejudice and intolerance is still unacceptable, especially those with a mean-social-distance (MSD) score of over 2.500. These categories would be quite vulnerable and the reasons for their relatively high MSD scores merit further research. Two subgroupings of categories are those who are victims of compulsive behaviour, i.e. *'Heavy Drinkers', 'Alcoholics', 'Drug Addicts',* and Middle-East categories. Negative social attitudes against people perceived to belong to compulsive behaviour categories militate against their rehabilitation and are likely to even worsen their problems. A more enlightened attitude towards people with compulsive behaviour problems is quite urgent!

17 Bogardus, Emory, 'Measuring Social Distance', in *Journal of Applied Sociology*, 1925.

'Admit to Kinship' and Mean-Social-Distance of all Stimulus Categories by Rank Order[18]

R/O	Stimulus Category	Admit to Kin-ship	MSD (1-7)	R/O	Stimulus Category	Admit to Kin-ship	MSD (1-7)
1st	'Roman Catholics'	91.1%	1.168	27th	'Socialists'	67.0%	1.990
2nd	'Working Class'	85.6%	1.228	28th	'Lithuanians' *	65.5%	2.044
3rd	'People-Physical Dis.'	83.0%	1.268	29th	'Russians'	63.9%	2.091
4th	'Irish Speakers'	84.4%	1.324	30th	'Coloureds'	58.7%	2.164
5th	'Unmarried Mothers'	82.4%	1.339	31st	'Jews'	60.7%	2.179
6th	'Welsh'	82.4%	1.388	32nd	'Indians'	57.2%	2.276
7th	'Gardaí'	81.4%	1.392	33rd	'Capitalists'	60.8%	2.297
8th	'Euro-Americans'	81.3%	1.416	34th	'Afro-Americans'	52.7%	2.342
9th	'English'	81.0%	1.422	35th	'Blacks'	52.6%	2.348
10th	'Canadians'	80.0%	1.430	36th	'Atheists'	52.5%	2.373
11th	'Scottish'	81.7%	1.436	37th	'Africans'	52.3%	2.440
12th	'Unemployed'	80.9%	1.446	38th	'Agnostics'	50.3%	2.554
13th	'Protestants'	78.4%	1.4827	39th	'Romanians' *	55.6%	2.566
14th	'French'	78.5%	1.4829	40th	'Heavy Drinkers' *	41.9%	2.626
15th	'British'	77.2%	1.488	41st	'Pakistanis'	49.4%	2.682
16th	'Trade Unionists'	77.8%	1.552	42nd	'Palestinians' *	49.4%	2.709
17th	'Northern Irish'	75.1%	1.603	43rd	'Nigerians'	50.5%	2.726
18th	'People-Mental Dis.'	74.4%	1.612	44th	'Israelis'	47.9%	2.842
19th	'Dutch'	74.2%	1.632	45th	'Iranians' *	47.5%	2.850
20th	'Germans'	73.9%	1.644	46th	'Arabs'	45.6%	2.908
21st	'Spaniards'	75.4%	1.660	47th	'Communists'	45.9%	2.920
22nd	'Italians'	73.0%	1.703	48th	'Alcoholics'	32.7%	2.937
23rd	'Polish'	69.6%	1.790	49th	'Travellers'	39.6%	3.030
24th	'Gay People'	62.8%	1.923	50th	'Muslims'	42.9%	3.066
25th	'Chinese'	63.0%	1.924	51st	'Drug Addicts'	19.7%	4.194
26th	'Unionists'	66.2%	1.944	---	---	---	---

* Five categories not included in the 1988-89 national survey questionnaire.

Notes: (1) 'Euro-Americans' refer to White Americans while 'Afro-Americans' refer to 'Black Americans'

18 See Mac Gréil, Micheál, *Pluralism and Diversity in Ireland*, Dublin, Columba, 2011, p515.

(2) Mean-Social-Distance (MSD) is the mean on a social-distance scale of one-to-seven:

1	2	3	4	5	6	7
Admit to Kinship (family)	Have as a Close Friend	Have as a Next Door Neighbour	Have as a Co-Worker	Have as a Citizen of Ireland	Have as a Visitor Only	Debar or Deport

Our attitudes towards Middle-East categories, i.e. *'Pakistanis'*, *'Palestinians'*, *'Israelis'*, *'Arabs'* and *'Muslims'*, are largely vicarious prejudices in Ireland. Irish people have not had any significant direct negative experience of members of any of the above five categories. We have absorbed negative dispositions from the media and from propaganda largely from the Western power-bloc of nations. Irish attitudes seem to be influenced by Anglo-American media and hostility towards nations in the Middle East! Such negativity can enhance an extremist response and continue to keep the Middle East unstable. Hopefully, this is not part of the grand strategy towards the region!

The position of 'Muslims' is particularly serious (MSD = 3.066). Followers of this religion seem to be 'demonised' because of the paramilitary behaviour of Muslim extremists, especially the merciless attack on the Twin Towers in New York and the Pentagon in Washington in 2001. It should not be forgotten that Muslim extremists are but a minority of the general Muslim population. The negative stereotype is reflected in the 2007-08 findings in the Republic of Ireland. Arising from the nature of the intergroup problem in the Middle East, it has become quite clear that an exclusively secular solution is unlikely to succeed. *Therefore, it appears imperative that an ecumenical (pluralist) coming together of Christians, Jews and Muslims is necessary for peace, justice and harmonious co-existence in the Middle East (and elsewhere in the world).* Prior to such a grand ecumenical pluralist unity, it is necessary for greater unity within the Christian Churches, i.e. Roman Catholics, Protestants and Orthodox, and within Islam, i.e. between Sunni and Shia Muslims. Such a coexistence of the major religions whose origin is in the Middle East is one of the major challenges facing the world in the twenty-first century! The findings of the 2007-08 national survey should be helpful in pointing to the extent of this challenge.

The level of racism or racialism, i.e. prejudice against people because of their genetically-inherited physical traits, has dropped substantially in the Republic of Ireland in recent decades. In 1988-89 some 29.7% would 'welcome black people into the family through marriage' while in 2007-08 the percentage 'admitting black people to kinship' was 52.6%. This is a nominal increase of 22.9%. At 52.6% admitting black people to the family is still far too low since the colour of one's skin is, humanly speaking, 'as significant as the size of one's boots'. The difference between Irish attitudes towards 'Euro-Americans' (white Americans) and 'Afro-Americans' (black Americans) confirms the presence in the Republic of Ireland of an unacceptable level of racism. Some 81.3% would welcome 'Euro-Americans' into kinship, while only 52.7% would admit 'Afro-Americans' into the family. This is a nominal percentage gap of 28.6%. Such a large gap was not anticipated in a year (2008) when an Afro-American was elected President of the United States, i.e. Mr Barack Obama. The careless use of the term racism by people when commenting on prejudice in the case of ethnic or social categories only tends to prolong this particular form of prejudice, which really became popular with the slave trade from Africa as part of European expansionism since the fifteenth century. The failure of the 'Enlightenment' to accept all peoples as equal is a painful legacy to civilisation. Native peoples from Africa, Asia, Australasia and the Americas were to become 'fair game' for the Eurocentric 'explorers'! The 'Enlightenment' also failed to accept women as equal to men! This is not to deny its progress in other areas.

The ethnic preferences of the Irish people are more or less as were expected (see the above Table). The Irish, British and American categories were the most preferred in the following order: *'Irish Speakers', 'Welsh', 'Euro-Americans', 'English', 'Canadians', 'Scottish', 'British'* and *'Northern Irish'*. The 'French' were more preferred than 'British' and 'Northern Irish'. (I have already commented on the latter and on the 'Afro-Americans'.) The next ethnic block of categories was Europeans with a clear preference for West Europeans. They were ranked (in order of preference) as follows: *'French', 'Dutch', 'Germans', 'Spaniards', 'Italians', 'Polish', 'Lithuanians', 'Russians'* and *'Romanians'*. A study of the Table shows a number of anomalies. 'Russians' and 'Lithuanians' were moderately low down the rank order of preference. Most serious of all is the position of 'Romanians' with an MSD of 2.566 and only 55.6% welcoming them into the family. Their association with Gypsies/

Travellers seems to increase our prejudice against them. (The recently reported horrific rape and murder of an innocent Romany minor, Marioara Rostas, highlights the dangerous expression of this widespread prejudice[19].)

The ethnic minorities from Asia and Africa are classified in *Pluralism and Diversity in Ireland* as ethnico-racial. Their rank order of preference (see Table) are as follows: *'Chinese', 'Indians', 'Afro-Americans', 'Africans', 'Pakistanis', 'Palestinians', 'Nigerians', 'Israelis'* and *'Iranians'*. This rank ordering of ethnico-racial categories show a mix of the ethnic and racial factor at work. If it were influenced only by racialism then the 'Afro-Americans', 'Blacks', 'Africans' and 'Nigerians' should be at the bottom of the scale, below the 'Pakistani, 'Palestinians', 'Israeli' and 'Iranians'. This highlights once again the serious position of the Middle-East ethnic categories, which would have dangerous consequences, should conflict begin to spread (assuming Irish attitudes reflect Western European ones). The level of negativity in our attitudes towards those people shows an above-normal potential for hate-attitudes, which could be manipulated in the event of a Middle-East war. The world mass-media must not inflame their viewers or listeners with further anti-locution deemed to incite greater social prejudice. Strict international regulation is necessary to prevent 'incitement to hatred' in media reporting, *et cetera. An integrated pluralist world requires vigilant control of print and electronic media reporting on different nationalities, ethnic, racial and social groups.* The United Nations has been remiss so far, in my opinion, in its failure to curb the propagation of negative stereotypes of peoples at the national and international levels via the media!

The social distance towards six religious categories was measured in the 2007-08 national survey. In terms of order of preference they were ranked as follows: *'Roman Catholics', 'Protestants', 'Jews', 'Atheists', 'Agnostics'* and *'Muslims'*. The first two categories, i.e. 'Roman Catholics' and 'Protestants', were rated as in-groups in Irish society. Ninety per cent of respondents declared themselves to be 'Roman Catholics', while 4.4% were 'Protestant', 2.7% were 'other religion' and 3.3% stated they had 'no religion'. In the context of affiliation, therefore, the above order of preference would be in accord with the *principle of*

---

19 See *The Irish Times*, 30.1.2012.

propinquity. The level of prejudice or social distance towards 'Jews' (MSD scores) is disappointing and I would say, disturbing. Irish Jews have been a most positive minority for a long time in this country and their current standing at MSD of 2.179 (which improved since 1988-89) is still lower than anticipated. The relatively low ranking of 'Israelis' on the scale probably indicates that the negative relations between Israelis and Palestinians is not helping the status of 'Jews' in the disposition of the Irish people. Recent history has shown how vulnerable the 'Jews' are to scapegoating and negative stereotyping. This is another reason for Christian-Jewish-Muslim pluralist ecumenism (see *Nostra Aetate* of Vatican Two). Our attitudes towards 'Atheists' and 'Agnostics' have improved significantly and substantially between 1988-89 and 2007-08, but there is still plenty of room for further improvement when one reflects on the finding that only half the population (as represented by the national sample) would welcome members of either group into their family. I have already commented on the intolerable position of our dispositions towards 'Muslims', who have given so much to European and World culture and civilisation.

The political attitudes measured in the Table printed above (page 418) reports on the social distance toward six different categories. They were ranked in the following order of preference: *'Gardaí', 'Trade Unionists', 'Unionists', 'Socialists', 'Capitalists'* and *'Communists'*. 'Gardaí' ranked as an in-group, i.e. with an MSD of 1.392 or less than 1.500. Admission to kinship was as high as 81.4%. It must be fairly rare to see the State's police ranked so highly in society. 'Trade Unionists' were on the verge of being an in-group at MSD 1.552. The high ranking of 'Trade Unionists' in a neo-liberal dominated society is interesting. It could be interpreted as a vote of support for social partnership, which influenced socio-economic policies in the Republic of Ireland for over thirty years. Does it not also reflect on a de-radicalising of Irish trade unions and a dominant influence of white-collar unions? I have already commented on the very positive performance of 'Unionists' in the 2007-08 national survey.

The standing of 'Socialists', 'Capitalists' and 'Communists' in the Republic of Ireland at 27th, 33rd and 47th respectively on a scale of fifty-one categories is interesting. The percentages admitting the three categories to kinship are also interesting, i.e. 67% for 'Socialists', 61%

for 'Capitalists' and 46% for 'Communists'. All three recorded decreases in mean-social-distance scores between 1988-89 and 2007-08, which indicate an increase in tolerance of each category. The relative standing of 'Socialists' and 'Capitalists' has reversed, with the former passing out the latter in the rank-order of preference. The fall of the Berlin Wall in 1989 (after the completion of the 1988-89 national survey) seems to have made left-wing ideologies more attractive or less threatening! The type of capitalists who dominated the 'Celtic Tiger' failed to maintain the category's place *vis-à-vis* the 'Socialists'. A moderate level of intolerance still remains in the case of 'Socialists' and 'Capitalists', while the level of social prejudice towards 'Communists' is still relatively severe at an MSD of 2.920. The demonisation of 'Communists' seems to have begun to fade out in the minds of some of the respondents.

In all, there were nine general social categories[20] among the fifty-one included in the 2007-08 national survey. This order of preference among Irish people in the Republic was as follows: *'Working Class', 'People with Physical Disability', 'Unmarried Mothers', 'Unemployed', 'People with Mental Disability', 'Gay People', 'Heavy Drinkers', 'Alcoholics'* and *'Drug Addicts'*. The first four of the above are now classified as in-groups in Irish society, i.e. 'Working Class' (MSD 1.228), 'People with Physical Disability (MSD 1.268), 'Unmarried Mothers' (MSD 1.339) and 'Unemployed' (MSD 1.446). 'People with Mental Disability' (MSD 1.612) were marginally above the in-group cut-off score of MSD 1.500. The performance of the above five minority groups speaks well of Irish society and the degree to which true Christian values have penetrated the culture (even if many people are turning their backs on religion, temporarily at least).

The social standing of the 'Working Class' is higher than one would have expected. The relatively high social standing of those with disabilities gives the 'green light' to Government to be adequate and generous when dealing with the needs of the two categories in question. Although the standing of the 'Unemployed' had slipped a little between 1988-89 and 2007-08, the category was still an in-group. This, hopefully, will stand to the greatly increased percentage of the workforce now unemployed.

The unchristian stigma against 'Unmarried Mothers', caused by

20 Attitudes toward 'Travellers' are examined separately in the text *Pluralism and Diversity in Ireland.*

societies severely negative sanctioning of illegitimacy to protect the transfer of private property, has, for all practical purposes, evaporated in the Republic of Ireland. This is good and will enable the children of unmarried mothers to get the maximum support and respect in their families of origin and in the community. This should not be interpreted as a vote against Married Mothers. Contrasted with their standing in Victorian and early-twentieth century times when unmarried mothers were negatively stigmatised by Church and State in Ireland (and elsewhere), their new in-group status is greatly to be welcomed.

Homophobia in the Republic of Ireland has been a serious prejudice and an unjust source of suffering (psychological and, at times, physical) for people who were/are homosexual in orientation, be they gay or lesbian. The change in attitudes towards 'Gay People' between 1988-89 and 2007-08 has been exceptionally positive, i.e. 'admission to kinship' went from 12.5% (in 1988-89) to 62.8% (in 2007-08), which means a nominal increase of 50.3%. An improvement in the rank order of preference in the case of the forty-six categories measured in both national surveys, 'Gay People' went from 45th in 1988-89 to 24th in 2007-08, i.e. a move up the order of preference of 21 places. This means an extraordinary change and a very substantial decrease in 'homophobia' in the Republic of Ireland. Another measure of the change of Irish attitudes can be gauged from the difference in replies to the opinion: *'Homosexual behaviour between consenting adults should be a crime'*. The percentages in favour and against criminalisation are given for each of the three major surveys on page 245 above.

From a global perspective there are different public attitudes and laws in various countries in relation to homosexual behaviour between consenting adults covering the whole spectrum from total tolerance to total intolerance. The decriminalisation of homosexual behaviour between consenting male adults in the Republic in the 1990s after a prolonged constitutional case, which ended in the European Court of Human Rights, has probably contributed significantly to the above change. The general increase in intergroup tolerance has also added momentum to the reduction of homophobia. Gay people were among the minorities whose members were put to death in Nazi concentration camps during the reign of the Third Reich in the Second World War. The change of attitudes towards 'Gay People' is something that should be welcomed.

The attitudes towards people with compulsive behaviour symptoms, i.e. *'Heavy Drinkers', 'Alcoholics'* and *'Drug Addicts'* are very worrying. In the course of history, people who live their compulsive behaviour addictions have gone through three phases in the public reaction, namely, demonisation, criminalisation and medicalisation[21]. The responses to the first two reactions are negative and penal, while 'medicalisation' elicits a response of helping to *cure* or/and *rehabilitate*. The areas of compulsive behaviours can vary, i.e. alcohol, drugs, gambling, sexual behaviour, *et cetera*.

The results of the 2007-08 survey of attitudes towards 'Heavy Drinkers' (MSD 2.626), 'Alcoholics' (MSD 2.937) and 'Drug Addicts' (MSD 4.194) are counterproductive and, for the most part, negative. Such negative attitudes indicate a lack of solidarity with the addicted, who need support in society to overcome or modify their behaviour. Such hostility could well lead to further indulgence. One has but to reflect on the approach to addiction of Sr Consilio Fitzgerald (Cuan Mhuire Rehab Centres) which exemplified an unlimited tolerance for the addicted with incredibly positive results. When one adds to the extent of negativity toward 'Heavy Drinkers' and 'Alcoholics' the contradiction of Irish society's tolerance of widespread use and abuse of alcoholic drink, it is necessary to take action on two fronts. In the first place, *we need to restrict and regulate more strictly the availability and use of alcoholic drink in Irish society*. Secondly, we must do more to support those who become addicted to alcohol and drugs and try to change the current attitudes found in the 2007-08 national survey. As already stated, I believe the drinks industry should bear a proportionate amount of the medical and other costs arising from the abuse of alcohol.

The position of the Irish Travellers in the attitudes of the adult residents in the Republic of Ireland is that of *'informal apartheid'*. A special chapter (XIII) of *Pluralism and Diversity in Ireland* is devoted to the *'Travelling People'* and the book itself is dedicated to their emancipation. The main social distance findings are mixed. There was a very substantial increase in the percentages who would welcome a Traveller into kinship, i.e. increase from 13.5% in 1988-89 to 39.6%

21 Medicalisation of the addicted can benefit from psychological, psychiatric and physiological care.

in 2007-08. This removed the *lower caste* classification from Travellers because such a high proportion would be willing to welcome them into their families. While these findings were a most positive change, it was more than neutralised by the fact that there was a substantial increase in the percentage willing to deny Travellers citizenship, i.e. increase from 10.0% in 1988-89 to 18.2% in 2007-08. Of that, 18.2% (some 8.9% would have them as 'visitors only' and 9.3% would 'debar or deport Travellers').

To add to the Travellers' difficulty, the response to the statement: *'I would be reluctant to buy a house next door to a Traveller',* only 20.5% disagreed and 79.6% agreed (39.9% strongly agreed, 18.9% moderately agreed, 20.8% agreed slightly). Following the *Housing (Miscellaneous) Act 2002*, Traveller families are criminalised if they camp on public-owned lands. On the positive side, the majority of respondents (59.0%) would be *'willing to employ a Traveller'* and 73.2% felt that Travellers were *'competent to serve on a jury'*.

In the overall, however, there is an urgent need to emancipate and assist our Travelling People, who constitute only 0.5% (22,369 persons) in the national population (*2006 Census*). At present, they have a significantly lower life expectancy and a higher fertility than the 'Settled Community'. Some 52.9% are under twenty years of age and only 4.0% are sixty years or older (while 15.3% of the national population are 60 years or older). Only 25% of the Traveller workforce had gainful employment in 2006 (in the time of the Celtic Tiger). I hope the above evidence – demographic and attitudinal substantiates my appeal for a complete change of approach to the Travelling People as an Irish Ethnic Minority, within the Irish population.

The above paragraphs on the findings of the 2007-08 national survey, which are reported, analysed and explained in *Pluralism and Diversity in Ireland* (Dublin, Columba, 2011) focus only on a number of main findings. The reader may wish to study the text further by reading the book. For me personally, I feel very grateful to God for enabling me to complete this *magnum opus* and getting the necessary resources in personnel and funding to carry out the full operation to a satisfactory conclusion within a reasonable time span.

16. Austerity, a Questionable Solution to Ireland's Economic Problem

Returning to political developments in Ireland and within the European Union, 2011 and 2012 have been most challenging times. Austerity policies were a desperate response to deal with the post-boom collapse and draconian budgets were imposed on the people to ensure the continuation of the liberal capitalist (globalised free-market) system. This naturally stifled economic growth and countries' capacity to recover through work as the only source of real wealth. Ireland, as a member state of the European Union, felt obliged to follow the austerity route. The *Fianna Fáil*/Green Party Government introduced three such budgets in 2009, 2010 and 2011 and agreed to follow a programme of cutbacks and tax increases until 2014.

The General Election in the Republic of Ireland of 25th February 2011 resulted in a crushing defeat for the Government parties and substantial increases in support for *Fine Gael*, Labour, *Sinn Féin* and Independents. The *Fianna Fáil* first-preference vote dropped from 44.1% in 2007 to 17.5% in 2011. This expressed the anger of the voters in reaction to the economic collapse and the severity of the recent budgets. *Fine Gael* and the Labour Party agreed 'a programme for Government' and formed a new Coalition Government in March 2011 with an overall majority of 109 deputies to 57 (one *Fine Gael* deputy became *Ceann Comhairle*). Since then the new Government (with Mr Enda Kenny TD[22], as *An Taoiseach* and Mr Éamon Gilmore TD, as *Tánaiste*) continued the austerity programme. Unemployment increased as did emigration and there was a lowering of the material standard of living of many of the people. By the end of December 2011, there were noises and signs of public unrest pending. The farming industry seemed to be improving while manufacturing and services were declining. Emigration returned to former heights with many of Ireland's best educated being lured to strong economies like Canada and Australia.

The crisis in the eurozone had become a major international issue during the autumn and winter of 2011. Numerous meetings of the EU

---

22 The election of Enda Kenny TD, as *Taoiseach* was a great honour for County Mayo. The appointment of Michael Ring TD (grandnephew of General Joe Ring) as Minister for state was welcomed by his native Westport Community.

bodies were held in an attempt to agree a solution. Greece, Italy and Spain, in addition to Ireland and Portugal, were among the problem nations. Great Britain refused to endorse a new integrated financial/budgetary control system. Instead a majority of the members supported a euro-nations fiscal control plan. By the beginning of 2012, there were signs of serious slow-down continuing in the global economy. Ireland returned to 'recession status' in April 2012, despite good exports and a 'boom' in agriculture.

The euro crisis and the 2012 austerity budget were to dominate the first year of the new *Fine Gael*/Labour Government in the Republic of Ireland. The pain and uncertainty inflicted on the citizens by the impositions of our EU masters and the IMF overseers are testing the patience of the people. Emigration and social welfare were the two safety valves to curtail social unrest. The level of involuntary unemployment continued at 14% plus throughout 2011 and early 2012. The spectrum of relative deprivation increased in the Republic of Ireland mainly because of the traumatic reduction in the incomes of hundreds of thousands of families and individuals due to unemployment, serious reduction in wages and various cutbacks in benefits and increases in taxes of various kinds. Austerity was beginning to hurt the ordinary citizen and also reduce his or her level of services in health, education, etc. The farming minority was experiencing the opposite effect because of an improvement in the demand for Irish produce abroad. There was also a growing problem of mortgage and negative equity in house prices.

The ongoing payment of the interest on the debts incurred by the former Anglo Irish Bank and other banking organisations to speculative lenders has raised serious questions among the public in the Republic of Ireland. Initially, we were given to understand that the State had to protect depositors from a total collapse of the Irish banking system. Bodies, such as local Credit Unions, for instance, would be in danger of going under if the banks were not underpinned in 2008. I have never been able to understand why bond-holders who speculated in lending money without sufficient collateral should not be forced to write-off the interest and capital 'owed' to them after the collapse of the 'bubble', which they (the bond-holders) caused to inflate in the first place? Maybe I am being too simplistic! Sooner or later this would have to happen if our little country is to survive. My fear is that bond-holders seem to be the real rulers of our economy at present (to a large extent). They are the powerful and often anonymous, the captains of neo-liberal, free-market capitalism, who have been exempt from effective regulation by the people. We must not forget the real source of wealth is the working people! *We should never forget that our capacity to provide for the needs and comforts of our people, i.e. our work, is the real wealth of the nation* (Adam Smith)[23].

The Cowen/Lenihan (2008-2011) programme of austerity has been continued by the new Kenny/Gilmore-Noonan/Howlin (2011-2012) regime. They have had little option within the 'recovery plan' of liberal-capitalist Europe. My real fear is that this crisis will have failed our people unless the structural causes of it are addressed, i.e. the liberal, free-market, self-regulated system. Also, the unchecked globalisation grand plan needs to be reappraised. It has taken power away from the people in various countries. The new *Fine Gael/Labour* government will find it difficult to satisfy the electorate because of their state of relative powerlessness within the EU which had failed its member states dramatically. The authorities are restrained by an ideology of liberal capitalism, which refuses to impose a maximum incomes policy within and between the nations.

For the very big multinational corporations, globalisation is a mechanism for profit without adequate redistribution. There is no protection against the corporation's right to transfer operations to places of low wages and relatively cheap raw materials without equity and control. The successful corporations seem to me to inflate the real significance of our exports in terms of benefiting our national economy. They make it difficult to operate an effective *maximum incomes level* or a *curtailment of the consumer's choice of the privileged*. This is not to deny the benefits to Ireland arising from the valuable employment provided for local workers in multinational factories, laboratories and bureaucracies.

17. THE 'ARAB SPRING'

During the year 2011, a widespread popular protest took place across North Africa, beginning in Tunisia and going on to Egypt and Libya resulting in the removal of the leaders. The revolt spread as a classic

---

23 Smith, Adam, *The Wealth of Nations,* 1776.

case of media-driven social contagion. The Western powers and Western media strongly supported those who rebelled.

The case of Libya was the most violent where NATO carried out thousands of bombing missions without reporting one casualty in its own forces. The authorisation for their activity meant the stretching of the United Nations mandate to protect unarmed protesters. In effect, it seemed to lead to almost outright military support for an armed uprising. France and Britain were most reported as providing the forces of intervention. *In the end, Colonel Gaddafi's regime was defeated and he was ignominiously and summarily executed on capture without due process.* This barbaric use of capital punishment without trial will leave an uncivilised legacy in the memory of Libyan people in time to come.

The net outcome of the popular uprisings in the long-run is likely to be a strengthening of Islamic rule in Egypt, Libya and Tunisia. Other Middle-East countries are also being destabilised by the spread of popular protest. Western media seem to be supporting this widespread destabilisation while, at the same time, giving support to those seeking a change of regime. It is to be hoped that participation in popular democracy will lead to a more pluralist regime in the countries concerned. Consensus government, as operating in Northern Ireland, would seem to me to be the most likely ruling system to succeed in countries with ethnic and religious minorities.

The position of Iran is causing great international concern because of the development of nuclear energy, which the Western powers, i.e. the United States and NATO, fear could be used to develop an atomic weapon. Iran is fearful of Israel using its atomic weapons against it. Iran began to feel the pressure of 'sanctions', which could lead to serious deprivation of its population. (The situation is ongoing.)

By the beginning of 2012, the popular uprising in parts of Syria had become more violent and destructive. From the outside, it appeared to have developed into the beginnings of a civil war with armed conflict on both sides. Some military personnel were reported to have deserted the state army and joined the rebels. An attempt to put through a motion against the Syrian regime at the United Nations Security Council was vetoed by Russia and China. In March 2012, a Security Council agreement was reached on a plan for reform in Syria with the cooperation of the Syrian government, but it did not materialise too much.

18. RELIGION IN THE 21ST CENTURY

This brings me on to considering the position of religion in Ireland and throughout the world in the first decade of the twenty-first century of Christianity. I suppose my first comment would be that religion has survived the ebb and tide of history despite various efforts to make it obsolete during the medieval, renaissance, enlightenment and scientific periods. This goes to confirm for me that there is a God and that we human beings are helped to live full lives with an awareness of His existence and our commitment (be it strong or weak) to live in society according to His guidance or will as revealed to us in His revelation and through our conscience. Faith, I believe, is a gift and, therefore, one can never blame or judge anyone for not being able to believe. I always respect people's agnosticism and their atheism, so long as they do not try to oppose the rights of those who do believe. I also (as a Christian) believe in the Church as *the corporate presence of Christ on earth through the indwelling of the Holy Spirit*. As such, the Church, which is the People of God, is obliged to hand on the basic truths of the Christian revelation to each new generation and guide each other on how to live out these truths in every generation. In life it is in getting to know and love our neighbour that we get to know and love God.

Since God is personal and wishes to relate to each person individually and collectively, personal prayer and collective worship are the proper response of the people to their God. In order to preserve the deposit of faith from generation to generation it is reasonable and necessary that selected members of the people of God would be called on and trained to teach and guide every generation of the faithful without deviation from the 'deposit of faith'. Likewise, it is necessary that certain people are chosen to lead the faithful in religious worship and to administer the sacraments. Spiritual leaders are also necessary to lead us in prayer and worship.

The Roman Catholic Church was and is, for me, the collectivity of the faithful, within the broader Christian family of Churches, into which I was born and reared. When I came to the age of rational self-consciousness, I gave my 'real assent' to my membership of the Catholic Church and tried, as best I could, to live up to its norms of worship and morality. Of course, I did not succeed in avoiding deviation from time to time. When I sinned I repented through the sacrament of penance, tried to amend my life and started out again. Before joining the Jesuits at the age of twenty-eight, I could be classified as an active lay member of the Church to some degree. This commitment to the Church was not due to my personal virtue but rather as a result of my parents and friends who inculcated in me and in my friends the importance of being open to the urgings of the Spirit and adopting a voluntary pastoral role.

To the outside observer, the state of the Roman Catholic Church in Ireland at the beginning of the 21st century is in a much-weakened position, when compared with its dominant role during the period 1920-1970. The drop in Church attendance began to accelerate in the 1980s and the authority of the Church leaders was publicly questioned in the media from time to time. In fact, there was a very significant change taking place within the Church itself after the deliberations at Vatican Two. The role of the laity and the move towards 'responsibility-sharing' had begun. There was a certain amount of disillusion when the expectations of Vatican Two seemed to be 'rolled back' somewhat by a more cautious authority in Rome and also by less adventurous local Church leaders in some dioceses. This was to be expected because of the nature of a Church, which was universal and seemed to move at the pace of the slowest culture.

The rise of the feminist movement, for instance, in the 1970s and 1980s was to challenge most social institutions, i.e. the polity, the economy, education and family and religion. In the Church, it could be said with justification, religious sisters and outstanding lay women exercised authority and a degree of autonomy that was not given them in the polity and in the economy. Nevertheless, the Church was seen to be predominantly male-dominated at the centre of its hierarchy. Unlike its Protestant counterparts, the Roman Catholic Church could not see its way to admit women to the priesthood. The majority of respondents in Ireland (64%), in the 2007-08 national survey, would be willing to accept the ordination of women in the Roman Catholic Church today, should the authorities agree to it. Many articulate women have advocated such a change and may feel alienated by the present situation. The place of women in the authority structure of the Roman Catholic Church needs to be addressed. I am not aware of why we could not have female 'cardinals' in our church! After all, women constitute 70% of the core Catholic in the parishes.

Since the 1970s there has been a very significant rise in materialism in Irish culture and a move towards consumerism and secularism. *The autonomy of the secular had been clearly recognised by Vatican Two*. The acceptance of the validity of the empirical sciences and their (hypothetical) findings were acknowledged. A new attitude prevailed towards the findings of psychologists, sociologists, anthropologists, palaeontologists and others. Their works were no longer viewed as '*adversarii*' (adversaries of the truth) by seminary professors. The classic case was that of the acceptance of the 'evolution hypothesis' as not being in conflict with the Church's understanding of 'ongoing creation'.

It is very difficult to realise now that during my first years as a student of philosophy, 1961-63, the writings of Teilhard de Chardin SJ, were banned because of his teaching on evolution. It took Pope John XXIII to remove the ban. The fact that we could accept the findings of empirical science (which of their nature are always hypothetical and open to change), did not, in my experience, weaken or threaten the validity of the metaphysical reality of religious belief and understanding. In a real sense, Christian revelation fitted on to natural sciences like 'a glove fitted on to a hand'. In the Incarnation, the physical/empirical and the Divine come together in 'Christ made human'. Those who see contradictions between science and the Christian religion create a false dichotomy. Of course, there is also the possibility of disagreement between the interpretation of theologians on the verified scientific findings or conclusions. The problem for some metaphysical agnostics is their faith in empirical science as the exclusive method of explaining reality. In such a view our lives are grossly limited. The more inclusive approach is to see the world/life as being both physical and metaphysical. Such is the Christian epistemology.

The rise of the exclusively empirical/scientific approach in modern, post-Enlightenment Irish society is related to the greater participation in third-level education which has been accompanied by a low level of religious and philosophical education. This, in all probability, may have weakened the faith and religious practice of a substantial proportion of the younger population at least for a time in their lives. The underlying need for meaning (as well as material interests) causes people to raise their sights beyond the mundane and material aspects of human life in later years. Therefore, it is very important that the Church or its spokespersons do not show animosity towards those who may have withdrawn from the religious practice in their youth. As Christ Himself warned us, we are not to judge others if we ourselves do not wish to be judged.

The Jesuits in Ireland, like the diocesan clergy and other religious orders and congregations, have suffered a serious decline in vocations (as brothers or as priests in the Society of Jesus) in the past few decades. This has been the case of most provinces in Western Europe, the United States and Canada and in Australia. Very worthwhile works and ministries had to be closed down because of the lack of manpower. Where possible, a serious effort has been made to hand over responsibility to committed lay believers – female and male. An attempt has been made to train lay leaders of our schools and other ministries in Jesuit spirituality. In the non-Western parts of the world, Jesuit vocations are encouraging. This is true also for other religious orders and diocesan clergy. The late Cardinal Tomás Ó Fiaich's prophesy that clergy and religious from the developing world would become evangelising missionaries in Ireland and in other Western so-called developed countries may be a reality sooner than we realise. The evangelisation of our consumer society will be much more difficult than the spreading of the faith in the poorer countries of Africa and Asia.

During my time in the Jesuit Order, there have been significant changes and achievements. On the changes' side we had a greater integration of the grades and the establishment of a better sense of brotherhood. While there are still some sociocultural remnants from the feudal era in which we were founded, i.e. in the sixteenth century, the de facto situation is moving towards equality. We are not yet fully egalitarian. The heroic work of Jesuits and other religious and clergy recently in Latin America and elsewhere, has been inspiring for religious in Ireland. During the past thirty years we have had the supreme witness of martyrdom in the cause of faith and justice.

At times, I have been very disappointed at the failure of the Jesuits (with notable exceptions) in Ireland to appreciate the importance of Irish language and culture, i.e. music and games. In fact, in my time, our all-Irish secondary school in Galway introduced English as a medium of instruction, at a time when the *Gaelscoileanna* at the primary level were increasing. In more recent years, there appears to be a growing focus on centralising our Order's structures towards Europe, which could result in the further weakening of the Irish cultural role. Of course, in times of declining numbers, centralisation and the merging of Provinces would appear to the culturally detached as rational and *ad majorem Dei gloriam!*

Despite our relatively small numbers, the Jesuits in Ireland have made a significant contribution to the spiritual, educational, cultural and social life of Irish society. The tragedy of the drop in vocations has been the more serious at a time when, with other Orders and Congregations, our services have become more necessary. Sometimes, I feel we must be prepared to almost die before we are reborn again. Our support for private secondary schools has raised serious questions among egalitarianists within and outside the Order. Such schools provide professionally qualified leaders who maintain our inequitable (at times) social system. Those who would argue in favour of Jesuit private schools point to the number of social radicals they have produced. Also, it could be argued the sons of the powerful were already from a dominant social background and the Jesuits could open them to the less privileged children of God. While respecting and acknowledging the good work of private schools, I feel it would be better for Jesuits to be identified more with the weaker sections of society. The current crisis in the Irish church gives the Irish province an ideal opportunity to respond to a real need in collaboration with the bishops, priests and laity.

It has been my opinion for some years that a successful future for single gender religious orders was less likely in the current culture. This is especially true for 'emancipated' Western Societies. Therefore, would it not be wise, to admit women to full membership of the Society of Jesus? Neither our pastoral ministries nor our spirituality are gender-bound. The fact that priests in the Roman Catholic Church are exclusively male and that the Jesuits are predominantly priests should not be an obstacle to female membership of the Order. What makes a person a Jesuit are the vows rather than ordination. Men and women are equally eligible for religious vows. The Order and its mission would benefit enormously from an inclusive Society of Jesus. In the end, the mission of the Church would reap the reward of such a progressive innovation. I pray that the Jesuit Order and the Church will be open always to the priority of equality in all aspects of life in the service of God and our neighbour.

435

19. Facing the Child-Abuse Problem in the Church

The public exposure of child abuse by a minority of priests and religious during the 1990s was a cause of great shame and regret to the faithful, including priests and religious. For the sake of justice to the victims of this child-sex-abuse it was good to have those involved brought to account. Although many of the cases (brought to light) of child-sex-abuse by clergy and religious had taken place in earlier decades, I was totally oblivious to them and nobody ever reported such abuse to me. I must admit I was shocked when the revelations came to public attention. It seems they were dealt with confidentially by the Church authorities. The fear of public scandal may have put pressure on the Superiors of the deviant clergy to keep the affairs confidential. Also, it was claimed that legal advice may have prevented a more open apology to the victims on behalf of the organisations. I would hope that those who have been abused will (for their personal freedom) get the grace to forgive those who have offended them. Forgiveness is necessary for the liberation of the offended and the rehabilitation of the offender. It is also at the core of our Christian faith.

Once the cases were brought into the public arena, the print and electronic media singled out the priests and religious abusers for headline reporting which was at times 'over the top'. The humiliation caused to the non-deviant vast majority of priests and religious was very great. This had the latent effect of making us more humble, which is good. The Church authorities produced child-protection policies, which were necessary. Hopefully, this sad chapter in the history of the Church will have taught us a lesson. Those who were injured by the whole sad series of crimes against children should be given priority in relation to professional and material support. Also, false accusations against innocent priests and religious need to be guarded against because of the ease with which such allegations can be made by people who may not be motivated by the pursuit of justice. There has been a danger of the demonisation of clergy and religious by some of those who are obviously prejudiced against the Church and its clergy and religious. This is something which we may have to 'grin and bear'!

The impact of the scandals on the life of the Church in Ireland has been serious but it should not be exaggerated. The causes of the decline in vocations and in the practice of the faith pre-dated the public exposure of the scandals. That is not to say that vocations to the priesthood and religious life have not been affected by the scandals. Of course, they must have had a negative impact. The only way to change that scene is by the total honesty and transparency of the Church authorities in dealing with the problem. The discovery that the authorities in the Diocese of Cloyne failed to implement the Church's strict guidelines has added insult to injury. This was discovered by the Catholic Church's own monitoring board which gives me more confidence in the bishops' adherence to their own rules. Inevitably, there will be mistakes and, maybe, excesses in the new regime. All regulations are tested only in their operation. We must constantly pray that the Holy Spirit will guide the Church through this emergency.

In a very positive article on the religious in Ireland in *The Irish Times* on the 20th May 2006, Senator Martin Mansergh (himself a member of the Church of Ireland) referred to the child-abuse scandals thus: '*Sorrow at abuses, which were a betrayal of trust, should lead to appropriate redress and better precaution, not to abandonment, marginalisation or expropriation*'. I would agree with the Senator's comment, which implies that we should learn from the mistakes and continue the task of preaching the word, worshipping God and striving for a more just and peaceful society. The tragic irony of the child-abuse scandals was its contradiction of the role of clergy and religious, which I had experienced throughout my life. I had known of so many times when priests, brothers and nuns were and still are ever-vigilant in protecting children from abuse or interference. It was always a top priority in the pastoral care of the young. And that was the way it should be. It is very important at this stage in the history of the Church in Ireland, having instituted the necessary precautions and procedures, not to lose its nerve in fulfilling its never-ending vocation and mission to the society of today, which includes the protection of children from sexual or other abuse.

Following the Cloyne Report (by Judge Yvonne Murphy) in 2011 on the failure of the diocese of Cloyne to implement the child-protection rules laid down by the Irish Bishops, *An Taoiseach,* Mr Enda Kenny TD, alleged that the Vatican obstructed the enforcement of the procedures. This was denied by the Vatican in its reply, which also noted the incorrect reference to such obstruction by the Vatican in the Murphy Report. The Irish Government did not acknowledge its inaccurate allegation.

In the 2011 pre-budget departmental cutbacks, *An Tánaiste* and Minister for Foreign Affairs, Mr Éamon Gilmore TD, proposed the closing of the Irish Embassy to the Vatican in Rome (together with embassies to Iran and East Timor) for economic reasons, i.e. to save €700,000 a year. The closing of this Embassy was an unnecessary insult to the vast majority of the Irish people. Hopefully the damage will be undone when wiser and fairer counsel will prevail.

How to interpret these two incidents in a country with over 84% of its population claiming Roman Catholic affiliation (in the 2011 Census) raised a serious dilemma for the people. It seems to me to be a deliberate admonition to the Irish Roman Catholic Church by our 'representative Government'. Considering the enormous contribution of the Roman Catholic Church to the spiritual and pastoral life of the people (at home and abroad), in education, medical care, social services, recreation and sport and in the cultural life of generations, the attempt to marginalise it has been a most ungrateful response to such immense generosity. 'Eaten bread is soon forgotten.'

There has been a degree of painful purification taking place among priests and religious over the past number of years (since the early 1990s), which will lead to positive renewal. The closer involvement of committed laity in the pedagogical, spiritual, liturgical and pastoral life of the parish will help priests and religious to cope with any problems of marginalisation or isolation caused by an often-imbalanced media. The priest who is close to the people can be reinforced by them in their joint mission. Reflecting on the approach of Saint Martin of Tours (d.397) and recognised as the father of Irish Christian Spirituality, it might be good if the Bishop and the priests of the Diocese would come together to pray even more regularly. This would result in a renewal and a reinvigoration of the priesthood. In this regard I would also recommend a greater role for women in the administrative, spiritual and pastoral leadership of the Church. The recently founded *Association of Catholic Priests* (2010) has engaged in deliberation and public consultation on the renewal of the Church in Ireland. It is too early to evaluate its contribution.

20. THE 50ᵀᴴ INTERNATIONAL EUCHARISTIC CONGRESS, DUBLIN, 2012[24]

The 50th International Eucharistic Congress took place in Dublin from the 10th to the 17th of June 2012. I had the privilege of taking part in the events of five of the eight days (including the closing Mass in Croke Park). It was a unique experience and did much 'to revive our drooping spirits'. Daily attendance (from Monday to Saturday) in the RDS ranged from thirteen to fourteen thousand pilgrims. The Eucharistic Procession on Wednesday, 13th of June, was almost more than a mile and a half long. In addition to those assembled in the RDS, special liturgies and spiritual events were organised in thirty-four designated churches throughout Dublin city and suburbs.

The major ceremonies and talks were transmitted on various Irish and international TV channels and radio stations. The organisation was efficient and unobtrusive. Hundreds of core-Catholics made up a team of volunteers who kept order and provided guidance for the thousands of pilgrims present. Clergy, laity and religious from all around the globe mixed and exchanged ideas as brothers and sisters. The weather was reasonable and we were able to cope with the odd shower of mild rain. The variety and quality of the programme kept up the pilgrims' interests. It was a special bonus for me that the patrician shrine at *Mámean* was duly recognised at the opening ceremony when An tAth Fiontan Ó Muineacháin placed a stone from St Patrick's Bed at the Congress Lectern.

The principal theme of the Congress was the place of the Eucharist in the life of the Christian Church today. Six specific topics were discussed and reflected on throughout the week. In chronological order they were as follows:

Monday: Ecumenism, Our Communion through Baptism;
Tuesday: Communion in Marriage and the Family;
Wednesday: Priesthood and Ministry in the Service of Communion;
Thursday: Reconciliation in our Communion;
Friday: Communion in Suffering and Healing;
Saturday: Communion in the Word through Mary.

---

24 This reflection of mine on the Eucharistic Congress has also been published in *Gold*, a quarterly publication on spirituality in later life, Dublin, 2012.

In all, over 160 workshops/talks were delivered on the above list of topics and most sessions were over-crowded despite the large size of the different halls. It was necessary to queue in advance of each workshop. The range of subjects and speakers gave the pilgrims a good choice. Plenary liturgies and talks were scheduled for the vast arena. I attended all the sessions I could and found the material interesting and, at times, stimulating. Of course, I would like to have discussed the contents of lectures and sermons with some speakers and look forward to the publication of the proceedings of the Congress. Such a publication would provide a good textbook for believers wishing to become active in the life of the Church. The Holy Father's address to us at the close of the Dublin Congress was brief but inspiring. I listened to him as the 'Vicar of Christ' on earth. Pope Benedict XVI spoke with authority, without being authoritarian.

One of the most attractive features of the Eucharistic Congress (for me) was the whole atmosphere of mutual respect and recognition of our common faith, irrespective of age, gender, nationality and position in the Church or Christian Denomination. We were truly a gathering of the 'People of God'. The experience was akin to being on a spiritual holiday in an 'oasis' away from the 'desert' of materialism and cynicism in a world that has lost its optimism and meaning. It was good to be there!

The fact that one day was centred on the theme of Christian Ecumenism and the Eucharist with participation of the Church of Ireland, Orthodox, Methodist, Presbyterian and other Churches was uniquely inspiring. In my opinion, the best sermon (in a week of good sermons) was preached on Monday by an Orthodox clergyman in the prophetic mode. It strengthened my desire for inter-communion and mutual recognition of Holy Orders. We badly need a renewed ecumenical movement to restore the vibrancy of Christianity in our pluralist and diverse world.

Another theme which was of special interest to me was 'Communion in Marriage and the Family'. *The Church is social*! The faith is dependent on family, neighbourhood and local community. It is transmitted (informally) from parents and grandparents to the children primarily in the home. Regrettably, the neglect of the domestic Church appears to have been taking place in Ireland for decades. I cannot see a revival of religion without its return to the family and local community, where we find our roots and nurture.

The global universality of the Roman Catholic Church was very evident during the Congress. The broad ethnic diversity of pilgrims from Europe, the Americas, Asia, Africa and Australasia integrated around their common belief. Irish missionaries from all over the world were present with the believers from their host nations. The Catholic Church in Western Europe would benefit greatly from re-evangelisation by missionaries (lay, religious and clerical) from South America, Africa and Asia where the level of commitment to Christ seems to be much more vibrant than ours.

Archbishop Diarmuid Martin, whose diocese hosted the 50th International Eucharistic Congress, and his able staff should be very pleased with the success of this major event in the life of the Church. They were first-class hosts. The Archbishop succeeded in setting an atmosphere of cordiality, equality and simplicity, which made us all feel at home as true pilgrims in the RDS and in Croke Park. It would be wonderful if such a '*leitmotif*' would begin to permeate Irish society, especially in and between our Christian Churches. With God's help this might be a product of the Congress. The next International Eucharistic Congress will be hosted by the diocese of Cebu in the Philippines in 2016. I hope to be able to attend this Congress, *le cúnamh Dé.*

21. *UACHTARÁN NUA*

In November 2011, Micheál D Ó hUigín, was elected *Uachtarán na hÉireann* to succeed Mrs Mary McAleese who served with distinction in that office for fourteen years (1997-2011). President Ó hUigín, who was a TD of the Irish Labour Party for Galway West for many years, also served in the office of *Aire na Gaeltachta* in the Governments led by *Taoisigh*, Albert Reynolds TD and John Bruton TD in the 1990s. Our new President had been very active in international civil rights campaigns during the post-Second World War period. In the 1960s and 1970s he led many protests at which I had the privilege of swelling the ranks. He was an articulate, insightful and courageous proponent of social justice. He was a senior lecturer in sociology and political science at University College Galway and this enabled him to diagnose and understand many of Ireland's and the world's structural social and cultural problems. His commitment to the Irish language and culture gives the people reassurance that we will not be totally absorbed or swallowed up in the current endless preoccupation with materialism. *Guím rath Dé ar thréimhse oifige ár nUachtarán Uí Uigín.*

Chapter Ten

EPILOGUE

1. INTRODUCTION

It was hoped originally to publish this book in the autumn of 2012 and complete the commentary on '*The Society and World in which I Grew up*' with a reflection on the International Eucharistic Congress in Dublin between the 10th and 17th of June 2012 and with a note of welcome to the new President of Ireland, Micheál D Ó hUigín. Owing to various pressures, including work on the Report *Westport Eleven-Twelve* (published in 2013), the date of publication was deferred to autumn 2014. This has given the author the opportunity to comment on developments and happenings over the two years 2012 to 2014 in the form of this *Epilogue*. Hopefully, this updating of the text will be of interest to the reader as the 'pilgrimage of life' continues in the never-over 'Ongoing Present'.

During the two years under review, Ireland and the world continued to struggle with the austere efforts to survive and recover from the economic/financial crash of 2008 in what could be aptly described as a state of 'economic convalescence'. Perhaps, the individual and collective experience will make us wiser and more realistic in relation to the folly of extravagant lifestyles and accept the need for universal maximum-income levels globally and nationally.

It was also an interesting period for the Roman Catholic Church, as it continued (in the West) to cope with materialism and a high degree of religious indifference. In Ireland, the new legislation for the protection of the mother at childbirth was seen as defective in part in that it opened the possibility of the unnecessary termination of the life of the unborn child in the case of threatened suicide. The proper reaction to threatened suicide is support and counselling to enable mother and child to survive. This new legislation has, in my opinion, damaged Ireland's heretofore legal protection for the unborn child. Let us pray that the facility provided by the legislation will never be used. Of course, the protection of the mother from life-threatening (physical) medical conditions is morally justified, even at the danger to the life of the unborn. This has always been the case in Catholic teaching.

On the positive side, the election of Pope Francis in March 2013 has been welcomed by believers and non-believers alike. His priorities and lifestyle have appealed to most people of goodwill. For Jesuits it was a unique experience to have a member of the Order as Bishop of Rome for the first time in our history. I was surprised and happy at Pope Francis' election. The Church seems to be recovering slowly from the scandal of child abuse by a very small minority of religious and clergy and has adopted new regulations to deal with it now and in the future. Society (including the Church) must study the causes of paedophilia as a form of compulsive behaviour and seek ways of curing it. At the end of the day, it is by our errors that we shall learn.

In the course of the following paragraphs, it is proposed to comment in greater detail on the following areas of interest, i.e. (a) Socio-political developments; (b) The impact of Pope Francis; (c) The current international scene; (d) Life goes on for me; (e) The legacy of the Celtic Tiger (1990-2008) and (f) *Focail Scoir.* Growing old in such exciting and challenging times, a person is kept mentally and emotionally alive by the ongoing evolution of human society with its highs and lows. We live in a wonderfully dynamic world in which we are all invited to become involved and make whatever positive contributions we are able to give.

The recent (April 2014) State Visit of President Micheál D Ó hUigín to the United Kingdom marked an important positive stage in British-Irish relations. This was in response to Queen Elizabeth's very successful visit to the Republic in 2011. Reading accounts of the exchanges, I was disappointed to observe little or no reference made to religion and the contribution of the Irish Catholic Chaplaincy to the support of Irish immigrants in England over the years.

2. SOCIO-POLITICAL DEVELOPMENTS (2012-14)

During 2013, we celebrated the centenary of the great test of the Trade Union Movement in Ireland by commemorating the 1913 Lock-Out in Dublin. Numerous articles, radio and television programmes, conferences and concerts were organised to mark the occasion. As a trade unionist and currently Honorary President of the County Kildare Congress Centres for the Unemployed, I was among the many guests at the Special Commemoration Garden Party in Áras an Uachtaráin, hosted by his Excellency, Micheál D Ó hUigín, *Uachtarán na hÉireann*. It was good to witness that the work of James Connolly, Jim Larkin and comrades was acknowledged at the highest level in the State.

In Ireland and throughout most of the European Union the people had to continue to endure the severe effects of the austere economic policies during 2012, 2013 and so far in 2014. Development and growth had almost stagnated. There was hardly a builder's crane to be seen on the Dublin sky-line! Agriculture, and the food industry, and a number of foreign-based pharmaceutical and electronic industries seemed to be doing relatively well and kept our exports high. In reality, there were relatively few jobs for the ordinary worker.

There was a haemorrhage of emigration of qualified Irish youth ('brain and brawn') who were forced to work abroad in the strong economies where they contributed to the wealth-generation of their host nations. To add insult to injury, the costly education and training of these young Irish emigrants had to be borne by the Irish people without any contribution from the host countries benefiting from their valuable work. I believe strongly that there should be *an immigrant tax paid by the host country to the country of origin*, i.e. €84,000 for every graduate and up to €250,000 for a qualified medical doctor or equivalent specialisation. It is sad to see the cost of emigration is still adding to Ireland's misery!

It appears that there are two diverse 'economic cycles' within the European Union. Germany, Benelux and the Scandinavian countries seem to be on a 'high', while Greece, Italy, Spain, Portugal, France, Ireland and even Britain are experiencing a 'low' at present. The reverse situation seemed to be in place during the so-called 'Celtic Tiger' years. For instance, when the Irish economy was overheating and would have benefited from higher interest rates, Germany needed low interest rates to sustain its development. Unfortunately for Ireland, the needs of Germany reigned within the eurozone. Is the common currency eventually going to force us into a common boom-burst cycle?

Looking to the future there are serious structural problems facing Ireland's job-creation policies. Employment in agriculture, fishing and the manufacturing industry is becoming more limited with the advance of technology. In years to come, the vast majority of human beings will be employed in the services, i.e. caring, communicating, entertaining, educating, spiritual guidance, infrastructure maintenance, transport, accountancy and finance, plumbing, electricity, tourism, art, music, drama, etc. The present policy, however, seems to curtail public service jobs and invest quite substantial sums in certain manufacturing industries which are not that labour-intensive and are often of little use to the ordinary skilled, semi-skilled and unskilled workers.

There appears to be a degree of class distinction in the State's support for job creation. This is borne out in the occupational make-up of our long-term unemployed. An economic system based on a liberal-capitalist free-market ideology is, in my view, of its nature anti-services. In addition to this ideological bias, we have an arbitrary job-prestige rating scale, which subjectively ranks white-collar professions higher than blue-collar skilled workers. (Jesus of Nazareth was a mere carpenter!)

As noted earlier in this book (see page 361), the indigenous or native-Irish have become 'lace-curtain Irish' and are keen that their children pursue white-collar professions to the neglect of the blue-collar trades and skills. During the boom years, immigrant workers from Eastern Europe and elsewhere had to fill the blue-collar vacancies and did so with commendable competence. The current structure of the Irish workforce is not conducive to the full employment of our blue-collar workers.

Uncontrolled globalisation, which exploits the weakest people and communities for the advantage of the rich and the strong, is structurally supportive of well-paid job-opportunities of minorities in weaker societies. It is also contributing to the unjust distribution of wages and job prestige in all societies. The industrial community in Ireland today also seems to have become engaged in the manipulation of blue-collar workers and embraces globalisation with open arms. Many of our manufacturing jobs have been transferred to countries where labour and raw materials are cheap.

Before leaving the post-2008 survival of the Irish economy, it would be unjust and ungracious not to acknowledge the main political leaders and assistants who, having chosen a policy of austerity, implemented it efficiently and courageously over a period of five years. As already stated (see pages 427ff), I feel that such a policy would not be my choice because it is too severe on the weaker sections of society. Nevertheless, it won public approval in *Dáil Éireann*. Great credit is due to the late Minister for Finance, Brian Lenihan TD, (who literally risked his life to save the country) and former *Taoiseach*, Brian Cowen TD (who was scapegoated and had to bear the anger of the people) for deciding on a five-year plan of recovery, even before the Troika forced themselves on us. Equally, credit is due to Minister for Finance, Michael Noonan TD, *Taoiseach* Enda Kenny TD, *Tánaiste* Éamon Gilmore TD and Minister for Public Expenditure and Reform, Brendan Howlin TD, who brought the agreed plan to fruition as outlined. Our exit from the control and support of the Troika was an achievement of both governments.

The social, economic and political 'fall-out' of the austerity budgets will be with us for a time to come and some of the more extreme decisions may have to be reversed when things improve. It would be 'a waste of a crisis' if some structural changes to the self-regulated liberal-capitalist free-market system did not take place. I sense two welcome changes, namely, strict regulation of the banks and State finances and moves towards maximum income-levels. It would be good to reduce the material standards of living of the strong societies so as to enable the weaker ones to live a decent way of life. Greater attention will have to be paid to the environmental impact of the lifestyles chosen by the people. I would like to see Ireland's material standard of living reduced for those of us with more than we actually need.

3. POPE FRANCIS

After just one year in office, Pope Francis has precipitated a new awakening among the 'people of God' and all people of goodwill. His election surprised me but it made me very happy that a pope with a grassroots background and a difficult life experience in his native Argentina would be able to identify with struggling humanity at this time. The Pope's approach is marked by a return to the simplicity and openness of Christ himself as a brother of all people, especially the poor and the marginalised.

It would be naive, however, not to acknowledge the immensity of the challenge facing the Church (which Francis compared to 'a field hospital after a battle') to motivate the people to return to a greater belief in God and the proactive pursuit of social justice, peace, charity, forgiveness and the protection of the absolute dignity of each human being. Respect for the physical environment is also an integral part of the Christian faith.

As most people who have had the experience of leading an organisation or a movement know, there are two types of change. One is 'total innovation', i.e. the setting up of new structures and the establishment of a new culture for the movement. The second is sometimes referred to as 'growth from strength', i.e. the identification of the strong aspects, and the development and renewal of them. The former would be radical and come close to revolutionary, while the latter would focus on the reform of the movement. I expect Pope Francis to arrive at a programme which combines both reform and revolutionary aspects.

It appears that he will be disposed to a more collegial model of the Roman Catholic Church. This is an opportune time to promote collegiality at all levels in the Church, i.e. parish, diocese, country, region and the highest level of Pope with his brother bishops and sister women leaders. Whatever structure is devised to give concrete expression to the collegial Church, it is very important to include women believers participating at each level of the 'collegial ladder'.

As has been mentioned a number of times in this book, the need to work for ecumenical (pluralist) unity within the family of Christian Churches is something Pope Francis will have as a priority. Following the work of his recent predecessor, Pope Benedict XVI, he seems to be keen to reach out to Jews and Muslims. World peace is very unlikely until the major religions of the world come together in an 'integrated pluralist' manner. I pray that the new Bishop of Rome will be able to advance inter-faith reconciliation.

Secular society's leaders need to be aware of the people's right to their religious beliefs and practices. Otherwise, they will incite religious extremism and the fundamentalism that was witnessed in the recent history of Iran/Persia under the rule of the Western-backed Shah. 'Extremely liberal Ayatollahs' tend to generate 'extremely religious Ayatollahs'!

The fact that Pope Francis is the first Jesuit to be elected Bishop of Rome is very significant and reassuring for the Society of Jesus and for me personally. I was ordained a priest on the same day (31st July 1969) as Pope Francis (in different locations, of course) and we probably studied similar courses in philosophy and theology, as decided by the Gregorian

University in Rome. He is six years my junior. Pope Francis' election has made the Jesuits an integral part of the Roman Catholic Church after two centuries of quasi-alienation.

The Jesuit Order had been suppressed by Pope Clement XI in 1773 at the behest of Voltaire, the Enlightenment, the Bourbon Monarchs, the Jansenists and others. We had been a thorn in the side of the European colonialists in South America because we defended the rainforest Indians from slavery (see the film, *The Mission*). The order was restored in 1814 by Pope Pius VII. The fact that Catherine the Great of Russia refused to sign the decree of suppression enabled a remnant of the Society to keep special contact between 1773 and 1814.

It is providential that Francis is Pope as we celebrate the bicentenary of the restoration of the Society of Jesus. When I was a student in the Catholic University of Leuven (Louvain) in 1964-65, I was reminded of the negative legacy of the Jesuit-Jansenist conflict in earlier years. When I joined the staff of St Patrick's College Maynooth in 1971, I often reflected on the possibility of coolness towards Jesuits by the senior academic staff, but it was not so. I was warmly accepted by the vast majority of the clerical academic staff.

If Pope Francis succeeds in changing and reforming the Roman Catholic Church, I believe a return to the faith and religious practice will follow. This, in turn, will be followed by an increase in religious and priestly vocations. Young idealistic people will be attracted to follow Christ more closely. Personally, I am hoping to see a greater number joining the Jesuits as Brothers and as Priests. They are badly needed at present.

4. THE INTERNATIONAL SCENE

The sad death of Nelson Mandela (1918-2013) elicited a genuinely universal grief. His wake and funeral were an amalgam of sadness for a real liberator by those he inspired and led to freedom, and a public act of contrition by the representatives of the class who suppressed him and opposed what he stood for throughout his long life. His legacy will help to continue the emancipation of post-colonial and post-racist Africa, based on peace and reconciliation. The world always needs role models like Mandela to give us the courage to keep going.

The so-called Arab Spring has turned nasty over the past three years. The military takeover of the government of Egypt from the duly elected President and the imposition of unrepresentative rule raise serious questions in relation to democracy and the possibility of representative government. The insurrection in Syria has turned into a civil war. The recent violent protests in Ukraine, with apparent European Union backing, could lead to conflict between Russia and the EU with the possible involvement of NATO, i.e. if confrontation is pushed beyond the point of no return. The Israeli-Palestinian dispute is at a standstill, despite the efforts of the Obama administration to create some movement.

The exit of NATO from Afghanistan could well mean the return of the Taliban government despite all the sacrifices and destruction the occupation has cost in terms of human life and widespread devastation. Recent moves towards talks between the United States and Iran give a 'ray of hope' in the cloudy sky of the Middle East. The legacy of death and destruction in Iraq is sadly still with us.

The violent conflict between Christians and Muslims in Central Africa is ongoing and becoming more serious. When religious and ethnic conflicts reinforce each other, the situation becomes more explosive and more difficult to reconcile. We have had examples of this in Northern Ireland over the past century. The social-class conflict dimension is also rarely absent in cases of ongoing ethnic-religious violence. The complex nature of current violence in Africa and the Middle East makes it difficult to reconcile. According as the world becomes more diverse in its religious, ethnic, political and cultural make-up, there is a greater need for integrated pluralism, which is a form of coexistence, which ensures inter-group equality while respecting and defending inter-group difference. It requires a degree of institutional duplication such as separate schools and places of worship. Bureaucracy does not favour 'institutional duplication', principally for financial reasons.

During 2013 and early 2014, communal violence seemed to be on the increase in South America, e.g. in Brazil and Venezuela. Outside vested interests are suspected of being influential in creating the causes of unrest. The drugs-related violence in Mexico and the generation-old conflict in Columbia seem to be endless! Structural poverty and injustice are rarely absent in areas of ongoing social unrest. The election of Pope Francis and the strength of belief among so many of the citizens of

South and Central America should be a source of collective pride for this neglected continent. In a real sense, the 'centre of gravity' of the Roman Catholic Church has begun to shift from tired and secular Europe to the more dynamic South and Central America. Europe has become 'mission territory'!

North America, i.e. Canada and the United States, is still dominant in the 'global playing field'. The US has begun to recover from the 2008 economic crisis, having pursued a non-austerity programme. The ugly spectre of Guantanamo Bay Concentration Camp is still there. Also the acceptance of capital punishment in some states is a sad reflection on this 'developed' country. President Barack Obama has tried hard to improve social conditions for many US citizens in a country that is ideologically divided. He has also succeeded in withdrawing the military from Iraq and Afghanistan. The phone-tapping scandal revealed by whistle-blower Edward Snowden was timely and a rude awakening as to the paranoia of 'Big Brother'! Is it not time to go back to the typewriter and postal service to ensure confidentiality? Despite his shortcomings, President Obama has been a positive influence overall during his time in the White House to date.

The rise of China as a major superpower has continued despite the decline of the Western developed countries. This shows to me the independent capacity of China and other countries in Asia, i.e. India, Eastern Russia, Indonesia, and other growing economies, to sustain their development. The degree of emancipation in Burma is to be welcomed and bodes well for the future. The instability of the Middle East is encroaching on Pakistan and also on Southern Russia. As noted earlier, I have grave worries about developments in Ukraine. If viewed as an attempt by the EU to annex that country, or part of it, we would be back in the 'cold war winter' or even worse. The situation in Turkey is going to be very challenging also, hence the need, once again, for making progress in inter-religious dialogue and pluralist integration before it is too late.

5. LIFE GOES ON FOR ME

Because of the nature of this book it ends abruptly in midstream. If I may quote my good friend and next-door neighbour, the late John Walsh, when commenting on my late father's health, at the end of his life, he reminded me not to be too optimistic because 'the mileage was there'! At eighty-three years of age, I accept I am beyond the current 'life-expectancy' figure, but I feel much younger and thank God for the gift of relatively good health. My hip trouble (caused by a fall in *Mámean* when carrying up material) I see as a 'mechanical replacement'.

Modern Western society does not seem to engage older people in the serious affairs of ongoing life as much as in earlier times. The concept of formal retirement is, for me, very much a bourgeois convention, which terminates social engagement outside the domestic and personal spheres at a prescribed age, irrespective of the capacity of the retiree. The cult of youth and middle-age dominates society to the exclusion of the wisdom and ability of older people. I may be fortunate not to have been 'closed-down' in cosy conditions at the statutory retirement age. Ageism deprives society of the benefits of experience and true wisdom.

All I am fairly sure of is that the loss to society of older people has become tangible in modern society. Cultural wisdom is cumulative and there is no substitute for real experience of living. Young, middle-aged and older citizens should live in continuous dialogue and cooperation irrespective of statutory age limits. Groups like Trades Unions need to examine their policy regarding compulsory retirement. With the dramatic reduction in fertility, economic pressures may force society to re-evaluate senior citizens as positive contributors to work. For those who are fit to do so, continuing to work and serve adds to the quality of their lives.

The sad and untimely death of my sister-in-law, the late Jackie McGreal (née Flanagan), wife of my younger brother Pádraig, took place on the 14th of March 2013 in her home in Westport. Her death was very sad for her immediate family, neighbours and friends. Jackie was one of nature's most attractive personalities. Her four children, Eoin, Gregory, Justine and Micheál, were at her bedside, together with their father, when she passed away. Her death was a great wrench for me and the rest of our family. *Ar dheis Dé go raibh a h-anam uasal.* As one grows older, more and more of our close friends have moved on to their heavenly home in the presence of God and all the saints!

In terms of research writing and publications, the last three years have been very productive for me. In addition to this current book, *The Ongoing Present*, the publication of *Pluralism and Diversity in Ireland* (based on a national study of Irish prejudices) in 2011 and *Westport Eleven-Twelve* (based on a survey of tourists to Westport and those involved in hosting them during 2011 and 2012) in 2013, were well received and generally favourably commented on by critical readers. As happened in the case of my first book on inter-group attitudes, there was some criticism of the empirical and 'positivist' nature of my research methodology in *Pluralism and Diversity in Ireland*, which annoyed some academics on reading this criticism. I am afraid that I am not convinced that there is a better or, should I say, more practical technique of measuring or gauging prejudiced attitudes than by national social survey. Participant observation is very good for measuring the attitudes and values of local or smaller groups.

I would like to see the study of inter-group relations in Ireland as a subject on the senior cycle of the second-level curriculum and young people becoming more aware of their own prejudices. The study of inter-group prejudice is quite self-therapeutic – as I have found out personally in the course of my liberation. This has been one of my main aims in publishing *Pluralism and Diversity in Ireland* in 2011 and the previous two texts in 1977 and in 1996.

In recent years, my pastoral workload has increased, i.e. Mass, baptisms, marriages, attending the sick and burying the remains of those who have gone home to the Lord. It is only the body that dies. The person lives on with God and the saints. This is the essence of the Christian belief. I spend midweek in Gardiner Street, Dublin, and the weekends in Loughloon, Westport, where I concentrate on writing and pastoral work in local parishes (especially in the Monastery Nursing Home in Corrandulla and in Aghagower and Leenaun parishes). The combination of the pastoral and academic work is so meaningful and stimulating humanly and spiritually. It is a most privileged life despite the effort and hardship involved at times. *Arís deirim 'munar lá crúógach é,* ní lá fós é' ('If it is not a hard day, it is not a day at all').

My involvement with the emancipation of the Travelling People (and, more recently, the Roma) has continued since 2012. The Report, *The Emancipation of the Travelling People* was published in 2010. To my surprise, on the strength of the Report and the book, *Pluralism and Diversity in Ireland*, I was invited to make a formal submission on the Travellers and the Roma as minorities before the Environmental and Social Committee of the *British-Irish Inter-Parliamentary Assembly* in Leinster House on Monday, 13th January 2014. The Committee of fourteen included Peers MPs, Members of the Northern Ireland, Scotland and Wales Assemblies and a Senator and a TD from the *Oireachtas*. My recommendations included the recognition of Travellers as an ethnic Irish minority and the convening of a special Inter-Parliamentary Commission on the Travellers and Roma minorities. I also recommended that one seat in the *Seanad* be elected by the Travellers.

6. THE LEGACY OF THE CELTIC TIGER (1990-2008) TODAY

Before concluding (for the present) this commentary on society, I would like to return to the legacy of the Celtic Tiger (1990-2008)[25], which still seems to preoccupy some politicians, journalists and 'experts' in an unfair and one-sided manner. The financial crisis of 2008, which was widespread throughout the EU and Western World, was largely due, in my view, to the defects and excesses of self-regulated liberal capitalism. The public reporting on this period of dynamic infrastructural development in Ireland has not received (so far) a balanced assessment. Developers and builders seem to have been demonised as a category and their lasting contribution to our infrastructure renewal is rarely recognised. Most political parties supported the work of the Celtic Tiger and welcomed its benefits for workers and for the people. Of course, mistakes made in some planning decisions, excesses in prices and deviant procedures should be investigated thoroughly and fairly.

During the Celtic Tiger period, Ireland experienced the greatest renewal and development of basic infrastructure since the foundation of the State. This included:

- Renewal of the housing stock and the provision of living accommodation;
- the building of a road and motorway network;
- the renewal of railway tracks and rolling stock (including *An Luas*);
- the renewal and building of new schools, colleges and universities;
- the construction of community water and sewerage schemes;

---

25 This comment was the subject of a letter of mine published in the *Irish Independent* on the 23rd of January 2014 and developed further in the *Mayo News* on the 28th of January 2014.

- the building of factories and office blocks;
- the transformation of Dublin docklands;
- the provision of modern sports and athletic amenities (including the re-building of Croke Park and Lansdowne Road stadia);
- the renewal of fishing ports and island quays;
- the development of cultural and social amenities;
- the expansion of hotel and other accommodation for tourists and visitors;
- the improvements in agricultural infrastructure;
- the upgrading of our airports and (sea) ferry ports; and
- other infrastructural projects.

The great thing about such an extraordinary development of basic infrastructure is the fact that it is there to be used by generations to come and be built on when the economy is allowed to function as it should in the interests of all the people.

Other related benefits were to come from the Celtic Tiger. It provided a background, which was conducive to the positive negotiations, which led up to the *Good Friday Agreement*. This, in turn, released the necessary energy for the people to develop post-Agreement Ireland (North and South). It also enabled the State to integrate a large influx of immigrant workers and other families in a relatively peaceful manner and cope with an increase of over 13% in the national population in a relatively short period of time. The increase in third-level education was also provided without much fuss or bother. The tragedy was that the capitalist neo-liberal system failed to prevent excesses in the 'free market'. The successful operation of social partnership gave us industrial peace for over twenty years. With regard to the Western Rail Corridor, I regret that the completion of its restoration was not achieved, i.e. from Athenry to Collooney *via* Tuam, Claremorris, Charlestown/Knock Airport.

When the good and the bad of the Celtic Tiger period for Ireland are put into the balance, the benefits greatly outweigh the deficiencies. Hence, the importance of a more balanced public appraisal of what was achieved in infrastructural renewal and due acknowledgement of workers, managers, and those who had the vision and courage to lead the workforce at different levels. Without such a balanced assessment we do those who developed and worked in renewing our infrastructure a great injustice and demoralise our young people by the obsession of some journalists and others who seem to be continuously emphasising and repeating the negative without pointing out the positive. We should remember that a lie is the absence of the whole truth! The net result of unbalanced negativity could well be the forcing of our young people to emigrate and deprive the country of their invaluable contribution to Irish society. The great thing about the Celtic Tiger infrastructural renewal was that it clearly confirmed the benefits of both white-collar and blue-collar workers cooperating on the site and on the farm! *Báil ó Dhia ar an obair*. What happened in Ireland can also happen in all countries when the people unite in positive work. Our people have the capacity to achieve great material and spiritual goals.

7. FOCAIL SCOIR

In the course of this long text, it has been possible 'to cast a cold eye' on modern society and appraise its perceived strengths and weaknesses. It is clear that greed and generosity have been present side-by-side. Despite significant advances in social welfare, structural imbalance in the distribution of wealth and opportunity both within and between societies is still a major matter of concern. The 'social-welfare approach' in itself is not enough without the obligatory introduction of maximum-income policies for all citizens, which will lead to greater justice and equality. This will result in the curtailment of the consumer's choice of the privileged leading to a reduction in the causes of unrest and violence. Such a major social change should guarantee greater peace and hopefully create a shift from profit motive to service motive, which is in line with basic Christian teaching.

On this optimistic note I end my commentary (for the present) as life continues on its exciting, creative and sometimes perilous evolution toward its completion. I am grateful to God and to so many, i.e. parents, family, relatives, friends, fellow-Jesuits, diocesan brother priests, neighbours, colleagues and comrades who have helped me on the way. The Irish State was only nine years old when I was born. My parents' generation suffered much sacrifice in winning independence and maintaining it through periods of economic and political difficulty and uncertainty. Hopefully, our generation took on its responsibility and carried 'the torch' to the third and fourth generations (at the helm of Irish society) in peaceful coexistence with the peoples of Britain, Europe and the rest of the world. We should all be grateful to each other. As we say in Irish: '*As scáth a chéile a mhairimíd*' ('We live in the shadow of each other'). Our generation may not have achieved as much as we wished. At least, we tried to sow the seeds for future generations to harvest!

For me personally, I would not have wished to live at any other time with any other family or friends and colleagues. I trust that the story and commentary narrated in the above pages will be of interest and helpful to the reader. I apologise to anyone who may in any way feel upset by any comment or remark, which unintentionally offended him or her. Because of the subjective nature of the account of the 'ongoing present', I apologise also for any errors due to mistakes of memory or misinterpretation. Thank you for reading this book and for your patient tolerance. *Rath Dé oraibh go léir.*

I give the last words to St Paul in his Letter to the Romans: '*The whole of creation is eagerly waiting for God to reveal his children. It was not any fault on the part of creation that it was made unable to attain its purpose, it was made so by God, but creation still retains the hope of being freed, like us, freed from the slavery of decadence, to enjoy the same freedom and glory as the children of God. From the beginning till now the entire creation, as we know, has been groaning in one great act of giving birth, and not only creation, but all of us who possess the first fruits of the Spirit, we too groan inwardly as we wait for our bodies to be set free.*' (Romans 8: 19-23[26])

Moladh go deo le Dia

---

26 These inspired words of St Paul to the Romans are said to have influenced the French Jesuit, Pierre Teilhard de Chardin (1881-1955), who was an eminent palaeontologist, geologist and philosopher. In his lifetime, he did much to influence Church leaders and others of the dynamic and evolving nature of the world and humanity.

INDEX